# HEBREWISMS OF WEST AFRICA

*From Nile to Niger with the Jews*


JOSEPH J. WILLIAMS, S.J.,
PH.D., LITT.D.

Fellow of the Royal Geographical and the American Geographical Societies, Member of the International Institute of African Languages and Cultures, Member of the Catholic Anthropological Conference,

Author of *Whisperings of the Caribbean,* etc. etc.




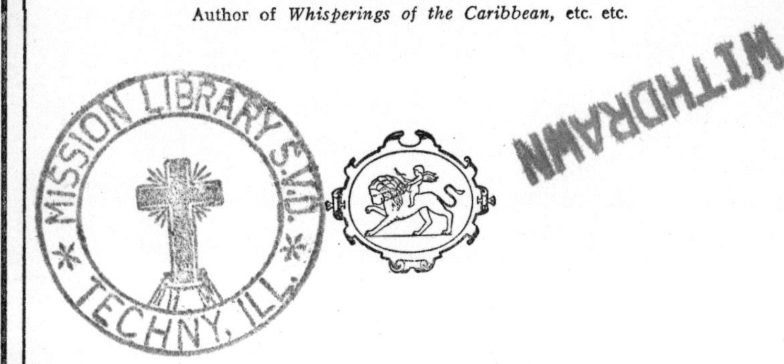



LINCOLN MAC VEAGH
THE DIAL PRESS
NEW YORK · MCMXXX
LONGMANS, GREEN & CO., TORONTO

MANUFACTURED IN THE UNITED STATES OF AMERICA
BY THE VAIL-BALLOU PRESS, INC., BINGHAMTON, N. Y.

# CONTENTS

## LIST OF ILLUSTRATIONS



## MAPS

# HEBREWISMS OF WEST AFRICA

*Introduction*

## ASHANTI INFLUENCE ON JAMAICA CUSTOMS

**Jamaica Negroes.**

Robert T. Hill of the United States Geological Survey, writing towards the close of the last century, was emphatic in his statement: "The Jamaican negroes are sui generis; nothing like them, even of their own race, can elsewhere be found—not even elsewhere in the West Indies. They are omnipresent. The towns, the country highways, and the woods ring with their laughter and merry songs: they fill the churches and throng the highways, especially on market-days, when the country roads are black with them: and they are witty and full of queer stories and folk-lore." [1] He is speaking of the native Blacks, the real peasantry of the Island.

During a five-years' residence in Jamaica, when much of the time was spent in the "bush" in close contact with the simple unaffected children of the soil, the present writer, in his turn, was deeply impressed by a striking difference between the Jamaican Black and all the other negro types that he had ever encountered.

**African Slaves.**

W. J. Gardner, in his *History of Jamaica,* states: "Great numbers of negro slaves were imported from Africa, representing tribes as diverse in character as different European nations. Among these the fierce Coromantyns occupied a very prominent place, but though their dangerous character was so well known, their superior strength was so highly valued as to lead to the rejection of all measures proposed to check their importation." [2]

**Koromantyns.**

Later on, the same author, while describing the various classes of slaves, tells us: "The Negroes from the Gold Coast were known generally as Coromantyns. The Ashantees and the Fans described

[1] Robert T. Hill, *Cuba and Porto Rico with the other Islands of the West Indies,* New York, 1898, p. 227.

[2] W. J. Gardner, *History of Jamaica,* London, 1909, p. 132.

by du Chaillu were included in this term. They were strong and active, and on this account valued by the planters. The Spanish and the French colonists shunned them on account of their ferocious tendencies; but attempts to prohibit their importation into Jamaica failed, though they were the instigators and leaders of every rebellion."[3]

**Bryan Edwards' Account.**

Bryan Edwards, the historian, for many years a resident of Jamaica and a member of the Council,[4] furnishes us with the most authentic description of these Koromantyn slaves, and as an appreciation of their characteristic traits will help to clarify what follows, a somewhat lengthy quotation from his graphic account may be pardoned. Speaking from his personal observations, he says: "The circumstances which distinguish the Koromantyn, or Gold Coast, Negroes, from all others, are firmness both of body and mind; a ferociousness of disposition; but withal, activity, courage, and a stubbornness, or what an ancient Roman would have deemed an elevation, of soul, which prompts them to enterprises of difficulty and danger; and enables them to meet death, in its most horrible shape, with fortitude and indifference. They sometimes take to labour with great promptitude and alacrity, and have constitutions well adapted for it; for many of them have undoubtedly been slaves in Africa:—I have interrogated great numbers on this subject, and although some of them asserted they were born free, who as it afterwards proved by the testimony of their own relations, were actually sold as slaves by their masters; others frankly confessed to me that they had no claim to freedom in their own country, and were sold either to pay the debts, or to expiate the crimes, of their owners. On the other hand, the Gold Coast being inhabited by various different tribes which are engaged in perpetual warfare and hostility with each other, there cannot be a doubt that many of the captives taken in battle, and sold in the European settlements, were of free condition in their native country, and perhaps the owners of slaves themselves. It is not wonderful that such men should endeavour, even by means the most desperate, to regain the freedom of which they had been deprived; nor do I conceive that any further circumstances are necessary to

[3] Idem, p. 175.
[4] Frank Cundall, *Historic Jamaica*, London, 1915, p. 308 ff.

prompt them to action, than that of being sold into captivity in a distant country. I mean only to state facts as I find them. Such I well know was the origin of the Negro rebellion which happened in Jamaica in 1760. It arose at the instigation of a Koromantyn Negro of the name of Tacky, who had been a chief in Guiney; and it broke out on the Frontier plantation in St. Mary's parish, belonging to the late Ballard Bechford, and the adjoining estate of Trinity, the property of my deceased relation and benefactor Zachary Bayly. On these plantations were upwards of 100 Gold Coast Negroes newly imported, and I do not believe that an individual amongst them had received the least shadow of ill treatment from the time of their arrival there. Concerning those on Trinity estate, I can pronounce of my own knowledge that they were under the government of an overseer of singular tenderness and humanity. His name was Abraham Fletcher, and let it be remembered, in justice even to the rebels, and as a lesson to other overseers, that his life was spared from respect to his virtues. The insurgents had heard of his character from the other Negroes, and suffered him to pass through them unmolested—this fact appeared in evidence. Having collected themselves into a body about one o'clock in the morning, they proceeded to the fort at Port Maria; killed the sentinel, and provided themselves with as great a quantity of arms and ammunition as they could conveniently dispose of. Being by this time joined by a number of their countrymen from the neighbouring plantations, they marched up the high road that led to the interior parts of the country, carrying death and desolation as they went. At Ballard's Valley they surrounded the overseer's house about four in the morning, in which eight or ten White people were in bed, every one of whom they butchered in the most savage manner, and literally drank their blood mixed with rum. At Esher, and other estates, they exhibited the same tragedy; and then set fire to the buildings and canes. In one morning they murdered between thirty and forty Whites, not sparing even infants at the breast, before their progress was stopped. Tacky, the Chief, was killed in the woods, by one of the parties that went in pursuit of them; but some others of the ringleaders being taken, and a general inclination to revolt appearing among all the Koromantyn Negroes in the island, it was thought neces-

**Slave Rebellion of 1760.**

sary to make a few terrible examples of some of the most guilty.

**Grewsome Reprisals.**

Of three who were clearly proved to have been concerned in the murders committed at Ballard's Valley, one was condemned to be burned, and the other two to be hung up alive in irons, and left to perish in that dreadful situation. The wretch that was burned was made to sit on the ground, and his body being chained to an iron stake, the fire was applied to his feet. He uttered no groan, and saw his legs reduced to ashes with the utmost firmness and composure; after which one of his arms by some means getting loose, he snatched a brand from the fire that was consuming him, and flung it in the face of the executioner. The two that were hung up alive were indulged, at their own request, with a hearty meal immediately before they were suspended on the gibbet, which was erected in the parade of the town of Kingston. From that time, until they expired, they never uttered the least complaint, except only of cold in the night, but diverted themselves all day long in discourse with their countrymen, who were permitted, very improperly, to surround the gibbet. On the seventh day a notion prevailed among the spectators, that one of them wished to communicate an important secret to his master, my near relation; who being in St. Mary's parish, the commanding officer sent for me. I endeavoured, by means of an interpreter, to let him know that I was present, but I could not understand what he said in return. I remember that both he and his fellow sufferer laughed immoderately at something that occurred—I know not what. The next morning one of them silently expired, as did the other on the morning of the ninth day."[5]

**New York Parallel.**

We may here be allowed to digress long enough to remark that while one cannot help being shocked at this inhuman treatment, it does not behoove us to reproach the Jamaica Planters. For, it is reported that after a negro insurrection in New York in 1741, no less than thirteen unfortunate Blacks were given to the flames, eighteen were imprisoned and eighty-eight deported.[6]

[5] Bryan Edwards, *History Civil and Commercial of the British West Indies*, London, 1793, Vol. II, p. 63 ff.

[6] Cfr. William S. Nelson, *La Race Noire dans la Démocratie Américaine*, Paris, 1922, p. 3.

**Koromantyn Indifference to Death.**

But let us now return to the narrative of Bryan Edwards. He continues: "The courage or unconcern, which the people of this country manifest at the approach of death, arises, doubtless, in a great measure, from their national manners, wars and superstitions, which are all in the highest degree, savage and sanguinary. A power over the lives of his slaves is possessed, and exercised too, on very frivolous occasions, without compunction and scruple, by every master of slaves on the Gold Coast. Fathers have the like power over their children. In their wars they are bloody and cruel beyond any nation that ever existed; for all such of their captives as they reserve not for slaves, they murder with circumstances of outrageous barbarity; cutting them across the face, and tearing away the under jaw, which they preserve as a trophy, leaving the miserable victims to perish in that condition. I have collected this account from themselves. They tell me likewise, that whenever a considerable man expires, several of his wives, and a great number of his slaves, are sacrificed at his funeral. This is done, say they, that he may be properly attended in the next world. This circumstance has been confirmed to me by every Gold Coast Negro that I have interrogated on the subject, and I have enquired of many. In a country where executions are so frequent, and human blood is spilt with so little remorse, death must necessarily have lost many of its terrors; and the natives in general, conscious they have no security even for the day that is passing over them, seem prepared for, and resigned to, the fate that probably awaits them. This contempt of death, or indifference about life, they bring with them to the West Indies; but if fortunately they fall into good hands at first, and become well settled, they acquire by degrees other sentiments and notions. Nature resumes her lawful influence over them. With the consciousness of security, the love of existence also, amidst all the evils that attend it in a state of slavery, gains admission into their bosoms. They feel it, and, such is the force of habitual barbarity, seem ashamed of their own weakness. A gentleman of Jamaica visiting a valuable Koromantyn Negro that was sick, and perceiving that he was thoughtful and dejected, endeavoured by soothing and encouraging language, to raise his drooping spirits. Massa, said the Negro, in a tone of self-reproach and conscious degeneracy, since me come to White man's country me lub (love) life too much!

"Even the children brought from the Gold Coast manifest an evident superiority both in hardiness of frame, and vigour of mind, over all the young people of the same age that are imported from other parts of Africa. The like firmness and intrepidity which are distinguished in adults of this nation, are visible in their boys at an age which might be thought too tender to receive any lasting impression, either from precept or example.— I have been myself an eye-witness to the truth of this remark, in the circumstances I am about to relate. A gentleman of my acquaintance, who had purchased at the same time ten Koromantyn boys, and the like number of Eboes, the eldest of the whole ap-

**Branding of Slaves.**

parently not more than thirteen years of age, caused them all to be collected and brought before him in my presence, to be marked on the breast. This operation is performed by heating a small silver brand, composed of one or two letters, in the flame of spirits of wine, and applying it to the skin, which is previously anointed with sweet oil. The application is instantaneous, and the pain momentary. Nevertheless it may be easily supposed that the apparatus must have a frightful appearance to a child. Accordingly, when the

**Timidity of Eboes**

first boy, who happened to be one of the Eboes, and the stoutest of the whole, was led forward to receive the mark, he screamed dreadfully, while his companions of the same nation manifested strong emotions of sympathetic terror. The gentleman stopped his hand; but the

**Bravado of Koromantyns.**

Koromantyn boys, laughing aloud, and, immediately coming forward of their own accord, offered their bosoms undauntedly to the brand, and receiving its impression without flinching in the least, snapt their fingers in exultation over the poor Eboes.

"One cannot surely but lament, that a people thus naturally emulous and intrepid, should be sunk into so deplorable a state of barbarity and superstition; and that their spirits should ever be broken down by the yoke of slavery! Whatever may be allowed concerning their ferociousness and implacability in their present notions of right and wrong, I am persuaded that they possess qualities which are capable of, and well deserve cultivation and improvement." [7]

**Dominant Influence in Jamaica.**

Who, then, were these Koromantyns, who as a matter of fact, maintained a commanding influence over all the other types of slaves, even imposing on them their own peculiar superstitions and religious practices, and who have left their impress on the general population of the Island to such an extent that they may undoubtedly be declared the dominant influence in evolving our Jamaica peasant of the present day?

**Origin of Koromantyns.**

The term Koromantyn, or as we frequently find it Coromantyn spelt with a C, was not the name of any particular race or tribe. Strictly speaking, it was applied in general to those slaves who were brought from the Gold Coast in West Africa and who measured up to a certain standard or quality. Its derivation can only be conjectured with more or less plausibility.

**"Memeneda Koromante."**

Captain Rattray, while describing the great oath of the Ashanti whereby they appeal for justice directly to the paramount chief, possibly throws some light on the subject. This solemn oath was taken merely by uttering the words "Memeneda Koromante," that is, literally, "Koromante Saturday," and the real import of the words was this: If the King or paramount chief did not render justice to the one who was making the appeal, might the same evil befall the people as had happened at Koromante on a Saturday. Thus the oath was in reality a conditional curse. The author then goes on to state, that it was at a place called Koromante that Ossai Panyin of Coomasie was defeated and slain, and adds: "This calamity was considered so terrible that even the name came to be proscribed and became known simply as ntam kese, the great oath." [8]

**Ashanti Defeat at Koromante.**

Lt. Col. Ellis, formerly of the lately disbanded West India Regiment, who spent many years upon the Gold Coast, thus refers to this incident which took place in a war between the Ashanti and the Akims: "As Osai Tuto was on his way to join this army with a

[7] Bryan Edwards, l. c. Vol. II, p. 64 ff.
[8] R. Sutherland Rattray, *Ashanti Proverbs,* Oxford, 1916, #496, p. 130.

small escort, he and his followers were suddenly attacked by a strong body of the enemy, which, lying in ambush, fell upon them as they were crossing the Prah. The King was wounded in the side at the first fire; but he threw himself out of his hammock, and was rallying his men, when a second volley was discharged, and he fell dead upon his face in the river."[9] The brother of Ossai Tuto shortly after crushed the Akims and completely obliterated the town of Koromante, or as Ellis calls it Acromanti, where "the party of Akims who had slain Osai Tuto was halted on the night previous to their attack, every living creature found in it being put to death, and every house razed to the ground."[10]

**Prisoners of War.**

As the main supply of slaves, especially at the start, was drawn from the prisoners taken in the endless tribal wars, it is just barely possible that the few captives taken at Koromante may well have been the first of a type that was henceforth to be classified as Koromantyns. Then, again, the great oath or curse might itself indicate a like origin of this particular class of slaves, as we shall see shortly. For aside from the prisoners of war, it was no uncommon thing for the native tribes to sell into bondage debtors and criminals generally.

**Slavery for Debt.**

Mungo Park, the intrepid adventurer of the closing days of the eighteenth century, who penetrated alone into the very heart of West Africa, and who lost his life there on the occasion of his second expedition of discovery, states from his own observations: "Of all the offences, if insolvency may be so called, to which the laws of Africa have affixed the punishment of slavery this is the most common."[11]

At times too, the petty chieftains helped along their revenues by assessing different villages a certain number of victims who were to be exchanged at the coast for rum and powder. What more natural then, than that the victim of his chieftain's greed should utter the great oath or curse against him, and with "Memeneda Koromante" on his lips that he should be started

[9] A. B. Ellis, *A History of the Gold Coast of West Africa,* London, 1893, p. 88.

[10] Idem, p. 88.

[11] Mungo Park, *Travels in the Interior Districts of Africa,* London, 1810, p. 441.

into bondage, his curse mistaken by the slavers for a homesick wail for his people and his country. This, however, is of course mere conjecture.

**Koromantyns: Generically Gold Coast Slaves.**

In any case, sufficient for our present purpose is the explanation of Ellis, when he writes: "The Gold Coast negroes are termed Koromantees or Koromantyns, in the jargon of the slave-traders, this name being a corruption of Coromantine, whence the English had first exported slaves. They were distinguished from all other slaves by their courage, firmness, and impatience of control; characteristics which caused numerous mutinies on board the slavers, and several rebellions in the West Indies. In fact every rebellion of Slaves in Jamaica originated with, and was generally confined to, the Koromantees; and their independence of character became so generally recognised that at one time the legislature of Jamaica proposed that a bill should be brought in for laying an additional duty upon the 'Fantin, Akin and Ashanti negroes, and all others, commonly called Koromantees,' that should be imported. The superior physique of the Gold Coast Negroes, however, rendered them very valuable as labourers, and this bill met with so much opposition that it was withdrawn; and, notwithstanding their dangerous character, large numbers continued to be introduced to the island." [12]

**Specifically Ashanti.**

While this derivation of the term would include both Fantis and Akims with the Ashanti, the real Koromantyn of type was preeminently an Ashanti, as Sir Harry Johnston clearly recognises.[13]

**Leaders of Maroons.**

Moreover, in connection with the fearless independence and uncompromising spirit of the Gold Coast Negro, whether we call him Ashanti or Koromantyn, it is well to remember that the Maroons of the Jamaica Mountains who wrote their own chapter of daring in the history of the Island were for the most part recruited, at least as regards their leaders, from the same group.[14]

[12] Ellis, *History of the Gold Coast,* p. 94.

[13] Harry H. Johnston, *A History of the Colonization of Africa by Alien Races,* Cambridge, 1913, p. 124.

[14] Note:—Commander Bedford Pim, R.N. on February 1, 1866, read a paper before the Anthropological Society of London, on the Negro and Jamaica, in connection with the then recent rebellion in the Island. In the course of the discussion which followed, a Mr. Harris, speaking from per-

**Sir Wm. Butler's Testimony.**

Sir William Butler, who arrived on the Gold Coast to take part in the Ashanti Campaign in October, 1873, tells us in his autobiography: "This coast has been for two hundred and more years the greatest slave preserve in the world. All those castles dotted along the surf-beaten shore at ten or twelve miles intervals were the prisons where, in the days of the slave-trade, millions of wretched negroes had been immured, waiting the arrival of slave-ships from Bristol or Liverpool to load the human cargo for West Indian or American ports. It would not be too much to say that from each of these prison castles to some West Indian port, a cable of slave skeletons must be lying at the bottom of the ocean. In that terrible trade the protected tribes of the coast were the prime brokers. They bought from the black interior kingdoms of Dahomey and Ashanti, and they sold to the white merchant traders of Europe; slaves, rum and gunpowder were the chief items in the bills of lading. The gunpowder went to the interior, the rum was drunk on the coast, the slaves, or those who survived among them, went to America. If two in ten lived through the horrors of the middle passage, the trade paid." [15] This would indicate, first of all, that the Koromantyn was not a native of the Coast, but was brought from the interior, and secondly, directly indicates the Ashanti as the source of supply.

**Confirmation of Folk-Lore.**

This theory, that the Koromantyns, at least as regards their leading spirits, were in reality Ashanti, is strongly supported by the folk-lore and present-day customs of the Jamaica "bush." Even Obeah, as it is practiced in the interior of the Island, with its cognate branches of Duppyism and Myalism, is directly traceable to the superstitions and practices of the Ashanti in West Africa.

sonal observation, said in reference to the Maroons of Sierra Leone who had been transported from Jamaica by way of Halifax: "The Maroons are principally descendants of the Gold Coast tribes, and still retain amongst them the same religious superstitions, customs, and common names, as, for instance, the naming of their children after the days of the week upon which they were born, such as Quamin (Monday), the son of Quacco (Thursday), each day being denoted by the masculine and feminine gender. They boast of being directly descended, or having been concerned in the Jamaica rebellion at the end of the eighteenth century, as partisans of King Cudjoe, their leader."—Cfr. Bedford Pim, *The Negro and Jamaica,* London, 1866, p. 64 f.

[15] W. F. Butler, *An Autobiography,* New York, 1913, p. 149.

Newbell Niles Puckett, it is true, shows that much of the negro folk-lore of our Southern States is due to a European origin. From Master to Slave, we are told, the stories passed, only to be preserved by the latter long after they had been forgotten by the Whites.[16] It is further stated concerning the folk-beliefs of the American Negro: "Purely local African lore would be apt to die out since its devotees in America were too few in number and too scattered to provide the constant repetition necessary for remembrance . . . only African beliefs of an universal nature would be likely to survive unless, perchance, many slaves from the same African locality were grouped on a single plantation." [17] This last condition was truly verified in Jamaica. The trouble-making Koromantyns, with the Ashanti as their leading spirits, while excluded from most other slave marts, were in great demand in Jamaica. Thus, to give but a single example, Messrs. Coppells, one of the leading slave dealers in Kingston, Jamaica, reported having imported and sold 10,380 slaves from November, 1782, to January, 1788, and that of this number no less than 5,724 were from the Gold Coast, that is, Koromantyns.[18]

**Anancy Tales.** Through the folk-lore of a people we may at times trace its origin as well as its contacts with other peoples. The Jamaica Anancy Tales, as has been shown elsewhere,[19] are clearly of Ashanti origin. They resemble in many ways the Brer Rabbit Stories of Uncle Remus, that are in one form or another common to all the tribes of Africa. However, as the name implies, in the Jamaica folk-lore it is the spider and not the rabbit or hare that forms the central figure, and here we have a strong indication of the source of the stories, as the Ashanti word for spider is ananse. Nay more, while the term is used in the folk-lore of the Gold Coast to-day under a slightly different form, Anansi,[20] we find that there the Spider's son is called Kweku Tsin, while among the Ashanti themselves the name is Ntikuma.[21] Is it a mere coincidence that the same individual is styled Tacooma in the Jamaica "bush"?

[16] Newbell Niles Puckett, *Folk Beliefs of the Southern Negro,* London, 1926, p. 2.
[17] Idem, p. 7.
[18] Cfr. Stephen Fuller, *Two Reports,* London, 1789, p. 22.
[19] *Whisperings of the Caribbean,* New York, 1925, Chapter VII.
[20] Cfr. Barker and Sinclair, *West African Folk-Tales,* London, 1917.
[21] Rattray, *Ashanti Proverbs,* #175, p. 73.

Incidentally, the Ashanti have a proverb, "No one tells stories to Ntikuma." Captain Rattray explains the meaning, that "as the spider is the fount and origin of all stories, the son, Ntikuma, would be supposed to know every story in the world, having heard them from his father. The saying is used in the sense of 'I know all about that, tell me something I do not know.' "[22] In Jamaica they say: "I'm not asking you, I'm telling you," with precisely the same meaning.

In this connection it may be objected that the Jamaica Anancy's wife is called Crookie, while the present-day Ashanti speak of her as Konori or Konoro, which would seem to militate against our argument. Let us see! Frank R. Cana makes the statement: "The most probable tradition represents the Ashanti as deriving their origin from bands of fugitives, who in the 16th or 17th century were driven before the Moslem tribes migrating southward from the countries on the Niger and Senegal."[23] Now among the Hausa of Northern Nigeria, where Major Tremearne assures us that distinction of sex is rare, the exception is made in favor of the spider—perhaps to mark its superior position, and while the male spider is called Gizzo in their folk-lore, the female is known as Koki.[24] Might not this imply that the Jamaica Crookie is a survival of the earlier term still in use when the first slaves were dragged from the Ashanti forests?

**Nanas.** The Jamaica Anancy Stories have been passed along in a living tradition by the old Nanas, or creole nurses, who correspond in many respects to the Mammies of the Southern States. The word Nana is itself pure Ashanti and means granny. Thus nana-barima, a maternal grandparent; oba-nana, a grandchild. To-day the term Nana has almost disappeared from common use in Jamaica, and in its place Granny is generally heard in reference to the type formerly called Nanas. And as Nana was generically applicable to either grandparent or grandchild, so even now granny is used in the same way, and elderly persons speak of any of their offspring beyond their immediate children by the general term "him me granny."

[22] Idem, #183, p. 76.

[23] Cfr. *Encyclopaedia Brittanica,* 11th Edition, Vol. II, Article: Ashanti, p. 725.

[24] A. J. M. Tremearne, *Hausa Superstitions and Customs,* London, 1913, p. 32.

**Fufu Yams.**

Again, the Jamaica peasant habitually makes use of words seemingly meaningless in themselves, and yet they also are pure Ashanti, and their signification has been preserved in use. To cite only an instance or two. The staple food of the Ashanti is fufu, which consists of mashed yam or plantain. Its derivation is from the word "fu," meaning white. In the Jamaica "bush" a very superior species of white yam is known as fufu yam, and none of the peasants seem to know the origin of the term. So too, in the Jamaica Mountains, there is a type of fowl with ruffled feathers and half-naked neck, as if it had been partially plucked. They are called sensey fowls, while the Ashanti word for the same kind of bird is Asense.[25]

**Sensey Fowls.**

**Proverbs.**

We see the same in some of the Proverbs of Jamaica.[26] Thus for example, "Poor man neber bex (vexed)," which Gardner explains by saying "he is humble, and cannot afford to take offence," [27] shows its derivation from the Ashanti "Ohiane bo mfuw," rendered by Rattray, "The poor man does not get into a rage." [28] In each case the meaning is the same, that a poor man cannot afford to take umbrage at those who are better supplied with this world's goods, and on whose charity he may be dependent.

**Funeral Customs.**

When we come to tribal customs, we find the same condition of things. And unless we are ready to accept these facts as a verification of the lasting influence which the Ashanti have exercised on the peasant population of the Island, we must ascribe them to a most extraordinary series of coincidences. Thus, for example, a "bush" funeral is almost invariably marked by a peculiar practice. Before starting for the burial ground, the coffin is raised and lowered three times. No one can give any real explanation for the act. Nor does local superstition seem to be attached to it. It is always done that way, and that is all there is about it. The very same practice has been in vogue among the Ashanti from prehistoric times.

[25] Rattray, *Ashanti Proverbs,* #697, p. 169.
[26] Note:—Professor Wallis states: "African culture is richly endowed with proverbs. . . . The distribution of proverbs suggests that the negro tribes acquired them from the Semitic peoples."—Wilson D. Wallis, *An Introduction to Anthropology,* New York, 1926, p. 324.
[27] Gardner, *History of Jamaica,* p. 392.
[28] Rattray, *Ashanti Proverbs,* #630, p. 159.

Captain Rattray thus explains the custom. "The coffin is now closed, and a hole is knocked in the wall; through this the coffin is carried by the asokwafo; on its arrival outside it is placed on the ground, but not without a pretence being first made to set it down twice before it finally comes to rest. The reason for this curious custom is undoubtedly to give Asase Ya (the Earth Goddess) due notice and warning." [29] Then, after a short ceremonial, "The sextons now raise the coffin to carry it away to burial; the same courtesies are paid to the Earth Goddess as when the corpse was set down." [30] So sacred has this custom become, that after the Ashanti had developed into a conquering nation, with the advent of the famous Golden Stool, the symbol of power and national vitality, on the occasion of each enthroning, or rather enstooling, of a new king, the ceremony required that he should feign three times to sit upon the Golden Stool, actually he may not rest upon it, raising and lowering his body three times as it will be raised and lowered after death.[31] It is almost as if he were reminded, "Dust thou art, and unto dust thou shalt return." [32] In many other ways also, as the present writer has noted elsewhere,[33] practices connected with the Jamaica "bush" funerals indicate their Ashanti origin.

**Hebrewisms in Jamaica.**

Now, as Gardner observes, even to-day in Jamaica the descendants of the old slaves retain a practice "that the room in which a person dies should not be swept or disturbed for nine days. Water and other requisites are placed in it and as among the Jews, a light is kept burning during the prescribed period." [34] Gardner, however, is in error, when he positively asserts that this practice is not of African origin.

**Hayti.**

As a matter of fact, Hebrewisms of African derivation are not confined to Jamaica among the West Indian Islands. Blair Niles in her recent delightful little volume, *Black Hayti,* speaking of the slaves from Africa, positively asserts: "Some were said to be descendants of Jews mixed

[29] R. Sutherland Rattray, *Religion and Art in Ashanti,* Oxford, 1927, p. 160.

[30] Idem, p. 161.

[31] R. S. Rattray, *Ashanti,* Oxford, 1923, p. 82.

[32] Gen. iii, 19.

[33] *Whisperings of the Caribbean,* Chapter VIII.

[34] Gardner, *History of Jamaica,* p. 391.

with negroes. These were tall, well built men whose features had a Caucasian cast and whose language was clearly Semitic in character." [35] Dr. Price-Mars, whom she quotes as an authority, also claims a distant Semitic infiltration in the antecedents of some of the San Domingo slaves.[36]

**Virgin Islands.**

This may seem to us less strange when we read the testimony of the Reverend Henry S. Whitehead who is speaking "'from information gained at first hand on the ground." While insisting that the opprobrious term "worthless old Cartegène," current to-day in the Virgin Islands is to be traced back to the African Carthage of the Punic Wars, he also remarks: "On the doors of the Negro cabins 'in the country,' i. e. outside the towns, crosses may be seen, much like those the Hebrews made with the blood of the Passover lamb. This is 'to keep out de wolf.' " [37]

**Johnston's View.**

It is interesting then, to find Sir Harry Johnston insisting: "The Elamites of Mesopotamia appear to have been a negroid people with kinky hair, and to have transmitted this racial type to the Jews and Syrians," [38] and further noting: "The Jewish hybrids with the Negro in Jamaica and Guiana reproduce most strikingly the Assyrian type." [39] Whatever we may think of this author's claim of a negro element in the ancient Hebrews, his attitude will make less shocking our present endeavour to show an infiltration of the same Hebrew stock in the evolving of certain distinctively Negro tribes in Africa.

**Grave Offering.**

It is surprising too, to find a Mississippi Negro attributing to the Jews the custom so prevalent in West Africa as well as in Jamacia in the slave days, of "putting food and money in the coffin with the dead so that he can eat and buy things when he gets to heaven." [40]

[35] Blair Niles, *Black Hayti,* New York, 1926, p. 113.

[36] Dr. Price-Mars, "Le Sentiment et le Phénomène religieux chez les nègres de Saint-Domingue,"—*Bulletin de la Société d'Histoire et de Géographie d' Hayti,* May 1925, p. 35 ff.

[37] Henry S. Whitehead, "Obi in the Caribbean,"—*The Commonweal,* June, 1, 1927, p. 94 f; July 13, 1927, p. 261.

[38] Harry H. Johnston, *The Negro in the New World,* London, 1910, p. 27.

[39] Idem, p. 102.

[40] Puckett, *Folk Beliefs of the Southern Negro,* p. 102. Note:—A. W. F. Blunt would make this a Canaanitish custom.—Cfr. *Israel before Christ,* London, 1924, p. 23.

**Koromantyn Accompong.**

Bryan Edwards, in his brief outline of the religious beliefs of the Koromantyn slaves, asserts: "They believe that Accompong, the God of the heavens, is the creator of all things; a Deity of infinite goodness." [41] In fact, we have in Jamacia to-day, in the Parish of St. Elizabeth, a Maroon town called Accompong which according to Cundall, the Island Historian, was so called after an Ashanti chief who figured in one of the early rebellions of the Island.[42] One's first impression would be that this chief had arrogated to himself the title of the Deity. But we are assured by J. G. Christaller that among the Ashanti the Divine Name was frequently given to a slave in acknowledgement of the help of God enabling the owner to buy the slave.[43]

**Ashanti Nyankopon.**

The Supreme Being among the Ashanti is Nyame,[44] whom we shall later try to identify with the Hebrew Yahweh. His primary title is Nyankopon, meaning Nyame, alone, great one.[45] Accompong then, appears to be the white man's effort to express the spoken Nyankopon as heard from the early slaves.

**Witchcraft**

When the slave trade was at its height, two Negro Nations shared the mastery of West Africa, the Ashanti and the Dahomans, and wherever the slaves of either tribe predominated, there we find the special forms of superstitions and witchcraft which were peculiar to that people. Thus in Cuba, San Domingo, Louisiana, etc. where the Dahomans

**Voodooism.**

were in the ascendency, the ophiolatry of Voodooism became prevalent.[46] In Jamaica, on the other

[41] Gardner, *History of Jamaica,* p. 90.
[42] Cundall, *Historic Jamaica,* p. 325.
[43] J. G. Christaller, *A Dictionary of the Asante and Fante Language,* Basel, 1881, p. 343, *Onyame.*
[44] Rattray, *Ashanti,* p. 86.
[45] Rattray, *Ashanti Proverbs,* #1, p. 19.
[46] Note:—Ellis says: "In the southeastern portions of the Ewe territory, however, the python deity is worshipped, and this vodu cult, with its adoration of the snake god was carried to Hayti by slaves from Ardra and Whydah, where the faith still remains to-day. In 1724 the Dahomies invaded Ardra and subjugated it; three years later Whydah was conquered by the same foe. This period is beyond question that in which Hayti first received the vodu of the Africans. Thousands of Negroes from these serpent-worshiping tribes were at that time sold into slavery, and were carried across the Atlantic to the western island. They bore with them their cult of the snake. At the same period, Ewe-speaking slaves were taken to Louisiana."—Cfr. A. B. Ellis, "On Vodu-Worship"—*Popular Science Monthly,* Vol. XXXVIII (1891), p. 651 ff.

hand, Voodooism is practically unknown,[47] while Obeah with its concomitant poisonings has been rife since the earliest days.[48]

**Obeah.** The word Obeah itself is really the Ashanti Obayifo, a witch or rather more properly, in practice as least, according to Captain Rattray, a wizard, being derived from bayi, sorcery.[49]

Now an Ashanti legend runs as follows. When Big Massa was busy with the work of creation, it happened that the little monkey Efo was making himself generally useful, and when the task was accomplished, he asked Big Massa, that, in return for the help rendered, all creatures should bear his name. To this Big Massa acceded to such an extent that henceforth certain classes of creatures added to their own proper names the suffix FO, in acknowledgment of the little monkey's part in the work.[50] Such is the Ashanti fable, and hence we find this suffix FO in the names of peoples, nations and occupations.

During the Haytian revolution many planters with their slaves took refuge in Cuba, whence some of them subsequently found their way to New Orleans. The Voodoo cult was thus established both in Cuba and in Louisiana.

[47] Note:—Ellis observes: "That the term vodu should survive in Hayti and Louisiana, and not in the British West India Islands, will surprise no one who is acquainted with the history of the slave trade. The tshi-speaking slaves, called Coromantees in the slave-dealers' jargon, and who were exported from the European forts on the Gold Coast, were not admitted into French and Spanish colonies on account of their disposition to rebel, and consequently they found their way into the British colonies, the only market open to them, while the French and Spanish colonies drew their chief supply from the Ewe-speaking slaves exported from Whydar and Badogry."—Cfr. A. B. Ellis, *The Ewe-Speaking Peoples of the Slave Coast of West Africa*, London, 1890, p. 29.

[48] Note:—Since the World War, I am told, Voodooism has spread in Jamaica, especially in the Parish of St. Catherine. In my own experience, only once did I find any indication of Voodooism and that was in upper Westmoreland in 1913.

[49] Rattray, *Ashanti Proverbs*, #56, p. 48. Note:—According to M. Oldfield Howey, one of the latest writers on the subject: "There are two distinct cults of fetish worship in the West Indies, Voodoo, or Voudou, and Obeah (Tchanga and Wanga). . . . But between the Voodoo and the Obeah cults are important differences. In the former the will of the god is communicated only through a priest and priestess; the ritual is carried out at night, and the serpent must be displayed in a cage. . . . The Obeah cult requires for its rites only a priest or a priestess, instead of the two, and the presence of the snake is not essential. Its sacrificial victims too are slain by poison instead of meeting a bloody death as in the rites of Voodoo."—Cfr. M. Oldfield Howey, *The Encircled Serpent*, Philadelphia, 1928, p. 246. As we shall see later, Howey is probably in error in requiring the serpent even as a concomitant of Obeah which strictly speaking is in no wise a form of ophiolatry.

[50] Rattray, *Ashanti Proverbs*, #78, p. 54.

Dropping this suffix then, from Obayifo, the resultant Obayi, as heard from the lips of the Koromantyn slaves, was variously rendered by the Jamaican Whites as obeah, obia, etc. For even now there is no agreement as to the correct spelling of the word. Of Obeah itself we shall have much to say, when we come to the consideration of Ashanti witchcraft and the source from which it was derived. For the present, let it suffice to note, that Jamaica Obeah is really a continuation of the Ashanti sorcery, just as Myalism in the Jamaica "bush" is a residue of the old tribal religious dance of the same African race.

Both with the Ashanti themselves and their descendants in Jamaica the word is commonly shortened into Obi. Thus we find the Obi-country referred to in the history of the Ashanti Fetish Priest, Okomfo-Anotchi, that is, Anotchi the priest. About the year 1700, after committing a capital offence, as Captain Rattray tells us, he "fled for his life to the Obi country. Here he had made a study of 'fetish' medicine and became the greatest 'fetish' man the Ashanti have ever had." Referring to the Obi country, Rattray notes: "I have so far been unable to trace this place,[51] but to this day in Ashanti any big fetish priest is called Obi Okomfo, that is, Obi Priest."[52] So also in Jamaica, in the practice of Obeah, the native "makes obi" even to-day. In fact what Captain Rattray witnessed among the Ashanti, e. g. his description of the making of a suman, or fetish charm,[53] has its counterpart in the weird incantation and grotesque fabrication of the Jamaica Obeah man, that produces a bundle of sticks as a protection against thief or evil spirit.

[51] Note:—Howey reports: "Among the Whydanese is a tribe called Eboes. Shepheard says this is 'a word of the same import as Oboes, which might mean the people or worshippers of Ob, the serpent-god. These people still practice a kind of serpent-worship—they worship the guana, a species of lizard.' "—The reference is to H. Shepheard, *Traditions of Eden,* London, 1871. Cfr. Howey, *The Encircled Serpent,* p. 28. Now while not agreeing with Howey as regards the identification of Ob with the serpent-god, as already noted, this citation may throw some light on the question of the Obi-country.

[52] Rattray, *Ashanti,* p. 288. Note:—Captain Newland states: "The Maguzawa, a section of the Hausa, may be found in the north of Togo and Cameroons." He notes that "Maguzawa" signifies "Magician and is a term applied by the Hausa Mohammedans to those of their kin who have remained pagans."—Cfr. H. Osman Newland, *West Africa,* London, 1922, p. 82. This may possibly be another clue to the Obi-country.

[53] Rattray, *Ashanti,* p. 310.

**Duppies and Mmotia.**

Moreover, is it merely another coincidence that the Jamaica duppies or ghosts are notorious for their stone-throwing propensities, pretty much the same as the Ashanti mmotia who, as A. W. Cardinall relates, "are pre-eminently mischief-workers, and are said to 'throw stones at one as one passes through the bush?' " [54]

**Oratory.**

Many years ago, John Beecham remarked of the Ashanti: "The natives of this part of Africa are remarkable for oratory, and will discourse fluently on a given subject for hours." [55] Any visitor to Jamaica who attends a school entertainment, especially in the country districts, will be impressed by the natural fluency and ease of manner in public appearances, on the part of even the smallest children. "Stage-fright" is positively unknown among them. And as for the peasantry themselves, how "dem do lub to argyfy" either in Court or along the public highway, wherever they can find an audience, however small.

**Songs.**

Again we are told by Ellis who primarily signifies Ashanti when he speaks of his Tshi group: "The Tshi songs consist of a recitative with a short chorus. The recitative is often improvised, one taking up the song where another is tired. Frequently the words have reference to current events, and it is not uncommon for singers to note the peculiarities of persons who may pass and improvise at their expense." [56] Had Ellis been writing of his experiences in Jamaica, and not of those on the Gold Coast, he would scarcely have changed a single word, except the subject of his remarks.[57] This is especially true in the heart of the "bush."

[54] A. W. Cardinall, *In Ashanti and Beyond,* Philadelphia, 1927, p. 224.
[55] John Beecham, *Ashantee and the Gold Coast,* London, 1841, p. 167.
[56] A. B. Ellis, *The Tshi-Speaking Peoples of the Gold Coast of West Africa,* London, 1887, p. 328.
[57] Note:—In connection with what is known as the Apo Custom, an annual festival among the Ashanti, there is a lampooning liberty which is thus described to Captain Rattray "by the old high-priest of the god Ta Kese at Tekiman."—"You know that every one has a sunsum (soul) that may get hurt or knocked about or become sick, and so make the body ill. Very often, although there may be other causes, e. g. witchcraft, ill health is caused by the evil and the hate that another has in his head against you. Again, you too may have hatred in your head against another, because of something that person has done to you, and that, too, causes your sunsum to fret and become sick. Our forbears knew this to be the case, and so they ordained a

**Jamaican Superiority.**

Having once established the dominant Ashanti influence in the formation of the Jamaica peasantry, it is easy to understand how the Blacks of the Island, if really representative of the higher caste, stand out above their brothers-in-color similarly situated in any other part of the world.

**Encomium of the Ashanti.**

After a careful study of his subject, W. Walton Claridge does not hesitate in his testimony to the truly remarkable innate ability of the Ashanti, both as individuals and as a Nation, when he says: "Although tradition asserts and other evidence favours the belief that this people and the Fantis and other Twi-speaking races are the offspring of a common stock, yet the Ashantis stand out in marked contrast to all the others, distinguished as much by their skill and bravery in war as by the patriotism and power of combination that ultimately led to the formation of the most powerful and in fact the only really important kingdom and empire that the Gold Coast has ever seen. From small beginnings these people gradually extended their power and authority, both by diplomacy and by force of arms, until in the end all the surrounding tribes owed allegiance to them and their countries became tributary provinces of Ashanti. Nor can there be the least doubt that that kingdom would, before the close of the nineteenth century, have included the whole Gold Coast, had not the seaboard tribes have been

[illegible] should have freedom to speak out just what was in their head, to tell their neighbours just what they thought of them and of their actions, and not only their neighbours, but also the king or chief. When a man has spoken freely thus, he will feel his sunsum cool and quieted, and the sunsum of the other person against whom he has now freely spoken will be quieted also. The King of Ashanti may have killed your children, and you hate him. This had made him ill, and you ill, too; when you are allowed to say before his face what you think, you both benefit. That was why the King of Ashanti in ancient times, when he fell sick, would send for the Queen of Nkoranza to insult him, even though the time for the ceremony had not come round. It made him live longer and did him good."—Cfr. Rattray, *Ashanti,* p. 152. Can this ceremony have given rise to the practice still in vogue in Jamaica of "throwing words at the moon?" You may tell the moon the most insulting things about a party within his hearing without being liable for libel as you would be if you addressed the same words to your victim or to another person. Thus you in turn may be called "a tief" or "a liar fee true," every word reaching you and those who are standing about, and yet if you ask your vilifier what he is saying, the answer will come: "Not you, sah. Him moon talk." It certainly "cools the sunsum" of the speaker who goes away contented and satisfied, though it must be confessed it has a far different effect on the object of the remarks. I speak from experience.

asssisted and protected by the Europeans, who feared their Settlements and trade might be endangered." [58]

A century earlier, Doctor Morse, of the Congregational Church in Charlestown, had already recorded his appreciation of the Ashanti, when he wrote: "To the English officer, who had very considerable opportunities of observation, the Ashantees appear a people decidedly superior to any other inhabitants of the Gold Coast. This superiority consists not only in military skill and valor, but as remarkably in moral feeling and intelligence." [59]

**Jamaica Peasantry.** The same might well be said of the descendants of the Ashanti in Jamaica. For, while you have in various parts of the Island many examples of the other negro types, still there stands out a strong distinctive element, that gives a tone to the general character of the peasantry, as it has all along left its impress on the folk-lore and superstitions that connect the entire Black population with their old haunts in Africa.

**Cleanliness.** A visitor to Jamaica from the States is immediately impresssed by the cleanliness of the native peasant in his habits and his fondness for bathing—a striking contrast with our Southern Negro, who too frequently seems to have a horror of water. In the Jamaica costal towns, the entire male population as a rule devotes a great part of every Sunday morning to swimming, so much so, that it frequently interferes with divine service, and even on weekdays, wherever water is plentiful, the morning bath is the rule rather than the exception.

In this connection it is interesting to find A. W. Cardinall writing: "The Ashanti are remarkable for their extreme cleanliness; and they take a pride in themselves, their clothing and their houses, which some of the other tribes do not, and many of the non-African population competely ignore." [60] Bowditch too, had noted the same characteristic of the Ashanti more than a century before: "Both men and women are particularly cleanly in their persons," he wrote of them, and adds that they washed "daily on rising, from head to foot, with warm water and

[58] W. Walton Claridge, *History of the Gold Coast and Ashanti,* London, 1915, Vol. I, p. 181.

[59] Jedidiah Morse, *The American Universal Geography,* Boston, 1819, Vol. II, p. 783.

[60] Cardinall, *In Ashanti and Beyond,* p. 48.

Portuguese soap, using afterwards the vegetable grease or butter, which is a fine cosmetic." [61] Is it a consequence of this use of Portuguese soap that in Jamaica to-day, perhaps no gift is more highly prized, even by the better class of the peasantry, than a cake or two of scented soap? On the occasion of my first Christmas in Jamaica, I was astonished by the number of gifts of soap, which almost seemed a reflection until I became better acquainted with the native customs.

**Conclusion.** To understand properly the spirit and aspirations of the better type of Jamaica peasant then, a close study of the Ashanti themselves became necessary, and this study, in turn, led to some rather startling results and conclusions, that have been incorporated into the following pages.

In the first place, many Hebrewisms were discovered in the Ashanti tribal customs. Then, several Ashanti words were found to have a striking resemblance to those of equivalent Hebrew meaning. Finally, the Supreme Being of the Ashanti gave strong indication of being the Yahweh of the Old Testament. The question naturally rose, how to explain these parallels of cultural traits? Should they be ascribed to mere coincidence—to independent development? Or, have we here a remarkable instance of diffusion across the entire breadth of Africa? Is it possible to establish even a partial historical contact between the Ashanti of to-day and the Hebrews of fully two thousand years ago, or more?

The problem might be approached, either by trying to trace the story of the Dispersion of the Jews, usually called the Diaspora, or by the study of tribal beliefs and practices and the records of early African travellers, particularly of those who had written of the manners and customs of the Negro before the inroads of Islamism had tended to utterly destroy all traditions of the past.

It was finally decided to attack the question from both angles. The worldwide diffusion of the Jews was followed in its manifold ramifications with a view of establishing every possible influx of Hebraic culture that might possibly at any time have reached the shores of Africa. After a general consideration of the Diaspora itself, the first line of investigation led from the Abyssinian centre of Hebraic influence, that dates back to a more or

[61] T. Edward Bowditch, *Mission from Cape Coast Castle to Ashantee,* London, 1819, p. 318.

less legendary origin, and which eventually built up the distinctively Jewish Falashas.

Then again, long before the destruction of Jerusalem by Titus, the Mediterranean shore of Africa had become lined with influential Jewish colonies which undoubtedly were in constant mercantile relations with the interior of the Dark Continent. But Egypt especially had been the haven of the refugees from Jerusalem at the time of the Babylonian Captivity, and for many subsequent centuries the Jewish element in the land of the Pharaohs continued to increase and prosper.

From all three of these sources, an Hebraic influence might well have penetrated to the very heart of Western Africa, especially along the general lines of commerce.

It was here that the study of the West African tribes themselves was undertaken, and every vestige of evidence recorded. It was indeed surpising how many Hebrewisms, either real or at least apparent, were to be found among the unislamised tribes.

The present volume is, then, the consequence of eleven years of intensive research, after the preliminary five years spent in Jamaica. It naturally follows along the line of study, with chapters parallel to the steps of the investigation, except that the Hebrewisms are, for the most part, grouped at the beginning of the work.

The argument at best must be a cumulative one, and as a single witness may be accused of bias or of being liable to error, quotations must necessarily be multiplied, even with a danger at times of becoming tedious. The two closing chapters will deal with a general summary and the author's personal deductions.

## *Chapter I*

## THE ASHANTI OF WEST AFRICA

**Admirers: Captain Newland.** Captain Newland, in his handbook of practical information intended for the guidance of officials and others in West Africa, writes: "Of all the Tshi-speaking races, the Ashantis have the most marked characteristics. Their skill and bravery in war, their diplomacy, and their singular patriotism and power of combination and organization, not only makes them the most formidable people in the Gold Coast, and the founders of the only important kingdom there, but also enabled them to become masters of the whole country and coast. Such was their ability and adaptabilty, that Lord Wolseley, who led the expedition against them in 1874, recorded: 'From the Ashantees I learned one important lesson, namely, that any virile race can become paramount in its own region of the world, if it possesses the courage, the constancy of purpose, and the self-sacrifice to resolve that it will live under a stern system of Spartan military discipline enforced by one lord, master or king.'

**Lord Wolseley.**

**Swanzy. Dupuis.** "Mr. James Swanzy, as long ago as 1816, in his evidence at the House of Commons, said: 'The Ashantees are the most civil and well-bred people that I have seen in Africa,' and Depuis, the British Consul in Ashanti, 1820, remarked that they professed never to appeal to the sword while a path lay open for negotiations, nor to violate their word, and he stated that their Moslem neighbours corroborated this assertion.

**Claridge.** "Dr. Walton Claridge, also, in his recent *History of the Gold Coast and Ashanti,* illustrates from the British wars in Ashanti at the end of the nineteenth century, the forbearance, the warlike skill, and courage of this race, whom he declares to be 'perhaps the most abused and least understood in Africa.'"[1]

**Ashanti Origin: Theories.**

Who then, are these Ashanti who have merited such unstinted praise even from those whom they have successfully opposed for nearly a hundred years before being finally subjected at the beginning of the present century?

**From Egypt: Arcin.**

Without adducing any proof, André Arcin positively asserts, in connection with the Arab invasion of Africa: "From Ethiopia, Middle Egypt and Central Sudan, descended the Ashanti and the tribes known as Bantu."[2] Whether, or not, there is ultimately any foundation for this assertion in the antecedents of the present-day Ashanti, we shall see later.

**From the North: Sir John Hay.**

Vice-Admiral Sir John Hay, who coöperated with General Wolseley in the campaign of 1874, makes the following observation: "When the Moslem invasion of Western Europe was stemmed, and the Christians reasserted their superiority in Spain, the Moors turned the tide of conquest towards Central Africa, and on the banks of the long mysterious Quorra or Niger established their seat of empire at Timbuctu. They advanced gradually to the Kong Mountains, pushing before them the aboriginal race of Central Africa; and having driven them into the low lying countries between the Kong Mountains and the sea, the tide of Mahometan conquest expended itself in establishing the kingdom of Gaman. The native tribes, which occupy the Countries now known as Ashanti and the Protected Territory, seem then to have been known as Ashanti, Fanti, Akim, Assin, Akuama, and Denkera."[3] However, in thus fixing the date of the Ashanti migration from the north, Sir John is evidently in error. The Moorish conquest of Timbuktu took place about the year 1591,[4] at a time when the Ashanti without a doubt had already been well established back of the Gold Coast.

**MacDonald.**

George MacDonald, who at one time was the Director of Education for the Gold Coast Colony,

[1] Newland, *West Africa,* p. 94.
[2] André Arcin, *La Guinée Française,* Paris, 1907, p. 169.
[3] John Dalrymple Hay, *Ashanti and the Gold Coast,* London, 1874, p. 22.
[4] Felix Dubois, *Tombouctou la Mystérieuse,* Paris, 1897, p. 255.

also thinks that the Ashanti were driven from the interior by the advancing Mohammedan tribes, and that they "settled in the countries round the Kong Mountains a district then known to the Arab traders as Wangara." [5]

**Captain Rattray.**

That they actually reached their present location from the north, there can be but little doubt. Captain R. Sutherland Rattray, who has spent more than a quarter of a century in Africa, and about twenty years of the time in the West, is without question the leading authority on all matters pertaining to the Ashanti. Great weight, then, must be attached to his statement: "All I can say so far about the origin of the Ashanti is that I feel sure they came from the North or North-West. They do not know this themselves, because all their myths record their origin as being from Ashanti proper." [6]

**Cardinall.**

In confirmation of this opinion of Captain Rattray, we find A. W. Cardinall reporting of the Northern Territory, that "as a matter of fact, the people here have many traditions concerning the Ashanti." [7]

**Ratzel.**

Friedrich Ratzel is also fully in accord with this view, when he observes: "As early as the sixteenth century, came in, it is said, from the Niger, the Intas, a race capable of founding states, who set up in Upper Guinea powerful states, especially Ashantee, which for some time embraced nearly the whole Gold Coast, with country a long way inland. . . . According to their own traditions, the Ashantee are decidedly a race of conquerors; and in the judgment of Europeans they are among the best breeds of Guinea—intelligent, industrious and courageous." [8]

**From the East: Johnston.**

Sir Harry Johnston, too, is quite positive in his opinion, that, "according to their language rela-

[5] George MacDonald, *The Gold Coast, Past and Present,* New York, 1898, p. 32.

[6] Personal letter dated Mampon, Ashanti, Oct. 5, 1925. Note:—Cfr. also Raymond Leslie Buell, *Native Problems in Africa,* New York, 1928, Vol. I, p. 785: "Originally occupying the northern part of what is now the Gold Coast, it is believed that the Akan people were gradually driven south by lighter-skinned peoples, and took up their abode in the forests which gave them protection against the cavalry attacks of the invaders." The Ashanti, of course, were a component part of the Akan.

[7] A. W. Cardinall, *The Natives of the Northern Territories of the Gold Coast,* London, 1920, p. 22.

[8] Friedrich Ratzel, *History of Mankind,* London, 1896, Vol. III, p. 142.

tions the Ashanti group of Negroes once came from the Niger north of Yoruba land, in the Borgu country." [9]

**Mockler-Ferryman.**

Now, as Lieut. Col. Mockler-Ferryman insists: "that the Borgus claim relationship with the Bornus," [10] and the Bornus are located to the southwest of Lake Chad, there is a far-reaching indication of the possi-

[9] Harry H. Johnston, *History and Description of the British Empire in Africa,* London, 1910, p. 293. Note:—As great stress is going to be placed on the testimony of the late Sir Harry Johnston in the course of the present volume, it may be well to record the following appreciation of the man and his work. At the general meeting of the Royal Geographical Society held June 18, 1928, Sir Charles Close in his Presidential Address said: "We have also to deplore the loss, during the past year, of that most accomplished and versatile traveller, explorer, and administrator, Sir Harry Johnston. He became a Fellow in 1883, he had been a Member of the Council and a Vice-President and was awarded the Founders Medal for his exploration in Africa in 1904. He died nearly a year ago, on 31 July 1927, in his seventieth year. He had lived a remarkably full life. Not only did he know Africa as few know it, . . . but in East Africa, and even more in Nyasaland, he took a prominent share in establishing the Government of this country. . . . In the midst of all this work he found time to write excellent accounts of the countries that he visited. . . . He was an intrepid explorer, he wrote admirably, he was a musician, and was a deep student of the customs and languages of the natives of Africa."—*The Geographical Journal,* London, Vol. LXXII (1928), p. 97 f. And the New York *Times* in its editorial of August 2, 1927, entitled "A Many-sided Englishman" says: "Sir Harry Hamilton Johnston was one of the most accomplished men of his time. He was not only a salient figure in the long line of British explorers, administrators, 'conditores imperii.' He was a student of architecture and painting, and his pictures of African scenes are said to have merit, though exhibited at the Royal Academy. He was master of some fifteen languages, eleven modern ones, and we don't know how many African dialects. He knew Arabic much better than the late Sir Mark Sykes, that engaging aristocrat who had some reputation as a linguist. He studied comparative anatomy at the Royal College of Surgeons. He was a Zoologist of note, whose services were recognized by the Zoological Society. To the knowledge of the flora and fauna as well as the geography of Africa he made important contributions. He was an apt after-dinner speaker. He was a man after Theodore Roosevelt's own heart and a friend of many other famous persons. In his sixties he began that brilliant series or continuations of renowned stories which made his name familiar here to a generation which had forgotten the expedition to Mount Kilimanjaro, the protectorates over the Niger delta and the Nyasa region and the grandiose 'Cape to Cairo'—Johnston was the first to use this phrase—plan, which the British Government allowed Germany to block. His works on Africa are many; some of them too loaded with detail for the easy-going reader to enjoy. But his work in Africa is a monument. He had ruled over enormous regions; had fought 'unofficial' wars, pacified the Niger delta, reorganized the administration of Uganda protectorate. The pompous term 'proconsul' is often applied to men like him. It was as a Vice-Consul or a Consul that Johnston most distinguished himself, though in British Central Africa he was British Commissioner and Consul General. It was not his G. C. M. G. or K. C. B. that honored him. We like to think rather of the Medalist of the South Kensington School of Art, the Honorary Life Member of the New York Zoological Society; of the young man who confabulated with Stanley on the Congo and was perhaps the third European of the early 80s to see that then almost

ble origin of the Ashanti, that carries us well on our way to the verification of the assertion of André Arcin, already quoted, that the Ashanti may trace their descent from distant Egypt.[11]

**P. Amaury Talbot.**

Moreover, P. Amaury Talbot who has spent many years in Nigeria, points out that "semi-white invaders appear to have penetrated by way of Borgu and Nupe into the Yoruba country about the eighth or ninth century, and to have supplied the ruling dynasty of these three tribes." [12]

**Ethnic Criteria: Dixon.**

Professor Roland B. Dixon of Harvard as we shall see is of the opinion that the oldest strata in Africa are represented by the Mongoloid—that is round-headed (brachycephalic) low-skulled (chamaecephalic) broad-nosed (platyrrhine) and the Proto-Australoid—that is long-headed (dolichocephalic) low-skulled (chamaecephalic) broad-nosed (platyrrhine)—types.[13] Speaking of the latter classification, Professor Dixon calls attention to the fact that this type "appears as a not inconsiderable element in the Abyssinian plateau and among the Ashanti of West Africa." [14] This might imply at least a partial derivation from a common source. He makes the further observation: "If we turn to archaeological data, it appears that the Proto-Australoid type was by a small margin dominant in Egypt in Pre-Dynastic times and de-

fabulous stream above Stanley Pool. It seems curious that the man who introduced the okapi to the world also gave us *The Gay Dombeys*."

[10] A. F. Mockler-Ferryman, *British Nigeria,* London, 1902, p. 144 N.

[11] Note:—According to Dr. Hermann Baumann of the Staatliches Museum für Völkerkunde in Berlin, the autochthonous African culture was characterized by the fact that the woman alone was the worker of the soil. On this native culture was superimposed a high-grade Asiatic civilization which swept from the East across the Sudan, leaving a notable impress, for example, in its method of field work by men. The West African civilization, he finds, "assimilated particularly elements of that 'new-Sudanese' culture, which transformed above all the real West African culture on the Gold and Slave Coasts and inland as far as Nigeria."—Cfr.Hermann Baumann, "The Division of Work according to Sex in Africa Hoe Culture,"*Journal of the International Institute of African Languages and Cultures,* London, Vol. I (1928), p. 298. Dr. Baumann further concludes that the Ashanti are to be classed with "the strongly Sudanese Yoruba and Nupe" who "follow the Sudanese method of work by the men."—l. c., p. 301.

[12] P. Amaury Talbot, *The Peoples of Southern Nigeria,* Oxford, 1926, Vol. I, p. 28.

[13] Roland B. Dixon, *Racial History of Man,* New York, 1923, p. 180.

[14] Idem, p. 181.

creased largely later except for a temporary rise in the fifth dynasty and again in Ptomemaic times." [15]

Again, according to Professor Dixon, among the Ashanti the brachycephalic Pigmy type forms less than ten per cent, while more than half belong to what he terms the Proto-Negroid type, that is Dolichocephalic Platyrrhine with high skull, medium broad face and moderate prognathism. Whence he concludes that the Ashanti "seem to be quite comparable to the Chad group in the Sudan." [16] It is further his opinion "that the early population of the Guinea-coast region was closely comparable to that of the Congo forest," that is, a Brachycephalic Pigmy type, "and that these have been overlaid by a strong immigration of typical Negroes," Dolichocephalic Platyrrhine with medium broad faces and moderate prognathism in which the high skulls greatly outnumbered the low skulls. [17] "This Negro immigration," he adds, "was in part a westerly drift from the Chad-Nile area, and in part a direct southward movement from the western Sudan and the Sahara borders, forced by the expansion in the Sahara region of the Caspian peoples who have poured into northern Africa since very early times." [18]

**Pittard.**

Eugene Pittard, the Anthropologist, basing his opinion on documents gathered by Ernest Chantre, formerly Sub-Director to the Société d'Anthropologie de Lyon, in 1919,[19] says of the Ashanti: "The marks of variability indicated by the stature, cephalic index and nasal index, shows us only that the Ashanti do not constitute a pure ethnic group. They appear to be—whatever future studies may show—an aggregate of negro types. They assuredly classify as a people of tall stature (height above the medium and tall stature), for the most part dolichocephals or sub-dolichocephals, and platyrrhine. But naturally, this is no more than a very general view. The proportion of short stature, of the brachycephalic and mesorhinian types, shows us clearly what a degree of heterogeniety this

[15] Idem, p. 181 f.
[16] Idem, p. 233.
[17] Idem, p. 500.
[18] Idem, p. 233 f.
[19] Cfr. Ernest Chantre, "Contribution à l'étude des races humaines de la Guinée, Les Aschantis."—Bulletin, *Société d'Anthropologie de Lyon,* 1919, p. 36.

people manifests." [20] Professor Pittard further expresses the opinion that the Ashanti reached their present location by emigration from the north-east.[21]

**Haddon.**

Doctor Haddon, in his turn, remarks: "Although dolichocephaly is a characteristic of the Negro, there is undoubtedly a broad-headed strain, the origin of which is obscure. In the third millenium B. C. the majority of the Negroes who came into Nubia were of the short, relatively broad-headed type. . . . An occasional broadening of the head extends as far west as the Kru and Vei and even among the Ashanti. Among the latter is a distinct proportion of short people, notwithstanding their mean high stature; they are also more downy and there is a tendency to extreme platyrrhiny. The broad-headed type thus extends from the western end to the eastern Sudan right across the continent, but it rarely appears in a pure condition. Its origin is doubtful; possibly it may represent an old migration from southern Arabia, and southward migrations from the central Sudan zone have broadened the heads of various peoples in several parts of the great Congo area." [22] Later Doctor Haddon adds: "The Ashanti and Fanti (of the Tshi-speaking group) should be regarded as probably a single people migrating coastward, part of which, the Ashanti, remained beyond the forest belt on the first terraces of the highlands, while the rest, the Fanti, reached the Gold Coast." [23]

**Summary of Claridge.**

Before going into this question more fully, let us quote the following summing up of Walton Claridge: "The records left by Europeans do not commence till the latter part of the fourteenth century, and none of them have left any account of any statements that may have been made to them by the people as to their past history. Very little is known, therefore, about the origin of these tribes, and such accounts as have been handed down and are current among them at the present time are purely traditionary. The Gold Coast African, however, seldom migrates. He will make long journeys for purposes of trade and may stay away for years, but he always tends

[20] Eugene Pittard, "Contribution à l'Étude Anthropologique des Aschanti,"—*L'Anthropologie,* Paris, Tome XXXV (1925), p. 464.
[21] Idem, p. 453.
[22] Haddon, *Races of Man and Their Distribution,* New York, 1925, p. 49.
[23] Idem, p. 51.

to return to his original home. The Linguists and better-class people, from whom these traditionary accounts of past events are obtained, belong to families which have had their home in one and the same place from time immemorial. Among such a people, tradition has a far greater value than among less settled races, for places and natural objects connected with their past history are constantly before their eyes, and assist in preserving the story from generation to generation.

"The general sum of these traditions is that the Fantis, Ashantis, Wassawa, and in fact all the Twi-speaking or Akan peoples were originally one tribe. They were a pastoral race and inhabited the open country beyond the forest belt and farther north than Salaga. A northern and lighter skinned people, which is commonly supposed to have been the Fulanis, commenced to encroach on their territory, and being stronger than they, seized their cattle and young women and made many of them slaves. After a time, the Akans began to migrate in small parties into the forest, where they built little villages and lived in hiding. As time went on, the number of these forest-dwelling fugitives increased, until, in the course of many years, their numbers became very considerable. Their oppressors then heard of them and made several attempts to conquer and enslave them, but were unable to fight in the dense forest, and, tiring of their want of success, eventually left them unmolested.[24] Living in peace, the people continued to increase, and gradually extended further south until they had populated the forest belt and eventually reached the coast."[25]

And again: "It is not known exactly when the Ashanti kingdom was first founded, and the law which makes any mention of the death of a king a capital offence has conduced to the loss of much of its earliest history. From the traditions that are now current it appears, however, that after the flight of the Akans from the districts that they had formerly occupied and the migration of the Fantis to the coast, the Ashantis remained and settled in the

[24] Note:—It has been suggested with much reason that the advance of Islam to the south was in reality checked by the tsetse-flies which destroyed the horses of the intruders. Unaccustomed to fight on foot, the Musulman was helpless without his mount.—Cfr. Haardt and Audouin-Dubreuil, *The Black Journey*, New York, 1927, p. 84.

[25] Claridge, *History of the Gold Coast and Ashanti*, Vol. I, p. 4 f.

northern portions of the forest country, where they established several minor kingdoms or principalities, which, though united by a common interest, were nevertheless independent of each other. By 1640 this confederacy had acquired considerable influence and was esteemed a powerful kingdom. With its allies, it was able to put an army of about 60,000 men in the field. They were armed principally with bows and arrows, and their valour and determination in battle soon gave their neighbours good reason to fear them. The seat of government is said to have been established sometimes at Chichiweri, at others at Bekwai or Dompoasi; but of their earliest rulers or wars nothing definite is now known, although several vague traditions exist.

"These traditions point to the Ashanti's first home as having been somewhere in the neighbourhood of the Adansi country—the 'Ananse' of Bosman. The first King whose name has been handed down is Chu Mientwi, who was succeeded by Kobina Amamfi. He is said to have reigned about 1600 to 1630. Gold was unknown during his reign, iron being used as currency. It is probable that there were at least two other Kings before him." [26]

**Contention of Bowditch.**

T. Edward Bowditch, who was the first European to come in close contact with the Ashanti and who subsequently published his impressions, records: "The men are very well made, but not as muscular as the Fantees; their countenances are frequently aquiline. The women are generally handsomer than those of Fantee, but it is only among the higher orders that beauty is to be found. . . . in many instances, regular Grecian features with brilliant eyes set rather obliquely in the head. Beauty in a Negress must be genuine, since complexion prejudices instead of imposes, and the European adjudges it to the features only, which appear in the class to be Indian rather than African." [27]

**Scoffed at by Freeman.**

Two years later, this same Bowditch sought to establish a connection between the Ashanti and the ancient Egyptians and Abyssinians. Richard Austin Freeman who gives little credence to the suggestion says of this essay or sketch: "I have elsewhere mentioned that when at Kumasi I was strongly reminded of ancient Egypt and its monu-

[26] Idem, p. 192.
[27] Bowditch, *Mission from Cape Coast Castle to Ashantee,* p. 318.

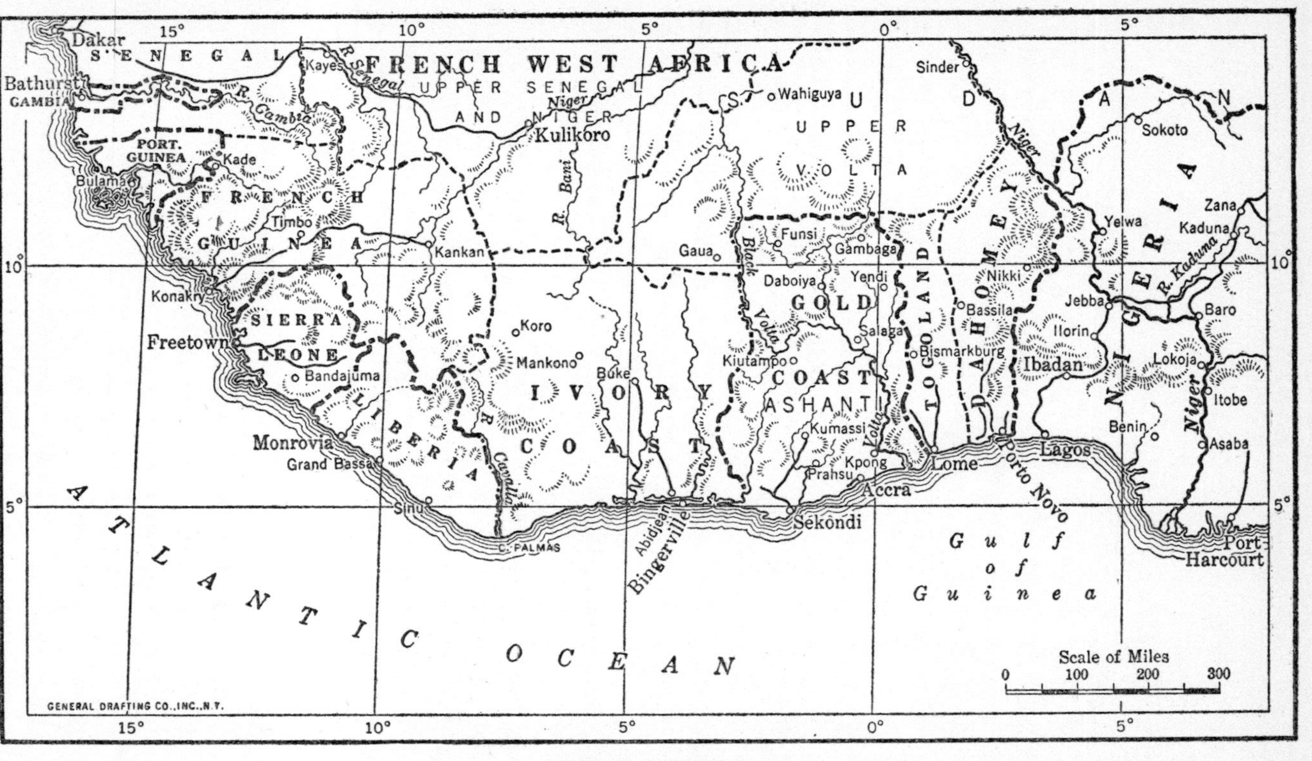
FRENCH WEST AFRICA
SENEGAL
UPPER SENEGAL AND NIGER
UPPER VOLTA
DAHOMEY
NIGERIA
FRENCH GUINEA
PORT. GUINEA
GAMBIA
SIERRA LEONE
LIBERIA
IVORY COAST
GOLD COAST
ASHANTI
TOGOLAND
Dakar
Bathurst
Bulama
Kade
Timbo
Kayes
Konakry
Freetown
Bandajuma
Monrovia
Grand Bassa
Sinu
C. PALMAS
Kankan
Kulikoro
Koro
Mankono
Buke
Abidjean
Bingerville
Gaua
Wahiguya
Funsi
Gambaga
Daboiya
Yendi
Salaga
Kiutampo
Kumassi
Kpong
Prahsu
Accra
Sekondi
Bismarkburg
Bassila
Nikki
Lome
Porto Novo
Lagos
Sinder
Sokoto
Yelwa
Zana
Kaduna
Jebba
Ilorin
Ibadan
Baro
Lokoja
Itobe
Benin
Asaba
Port Harcourt
R. Senegal
R. Gambia
Niger
R. Bani
Black Volta
Volta
R. Cavalla
R. Kaduna
ATLANTIC OCEAN
Gulf of Guinea
Scale of Miles
0
100
200
300
15°
10°
5°
0°
GENERAL DRAFTING CO., INC., N.Y.

WEST AFRICA

ments; but when I endeavoured to account for this impression I was unable to find that it was based upon any real resemblance excepting that the curious birdlike figures sculptured on some of the houses were singularly like some that I had seen in Egyptian monuments.

"I suspect that Bowditch received a similar impression and endeavoured, after leaving the country, to 'work up' a theory on the subject, for whereas his hypotheses are numerous and learned, his facts are extremely scanty, and his arguments in general more ingenious than convincing.

"Nevertheless his book is not without interest, and some of the analogies which he mentions are certainly striking." [28]

**General Theory.**

While then, many of Bowditch's observations must be rejected as specious, some of them at least deserve mention here. It is true, that they may be of little value in themselves, but certain facts adduced will tend to strengthen our own general theory, that somewhere in the remote past, there was an infiltration of the ancient Hebrews in the parent stock from which the present Ashanti were evolved. As our argument, we have seen, must be a cumulative one, no point can be considered so trifling as to be overlooked.

**Infiltration from Egypt.**

Bowditch thus enunciates his thesis. "The traditions of emigration, not of the whole population but of particular families, so current in Ashantee and neighbouring nations, the numerous exceptions to the negro countenance, and the striking similitude of most of their more extraordinary superstitions, laws, and customs to those of ancient Egypt, persuade me that most of the higher classes are descended from eastern Ethiopians who had been improved by an

[28] Richard Austin Freeman, *Travels and Life in Ashanti and Jaman,* Westminster, 1898, p. 433 f. Note:—Too much value is not to be given to the opinion of Doctor Freeman in such matters. His reputation was established, not as a historian, but rather as the writer of fiction, as the following sketch shows. R. Austin Freeman "in 1887 went to Accra in the West Coast of Africa, to take up an appointment as Assistant Colonial Surgeon. In 1888 he was attached to a mission to Ashanti and Jaman as medical officer, naturalist and surveyyor. He contracted blackwater fever, and was invalided home in 1892. For five years he practiced medicine in England, and at one time was Deputy Medical Officer of Holloway Prison. Dr. Freeman is also a landscape and marine painter, a sculptor, a plaster moulder, a worker in wood and metal, and a bookbinder. His twenty-odd novels fall into two classes—adventure romance and detective stories."—Willard Huntington Wright, *The Great Detective Stories,* New York, 1928, p. 196.

intercourse with the Egyptian emigrants and colonists."[29] To this general thesis of Bowditch we are going to subscribe later, with this modification, that we hope to show in due course, that the specific influence from Egypt, that improved and as it were elevated the Ethiopians to a higher plane of civilization, was in all probability a continuous influx of Jewish colonists, trekking up the Nile, an influence that was eventually to spread itself clear across Africa to the Niger, and thence over pretty much the whole of West Africa, where it coalesced with an earlier Semitic influence that had swept down from the North. With this preamble, let us now seriously consider, somewhat in detail, the facts adduced by Bowditch.

**Parallel Customs.**

Relying principally on Salt's *Voyage en Abyssinie* as an authority on Abyssinian customs, Bowditch makes good use of his own experience amongst the Ashanti and establishes many parallels in the habits and manners of the two peoples. Thus he states: "The following customs will be recognised as Abyssinian. The king of Ashantees is never to be presumed to speak but through his ministers or interpreters, who invariably repeat his ordinary observations, however audible, with the Abyssinian exordium, 'Hear what the King says!' "[30]

Again he finds in the prefix Sai or Zai to the names of the Ashanti kings a remnant of the Abyssinian Za or Zo, prefix of the Shepherd kings or original Ethiopians, which was sometimes pronounced or written, he says, Zai or Sai.[31] So, too, he traces eleven early Ashanti kings, whose names are strikingly similar to a like number of Abyssinian kings given by Salt.[32]

The practice of ablutions among the Ashanti he would have of Abyssinian origin, and would ascribe to Ethiopic influence the part played by the women in the succession of the Ashanti kings.[33] This succession is had not from father to son, but

[29] T. Edward Bowditch, *An Essay on the Superstitions, Customs and Arts, common to the Ancient Egyptians, Abyssinians, and Ashantees,* Paris, 1821, p. 5.

[30] Idem, p. 16.

[31] Idem, p. 17.

[32] Idem, p. 18.

[33] Idem, p. 26. Note:—In reference to the early Egyptians Gaston Maspero writes: "Paternity was necessarily doubtful in a community of this kind, and hence the tie between fathers and children was slight; there being no family, in the sense in which we understand the word, except as it centred around

through the sister of the late king to his nephew.[34] In Abyssinia, too, Bowditch finds a parallel for the custom of 'swearing on the king's head' [35] already referred to as the great oath.[36]

Again, he says: "The Abyssinians like the ancient Egyptians, never fight in the night, neither do the Ashantees, not even after sunset, whatever advantages they may lose. The Gallas never fight on a Friday, the Ashantees never on a Saturday." [37] This last rather savors of Judaism!

Stripping to the waist as a sign of respect, Bowditch finds among the Abyssians and Ashanti alike,[38] and both nations begin their year at about the same time, in the Autumn.[39] The Civil New Year of the Jews (Rosh Ha-Shanah) also occurs in September or early October.[40]

Of facial expressions, Bowditch claims: "Browne's description of the aquiline nose and thin lips of the modern Copts, agreeing

the mother. Maternal descent was, therefore, the only one openly acknowledged, and the affiliation of the child was indicated by the name of the mother alone."—Gaston Maspero, *History of Egypt,* trans. M. L. McClure, London, 1906, Vol. I, p. 64. While it seems difficult to admit such a decadence in pre-historic Egypt, the citation is given for what it is worth.

[34] Note:—Francis Rennell Rodd after stating, "It seems clear that before the advent of Islam, which has tended to modify the system, the Tuareg had a complete matriarchal organization," adds, "I know of no reason to suppose that these matriarchal customs were derived from association with the negro people; the reverse is quite likely to have occurred." He then states: "The matriarchate is known to have existed in classical times as far south as Aethiopia, in the Meroitic kingdom as well as in early Egypt."—Cfr. Francis Rennell Rodd, *People of the Veil,* London, 1926, p. 152. Cfr. also E. L. Gautier, La Conquête du Sahara, Paris, 1925, p. 191: "At Hoggar, the father has no legal existence; he has without doubt, full realization of his paternity, he is father from the sentimental and domestic view-point, but his children are legal strangers to him. They belong to the tribe of the mother, they have only such heritage and rights as she transmits to them, their nearest male parent is the maternal uncle. It is this last who is the true head, the great dignitary of the Tuareg matriarchal family, the object of the greatest respect; a great political chief at death transmits his authority, not to his sons, but to the sons of his sister." The Ashanti has successions through both parents, but the great "blood succession" (abusua) is through the mother.

[35] Bowditch, l. c. p. 27.

[36] Cfr. Page 7.

[37] Bowditch, l. c. p. 32.

[38] Idem, p. 33.

[39] Idem, p. 34.

[40] H. St. John Thackery, *The Septuagint and Jewish Worship,* London, 1921, p. 137, Appendix V. Cfr. also Professor J. F. McLaughlin: "In the earliest times the Hebrew year began in autumn with the opening of the economic year. . . . This system of dating the New-Year is that which was adopted by the Semites generally, while other peoples, as the Greeks and Persians, began the year in Spring."—*Jewish Encyclopedia,* Vol. IX, Article "New-Year," p. 254.

with the ancient Egyptians paintings and sculpture, is also applicable to many of the higher class of Ashantees, although the dirty brown complexion is rare among them; a clear brownish red being a frequent variety, but the deep black the general color." [41]

He finds an Egyptian character in "the larger ornaments of the bases of the Ashantee buildings," [42] and considering all the similarities between the Abyssinians and Ashanti, he argues to a common origin "from the civilized Ethiopians of Herodotus," [43] and continues: "I will now show, that the Ashantees seem to have preserved the superstitions and customs, which the Egyptian colonists and visitors introduced amongst them, much more tenaciously than the Abyssinians, who must have abandoned many on their conversion." [44]

**Religious Observances.**

Turning to religious observances, Bowditch maintains: "The priests in Ashantee, as in ancient Egypt, are attached in bodies to particular deities, and enjoy a portion of the offerings. . . . The priesthood is also hereditary in particular families; they are exempt from all taxes; are supplied with meat and wine; consulted by the king before he undertakes war; do not pretend to divine of themselves, but simply to utter the voice or disclosure of the Deity; and shave their heads and bodies carefully and frequently; the same particulars are recorded of the priests of ancient Egypt." [45] Might not most of this be said with equal truth of the priests of the temple in Jerusalem? [46]

Again Bowditch assures us: "White is a color as sacred in Ashantee as it was in Egypt; the priests are not only distinguished by a white cloth, but frequently chalk their bodies all over. The king, and all but the poorer class of his subjects, wear a white cloth on their fetish days or Sundays, which is not the same in all families, and also on the day of the week on which they were born. The acquitted are always sprinkled with white chalk by the king's interpreters, as a mark of their innocence. The king always swears

[41] Bowditch, l. c. p. 35.
[42] Idem, p. 37.
[43] Idem, p. 40.
[44] Idem, p. 41.
[45] Idem, p. 45.
[46] Cfr. Ezech. xliv, 20. The reiteration of Ezechiel of the prohibition of Leviticus against the shaving of the head, might imply that the priests had grown remiss in this regard, and fallen into gentile ways.

and makes others swear on a white fowl, and three white lambs is the sacrifice appointed to be made before his bed-chamber." [47]

And further Bowditch informs us: "The kings of Egypt assisted in a morning sacrifice, soon after rising; after which, some wise maxims or great actions were read to them from the sacred books; the king of Ashantee always assists in the morning sacrifice, at the fetish temple, Himma, adjoining the palace; pouring the blood of the sheep over his royal stool, and afterwards rubbing it with the juice of the sacred oranges with his own hands." [48]

**Legal Procedure.**

Legal procedure, also, lends support, in Bowditch's point of view. According to him: "The following remarkable coincidence between the laws of the Ethiopians and those of the Ashantees, are still more interesting by the assurance of Diodorus, that the laws of the Egyptians were, in substance, the same as those of the Ethiopians. 'According to the established order of succession amongst some Ethiopic nations, upon the death of the king, his sister's son mounted the throne.' " [49] This is, as noted before, the rule among the Ashanti.

**Architecture.**

One of Bowditch's chief arguments, however, he has reserved for the end. It may bear quotation at length. "The freedom and simplicity of the larger ornaments of the Ashantee architecture are truly Egyptian, originating from the calix or corolla of a flower, as Denon suggests, or from the young leaves of those immense palm-like filices, representing, at their birth, the voluta of the Ionic capital, of which they are supposed to have furnished the idea. The more Etruscan patterns are the same as those in the tombs of the kings of Thebes, and several of the smaller base ornaments are to be recognised at Tentyris and Latopolis; the figure of the sacred bird is also remarkable. The sandal on the figure in the entry of the fifth tomb of the kings of Thebes, is precisely Ashantee; the tye, or courrois, as the artist observes, passing between the first and second toe, and M. Caillaut has just sent home one dug up near Thebes, exactly the same. It is more extraordinary and satisfactory, however, to find a long string of aggry beads amongst the fruits of excavation lately ad-

[47] Bowditch, l. c. p. 46.
[48] Idem, p. 52.
[49] Idem, p. 53.

dressed by the traveller to the Bibliothéque du Roi. I have drawn three of them, the first being the counterpart of one I presented to Baron de Humboldt, which he has sent to Berlin, and the others similar to those in the British Museum. I am inclined to think these aggry beads might have been emblematic of Osiris, from their prevailing pattern resembling rude eyes, and I once saw a bead in which these circles or eyes had evidently been inserted separately, for one had dropped out." [50]

**Names.**

Finally, in his supplementary notes, Bowditch calls attention to many striking similarities in names of cities, etc. among the Egyptians and the Ashantis.[51] But the chances are, of course, that these are coincidences and nothing more.

**Freeman's Admission.**

While rejecting Bowditch's theory in its entirety, Freeman himself had admitted, when speaking of his formal reception by the King at Kumasi: "As I listened to the strange solemn monotonous music and watched the various changes in the intricate, evidently symbolical ceremonial, while my eyes were dazzled by the gorgeous colours of the garments, the gaudy umbrellas and the glitter of the massive gold ornaments, I was irresistibly reminded, I cannot exactly tell why, of the life of Ancient Egypt and Assyria." [52]

**Stanley's Observations.**

Others, too, have been reminded of Ancient Egypt by what they have beheld among the Ashanti.[53] Thus Sir Henry M. Stanley, at the time a reporter for the *New York Herald,* writing from Kumasi, after its capture in 1874, observes: "Many little things which we see about us evince the taste and industry of the Ashantees. Take one of their stools for instance and examine it. Formerly it was one square block of white wood, very like sycamore. An artisan has chiselled and shaped a beautiful stool which any drawingroom might possess for its unique shape, design and perfection of workmanship. The seat is

**Ashanti Stools.**

[50] Bowditch, l. c. p. 60 f.
[51] Idem, pp. 57, 62.
[52] Freeman, *Travels and Life in Ashanti and Jaman,* p. 102.
[53] Note:—It may seem surprising to find Maspero recording that the Egyptians of the Pharaonic age preferred castor oil before all else in flavoring their food.—Cfr. Maspero, *History of Egypt,* Vol. I, p. 83. Among the descendants of the Ashanti in Jamaica I have found the same unaccountable predilection for castor oil which is taken with great relish.

crescent shaped, the ends of which when we are seated in it come up half-way to the hips; a central column beautifully carved, resting on a flat board twelve or fifteen inches in length by about eight in breadth supports it; on each side of the column, is a side support chipped until it resembles a lace-work pattern. There is art in this stool, and whether it is original with the Ashantees, or borrowed from strangers, it is certainly a most interesting specimen of woodwork, the whole of which is cut from a solid block of wood. I think I have seen the shape of a stool similar to it painted on one of the tombs of Thebes." [54]

Stanley had said, à propos of the interior of an Ashanti courtyard: "A strangely original people have been found in the Ashantees, infinitely superior to the Fantees and Assins, whose countries we have just traversed." [55] He further comments on the ornamentation of the walls: "Designs in alto-relievo, half an inch thick,

**Scroll-work.**

cornices are set off in many grooves, friezes with singularly bold diamond-shaped designs with embossed centres, pediments are something of the ionic order, severely plain and square, the walls with intricate scroll-work relieved by corollas in alternate squares." He goes on to mention

**Sandals.**

the sandals of the Ashanti: "You might almost declare upon oath that they are as good as anything worn by a middle-class Turk or Egyptian. Sandals! At the very repetition of the word one's thoughts revert to the inhabitants of Egypt, Syria and Asia Minor." [56] He then suggests that Moorish influence might be responsible for all this, as a consequence of the Moorish tribes. But the Mohammedans never gained any influence over the Ashanti, either politically or socially, and a distant Egyptian, or rather Hebraic, influence, as we hope to show, will explain it just as effectively.

**Cardinall's Impressions.**

Even quite recently, A. W. Cardinall, a Resident Magistrate and District Commissioner of the Gold Coast, speaking of typical Ashanti houses, thus records his own impressions: "This Ashanti type is quite characteristic, and lends itself to development. The houses devoted to the custody of the altars and shrines of the gods are often decor-

[54] Henry M. Stanley, *Coomassie and Magdala,* New York, 1874, p. 167.
[55] Idem, p. 166.
[56] Idem, p. 168.

ated in stucco mouldings, somewhat reminiscent of Egyptian and Eastern scroll-work." [57]

**Conclusions.** We may here safely conclude from the present data on hand, that the Ashanti constitute an Ethnic Complex. They form for the most part, a mixture of narrow and broad-nosed long-headed peoples, with moderate prognathism; and although the distinctively negro type is dominant, there is a small percentage of the early pigmy type. We may also conclude, that the Ashanti are not autochthonous to their present habitat, but are comparatively recent arrivals from the district of the Upper Volta, whither they had in all probability been driven from the vicinity of the Niger by the advance of Islamism.

The testimony of Dixon, Pittard and Haddon would further imply that they have a distant affiliation with the tribes of the Nile-Chad region, and the facts adduced by Doctor Baumann certainly suggest that they are a kindred people to the Yorubas. Finally, while it is not well to stress too much the evidence of Bowditch, there are strong indications of cultural contact, probably in the remote past, with Egypt or Abyssinia.

Let us now approach the question of possible traces of Hebraic culture in the tribal development of the Ashanti.

[57] Cardinall, *In Ashanti and Beyond*, p. 51.

## *Chapter II*

# ASHANTI HEBREWISMS

**Jamaica Obeah.**

As noted in the Introduction, Jamaica Obeah is directly traceable to the Ashanti, and the word itself is presumably derived from Obayifo, a witch. Captain Rattray tells us: "The word for witchcraft in Ashanti is bayi and for witch obayifo and bonsum, which are feminine and masculine respectively. The bonsum appear to be much less common than the female obayifo." [1] J. G. Christaller would seem to indicate the possible derivation of the word obayifo from obayen, which is itself compounded of ob and ayen, a wizard; so that its strict meaning would become an Ob-wizard.[2] However, Captain Rattray, whose authority is paramount in these matters, insists that while ayen is also used, this word is really Fanti and not Ashanti.[3] But as the Ashanti and Fanti are kindred people with a common origin, the ultimate root of both bayi and ayen may be the same.

In any case, the term obeah, obiah, or obia, there is no agreement as to the spelling, is usually regarded as an adjective, while obe or obi is the noun.[4] A description of Obi, transmitted some hundred and fifty years ago by the Agent of Jamaica to the Lords of the Committee of the Privy Council in England and by them subjoined to their report on the slave trade, would trace the etymology of the word Obi to the Egyptian Ob, a serpent, thus making the practice ultimately a form of Egyptian Ophiolatry.[5] However, one of the fragments of Sanchoniathon preserved for us by Eusebius of Caesarea in his *Praeparatio Evangelica,*[6] indicates

[1] Rattray, *Religion and Art in Ashanti,* p. 28.
[2] Christaller, *Dictionary of the Asante and Fante Language,* pp. 9, 561.
[3] Rattray, l. c. p. 28 N.
[4] Edwards, *History Civil and Commercial of the British West Indies,* Vol. II, p. 88.
[5] Idem, Vol. II, p. 89.
[6] Bk. I, Chap. 10.

that this form of idolatry, together with the word Ob itself, did not originate with the Egyptians.[7] In fact, John Bathurst Deane positively asserts: [8] "The origin of the terms Obeah and Obi may be traced to the Canaanitish superstition of the Ob or Oub,[9] which Bryant has so ingeniously detected in his remarks upon the witch of Endor." [10]

It was probably from Canaanitish origin also that the Hebrew word 'OB [11] was derived, and the uncertainty of its precise meaning renders difficult the translation of those passages of the Old Testament where it occurs. Many even to-day follow Godwyn in his explanation: "Ob signifieth properly a bottle, and is applied in divers places of Scripture to Magicians, because they being possessed with an evil spirit speak with a soft and hollow voice, as out of a bottle." [12]

While accepting the original meaning of the word to be a bottle, that is, a water-skin, we need not admit the subsequent reason adduced by Godwyn. As a matter of fact, in "making obi" to-day, one of the essential elements seems to be a bottle, in which various ingredients of the spell or bewitchment are placed. In this we have practically a clear differentiation between the making of a fetish and the making of obi. For, while poisonings are fre-

[7] Cory's *Ancient Fragments,* ed. E. Richmond Hodges, London, 1876, p. 22.

[8] John Bathurst Dean, *The Worship of the Serpent,* London, 1833, p. 173.

[9] Note:—M. Oldfield Howey who, as we think erroneously, would make Obeah a form of ophiolatry, says: "In Canaan the Hivites were serpent worshippers, and actually derived their name from the practice. According to Bochart the word is derived from Hhivia, a serpent, the root of which is Eph or Ev—one of the variations of the original Aub. This word was variously pronounced in different dialects, Aub, Ab—Oub, Ob,—Oph, Op—Eph, or Ev—the Greek ophis, a serpent, being formed from the same root." Cfr. Howey, *The Encircled Serpent,* p. 85. Later he adds: "In the Egyptian language the serpent is called oub, and Moses, born and educated in Egypt, doubtedlessly used the word in this sense, though our translators have rendered it 'familiar spirit.'"—l. c. p. 218.

[10] Potter, *Archaeol. Graeca,* Vol. II, p. 251. Note:—Howey remarks: "The witch of Endor is spoken of as an ob or oub, and was applied to by Saul for an oracle. To-day among the negroes the same is found, and the obi-man, or obi-woman is habitually consulted in any case of doubt and difficulty, just as was the ob-woman, or oub-woman of Endor by Saul."—Howey, l. c. p. 219.

[11] אוב

[12] Thomas Godwyn, *Moses and Aaron, Civil and Ecclesiastical Rites used by the Ancient Jews, London,* 1678, Lib. IV, Chap. X, p. 175. Note:—Professor Ludwig Blau declares: "'Ob' is said to denote the soothsaying spirit . . . or the ghost of the dead. . . . Jewish tradition says: 'Ob is the python, who speaks from his armpits. . . . The 'possessor of the ob' stooped while speaking, to make it appear as if the spirit spoke from his joints and arms."—*Jewish Encyclopedia.* Vol. IX, Article, "Necromancy," p. 204.

quently concomitant circumstances, if not the primary object in the practice of obi, the real incantation consists precisely in the forming in a bottle of a concoction that might well remind one of the formula made use of by the weird sisters in Macbeth.

**Implements of Obeah.**

The *Sub-Officers' Guide of Jamaica*[13] defines the implements of Obeah as follows: "Grave dirt, pieces of chalk, packs of cards, small mirrors, or bits of large ones, beaks, feet, and bones of fowls or other birds, teeth of dogs and alligators, glass marbles, human hair, sticks of sulphur, camphor, myrrh, asafoetida, frankincense, curious shells, china dolls, wooden images, curiously shaped sticks, and other descriptions of rubbish." To my own personal knowledge, after five years of close contact with the Jamaica "bush," in the midnight incantation of Obi, a perfect farrago of these and similar ingredients is invariably placed not in a box or package, but in a bottle, which must be duly buried near the dwelling of its intended victim, or openly suspended from tree or post, if it is to be a protective agency and not a vindictive one. The bundle of sticks, feathers, egg-shells, etc. which one so often sees stuck in the thatch of the hovel or suspended openly, though likewise produced by the Obeah-man, strictly speaking is not an instrument of Obi, but a fetish pure and simple. Its purpose is specifically preventive and it has no active potency as in the case of real Obi.

**Make Obi.**

The very term used by the native, to "make obi," which has come to Jamaica through the old Ashanti slaves, is idiomatically the same as the Scriptural ᶜASA 'OB,[14] one of the crimes charged against King Manasses, and which literally means "he made ob."[15] Is this still another mere coincidence? Or may it not indicate that the Ashanti ultimately

[13] *The Sub-Officers' Guide of Jamaica,* publ. by Harry McCrea, Inspector of Police, Kingston, 1908, Chap. XXX, No. 9, p. 83.

[14] עָשָׂה אוֹב Cfr. IV Kings, xxi, 6; II Paral. xxxiii, 6.

[15] Note:—The late Doctor J. M. Casonowicz of the United States National Museum, in a personal letter, dated July 13, 1926, disagreed with me on this particular point. It was his view that the function of the 'OB "was totally something different from the practice of obeah. The former had nothing to do with witchcraft or poison mongering, but was mantic, or necromancy, specificially, to call up a ghost in order to obtain information from it." And again, of the expression ᶜASA 'OB, he wrote: The expression . . . cannot mean that the king prepared a concoction similar to that of the obeah but has here the meaning: he instituted or established the institution of these special diviners, cf. I Kings, xii, 31; which means he installed priests."

trace some connection with the contemporaries of Manasses and the various forms of witchcraft then in vogue?

Brown, Driver and Briggs' Lexicon [16] while giving the primary meaning of 'OB [17] as "skin-bottle" and observing that in certain passages of the Scriptures it "is usually interpreted as ghost or familiar spirit conceived as dwelling in a necromancer," takes care to add: "But this apparently was not the ancient conception." The present suggestion, then, by tracing the Ashanti Obi to the Hebrew 'OB, might tend to clarify the original meaning of the word and explain one form of witchcraft practiced by the ancient Hebrews.[18]

[16] *Hebrew and English Lexicon of the Old Testament,* Boston, 1907, p. 15.

[17] אוֹב

[18] Note:—Eduard König writing on the forbidden media which superstitions had introduced among eastern peoples, gives his own explanation of the Hebrew 'OB, thus: "One of the soothsaying media was the 'OB (plural 'OBOTH). It had to do with the dwellers of the Kingdom under the earth.

1. Its real meaning is to be derived from Is. 8. 19, 'And when they shall say to you, seek of 'OBOTH and YIDDEᶜONIM, who mutter (Hebr. pipientes et murmurantes) . . . should not a people seek from its own God; should it seek the dead for the living.' Here the 'OBOTH and YIDDEᶜONIM are made parellel with the 'dead.'

2. In its derivation as a form 'OB is the active participal of a verb 'UB, corresponding to the Arabic ABA. It means rediens, reveniens. This is the derivation which Hitzig suggested as early as 1832. It forms like the participle active of KUM in KOM of 2 K.16.7b. The word therefore means a 'spirit,' such as men think find no rest in the grave, or one that returns from the kingdom of the dead,—a revenant. In later Jewish thought this same notion was supposed. These same spirits or 'OBOTH, under another aspect were YIDDEᶜONIM, scil. 'knowers,' that is of the secrets of Sheol and hence of Hades.

3. Since the 'OBOTH were considered special spirits among the dead, the ordinary dead could be reached through them (Deut. 18.11 against the opinion of Knobel). Moreover that the YIDDEᶜONIM were considered such spirits is sustained in Lev. 20.27, 'A man or woman *in whom* there is an 'OB or a YIDDEᶜONI, dying let them die.'

4. Those who invoked the dead were known:

a) sometimes as the 'dwelling places' of the 'OB or YIDDEᶜONI as in Lev. 20.27.

b) sometimes as the 'possessors of an 'OB as in I Sam. 28.7, where we have BAᶜALATH 'OB.

c) sometimes by an abbreviation of the expression, simply as 'OBOTH and YIDDEᶜONIM. Thus I Sam. 28.3 where Saul drives them from the land. Cf. also 2 Kings, 21.6; 23.24 and II Paralip. 33.6. In this latter use, we have of course a derived, extended meaning of 'OB.

For the above reasons, the word 'OB cannot have the original meaning 'gourd.' This derivation depends on the translation of the LXX ἐγγαστρίμυθος ventriloquists, and derives 'OB from a possible 'UB, to be hollowed out, to be bellied out. This derivation was held by Delitzsch, Dillman and de Buadissin. The parallelism of 'OB and YIDDEᶜONI is again the meaning of 'gourd' for 'OB. How after all could one speak of a 'man or woman in whom there is a GOURD,' Lev. 20.27, or the 'possessor of a bottle' as in I Sam. 28.7? Of

**Poison and Fear.** Voodooism, as we have seen, is essentially connected with serpent worship. Obeah, on the contrary, despite the fact that occasionally traces of ophiolatry are said to be found in particular instances, may be practically confined to witchraft wherein the end is attained through poison and fear. Hesketh J. Bell, who spent many years in the British Colonial Service of the West Indies, and who has only quite recently retired as Governor of Mauritius, speaks of the "Obeah bottle stuck in the thatch of a hut, or the branches of a plantain tree to deter thieves," and adds: "The darker and more dangerous side of Obeah is that portion under cover of which poison is used to a fearful extent, and the dangerous and often fatal effects of many a magic draught are simply set down, by the superstitious black, to the working of the spells of Obeah, and never to the more simple effects of the scores of poisonous herbs growing in every pasture, and which may have formed the ingredients of the Obeah mixture." [19]

As the Encyclopedic Dictionary states; successful Obeah is "either the effect of a disorderly imagination, or, more probably poison." [20] For, in practice, after the nocturnal incantation with

such a person there is no question of calling up a bottle! He calls up one of the spirits of the dead. How would the possession of a bottle give him authority? And finally how can there be any connection between the dead spirit which Is. 29.4. describes as 'pipiens' hollowly from the earth and 'OB a GOURD?"—Cfr. Eduard König, *Die messianischen Weissagungen des Alten Testaments,* Stuttgart, 1925, p. 14 f.

But König's whole argument is based on a presumed parallelism, that is not established, in Is. 8.19. "When they shall say to you, consult the 'OBOTH and YIDDE<sup>c</sup>ONIM, shrilly squeaking and murmuring—Will not a people consult ITS OWN God? (Will it consult) THE DEAD (for favors) for the LIVING?" While the Vulgate does not separate the two questions, and hence labors with some obscurity, the LXX makes the double question clear. The Prophet fails to supply the independent clause from which the "when" clause depends. After proposing the "when" clause, he breaks off abruptly and may be regarded as giving the answer in the form of a question. Or, perhaps more probably, he dramatically drops the original thought altogether, to break out with his own words to the people, lashing them with two ironic sentences. While, too, there is strong probability established that the DEAD are the 'OBOTH, the word is not absolutely dissociated from the meaning "gourd." The argument which König bases on Lev. 20.27, "A man or woman IN WHOM there is an 'OB," takes it for granted that the preposition B$^{e}$ in the text has exclusively the sense of IN, whereas, with the LXX reading, it may well be understood as the B$^{e}$ of Accompaniment or Association, so that the passage becomes "A man or woman WITH WHOM there is an 'OB." That is one who keeps an 'OB, etc. for superstitious practices. And in this sense the term "gourd" or water-skin is quite admissible.

[19] Hesketh J. Bell, *Obeah Witchcraft in the West Indies,* London, p. 9.

[20] *Encyclopedic Dictionary,* Philadelphia, 1894, Article, OBI.

the preparation of the bottle, the Obi-man may give his patron a powder to be dropped into the food or drink of the intended victim,[21] or, if this is not done, the fact that obi is being made against the individual is bruited abroad and quickly comes to the unfortunate's knowledge with consequent loss of peace of mind. Nervous worry and anxiety will do the rest, and not unfrequently the wretched man will waste away and actually die of fear.[22] Nevertheless, it is the Obi-man's persistent claim that it is solely his incantation over the bottle and its ingredients that produces the effect.[23]

**Bottle Witchcraft.**

In our supposition, then, if the "making of 'OB" among the Hebrews was like the "making of obi" in the Jamaica "bush" to-day, primarily a form of witchcraft as a shield to active poisoning, how could the desired end be more expediously affected than through the use of the skin-bottle so necessary in every household? A claw or tooth, or any other of the usual ingredients of Obeah might well have been placed in the water-skin as a cover for the poison which was to do the real harm. The skin-bottle might be said to be bewitched by the claw or the tooth. It would be bottle-witchcraft.

[21] Note:—Sumner, Keller and Davie, who do not clearly distinguish between Obeah and Voodooism in their Science of Religion Case Book, record: "Among the most dangerous articles sold by the voodoo man is the mixture of ground glass with water. This is known as 'obi water.' . . . In small doses obi water produces a sort of dysentery, and if the doses are repeated a miserable death, after protracted sufferings, is sure to follow."—Cfr. Summer, Keller and Davie, *The Science of Society,* New Haven, 1927, Vol. IV, p. 706. Even to-day in the Jamaica "bush" revenge is had on an enemy by administering 'obi water' to his live stock.

[22] Cfr. Gardner, *History of Jamaica,* p. 187.

[23] Note:—According to Wallis Budge, "It would be foolish to blink the fact that in ancient Herbals medicine and magic are almost inextricably mixed together; but the broad fact remains, and it is admitted by all competent authorities, that the compilers of the oldest Oriental Lists of Plants and Herbals had a very real knowledge of primitive medicine."—E. A. Wallis Budge, *The Divine Origin of the Craft of the Herbalist,* London, 1928, Prefatory Note, p. v. Of early Egyptian Medicine, he says: "The majority of practitioners relied on the use of spells and magical ceremonies, and made their treatment to suit the views of their patients, who as a whole believed in Magic. The progress of herbal science was strangled by the belief in magic which was general among the people."— l. c. p. 27 f. Any one who has lived for some time in Jamaica has come in contact with really marvellous "bush remedies." For example, fever is broken effectively by a "bush tea" made from certain leaves and twigs known only to the old woman who gathers them, and a throbbing headache is quickly relieved by the application of split cactus. Too frequently, the Obi-man makes use of this knowledge of herbals in connection with his art.

All this, of course, is mere conjecture, but it would have plausibility in its favor, at least more so than the claim of ophiolatry.

**Suggestion from Philo.**

The observations of Philo's *Biblical Antiquities* may throw a little further light on the subject. These so-called *Biblical Antiquities* of Philo, according to M. R. James who has published an English translation, are erroneously attributed to the famous Jewish Philosopher of the first century, but they carry great weight, as they were in all probability originally written in Hebrew shortly after the destruction of Jerusalem by the Romans in 70 A. D.[24] Referring to the period just prior to Gedeon,[25] this Pseudo-Philo relates: "And at that time there came a certain Aod of the priests of Madian, and he was a wizard." [26] Later on he gives Sedacta as the name of the witch of Endor, whom Saul consulted, and makes her the daughter of the aforementioned Aod.[27] In all probability, this Aod might be Aob. It is hard to distinguish the second and fourth letters in early Aramaic-Hebrew manuscripts. In fact in the old Aramaic itself, the essential difference is merely a turn to the left of one downward stroke.[28] Moreover, as Philo's work has come down to us only in a Latin translation, which was made from the Greek, and that again from a Hebrew original,[29] it is easy to understand how this alteration of a letter might well creep in. Furthermore, it may in itself be another form for the same word, as in the Hebrew we find NOD [30] of unknown root, signifying skin-bottle, as well as the usual 'OB.[31]

[24] *The Biblical Antiquities of Philo,* trans. M. R. James, London, 1917, Introduction, p. 7.
[25] Cfr. Judges, vi, 1–10.
[26] Philo, *Biblical Atiquities,* xxxiv, 1; l. c. p. 180.
[27] Idem, lxiv, 3; l. c. p. 240. Note:—Philo Judaeus was born at Alexandria probably between 20 and 30 B. C. He came of a noble, possibly a priestly, family, and his nephew became Alabarch or Prefect of the Alexandrine Jews. Cfr. Francis X. Kortleitner, *Archaeologia Biblica,* Innsbruck, 1917, p. 8, who considers the *Biblical Antiquities* as the work of Philo himself.
[28] Cfr. Table of Alphabets, Gesenius' *Hebrew Grammar,* ed. E. Kautzsch, Oxford, 1910, Insert, p. 10.
[29] Philo, l. c. p. 7.
[30] נאד
[31] Brown, Driver and Briggs, *Hebrew Lexicon,* p. 609. Note:—At Jado in the Jebel Nefussa, once a famous Jewish center, one still hears tales of a legendary Jewess who bore the significant name of "Umm el Ghrib," the Mother of Bottles.—Cfr. Nahum Slouschz, *Travels in North Africa,* Philadelphia, 1927, p. 178. Her memory is held in the highest veneration by the superstitious Berbers. l. c. p. 181.

**Conclusion of Deane.**

John Bathhurst Deane, after claiming to connect the Obeah of the West Indies with the ophiolatry of the Phoenicians and Egyptians, concludes: "Hence there is room for one of these two conclusions; that the Gold Coast was either colonized from Canaan, or from Egypt; the former of which is perhaps the more probable, from the greater facility afforded to the Phoenicians by navigation than to the Egyptians, who would have to cross deserts, and overcome many other physical difficulties in their distant march." [32] In due course, we hope to establish the existence of a regular line of trek from the Nile to the Niger, and while not wishing to deny the direct traffic with the Gold Coast by sea on the part of the Phoenicians and more especially by the Carthaginians, we are inclined to choose the land route as the way by which the principle Semitic influence ultimately reached West Africa, and that, too, through migratory bands of Hebrews.

**Semitic Influence.**

**Religious Dance.**

We are informed by Wallis Budge, that from early dynastic times dancing formed an intimate part in the religious functions among the Egyptians.[33] The Children of Israel carried this custom with them in their migration from Egypt, and we find it recorded in Holy Writ that when the Ark of the Lord was removed from the house of Obededom the Gethite, to be brought into the Holy City, King "David danced with all his might before the Lord: and David was girded with a linen ephod." [34]

In this connection Edward Scott remarks: "Among the Jews dancing was always regarded as a becoming expression of religious fervor and joyful emotion." [35] And again he tells us: "The Jews in early times, like the Greeks and Egyptians, introduced dancing in all their great religious festivals. For instance, at the festival of the first-fruits the whole population of a town would turn out. A procession was formed, headed by flute players, and the virgins danced to the music as they went along. At the feast of Tabernacles or of Ingathering, also, the young people danced around the altar, which was decorated with bunches of poplar-

[32] Deane, *Worship of the Serpent,* p. 176.
[33] E. A. Wallis Budge, *The Book of the Dead,* London, 1923, p. xxxv.
[34] II Kings, vi, 14.
[35] Edward Scott, *Dancing in All Ages,* London, 1899, p. 93.

osiers. On the day of Atonement there was dancing in the vineyards, and chain dances were formed." [36]

In the same manner, dancing forms a very essential part of the Ashanti worship to-day, and we are told that the Ashanti dance "invariably has a religious significance." [37] So also we find in the Myal dance of the Jamaica "bush" and the fanaticism of Myalism as manifested in the "digging up" or "pulling of Obeahs," [38] as it is called, one of the strong indications of the Ashanti's dominance among the descendants of the slaves in the Island, and possibly the survival of another Hebraic influence.[39]

**"Amen."** In his work on Ashanti Proverbs, Captain Rattray cites an Ashanti hymn of thanksgiving to the Supreme Being. It closes with the word Amen which, however, he avers, "it would be erroneous to ascribe to Christian origin." [40] It antedates the advent of Missionaries to West Africa, he assures us. But why may it not ultimately be of Hebrew origin?

**Vowel Value.** In another place the same author calls attention to the fact that in Ashanti there are many instances of words spelt alike, save for the prefix vowel which is generally omitted, and distinguished one from another only by accent or change in the shading of the vowel. "It is this variety of vowel sounds," he adds, "which, in words otherwise spelt the same alters the entire meaning, that makes the Twi language one of exceptional difficulty for the European to master." [41] Compare this with that we read in Gesenius' Hebrew Grammar: "The vowels are subject within the same consonantal framework, to

[36] Idem, p. 97.
[37] Rattray, *Religion and Art in Ashanti,* p. 184.
[38] A. J. Emerick, *Jamaica Mialism* (Privately Printed). Woodstock, 1916, p. 45.
[39] Note:—Professor Keller speaking of witchcraft, distinguishes between "White art" and "Black art" in as much as the practitioners of the former act in consonance with the orthodox cult, and the devotees of the latter in contravention of the same.—Cfr. Sumner, Keller and Davie, *Science of Society,* Vol. II, p. 1335 ff. According to this distinction Obeah must be classed as "Black art" and Myalism which is an expression of the orthodox cult of the Ashanti, as preserved in Jamaica, is merely to be regarded as "White art," although the uninitiated might find it impossible to distinguish between the two in practice, save that the noisy concomitants of the Myal dance are always wanting in the "making of obi" which is essentially hidden and secretive, and might betray itself, if employing the bustle and excitement of the sanctioned Myal practices.
[40] Rattray, *Ashanti Proverbs,* #1, p. 23.
[41] Idem, #83, p. 55.

great changes in order to express various modifications of the same stem-meaning." [42] While then, the consonantal stem or root is usually regarded as the basis of similarity between languages, in both Ashanti and Hebrew the traditional vowel-sound is equally important for the true signification of words. This is a fact which may be noted in many of the examples given in the course of the present work.

**Patriarchal System.**

Doctor Claridge in passing calls attention to the fact that the family or patriarchal system is the fundamental principle of the Ashanti and allied Tribes.[43] In this, again, they are not unlike the Children of Israel.

**Ashanti Stool.**

But let us now come to an even more striking phase of the question. Among the Ashanti, the stool, so well described by Sir Henry M. Stanley,[44] occupies a very peculiar position. P. Amaury Talbot unhesitatingly derives it from the "wooden head-rest, which is found in Egypt from the IInd dynasty," and adds: "It was used not only for its original purpose, but also increased in size and developed into the large wooden stool, such as is now identified with the Akan or Twi-speaking peoples." [45]

Now the Ashanti word for stool is Agwa, something carved; from Gwa, to carve.[46] Incidentially, the Hebrew verb "to carve" is QALA$^{c}$.[47] But, as Ellis further assures us that in the Ashanti dialect, "There are no words, as far as I can ascertain, in which the letter L occurs," [48] and as he gives another spelling for Agwa as Egwah,[49] indicating a final-aspirate sound, would it not seem possible that this Gwah of the Ashanti may have been derived from the Hebrew QALA$^{c}$? For, even in Gesenius we are warned: "No system of writing is ever so perfect as to be able to reproduce the sounds of a language in all their varying shades." [50] How much more true is this in the case of an un-

[42] Gesenius' *Hebrew Grammar,* ed. c. p. 3.
[43] Claridge, *History of the Gold Coast and Ashanti,* Vol. I, p. 8.
[44] Cfr. Page 40 f.
[45] Talbot, *Peoples of Southern Nigeria,* Vol. I, p. 21.
[46] A. B. Ellis, *The Yoruba-Speaking Peoples of the Slave Coast of West Africa,* London, 1894, p. 219.
[47] קָלַע
[48] A. B. Ellis, *The Tshi-Speaking Peoples of the Gold Coast of West Africa,* London, 1887, p. 324.
[49] Idem, p. 322.
[50] Gesenius' *Hebrew Grammar,* ed. c. #1 K.

written language, especially in the development of a word through varying conditions, when the white man undertakes to record the sound he more or less perfectly comprehends?

**Symbol of Authority.**

In any case, among the Ashanti, the stool is a symbol of authority and very much more besides. In some inexplicable way, the vitality of an individual, of a family, or, in the case of the Golden Stool, of the entire nation, is thought to be essentially linked up with the respective stool. In fact, certain inheritance rights are transmitted with the stool.

More than one uprising of the Ashanti was in defence of their Golden Stool, which is not only an emblem of national unity, but is supposed by the Ashanti to contain the national Sunsum or spirit.[51] After repeated futile attempts to gain possession of this Golden Stool, finding the Ashanti ready to die to a man rather than disclose its hiding place, British Officials finally awoke to the realization of the quasi-sacred character of this symbol of national vitality. With the assurance that they would not again be asked to surrender what they valued more than life itself, the Ashanti quickly became reconciled to British rule, and during the World's War they proved their loyalty.

In 1922, on the occasion of the wedding of the Princess Mary, the Queen Mothers of Ashanti sent as a wedding-gift, a silver stool which was a replica of that belonging to the late Queen Mother of Mampon. Their address to Lady Guggisberg, wife of His Excellency the Governor, gives us some idea of the reverence in which the Ashanti hold the stool, as well as its symbolism.

"I place this stool in your hands. It is a gift on her wedding for the King's child, Princess Mary.

"Ashanti stool-makers have carved it, and Ashanti silversmiths have embossed it.

"All the Queen-Mothers who dwell here in Ashanti have contributed towards it, and as I am the senior Queen-Mother in Ashanti, I stand as representative of all the Queen-Mothers and place it in your hands to send to the King's child (Princess Mary).

"It may be that the King's child has heard of the Golden Stool of Ashanti. That is the stool which contains the soul of the Ashanti nation. All we women of Ashanti thank the Governor ex-

[51] Rattray, *Ashanti,* p. 46.

ceedingly because he has declared to us that the English will never again ask us to hand over that stool.

"This stool we give gladly. It does not contain our soul as our Golden Stool does, but it contains all the love of us Queen-Mothers and of our women. The spirit of this love we have bound to the stool with silver fetters just as we are accustomed to bind our own spirits to the base of our stools.

"We in Ashanti here have a law which decrees that it is the daughters of a Queen who alone can transmit royal blood, and that the children of a king cannot be heirs to that stool. This law has given us women a power in this land so that we have a saying which runs:

'It is the woman who bears the man,'

(i. e. the king). We hear that her law is not so, nevertheless we have great joy in sending her our congratulations, and we pray the great God Nyankopon, on whom men lean and do not fall, whose day of worship is a Saturday, and whom the Ashanti serve just as she serves Him, that He may give the King's child and her husband long life and happiness, and finally, when she sits upon this silver stool, which the women of Ashanti have made for their white Queen-Mother, may she call us to mind.

"(Signed) Amma Sewa Akota,

"X her mark." [52]

In addition to the Golden Stool, on which he is never allowed to sit, each king in turn has his own royal stool. Of these Captain Rattray tells us: "After the death of a wise ruler, if it is desired to perpetuate his or her name and memory, the late owner's 'white' stool is 'smoked' or blackened by being smeared all over with soot, mixed with the yoke of egg. It then becomes a 'black' stool, and is deposited in the stool house and becomes a treasured heir-loom of the clan. The stool which during the life-time of its possessor was so intimately bound (literally and metaphorically speaking) with the owner's sunsum or soul,[53] thus becomes after death a shrine into which the departed spirit may again be called

[52] Rattray, *Ashanti,* p. 294.

[53] Note:—Rattray remarks in a foot-note: "Fetters are put on a stool with the idea of binding to it the owner's soul."—Idem, p. 92 N.

upon to enter on certain special occasions, . . . that it may receive that adulation and those gifts that were dear to it in life, and so be induced to continue to use its new and greater spiritual influence in the interest of those over whom it formerly ruled when upon earth." [54]

**Chair of Moses.** This deep veneration of the stool as a symbol of more than human authority and power appears to require some deep-seated superhuman tradition in the early stages of the development of the Ashanti Nation. Christ's warning, "On the chair of Moses have sitten the Scribes and Pharisees, etc." would imply just such a spiritual force in the figure of speech used. The "Chair of Moses" must have been an expression symbolic of authority and legitimate succcession to the law-giving power of the Prophet.

**Chair of Elias.** Even to-day, there is some such symbolism in the Chair of Elias which is used in the Jewish ceremony of circumcision.[55] After the father of the child has proclaimed his readiness to comply with the precept of the Creator, "the operator places the child, then, upon a chair symbolical of the throne of Elijah, Elijah being the angel of the covenant, according to the prophet Malachi, and says, 'Behold I will send my messenger, and he shall prepare the way before me.' The operator thereupon recites: 'This is the throne of Elijah—may he be remembered for good,' etc." [56]

**Enthronement of Conyonk.** In 1246, two Franciscan Fathers set out as missionary ambassadors of the Holy Sea for Tartary and eventually reached the imperial residence near the Dnieper. The Khan Dgotai had just died and Carpini, one of the missionaries, describes the election and enthronement of his son Conyonk in his stead. The choice of the assembled princes was unanimous, and they put a golden seat in their midst and seating Conyonk on it addressed him as follows: "We will,

[54] Idem, p. 92.

[55] Note:—What is said in this regard of the present day only carries out an ancient tradition. For, while describing the ceremonial of circumcision as practiced by the Jews at Fez in Morocco, in the middle of the seventeenth century, Lancelot Addison states that a seat was set close by for Elias, "whose presence they still expect at this solemnity."—Cfr. Lancelot Addison, *Present State of the Jews,* London, 1675, p. 62.

[56] William Rosenau, *Jewish Ceremonial Institutions and Customs,* New York, 1925, p. 133.

we pray, and we command, that you have power and dominion over us all." [57]

This function has many characteristics in common with the enthronement of an Ashanti king—characteristics that may in both cases be ascribed perhaps to a common origin, and that quite possibly an Hebraic one. For a strong influx of Hebrew culture may be traced well beyond the Dnieper into the very heart of Mongolia itself.

Furthermore, is it entirely without significance that Vernon Blake, in contributing a chapter on the Aesthetics of Ashanti to Captain Rattray's latest volume, remarks in connection with the Ashanti stools: "I cannot prevent myself, every time I look at these stool designs, from immediately remembering certain sides of Chinese art . . . and indeed the greater number perhaps of the designs, might almost pass for having a Chinese origin." [58] Again, we repeat, may not the Hebrews be the common source of both?

**Jews of Caifomfou.**

In this connection, it is most interesting to read, that in an ancient synagogue of the Jews at Caifomfou,[59] capital of the Province of Honan, in China, the center of the room of prayer was occupied by a raised chair with richly ornamented cushions, upon which the scroll of the Law was placed when it was being read. And even in comparatively recent times, this stool or chair was called by the members of the Synagogue, "the Chair of Moses." [60] These Jews supposedly found their way into the far East about the beginning of the Christian era, as we shall see in a subsequent chapter.

**Language Indications.**

J. G. Christaller in the Grammatical Introduction to his Ashanti dictionary, remarks how a relative particle "serves to make up for the want of relative pronouns, as in Hebrew," [61] and a careful study of Captain Rattray's *Ashanti Proverbs* discloses not a few indications of seeming Hebrew affinity or rather influence. Thus in the con-

[57] Pamfilo da Magliano, *St. Francis and the Franciscans,* New York, 1867, p. 447.
[58] Rattray, *Religion and Art in Ashanti,* p. 369.
[59] Cfr. Nicalaus Trigault, *De Christiana Expeditione apud Sinas suscepta ab Societate Jesu ex P. Matthaei Ricii ejusdem Societatis Commentariis,* Augsburg, 1615, p. 118 ff.
[60] *Recueil d'Observations Curieuses,* Paris, 1749, Tome II, Chap. VI, p. 103.
[61] Christaller, *Dictionary,* Gram. Introd. p. xix.

jugation of the verb the Ashanti prefix the personal pronouns to the verb-stem,[62] the same as is found in the Imperfect of the Hebrew.[63] In Ashanti the past tense is formed by lengthening the final vowel,[64] which would be equivalent to deriving the present from the past or perfect tense by shortening the final vowel. This would show some analogy to the Hebrew, where the imperfect is formed from the abstract form of the stem.[65]

In Ashanti, the comparative degree of the adjective is expressed by using the verb kyen or sen, meaning to surpass, or to be "more than," [66] and in Hebrew "to express a comparative, the person or thing which is to be represented as excelled in some particular quality is attached to the attributive word by the preposition MIN,[67] where the general sense of the word is also "more than." Now just as in Hebrew "all words, which by usage serve as prepositions, were originally substantives," [68] and these substantives in turn are for the most part traced back to the third person singular of the perfect Qal as a root, so also in Ashanti there is strictly speaking no such thing as a preposition. The words used as such are really verbs,[69] or nouns in certain circumstances.[70]

There is no indefinite article in Ashanti any more than there is in Hebrew, and the force of the definite article in the former language is usually obtained by the use of a pronoun,[71] just as in the Hebrew the definite article "is by nature a kind of demonstrative pronoun." [72]

The essential characteristics of the Hebrew Niphal conjugation consist in a prefix to the stem. This is supplied by the prepositive NA, which in strong verbs is attenuated to NE, or by the proclitic IN. The feature, then, of the Participle and its derivative Nouns is the prefix NUN.[73] While the real meaning of Niphal

[62] Rattray, *Ashanti Proverbs,* #22, p. 32.
[63] Gesenius, l. c. #30.
[64] Rattray, l. c. #4, p. 24.
[65] Gesenius, l. c. #47a.
[66] Rattray, l. c. #261, p. 89; #653, p. 162.
[67] מִן (מִ־)Gesenius, l. c. #133a.
[68] Idem, #101a.
[69] Rattray, *Ashanti Proverbs,* #317, p. 97.
[70] Ellis, *Tshi-Speaking Peoples,* p. 311.
[71] Idem, p. 311.
[72] Gesenius, l. c. #35a.
[73] Idem, #51a & b.

bears some resemblance to the Greek Middle Voice with its reflexive force,[74] many of the nouns derived from its participle and infinitive are to be found only in the plural number, e. g. NIPHLAOTH,[75] wonders; NIPHTULIM,[76] wrestlings. Ashanti words prefixing N have usually a plural force, implying multitude or masses, collectively or in the abstract,[77] pretty much the same as the plural abstracts of the Hebrew.[78]

In Ashanti the negative is usually formed by the prefix N, "not" [79] sometimes written M, and in certain cases by Yen.[80] Similarly, in Hebrew, noun-clauses are negatived by the adverb EN,[81] literally (it is) not.[82] A negative effect is also produced by the use of the prefix MIN,[83] usually written MI,[84] or ME.[85] In Hebrew, also, "two negatives in the same sentence do not neutralize each other, but make the negation more emphatic." [86] In Ashanti, the use of the double negative is the regular construction.[87] Moreover, the parallelism so distinctive of Hebrew poetry is also to be noted in the Ashanti.

While contending that primitive verbs in Ashanti and kindred languages are monosyllabic, Ellis admits: "The sound of the consonant can, however, frequently only be expressed by a combination of two of the consonants of our alphabet." [88] This monosyllabic system of primitive words is claimed as the distinctive groundwork of all Negro languages,[89] and would seem at first glance to preclude any possible similarity to the Hebrew, where the stems as a rule consist of three consonants.[90] But as a matter

[74] Idem, #51c.
[75] נִפְלָאוֹת
[76] נִפְתּוּלִים
[77] Ellis, *Yoruba-Speaking Peoples,* p. 219.
[78] Gesenius, l. c. #124a.
[79] Rattray, *Ashanti Proverbs,* #439, p. 118.
[80] Ellis, *Tshi-Speaking Peoples,* p. 315. Note:—Yen seems to be made up of ye or yeh, to be, and the negative N, not.
[81] אַיִן
[82] Gesenius, l. c. #152a.
[83] מִן
[84] מִ
[85] מֵ Gesenius, l. c. #119y.
[86] Idem, #152y.
[87] Rattray, l. c. #33, p. 35.
[88] Ellis, *Tshi-Speaking Peoples,* p. 305 f.
[89] A. Werner, *The Language Families of Africa,* London, 1925, p. 36.
[90] Gesenius, l. c. #30.

of fact there is a group of scholars who maintain that fundamentally at least the Semite languages were built up on a biliteral base, and it is even disputed whether these biliterals were monosyllabic or dissylabic.[91] Doctor Hurwitz observes: "We may hold, with König, that this biliteral base, as the fundamental root, is a theoretical abstraction which never actually existed in the living language; or we may prefer the other alternative, maintaining that the biliteral root once had an independent existence, and that it developed into its present style by the affixation of formative increments or determinatives." [92] In the same way, when Ellis and others would make the monosyllabic root the foundation of Negro languages, it would be difficult to prove that they are arguing for anything more than the most primitive forms confined to theoretical existence only, and forerunners to the actual spoken language, and consequently of little use outside the field of pure etymology as Hurwitz concludes concerning biliteral Semitic stems.[93]

**Verbal Ingrafts.**

However, it is far from the present intention to even hint that Hebrew and Ashanti may be of the same linguistic family or stock. Neither is it the purpose to claim that they are of similar type. We are warned by Edward Sapir: "The historical study of language has proven to us beyond all doubt that a language changes not only gradually but consistently, that it moves unconsciously from one type towards another, and that analagous trends are observable in remote quarters of the globe. From this it follows that broadly similar morphologies must have been reached by unrelated languages, independently and frequently." [94] A. L. Kroeber, too, sets it down as a principle: "Before genetic connection between two languages can be thought of, the number of their words similar in sound and sense must be reasonably large. An isolated handful of resemblances are either importations—loan words—or the result of coincidence." [95] But to quote Sapir again: "One can almost

[91] Solomon Theodore Halevy Hurwitz, *Root-Determinatives in Semitic Speech,* New York, 1913, especially p. 107ff.

[92] Idem, p. 13.

[93] Idem, p. 108.

[94] Edward Sapir, *Language,* New York, 1921, p. 128 f.

[95] A. L. Kroeber, *Anthropology,* New York, 1923, p. 90. Note:—Cfr. also Edward Sapir, *Language,* p. 57: "The objective comparison of sounds in two or more languages is, then, of no psychological or historical significance

estimate the rôle which various peoples have played in the development and spread of cultural ideas by taking note of the extent to which their vocabularies have filtered into those of other peoples." [96]

By the present writer then, the most that is suggested is that not a few Hebrew words and possibly certain distinctive Hebrew constructions have been ingrafted on the native language of the Ashanti.[97] Moreover, if some scholars find similarities between the Sumerian of early Babylonia and Modern African languages, why should we be surprised at apparent traces of Hebrew in the Ashanti language of to-day? [98]

**Derivation of Ashanti.**

The very name Ashanti has itself a strong Hebraic flavor. For, while some would derive the word from "Shan" the name of a plant, and "dti," to eat, claiming that the title must have been acquired in the time of a great famine, when they found sustenance in the plant in question,[99] this is mere guesswork. Actually, the termination "ti" or "tie" in the names of West African Tribes has usually the general meaning of "the race of," "the men of," "the children of." [100] This would make Ashanti, "the people of Ashan." There was as a fact, a town of the name of Ashan in the domain of Juda.[101] Priests were in residence there according to the First Book of Chronicles,[102] where the word is spelt ᶜASHAN,[103] though in the corresponding passage of Joshue [104] it is spelt ᶜAIN,[105] which

unless the sounds are first 'weighted,' unless their phonetic 'values' are determined. These values, in turn, flow from the general behaviour and functioning of the sounds in actual speech."

[96] Sapir, l. c. p. 209 f.

[97] Note:—Sapir maintains: "The language of a people that is looked upon as a center of culture is naturally far more likely to exert an appreciable influence on other languages spoken in its vicinity than to be influenced by them."—Sapir, l. c. p. 205.

[98] Cfr. Kroeber, l. c. p. 450: "The languages of these early west Asiatic peoples have not been classified. Sumerian was non-Indo-European, non-Semitic, non-Hamitic. Some have thought to detect Turkish, that is Ural-Altaic, resemblances in it. But others find similarities to modern African languages. This divergence of opinion probably means that Sumerian cannot yet be safely linked with any other linguistic group."

[99] Claridge, *History of the Gold Coast and Ashanti*, Vol. I, p. 5.

[100] Louis Desplagnes, *La Plateau Central Nigérien*, Paris, 1907, p. 106.

[101] Joshue, xv, 16.

[102] I Paral. vi, 59.

[103] עָשָׁן

[104] Joshue, xxi, 16.

[105] עַיִן

the Jewish Encyclopedia suggests "may simply be a corruption of Ashan." [106] Now is it a mere coincidence again, that Erwin de Bary, referring to Aïr or Asben, north of Agades, calls it Ain? [107] And, further, can its other name be a corruption of Ashan? [108]

The primary meaning of the Hebrew word ᶜASHAN [109] is smoke, and it is used primarily of a burning city; and secondly figuratively of the destruction of Israel.[110] The latter meaning would be significant and certainly applicable to fugitives from the destroyers of Jerusalem, whether they were the Assyrians or the Romans.

**Endogamy.**

Reading Captain Rattray's latest work, entitled *Religion and Art in Ashanti,* one cannot help being impressed by the number of customs and practices there described that find their counterpart among the ancient Hebrews. Thus, for example, the Mosaic Law of intra-tribal marriages,[111] which was devised expressly to preserve the inheritance of the daughters "in the tribe and family of their father," [112] finds a close verification among the Ashanti of to-day, and the cross-cousin marriages, so characteristic of the latter,[113] are strictly similar to that of the daughters of Salphaad who wedded "the sons of their uncle by their father." [114]

**Cross-Cousin Marriages.**

**Familial Names.**

Again the preserving of certain names in a family is as much sought after by the Ashanti [115] as it was of old among the Hebrews, as shown in the case of the naming of John the Baptist, when the objection was

[106] עָשָׁן

[107] "Ghat et les Tuareg de l'Ain,"—cfr. *Jewish Encyclopedia,* Vol. IV, p. 410.

[108] Note:—According to Maurice Abadie the word should be Absen and not Asben. The Hausa, he claims, would find it too difficult to pronounce the S before the B, while the inverted order of these letters is usual with them.—Cfr. Maurice Abadie, *La Colonie du Niger,* Paris, 1927, p. 40. But the name itself is not of Hausa origin. Francis Rennell Rodd thinks that Asben or Absen was the "original name given to the area by the people of the Sudan before the advent of the Tuareg." Cfr. Francis Rennell Rodd, *People of the Veil,* p. 28.

[109] עָשָׁן

[110] Brown Driver and Briggs, *Lexicon,* p. 798.

[111] Num. xxxvi, 5–12.

[112] Num. xxxvi, 12.

[113] Rattray, *Religion and Art in Ashanti,* Chapter XXIX.

[114] Num. xxxvi, 11.

[115] Rattray, l. c. p. 323.

made; "There is none of thy kindred that is called by this name." [116]

**Marriage Rite.** So also, the remarkable simplicity of the Ashanti marriage and the distinctive part that wine plays in the ceremonial remind one of the ancient Hebrew rite. Thus Captain Rattray remarks the noticeable absence of such rites as are observed in connection with birth and puberty.[117] However, he states: "Before a proposal of marriage, and the subsequent seeking of the consent of the parents . . . and the exchange of gifts, it is the business of the young people to satisfy themselves that their union would not violate any of the forbidden degrees of consanguinity." [118] The ancient Hebrews themselves could not have been more particular in this regard. They having obtained the parents' consent, the Ashanti youth will make them small gifts and pay the bride-price including the wine offering,[119] and as Captain Rattray insists: "The parents' consent, the presentation and acceptance of these gifts, and the aseda (bride-price) are the only formalities that are necessary to constitute a valid marriage." [120] Later Captain Rattray adds: "I am of the opinion that the payment or passing of wine as a part of the 'tira aseda,' or 'bride-price,' was originally a very important, if not the essential part of the ceremony. This wine is used in the religious part of the marriage rites . . . and is also handed round to those who are present, who, along with the ancestral spirits, thus become the witnesses of the marriage contract." [121] In the case of a princess, some of the wine is poured over the ancestral stools, otherwise "wine is poured on the ground for the spirits of the ancestors, and the remainder shared by those present." [122]

In close parallelism with the foregoing, in the ancient Hebrew marriage, the ceremony was performed in a private house, without the necessary presence of priest or rabbi. An elder invoked the benediction and gave a cup of wine to the contracting parties who pledged each other. The bridegroom, after drinking his portion, dashed the cup to the ground and crushed it under his

[116] Luke, i, 61.
[117] Rattray, l. c. p. 77.
[118] Rattray, *Religion and Art in Ashanti,* p. 79.
[119] Idem, p. 80.
[120] Idem, p. 81.
[121] Idem, p. 84.
[122] Idem, p. 85.

heel. The marriage contract was then read and attested by the drinking of a cup of wine by each person present." [123]

**Uncleanness After Child-birth.**

Not only in the marriage ceremony itself, but also in after-marriage customs there is a strange similarity between the Ashanti and the Hebrews. Thus, for example, for eight days after the birth of a child the Ashanti "mother is considered as unclean." [124] It is only on the eighth day, at the Ntetea rite, as the Ashanti call it, that the child receives its personal name,[125] and on the fortieth day a still further ceremony has to be observed.[126] In all this we are certainly reminded of Hebrew customs.

**Purification Ceremony.**

**Menstrual Seclusion.**

Furthermore, the restrictions and taboos of the Ashanti woman at the menstrual period, even to the retirement to the bara hut,[127] read like a page borrowed from the Book of Leviticus,[128] and the system of Ashanti ablutions to prevent legal uncleanness constantly brings to mind similar practices which were common among the Hebrews.

**Ceremonial Ablutions.**

**Dupuis' Account.**

Joseph Dupuis, after a lengthy residence in Barbary, where he had become proficient in the Arabic language, was sent in 1818, as His Britannic Majesty's Envoy and Consul to the Ashanti, and while on that mission, through his acquaintance with the Moors of the district, collected much valuable information about the interior of Africa, chiefly from the Arabic Manuscripts and the traditions of the Moslems. As a result of his investigations, he explains the origin of the Ashanti as follows: "The growth and consolidation of this comparatively great empire, is much talked of by the Heathens as well as Moslems; and both are agreed, that the tribes of Ashantee, Gaman, Dinkira, and Akim, were driven by the believers, in the early age of Islam, from their original inheritances in Ghobagho, Ghofqa, and Tanouma,[129] to the forests of Wangara, i. e. the states of Ashantee inclusively, and the south-

[123] Cfr. E. L. Urlin, *A Short History of Marriage,* London, 1903, p. 108 f.
[124] Rattray, Religion and Art in Ashanti, p. 59
[125] Idem, p. 62.
[126] Idem, p. 65.
[127] Idem, p. 75.
[128] Leviticus, xv, 19–29.
[129] Placed by Dupuis along the longitude of Greenwich and about 10° N.

eastern parts of Gaman, where they maintained their independence at the expense of much blood, and defended the country gifted with the precious metal, against the most vigorous efforts that were made to bereave them of it."[130]

**Yahoodee.** Later, while criticizing a map that had been published by T. Edward Bowditch in 1819,[131] he says: "Beginning then at the top of the map, I find a place called Yahoodee, a country or town of non-existence. Yahoodee simply implies Jews, the tribes of Jews, etc. which term the Moslems apply to those people of the Mosaic faith who inhabit the lower Atlas, and the districts of Suse.[132] They also apply the term Yahoodee to the Hebrew or Jewish tribes, whether native Africans or not, who inhabit Maroa, some parts of Fillany,[133] and the neighborhood of Timbuctoo. Of these people I imagine the author of the information spoke, when he endeavoured to make Mr. Bowditch comprehend the import of the word Yahoodee. As a nation or a tribe they cannot be inserted with propriety in any map, for they exist even in a more deplorable state of servitude and humiliation in those districts than in the empire of Morocco."[134]

In passing, it should be remarked, that whenever it is at all possible, Dupuis takes exception to the statements of Bowditch, and aligns himself against his predecessor's view. It should also be remembered that Dupuis is drawing his information for the most part from the Moors, while Bowditch records the traditions of the Ashanti themselves. In the present instance, however, Bowditch would appear to have the better claim for credibility, as only six years after the publication of Dupuis' criticism, it was emphatically refuted by two travellers who actually passed along the Niger and entered in their Journal under date of Wednesday, July 7, 1830: "Yahoorie (sic) is a large, flourishing and united kingdom. It is bounded on the east by Haussa, on the west by Borgoo, on the north by Cubbie, and on the south by the kingdom of Nouffie."[135] The position indicated by the

[130] Joseph Dupuis, *Journal of a Residence in Ashantee,* London, 1824, p. 224.
[131] Wherein Bowditch places Yahoodee about 20° N.; 2° E.
[132] Suse he places 30° N; 7° W.
[133] He places Maroa 18° N; 6° E; and Fillany 15° N; 2° E.
[134] Dupuis, l. c. Part II, p. xxii.
[135] Richard and John Lander, *Journal of an Expedition to Explore the Course and Termination of the Niger,* London, 1838, Vol. I, p. 240.

travellers on the map,[136] would place it on the Niger River, about midway between the present Bussa and Gomba, in Northern Nigeria.

**Sudanese Jews.** But let us return to Dupuis' narrative, where we read: "The Jews of Soudan are, according to my informers, divided into many large and small tribes, with whose names they are unacquainted. Their mode of life in some countries is pastoral; but the towns are filled with traders and artificers of that faith, who gain a subsistence at their several employments, in the service of the Moslems, under whose government they live as vassals. This, in reference to Mr. Bowditch's kingdom of 'Yahoodee,' I may be permitted to say, is the only state of society in which that oppressed nation is suffered to live; and the tribes, without security in their possessions, without public revenues or arms, are hourly exposed to insult and rapine from the blind zeal and active bigotry by which their lords are animated in these countries. The lands occupied by these people cover a wide extent, between Massina[137] and Kaby.[138] They are said to be mingled also with the upper Foulaha tribes, eastward of Timbuctoo, and in many parts of Marroa they have inheritances or are employed as artificers in the cities and towns; 'As we live among the heathens,' said Bashaw,[139] 'so do the Jews in Marroa and Fillany with our brethren; but they are not esteemed like us, for they are a people hardened in their sins and obstinate in infidelity; the anger of God is upon them, and therefore are they given to the rule of the Moslems until they shall become incorporated with the faithful.' The tribes are not black, but of a colour resembling the Arabs of the north. But what is more material, these Soudanic Jews are reported to have been the original inhabitants thereabout, after the Arabs were acquainted with central Africa." [140]

Whence came these Jews, and what influence did they exert, if any, upon the Ashanti in bygone days? This question will be taken up after we consider the Supreme Being of the Ashanti

[136] Idem, Vol. I, p. xl.
[137] Massina is located 16° N; 2° W.
[138] Kaby is located 6° N; 5° W.
[139] Note:—Bashaw was the leading Moor among the Ashanti at the time of Dupuis' stay there.
[140] Dupuis, l. c. Part II, p. cvi.

and His possible identification with the Yahweh of the Old Testament. For perhaps the most striking of what might be called Ashanti Hebrewisms is the remarkable similarity between the Ashanti tribal God and the Hebrew Yahweh. So important is this link in our chain of evidence, that it seems well to devote to it a separate chapter.

**Summary.** Thus far, however, we have shown certain cultural elements common to the Ashanti and the ancient Hebrews, such as Ob cult, religious dances, use of "Amen," vowel value, patriarchal system, parallel symbolism of authority in "stool" and "chair," endogamy, cross-cousin marriages, familial names, exogamy, simplicity of the marriage rite and the part that wine plays in the ceremony, uncleanness after child-birth, purification ceremony, menstrual seclusion, and ceremonial ablutions; besides Ashanti loan words of apparent Hebrew origin. While individually each of these traits might well be of independent origin, collectively they would appear to postulate diffusion at least from a common center.

## *Chapter III*

# THE SUPREME BEING OF THE ASHANTI

**Assertion of Ellis.**

On all questions pertaining to the Ashanti, no authority is more widely quoted than that of the late Sir Alfred Burton Ellis, who was for many years an officer in a colored West India Regiment, that alternated, usually at three-year intervals, between the Gold Coast and Jamaica. It is a little surprising then, to find Sir Alfred making the unqualified assertion, that the concept of a Supreme Being in the minds of the Ashanti was entirely due to the influence of Christianity, and was unknown previous to the advent of the Missionary. In other words, that the traditions of the Ashanti, as a tribe, preclude a Supreme Being, and that their native religion was circumscribed by polytheism and fetishism.

After quoting from Professor Waitz,[1] to the effect that "The original form of all religion is a raw, unsympathetic polytheism," Ellis adopts the opinion as his own, and enunciates the thesis, that in the case of the Negro of the Gold Coast, "all the deities are of the earth, and their worship is born of fear of some possible ill, or of a desire of some possible good." [2]

Under the caption "General Deities," Ellis further evolves his theory as follows. Among the Northern Tribes of the Gold Coast Negroes, which classification includes the Ashanti, the highest deity generally worshipped, he calls Tando, a preternatural, not a supernatural, being. Intercourse with the European in time led to the introduction of a new deity named Nana-Nyankupon, the Lord of the Sky. This God of the Christians had no temple and no priesthood. The negro mind classified Him with their own deities in a way, but conceived Him as altogether "too distant and too indifferent to interfere directly in the affairs of the

[1] *Introduction to Anthropology,* p. 368.
[2] Ellis, *Tshi-Speaking Peoples,* p. 21.

world." [3] This Nana-Nyankupon, frequently styled merely Nyankupon, according to Ellis, gradually became regarded as "the lord over the local deities." "To the anger of Nyankupon was also ascribed the thunder and lightning, the tornado and the flood. To these were added special attributes, the result of their contact with Europeans." Thus small-pox and famine came to be regarded as "Nyankupon's own special modes of displaying anger." [4]

Ellis then continues: "Within the last twenty or thirty years the German missionaries, sent out from time to time by the mission societies of Basel and Bremen, have made Nyankupon known to European ethnologists and students of the science of religion; but being unaware of the real origin of the god, they have generally spoken and written of him as a conception of the native mind, whereas he is really a god borrowed from Europeans and only thinly disguised. Hence some scholars have expressed surprise that the negro tribes of the Gold Coast should have progressed so much further in their religious development than many other peoples occupying positions higher in the scale of civilization, as to have formed a conception of a quasi-omnipotent god, residing in the heavens instead of upon the earth, and approachable by sacrifice. Finding many points of similarity between the Jahveh of the Jews and Nyankupon, the missionaries have made use of the latter name to express the word 'god' in their sermons and discourses, thus reversing the process which the natives had themselves performed some two or three centuries earlier. But, to the native mind, Nyankupon is a material and tangible being, possessing a body, legs, and arms, in fact all the limbs, and the senses, and faculties of man. He is also believed to have passions similar to those of men. This, however, is but natural, and to the uncultured mind the conception of an immaterial being is impossible." [5]

**Refutation of Rattray.**

Shortly before the World War, R. Sutherland Rattray, the Ashanti District Commissioner, published a volume of *Ashanti Proverbs,* and while giving due credit to Ellis for what the latter had accomplished, he seriously took exception to his viewpoint as regards the

[3] Idem, p. 22.
[4] Idem, p. 27.
[5] Idem, p. 28.

Ashanti concept of a Supreme Being. Citing the very passage just quoted from Ellis, he objects: "The writer can hardly allow these statements to remain unchallenged, as careful research has seemed to him so totally to disprove them. Now the first credentials the present writer would ask of any one who was advancing an opinion, as the result of independent research, into native customs and beliefs such as this, would be the state of proficiency that the investigator had acquired in the language of the people whose religion and beliefs he was attempting to reveal.

"The standard we would ask would be a high one. Had the investigator real colloquial knowledge of the language of the people whose inner soul he was endeavouring to lay bare? Such a knowledge as is gained only after years of arduous study and close intercourse, a knowledge that will enable the possessor to exchange jokes and quips and current slang, and to join in a discourse in which some dozen voices are all yelling at once? Such a knowledge of a language is a very different thing from an academic acquaintance with it, which might fit the possessor to write an excellent grammar, dictionary, or some other treatise.

"Judged by such a standard the late Major Ellis must have been found wanting." [6]

Nine years later, the same author, who during the war had become a Captain in His Majesty's Service, published another volume entitled *Ashanti,* wherein he returns to the same subject. After styling Sir Alfred Ellis "our great authority upon the region," he cites again the passage already mentioned, and then continues: "I quoted the above extract in a previous work, and therein stated at some length that I wholly disagree with the opinion and statement of Ellis upon this particular subject.

"Further research, embodying a much fuller investigation into Ashanti religious beliefs than was before possible, has only served to strengthen the opinion which I formerly expressed.

"It is surprising to find that Ellis, who, considering his many difficulties in working with an interpreter, made such good use, on the whole, of his opportunities, was so greatly misled with regard to such an important question. He was, moreover, a close student of Bosman, whom he constantly quotes, but he appears to have missed or ignored what the Dutchman wrote upon this

[6] Rattray, *Ashanti Proverbs,* #1, p. 18.

subject more than 150 years before those 'German missionaries' ever set foot upon the Coast.

"Bosman says: 'It is really the more to be lamented that the negroes idolized such worthless Nothings by reason that several amongst them have no very unjust idea of the Deity, for they ascribe to God the attributes of Omnipresence, Omniscience, and Invisibility, besides which they believe that He governs all things by Providence. By reason God is invisible, they say it would be absurd to make any Corporeal Representation of him, . . . wherefore they have such multitudes of Images of their Idol gods which they take to be subordinate deities to the Supreme God, . . . and only believe these are mediators betwixt God and men, which they take to be their idols.' [7]

"How accurate in some respects Bosman's statement is will be clear from an examination of the religious ceremonies which are here recorded." [8]

**Partial Retractation.**

In due course, Ellis himself acknowledged that his position was untenable, but as so often happens in similar cases, the original assertion has been broadcasted and quoted innumerable times, while the retractation has been for the most part ignored.

Three years after his earlier volume, Ellis returned to the question in his *Ewe-Speaking Peoples,* and while treating of Mawu, stated: "While upon the subject of this god, I may as well say that, from additional evidence I have since collected, I now think that the view I expressed concerning the origin of Nyankupon, the parallel god of the Tshi-Speaking peoples, was incorrect; and that instead of his being the Christian God borrowed and thinly disguised, I now hold he is like Mawu, the sky-god, or in-dwelling spirit of the sky; and that, also like Mawu, he has been to a certain extent confounded with Jehovah." [9] But even here,

[7] This quotation is from William Bosman, *A New and Accurate Description of the Coast of Guinea, divided into the Gold, the Slave and the Ivory Caosts,* London, 1721, p. 179 ff.

[8] Rattray, *Ashanti,* p. 139.

[9] A. B. Ellis, *The Ewe-Speaking Peoples,* p. 36. Note:—An article in the *New York Times Magazine* is introduced by the following comment: "Impressions of savage and remote parts of West Africa are recorded in the following article by Dr. Ossendowski, who recently completed an extensive journey through this primitive expanse of the Dark Continent." In the course of this article, we read: "West Africa is a jumble of many religions. Some of those that have disappeared for centuries from the rest of the earth persist

of course, he does not give Him the full rating of a Supreme Being.[10]

This modification of Ellis' view detracts nothing from the stand of Captain Rattray. In fact, it only confirms the justness of his criticism. For had Ellis enjoyed a conversational knowledge of the languages that he was treating through means of an interpreter, he would scarcely have made the blunder he did in the first place.

**Rattray as an Authority.**

That Captain Rattray personally is fully qualified to judge in the matter, even according to the severe conditions that he has himself set down as a norm, in rejecting Ellis as a competent witness, there can be no question. Not only is he a master of the Ashanti language and an official interpreter in several other dialects, but his many years among the Ashanti and kindred peoples have familiarized him with their mode of thought, and have enabled him to win the unreserved confidence of the negro, which in turn has gained for him admission to their most hidden ceremonies and has unlocked the secrets of the Queen Mothers, who have freely satisfied his every inquiry. As a matter of justice, the very title of "our great authority upon the region," which in his modesty he has so graciously yielded to Ellis, in all truth belongs to Captain R. Sutherland Rattray himself and to no other.

**Supreme Being of the Ashanti.**

Great weight then, must be given to Captain Rattray's statement: "I am convinced that the conception, in the Ashanti mind, of a Supreme Being, has nothing whatever to do with mission-

among these wild peoples, mingled with later religions down to those of to-day. The result is a theological confusion difficult to analyze. Roman, Phoenician, Syrian, Egyptian mythologies and the earlier Christian teachings have left their mark on the tribes, and all these cults are criss-crossed with primal nature worship that may be older than any of them. Most of the tribes of West Africa have lost their individuality through intermarriage with other tribes; and their present-day religion, too, is conglomerate." However, he numbers the Ashanti among the tribes that "have remained most nearly pure in blood."—Cfr. Ferdinand Ossendowski, *Cruel Gods Fill the African Olympus —New York Times Magazine,* May 13, 1928, p. 13.

[10] Note:—Four years later, Ellis makes even a further concession. After asserting: "Olorun is the sky-god of the Yorubas . . . just as Nyankupon is to the Tshis" (Cfr. *Yoruba-Speaking Peoples,* p. 35) he states: "Like Nyankupon . . . Olorun is considered too distant or too indifferent, to interfere in the affairs of the world" (l. c. p. 36) and then admits: "The name Olorun, however, occurs in one or two set phrases or sentences, which appear to show that at one time greater regard was paid him" (l. c. p. 37).

ary influence, nor it it to be ascribed to contact with Christians or even, I believe, with Mohammedans." [11] And again: "In a sense, therefore, it is true that this great Supreme Being, the conception of whom has been innate in the minds of the Ashanti, is the Jehovah of the Israelites." [12]

**Mixed Religion.** In the very fact that the Hebrews, despite their service of the True God, frequently relapsed into idolatry, Captain Rattray finds a parallelism with the Ashanti, where, as Bosman noted, one finds a belief in a Supreme Being side by side with "multitudes of their Idol gods." The Captain continues: "As will be seen presently, every Ashanti temple is a pantheon in which repose the shrines of the gods, but the power or spirit, that on occasions enters into these shrines, is directly or indirectly derived from the one God of the Sky, whose intermediaries they are. Hence we have in Ashanti exactly that 'mixed religion' which we find among the Israelites of old. They worshipped Jehovah, but they worshipped other gods as well." [13]

**Judaism.** Professor George Foot Moore, treating of the character of Judaism, after declaring: "The foundation of Judaism is the belief that religion is revealed," and that, "There could be but one religion properly deserving the name, for God is one: and revelation was not only consistent but identical throughout, for God is ever the same," shows that in practice at times: "The forefathers had fallen away from the true religion, not only by worshipping other gods, and by worshipping their own God in a heathenish way, but by tolerating injustice and immorality." And yet nevertheless this serious infraction of the Law in no way affected the religion itself, which was "perfect from the beginning, and therefore unalterable." [14]

**Idols of Canaan.** R. L. Ottley has summed up this seemingly paradoxical condition of things. He writes: "The Hebrews did not indeed openly abandon their allegiance to Jehovah, but they co-ordinated and sometimes even identified, their national Deity with one or other of the gods of Canaan, and thus the simple and pure worship of Jehovah was

[11] Rattray, *Ashanti,* p. 140.
[12] Idem, p. 141.
[13] Idem, p. 141.
[14] George Foot Moore, *Judaism in the First Centuries of the Christian Era,* Cambridge, Mass. 1927, Vol. I, p. 112.

gradually corrupted by the admixtures of usages and symbols borrowed from the nature worship of the Canaanites." [15] But let us go into this question a little more in detail.

**Hebrew Monotheism.**

The condition of Israel then, was not idolatrous in the strict sense of the word, viz. the absolute cult of a false god.[16] Vigouroux makes this clear when he says: "The Children of Israel who sacrificed to idols, did so through frailty, through passion; but these infidelities of the Chosen People, these 'adulteries' as the Prophets called them in their forcible language, however culpable they were, nevertheless did not change the nature of the religion proper of Israel. King Solomon affords us the type of the weak and inconstant child of Jacob. He knows the unity of God, he confesses it and praises it in chant, and despite all this, yielding to ignoble weakness, he prostrates himself before shameful idols." [17] The same author elsewhere quotes approvingly the words of F. Pret: "The idolatry of the Hebrews was less an apostasy, than the adoption of strange practices or ceremonies. One did not abjure Jahve, who remained the only legitimate God of Israel; but, by impulse or through interest, one associated with His worship what He reproved." [18]

**Divided Service.**

This state of affairs is well illustrated in the reign of the Reformer, King Josias, when "the priests of the high places came not up to the altar of the Lord in Jerusalem; but only ate of the unleavened bread among their brethren." [19] Josias, according to the Scripture account, was

[15] R. L. Ottley, *A Short History of the Hebrews to the Roman Period,* New York, 1923, p. 102.

[16] Note:—Writing of the days of the Monarchy, Blunt observes: "The Canaanite culture remained engrafted in Yahwism. The bull-worship of Yahweh in Bethel and Dan was maintained by kings and priests, and did not receive its death-blow till the destruction of Samaria. There are occasional references to the practice of witchcraft and sacred prostitution, and numerous evidences of the continued use of images, pillars and poles."—A. W. F. Blunt, *Israel before Christ,* London, 1924, p. 70. And again: "The cultus, therefore, remained much the same as it had been in pre-monarchic times. But in the train of the foreign connexions which were established under the monarchy, foreign influences in religious practices began to flood the country. Solomon's importation of Egyptian and other gods set the example. . . . The fact was that, as relations with foreign countries developed, hospitality to foreign gods seemed natural."—l. c. p. 71.

[17] F. Vigouroux, *La Bible et les Découvertes Modernes,* Paris, 1884, Vol. III, p. 33.

[18] F. Vigouroux, *Dictionnaire de la Bible,* Paris, 1895, Vol. III, p. 815.

[19] IV Kings, xxiii, 9.

slain at Mageddo by the Pharaoh Nechao, about 610 B. C.[20] and was succeeded by his son Joachaz, who after a reign of only three months [21] was dethroned by the Pharaoh Nechao and carried into Egypt where he died. As the Babylonian captivity began about 585 B. C. the religious condition of the Hebrews was most deplorable just at this period.

**Rattray's Views.**

That Captain Rattray has no preconceived notions which he was trying to substantiate, and was in reality entirely oblivious of the fact that his very words indicate a connection between the Supreme Being of the Ashanti and the Yahweh of the Hebrews, is shown from a personal letter written from Mampon on May 5, 1925, wherein he differs with my view of the matter, saying: "I am afraid I can't follow you in any attempt to trace Hebrew affinities in race and language," though he admits: "Many curious parallels certainly exist." Later, however, after further correspondence on the subject, he apparently modifies his view somewhat, when he writes, again from Mampon, on October 5, 1925: "I am so wholly ignorant about all things HEBREW that I am never in a position to trace and to follow up possible clues to your theory of the possible Semitic origin of some of Ashanti customs. I am aware of course, that such a possibility has been suggested. Many times, however, even with my scrappy information on the subject, I have been struck with curious little points, such as the 40 day periods, etc." Then with his characteristic modesty, he remarks: "All I can do to help scholars like yourself, is to record accurately what I find here. That my knowledge is limited to the Ashanti is possibly all for the best, for I do not bring in preconceived notions and theories which might unconsciously influence my work." Before closing, he adds: "I think you are possibly on the right track, but we have to be extraordinarily careful not to be too ready to jump to conclusions from what may after all be just one or other of those strange coincidences which crop up in the comparison of any two languages of peoples."

**Ashanti Nyame.**

Keeping this warning in mind, we may now approach the consideration of our subject in somewhat of a critical spirit. The full name of the Su-

[20] IV Kings, xxiii, 29.
[21] IV Kings, xxiii, 31.

preme Being among the Ashanti is Onyame, but in conversation the nominal prefix O is generally elided,[22] and we usually find the word even in writing 'Nyame, "a" being pronounced as in "bat" and "e" as in "met".[23] Moreover the prefix N, which is placed before verbs to form nouns that convey the idea of immensity or numbers collectively or in the abstract,[24] would leave as the significant part of the word Yame. Now, on the one hand, we have no less an authority than Professor Albert T. Clay, of Yale University, that "some Semites used M and others W to represent the same sound," [25] and on the other hand, Captain Rattray assures me that in Ashanti the letter M interchanges with W, and quotes Christaller [26] as confirmatory authority. This establishes a surprising similarity between the Ashanti Yame and the Hebrew Tetragrammaton, Yahweh.[27] And the fact that the latter is commonly regarded as having been derived from the verb HAYAH,[28] "to be", which in turn has an equivalent in Ashanti, "yeh" [29] also meaning "to be", only strengthens the presumption that the one was derived from the other, or that both came from the same Semitic root.

**Identification with Yahweh.** Furthermore, among the attributes of the Ashanti 'Nyame, stands out Bore-bore, meaning Creator,[30] the exact equivalent, in sound and signification, with the participle BORE [31] of the Hebrew verb BARA,[32] "to create" Again, 'Nyame is called 'Nyankopon, signifying 'Nyame, alone, great one,[33] and 'Nyankopon Kwame, which means 'Nyame, alone, great one, to whom Saturday is dedicated,[34] which is assuredly an easy equivalent for "the Lord of the Sabbath."

We might even draw a confirmatory argument from the fact

[22] Ellis, *Tshi-Speaking Peoples,* p. 309.
[23] Idem, p. 307.
[24] Ellis, *Yoruba-Speaking Peoples,* p. 219.
[25] Albert T. Clay, *Empire of the Amorites,* New Haven, 1919, p. 72.
[26] Christaller, *Dictionary,* p. 291.
[27] יהוה
[28] הָיָה
[29] Ellis, *Tshi-Speaking Peoples,* p. 315.
[30] Rattray, *Ashanti Proverbs,* #1, p. 18.
[31] בּוֹרֵא Cfr. Isaias, xlii, 5.
[32] בָּרָא
[33] Rattray, l. c. #1, p. 18.
[34] Rattray, *Ashanti,* p. 51.

that 'Nyame has the prefix N, which would imply that it is a collective noun, as we have already noted. For, just as we find in the Hebrew the plural form ELOHIM [35] when the Supreme Being is indicated, so the same general principle would apparently here assert itself in the Ashanti concept in this use of a collective noun—in both instances perhaps there is a veiled reference to the Trinity by implication. And what is even more strange, while the accepted rule in Ashanti is that descriptive nouns are generally compounded of a verb with the prefix O and the suffix FO to imply personality,[36] in the present instance the personal suffix is wanting, as if the traditional concept of the Trinity precluded the idea of a single personality from 'Nyame.

**Testimony of Queen-Mothers.**

That the present-day Ashanti themselves regard their tribal God as identical with the one True God of Christendom, who is in reality the Yahweh of the Hebrews, is clear from the address of the Queen-Mothers that accompanied the silver stool which they presented to Viscountess Lascelles as a wedding present. The letter appeared in full in the previous chapter, but we may be permitted to repeat here a single passage that is much to our purpose: "And we pray the great God Nyankopon on whom men lean and do not fall, whose day of worship is a Saturday, and whom the Ashanti serve just as she serves Him, that He may give the King's child and her husband long life and happiness." [37]

**Rattray's Argument.**

Well then, did Captain Rattray write in 1914: "In Ashanti, in remote bush villages, buried away in impenetrable forest, and as yet even untouched by European and missionary influence, it would seem incredible that the Christian idea of a one and Supreme Being should, if a foreign element of only some two or three hundred years' growth, have taken such deep root as to affect their folk-lore, traditions, customs, and the very sayings and proverbs with which their language abounds. These proverbs and traditions, moreover, which speak of and contain references to a Supreme Being, are far more commonly known among the greybeards, elders, and the fetish priestly class themselves than among the rising younger genera-

[35] אֱלֹהִים

[36] Ellis, l. c. p. 308.

[37] Cfr. Page 54 f.

tion, grown up among the new influences and often trained in the very precincts of a mission. Fetishism and monotheism would at first sight appear the very antithesis of each other, but a careful investigation of facts will show that here in Ashanti it is not so." [38]

**Ashanti Proverbs.**

Among the proverbs adduced by Rattray are the following:—"Of all the wide earth, Onyame is the elder."

"If you wish to tell anything to Onyankopon, tell it to the winds."

"The hawk says, 'All things that Onyame made are beautiful (good).' "

"I who lie on my back looking upwards, do not see Onyankopon, so what do you expect who are sprawling on your belly!"

"Because Onyankopon did not wish any bad words, He gave a name to each thing, one by one."

"The words that Onyame had beforehand ordained, a human being does not alter."

"If Onyame gives you sickness, He gives you medicine."

"It is Onyame who pounds the fufu for the one without arms."

"All men are the children of Onyame, no one is a child of earth." [39]

**Priests of Nyame.**

Despite the assertion of Ellis, already quoted,[40] that the deity whom he calls Nana-Nyankupon had no temple and priesthood, Rattray positively proves the contrary, and shows moreover that the priests of 'Nyame are dedicated to Him for life. The ceremony of dedication requires that white clay be smeared in three lines on parts of the head, arms and chest, the prayer of invocation being: 'Nyankopon Kwame wo huiri eni o,—God, Kwame (i. e. whose day of service is Saturday) this is your white clay, life to our master." . . . "After this ceremony the priest must sleep in the 'Nyame dan, temple of the Sky god, for eight nights." [41]

The candidate for the priesthood must spend three years of novitiate in preparation for the office, and it is during his third year of training that he utters a prayer containing these words:

[38] Rattray, *Ashanti Proverbs,* #1, p. 19 f.
[39] Rattray, *Ashanti Proverbs,* #1, 2, 6, 7, 8, 10, 13, 14, 15, p. 17 ff.
[40] Cfr. Page 67.
[41] Rattray, *Ashanti,* p. 144.

"Supreme Being, who alone is great, it is you who begat me, etc." [42] and there is a common saying among the Ashanti: "No priest may look upon the face of his God and live," [43] which sounds remarkably like an echo of Yahweh's warning to Moses at Mount Sinai: "Thou canst not see my face: for man shall not see me and live." [44]

**Redeemer.** One Ashanti proverb is particularly striking. "The Creator created death only for death to kill Him." On which Rattray comments: "This saying illustrates in a wonderful epigrammatical manner the power of death." [45] But does it not rather resemble, either a Christian reference to Calvary, or else a prophetic utterance worthy of Isaias or some other of the ancient Hebrew prophets? [46]

**Ta Kora.** In connection with the same concept of Redeemer, we might call attention to "Tano or Ta Kora, the greatest of the Ashanti gods upon earth." [47] He has a material element about him, and yet "is considered as the 'son of the Supreme God,' " [48] and we find his invocation: "Ta Kora, that great spirit which is everywhere." [49] According to Captain Rattray who had requested the priests to make him a new shrine, this answer to his request came, supposedly from Tano himself, but throught the priest who appeared, or at least feigned, to be in a trance: "I am not named 'Akora because I am old (akora, an old man), but I am called Ta Kora; if it be that anything is spoiled I mend it (kora, to mend). Now if he had come to me and said that something of his was spoiled and had asked me to mend it, then had I seen the path clear, but he says that I must take one of my sons and give him, but that I am unable to do. . . . In my own being I am the son of God, and if any of my grandchildren say that the white man loves me and has drawn nigh to me, I, too, shall stand behind him." [50]

[42] Rattray, *Religion and Art in Ashanti,* p. 45.
[43] Idem, p. 41.
[44] Exod. xxxiii, 20.
[45] Rattray, *Ashanti Proverbs,* #16, p. 28.
[46] Note:—In his latest volume Rattray renders the proverb: 'Odomankoma bo owuo kum no' (The Creator created death and so caused his own death). Cfr. Rattray, *Religion and Art in Ashanti,* p. 151.
[47] Rattray, *Ashanti,* p. 172.
[48] Idem, p. 54.
[49] Idem, p. 196.
[50] Idem, p. 180 f.

Only after the beginning of the nineteenth century was there a shrine for Ta Kora, which is abbreviated for Tano Kora, or Tano the Mender. Prior to that date he was supposed to dwell in a cave near the source of the River Tano.[51]

**Ashanti Myth.**

Once more let us quote from Rattray. "There is known from one end of Ashanti to the other, a popular myth, which I shall here only outline very briefly; it gives in simple and childish form the very basis of Ashanti theological beliefs. This myth recounts how 'Nyame—the Sky God—had various sons of whom one in particular was a bayeyere (favorite son). 'Nyame decided to send these children of his down to the earth in order that they might receive benefits from, and confer them upon, mankind. All these sons bore the names of what are now rivers and lakes." [52]

**Semitic Heathenism.**

In speaking of what he terms "Semitic Heathenism," W. Robertson Smith declares: "It was the community, and not the individual, that was sure of the permanent and unfailing help of the deity. It was a national not a personal providence that was taught by ancient religion. So much was this the case that in purely personal concerns the ancients were very apt to turn, not to the recognised religion of the family or of the state, but to magical superstitions." [53]

[51] Note:—With the Ibos of Nigeria a female deity is the mother of the highest god, the Thunder God, and of all created things.—Cfr. D. Amaury Talbot, *Woman's Mysteries of a Primitive People,* London, 1915, p. 8ff. Some such concept may be at the root of the Songhois legend that the Chief of the Gow or mythological Hunters of the Niger, was Mousa-Gnamé, whose father was a Djinn and whose mother's name was Gnamé.—Cfr. A. Dupuis-Yakouba, *Les Gow,* Paris, 1911, p. 5. This last name pronounced according to its French spelling is identical with the Ashanti Nyame. The Songhois, with whom we are going to connect the Ashanti, have been under a strong Moslem influence for many centuries which explains the introduction of the Djinn. As regards the confusion of gender in the parent deity, this is a common occurrence in mythology.

[52] Rattray, *Ashanti,* p. 143.

[53] W. Robertson Smith, *Lectures on the Religion of the Semites,* London, 1923, p. 263 f. Note:—According to some the very fetishism of the West African is not entirely at variance with Hebraic practice. Thus, Professor Wallis expresses the opinion: "Many Hebrew ornaments seem to have had their origin as charms, particularly those designed to protect the orifices of the body against the entrance of evil demons. Among the Jews the amulet was in common use." Cfr. Wallis, *Introduction to Anthropology,* p. 280. And Blunt is even more specific: "To a late date, as excavations prove, the Israelites continued to use models of cows and plaques of Astarte as amulets."—Cfr. Blunt, *Israel before Christ,* p. 72.

**Ashanti Religion.**

Just some such condition of affairs, it would seem, characterized the tribal religion of the Ashanti, at least in practice. For even independent of the superstitions of Obeah, under the heading of "Ashanti beliefs in non-human spiritual powers," we find Captain Rattray stating: "In the latter category are included all deities, from the Supreme Being, 'Nyame or Nyankopon, who dwells somewhere aloof in His firmament, down to those to whom He delegates some of His powers, as His vice-regents upon Earth. There are the lesser gods, who in their turn are graded in a regular descending scale, until they reach, or at times almost merge into, that class which the Ashanti themselves name suman, who are the lowest grades of superhuman powers. I have given elsewhere some accounts of ceremonies, which afford us examples of animism in its simpler forms." [54]

**Sterility a Curse.**

In another place Captain Rattray writes: "Yet again, unless we understand the full significance underlying that aspect of Ashanti religion which enjoins that the spirits and memories of famous ancestors be venerated and propitiated, we cannot fully grasp what a calamity in the Ashanti mind, the extinction of his clan entails." [55] The same overmastering desire that the family should be perpetuated, made sterility a seeming curse among the ancient Hebrews. To their ancestors, too, did they pay veneration and respect,[56] though not to such a degree, it is true, as do the Ashanti.

**Nyame is Yahweh.**

For the present then, we feel safe in concluding, that, whatever its source of enlightenment, whether by direct tradition effected by a considerable infiltration of Hebrew stock, or through the instruction of missionaries in Christian times, the Supreme Being of the Ashanti is identical with the God of the Christians, the Yahweh of the Old Testament; and further that their tribal worship is strangely parallel to that of the divided worship that existed in Jerusalem immediately prior to the Babylonian exile, as we will see later more in detail.

[54] Rattray, *Ashanti,* p. 86.

[55] Idem, p. 79.

[56] Note:—So great was the Hebrew's respect for the memory of his forefathers that it has misled some into believing that ancestor worship actually prevailed among the Chosen People.—Cfr. Maurice H. Farbridge, *Studies in Biblical and Semitic Symbolism,* London, 1923, p. 217 f.

In this connection, and by way of further proof that in all probability the Ashanti Nyame is but another form of the Hebrew Yahweh, it is interesting to quote from Professor Clay, who assures us that "in the Murushu archives found at Nippur, belonging to the reigns of Artaxerxes and Darius, the divine element in Hebrew names is written Ja-a-ma for Jawa." Clay also mentions a tablet found at Taᶜanach which "contains the divine name of Israel's God written Ja-mi." [57]

Nor can it be objected that in view of the Hebraic prohibition against the use of the Divine Name the common invocation of Nyame among the Ashanti militates against our theory. For Kortleitner assures us that it was only after the Babylonian Captivity that the pronouncing of the terragrammaton was prohibited.[58] Consequently the most that could be implied would be that whatever Hebraic cultural influence may have reached the Ashanti, must probably trace its origin back to Pre-Babylonian Hebrews. And this is precisely what we hope to establish before the close of the present work.

**Altar to Nyame.**

Among the stamp patterns of the Ashanti cloths recently reproduced by Rattray, there is one of rather striking design known as "Nyame dua" or "Altar of Nyame." [59] If we may conceive in the case of the Mosaic Altar of Sacrifice the horns at the corners being turned in and not outwards,[60] the visualization of the one from the other becomes easy.[61]

**Breastplate.**

But before leaving this subject, we must refer to what may well be regarded as a possible vestige of the Office of the Jewish High Priest to be found among the Ashanti.

Ellis relates, how in 1881, when messengers came to Mr. Griffith, the Lieutenant-Governor of the Gold Coast, while relations between the Ashanti and the British were strained, that

[57] Clay, *The Empire of the Amorites,* p. 54.

[58] Cfr. Francis X. Kortleitner, *De Polytheismo Universo,* Innsbruck, 1908, p. 299.

[59] Rattray, *Religion and Art in Ashanti,* p. 267 f.

[60] Exod. xxxviii.

[61] Note:—In the *Jewish Encyclopedia,* Vol. I, p. 466, we find an illustration with the caption, "Bronze Altar of the Temple, Restored (after Calmet)," which actually represents the "Horns of the Altar" inclined inward and not outward.

official, apparently through ignorance of local customs, asked them, how he was to know that they really came from the King of the Ashanti. "They pointed to the gold plates on their breasts as being their insigna of office."[62]

We have a remarkable sketch of this breastplate, which appeared originally in the *Illustrated London News*,[63] and was reproduced without any acknowledgment by Sir Henry M. Stanley in his volume entitled *Coomassie and Magdala*.[64] It is inscribed "Ashantee Ambassadors Crossing the Prah." The breastplate on the central figure, the Herald (Osene), who is called by Stanley the Town-crier, is strikingly similar to the breastplate of the High Priest among the ancient Hebrews, even to its division into twelve parts.

**Misnefet.**

The head-dress of the Herald, too, with its gold disc in front[65] satisfies the description of the miznefet, as given in the Jewish Encyclopedia, "A tiara, or perhaps, a peculiarly wound turban, with a peak, the front of which bore a gold plate with the inscription 'Holy unto Yhwh.' "[66]

**Vestige of High Priest.**

At first glance, this would appear to be unquestionably a vestige of the High Priest of the Hebrews. But it is well to remember that Professor Clay holds that the breastplate was not peculiar to the Hebrews. It was to be found as well in Egypt and probably elsewhere.[67] However, the division of the breastplate into twelve parts is certainly distinctive. So also is the head-dress with the gold disc in front.

**Grebo Bodia.**

In this connection it is interesting to note how Sir James George Frazer records: "Among the Grebo people of Sierra Leone there is a pontiff who bears the title of Bodia and has been compared, on somewhat

[62] A. B. Ellis, *The Land of Fetish*, London, 1883, p. 221.

[63] "From Cape Coast to Coomassie," From the *Illustrated London News*, London, 1874, p. 28.

[64] Note:—As the signature in the original is an H and S superimposed,—the reproduction has been cut down, so that the signature has disappeared—presumably the picture was sketched by Stanley himself, who had gone out to the Ashanti War as a Newspaper correspondent for the New York *Herald*. —Cfr. *Autobiography of Sir Henry Morton Stanley*, ed. Dorothy Stanley, Boston, 1909, p. 291. We may absolve Stanley then from any plagiarism.

[65] Cfr. Rattray, *Ashanti*, p. 282, note 5: "The head-dress of a herald is a cap made from the skin of a Colobus monkey with a gold disc in front.'"

[66] *Jewish Encyclopedia*, Vol. VI, p. 390, Article, "High Priest."

[67] Albert T. Clay, *Origin of Biblical Traditions*, New Haven, 1923, p. 37.

ASHANTI AMBASSADORS CROSSING THE PRAH
*(From a drawing by Sir Henry Morton Stanley)*

slender grounds, to the high priest of the Jews. He is appointed in accordance with the behest of an oracle. At an elaborate ceremony of installation he is anointed, a ring is put on his ankle as a badge of office, and the door-posts of his house are sprinkled with the blood of a sacrificed goat. He has charge of the public talismans and idols, which he feeds with rice and oil every new moon; and he sacrifices in behalf of the town to the dead and to demons." [68] Naturally Sir James accentuates the "somewhat slender grounds" on which the tradition rests, but his mere admission that such a tradition has any foundation at all, is greatly to our present purpose. But now let us return to the Ashanti official with his breastplate and peculiar head-dress with its golden disc.

**Ashanti Osene.**

The word for "Crier" or more properly "Herald" in Ashanti is Osene. According to Rattray: "The Ashanti have a myth which states that the Creator made a herald (osene), a drummer (okyerema), and an executioner (obrafo), and that the precedence of these officials in the Ashanti Court is in that order." [69] Can this have any reference to the beginning of the Mosaic Revelation from the burning bush? [70] The word for bush in Hebrew in S$^e$NE,[71] which might possibly indicate the origin of the Ashanti Osene, the Herald, after dropping the prefix O. The drummer, Okyerema, again dropping the nominal prefix O, might then be derived from KHOREB [72] the western height of Sinai; and the Executioner, Obrafo, after dropping the prefix O and the nominal suffix FO, might be derived from B$^e$RITH,[73] a covenant or alliance. The Ashanti Myth might thus record progressive stages in the manifestation of Yahweh to the Hebrews:—The burning bush; Sinai; and, the Covenant, that established the Nation as God's Chosen People.

The Drum History of Mampon declares: "The Creator made something. What did he make? He made the Herald. He made the Drummer. He made Kwawuakwa, the Chief Executioner. They all, they all, declare that they came from one Ate pod

[68] James G. Frazer, *The Golden Bough,* London, 1920, Vol. III, p. 14 f.
[69] Rattray, *Ashanti,* p. 263.
[70] Exod. iii, 2 ff.
[71] סְנֶה
[72] חֹרֵב
[73] בְּרִית

(Tabena). . . . Come hither, Oh Herald, and receive your black monkey skin cap.[74] What was your heritage? Your heritage was a good master. Your heritage was the death dance. (Atopere)." [75]

That the office of Ashanti Herald may possibly have some distant relationship with the high-priesthood of the ancient Hebrews might be further indicated by some of his privileges and duties. Thus Captain Rattray records: "It is always the herald's privilege to drink first from the wine cup, before the king, before any chief, and even before the spirits themselves." [76] And again: "A herald's duty also included that of town sanitary inspector and tax-gatherer on the main cross-roads, where tolls and duties are collected for the King of Ashanti." [77]

**Twelve Tribes.** Once more, have the twelve divisions on the breastplate anything to do with the tradition recorded by Bowditch,[78] and extended by Beecham,[79] that the Ashanti and allied peoples were originally derived from twelve tribes or families? Another possible indication of some affinity with the twelve tribes of Israel!

In this connection, while speaking of the Ashanti and kindred tribes, Friedrich Ratzel asserts without hesitation: "There are twelve stocks, the members of which are distributed promiscuously throughout these tribes, however remote they may be in situation, or politically separated. . . . Perhaps, however, the basis is not in all cases common descent, but the 'servants' may have been a subject class, as the oil-palm clan, into which the Portuguese are adopted, embraces the trading people." [80] This, however, is merely a conjecture, but it deserves consideration.

**Hebrew Tribes.** With equal assurance, while discussing Totemism, P. Amaury Talbot expresses the opinion: "In

[74] Note:—As noted before the head-dress of the Herald is a cap made from the skin of a Colobus monkey with a gold disc in front.

[75] Rattray, *Ashanti,* p. 282.

[76] Rattray, *Religion and Art in Ashanti,* p. 279.

[77] Idem, p. 279.

[78] Cfr. Bowditch, *Mission from Cape Coast Castle to Ashantee,* p. 229: "One curious evidence, however, may be added of the former identification of the Ahanta nations; which is a tradition that the whole of these people were originally comprehended in twelve tribes or families; the Aquonna, Abrootoo, Abbradi, Essena, Annona, Yoko, Intchwa, Abadie, Appiadie, Tchweedam, Agoona, and Doomina; in which they class themselves still, without any regard to national distinction."

[79] Beecham, *Ashanti and the Gold Coast,* p. 6.

[80] Ratzel, *History of Mankind,* Vol. III, p. 129.

these beliefs there is a strong resemblance to those prevailing in Egypt, where the tutelary deity of each nome, or province, was thought to be incarnate in the animal or plant, etc. after which it was named." And he adds: "The Hebrew tribes also had animal standards." [81] In this last statement, for which he adduces neither proof or reference, he is certainly at odds with W. Robertson Smith, no mean authority on the subject, and who states positively: "On the other hand, it may be argued with more plausbility that totemism, if it ever did exist, disappeared when the Semites emerged from savagery," [82] which was certainly long before the days of Abraham, even were we inclined to admit that the Semites actually did evolve from savagery.

**Parallel to Elias.**

If we might here digress for a moment, it is worth remarking how the story of the great famine that affected Israel, when Elias was miraculously fed by ravens,[83] and the prophets' subsequent destruction of the devotees of Baal,[84] finds its counterpart in Ashanti folk-lore. Speaking of the spirit that is said to dwell in a great rock near Min Mahon, to the west of the river Tano, Cardinall relates: "The spirit was said to be the son of the spirit of the holy River Tano, and had revealed himself in a way reminiscent of Jewish history; for it was the tradition that a certain hunter had been lost in the forest here, and he came to this rock. There he rested, and almost dying of hunger, had prayed to his ancestors and his gods for help. To his surprise, the next day, and every day for seven years, food was brought to him by vultures. The god evidently revealed himself to the man, for he learned many languages and acquired much magic, and eventually found the way back to his people. His reception was far from cordial, but by his magic he overcame their terror, and led them to the dwelling-place of the spirit which had helped him." [85]

**Ashanti New Year Festival.**

We find, too, among the Ashanti what might well be an Hebraic touch in their celebration of the New Year. The Afahye ceremony of the Ashanti is defined by Captain Rattray as "an annual cus-

[81] Talbot, *Peoples of Southern Nigeria,* Vol. II, p. 252.
[82] W. Robertson Smith, *Religion of the Semites,* p. 137.
[83] III Kings, xvii, 6.
[84] III Kings, xviii, 1–40.
[85] Cardinal, *In Ashanti and Beyond,* p. 86.

tom held in connection with the eating of the first crop." [86] The same author who translates the word Afahye as "an appointed festival," [87] goes on to describe the ceremony as he witnessed it towards the end of October in 1921, the Ashanti New Year beginning on the last day of that month.[88] The entire function is remarkably suggestive of the old Hebrew Feast of Ingathering which is known also as the Feast of Tabernacles or simply The Feast.

**Feast of Tabernacles.**

H. G. Friedman states: "From the frequent notices of it, as well as from its designation as 'The Feast,' it would seem that the Feast of Tabernacles held the most prominent place among Israel's festivals. That it was agricultural in origin is evident from the name 'Feast of Ingathering,' from the ceremonies accompanying it and from the season and occasion of the celebration; 'At the end of the year when thou gatherest in thy labors out of the field.' " [89]

The Feast was featured by dances of the maidens in the vineyards [90] and by bringing to Jerusalem the first-fruits as prescribed in Deuteronomy.[91] It lasted seven days [92] to which an eighth day was added [93] "as a concluding festival" that came to be known as "Hasereth" [94] Drink offerings were made and bullocks, rams and lambs were sacrificed [95] with the customary sprinkling of blood upon the altar.[96] Drawing his information from Post-Biblical Literature, Friedman further observes: "Practices, some perhaps of ancient origin, grew up, prominently the libations of water and the rejoicing connected therewith on the second evening of the festival." [97] The same author thus describes the ceremony in further detail. "A golden pitcher holding three logs was filled by a priest with water at Siloah, and brought through the water-gate, the multitude reciting Isa. xii, 3. Amid trumpet-blasts

[86] Rattray, *Ashanti,* p. 203.
[87] Idem, p. 203.
[88] Idem, p. 203 ff.
[89] Exod. xxiii, 16; xxxiv, 22.—Cfr. H. G. Friedman, *Jewish Encyclopedia,* Vol. IX, Article, "Tabernacles," Feast of. p. 656 ff.
[90] Judges, xxi, 21.
[91] Deut. xxvi, 1–11.
[92] Levit., xxiii, 34.
[93] Levit., xxiii, 39.
[94] Friedman, l. c. p. 658.
[95] Num. xxix, 12–38.
[96] Levit., i, 5.
[97] Friedman, l. c. p. 660.

the water was poured simultaneously with a libation of wine into a tube in the altar, through which it flowed, mingling with the libation of wine, by an underground passage to the Kedron." [98] And again: "In the brilliantly illuminated court of the women, before the assembled multitude occupying the double gallery erected by the Priests and Levites, the most prominent Israelites took part in a torch-dance, reciting at the same time hymns and songs of praise. . . . The celebration continued till cockcrow." [99]

**Ashanti Parallelisms.**

Turning now to the Ashanti festival, as described by Captain Rattray, we find many parallelisms. For all these functions the Ashanti assembled not only the drummers but also the horn-blowers, whose horns manufactured from elephant-tusks might well have replaced the trumpets of the Temple.[100]

The ceremony began with the washing of the chief's "white stools," [101] the supposed repository of the owner's vital spirit.[102] The following day, the chief with some companions entered the stool-house of the "black stools," which are regarded as the shrines of the ancestral spirits [103] to pour wine on them with this invocation: "Grandsires, come and receive wine and drink, for to-day the edges of the year have met (i. e. the new and the old), and to-day I am taking you to the stream to sprinkle you with water." [104] The stools were forthwith carried to the river to be sprinkled and then returned to the stool-house, where a sheep was killed, and "blood smeared, with the hand, upon the seat and edge of each stool in turn." [105] Then "pieces of the sacrifice were placed on the stools along with new yams sliced and boiled. The remainder of the yams were sent to the chief's house, and he and certain other persons were now permitted to eat them for the first time that season." [106]

As Captain Rattray remarks: "The ceremony so far, it will have been noted, has reference to ancestral spirits. . . . The next

[98] Idem, p. 661.
[99] Idem, p. 661.
[100] Rattray, *Ashanti,* p. 94.
[101] Idem, p. 203.
[102] Idem, p. 298.
[103] Idem, p. 92.
[104] Idem, p. 204.
[105] Idem, p. 97.
[106] Idem, p. 205.

half of the ceremony was more concerned with the gods than with disembodied human spirits."[107] About midnight, at the opening of the Ashanti New Year (October 31st) the drums began to "talk" and the singers assembled in the court-yard of the temple to intone the invocation to the gods.[108] The ceremony proper commenced at 4 A. M. with dancing and chants of priestesses all white with powdered clay.[109] Bundles of yams had been placed in front of the temple and the dance continued until shortly before dawn.[110] Soon after midday the celebration was taken up again. All the "shrines of the gods" were brought out and taken in procession to the river where they were sprinkled with water.[111] The shrines were then escorted back to the village "amid firing of guns." They were first carried to the stool-house and then returned to the pantheon. One priest with shrine on head, now danced before the temple, and he was shortly joined by other priests and priestesses.[112] This dance continued till about eight o'clock, when gifts from the chief, a sheep, yams, salt, and a money offering, were brought to the pantheon with this prayer: "The edge of the year has come round and your people hold a sheep for you saying: partake of yams, and let what comes after, fall peacefully. Permit the year to come round once more and all people once again to bring you new yams just as we are giving you this day." The blood was forthwith sprinkled on the top of the shrines in the usual manner and then yams were placed before them.[113]

**Taboo Violated.**

Another strange practice connected with an end-of-the-year festival is also recounted by Captain Rattray. The golden state sword is known as Bosummuru, since it is regarded as the shrine of the vital spirit or ntoro of the clan of that name, to which many of the Ashanti kings belonged. To clan, and consequently to the sword also, an ox is taboo. To the uninitiated then it seems inexplicable to find an ox dragged before the king who takes the state sword in hand and strikes the ox three times with the words, "This is yours!

[107] Idem, p. 205.
[108] Idem, p. 207.
[109] Idem, p. 209.
[110] Idem, p. 210.
[111] Idem, p. 210.
[112] Idem, p. 211.
[113] Idem, p. 212.

This is yours! This is yours!" [114] For as Captain Rattray comments: "Here we have a deliberate and public violation of a taboo and pollution of the potential dwelling place of a sacred power. Such an act would in ordinary circumstances be expressed by the phrase 'They have poisoned it.' " [115] On the day following this seeming desecration, the king publicly sacrifices a sheep which he holds over the golden sword, the shrine of Bosummuru. The throat of the sheep is then pricked and the blood is allowed to fall on the sword, which is also sprinkled with water from the sacred rivers. The accompanying invocation is suggestive: "O Bosummuru, the edges of the year have met: you were sharp but I took that thing which you abhor and touched you (with it) but to-day I sprinkle you with water in order that your power may rise again, etc." [116]

This peculiar rite is connected with an Ashanti custom, "an annual ceremony held in September in honour and propitiation of the Ashanti kings who 'have gone elsewhere,' and for the cleansing of the whole nation from defilement," as we are told by Captain Rattray who has already stated: "Its proper title is Odwira, concerning the derivation of which there is no possible doubt. Dwira means 'to purify' or 'to cleanse,' and Odwira means simply 'purification' or 'cleansing.' " [117] Can this annual violation of a sacred taboo have anything in common with the annual exception made in the case of the Hebraic taboo against passing the Veil of the Temple? This occurred just five days before the beginning of the Feast of Tabernacles, on the Day of Atonement, when the priest entered the Holy of Holies to sprinkle the mercy seat with the blood of a bullock, his personal sin-offering, and that of a ram, the sin-offering of the people.—"For on that day shall (the priest) make an atonement for you, to cleanse you, (that) ye may be clean from all your sins before the Lord." [118] The Hebrew word here meaning to cleanse is TAHER [119] and the substantive 'Cleansing' is TAHORRAH [120] which radically

[114] Rattray, *Religion and Art in Ashanti,* p. 136.
[115] Idem, p. 137.
[116] Idem, p. 137.
[117] Idem, p. 127.
[118] Literal translation from the Hebrew of Levit. xvi, 30.
[119] טַהֵר
[120] טָהֳרָ

is not entirely unlike the Ashanti Dwira as the emphatic T (teth) might easily have become a D.

**Ashanti Ntoro.**

Finally Captain Rattray writes: "The Ashanti believe that it is the male-transmitted ntoro, mingling with the blood of the female (mogya), which accounts for the physiological mysteries of conception. I have stated that the ntoro may perhaps be translated by 'spirit.' Indeed, it appears to be used at times synonymously with Sunsum, that spiritual element in a man or woman upon which depends—not life, i. e. breath, for that is the okra or kra—but that force, personal magnetism, character, personality, power, soul, call it what you will, upon which depend health, wealth, worldly power, success in venture, in fact everything that makes life at all worth living." [121] Possibly Vitality might come nearest to express this indefinable something thus described.

**Hebrew Torah.**

But, if the Ashanti Ntoro could be derived from the Hebrew TORAH,[122] Law,[123] the following explanation of the term might suggest itself. While descent among the Ashanti is through the woman (mogya), the lawful seat of authority is not the woman but the man, whether as head of the family or of the entire Nation. It is this right of authority, this right to command, if properly exercised, that assures success, as well in the case of the family as of the Nation. And although this right in itself descends from father to child, it is only the son who is able to transmit it in turn, just as the mother's mogya, or blood, it is believed, is only transmitted by the daughters. In this way, the Ntoro's field of activity is determined by the rights of Mogya, for, again, "It is the woman who bears, i. e. makes the man." [124]

**Natural Law.**

The Ntoro then, might be defined as a spiritual something in man, the possession of which constitutes lawful authority, such authority as is built up on the fundamental Law, whether we regard is as the Natural Law or the Divine Law, since the one is but the declaration of the other. This authority, if properly exercised, necessarily implies respect

[121] Rattray, *Ashanti,* p. 46.
[122] תּוֹרָה

[123] Note:—The prefix N in Ntoro merely signifies a collective noun, and may be disregarded in seeking the derivation of the word.
[124] Cfr. p. 54.

for higher authority, respect for Law, and it is that dictate of the intellect, usually called Conscience, which practically directs, whether or not an action is in conformity with the principles of right and wrong. For certain principles of right and wrong are necessarily impressed on human reason. Conscience brings home this fact from time to time, saying, "This should be done," or "It is wrong to do that." At the beginning of the human race, this Law of Nature, or the Natural Law as it is called, was sufficient for man, acting under the influence of grace, in his relations with God and his fellow men. But sin quickly obscured the natural light of reason, and it became necessary that these same precepts and prohibitions should be given to man in clearly defined terms, that he might not plead ignorance as an excuse for transgression. That is precisely what Almighty God did on Mount Sinai, in giving us the Ten Commandments. He reduced to unmistakable formulae of "Thou shalt" or "Thou shalt not," all those general, time-honored, rules which we should recognize from our own sense of right and wrong as manifested by our consciences.

With the promulgation of the Decalogue on Mount Sinai, was laid the foundation of the Torah. The Deuteronomic Code was the fuller expression and detailed application of the Law, which became the great guiding principle of every God-fearing Hebrew, and it was the spirit of conformity to the Torah that meant real success and attainment for the true Israelite, since it assured participation in the National Promises of Yahweh. It was this respect for the Law, too, that after the close of the Babylonian Captivity, developed into an almost fetish reverence, so much so, that every letter was stressed and strained, until the real spirit of the Law itself was obscured in the school of the Pharisees.

As regards the Ashanti, there exists a like veneration and respect for authority and Law. This is one of the very points, as we have seen, that most impressed Lord Wolseley.[125] While utterly unable to define their own intellectual emotions and subconscious deductions, they show an inherent regard for the Natural Law as well as for their racial traditions, which have for them the force of Law. They reason, too, that there must be some innate quality in man that will not only respect the rights and authority of those above him, but which will also enable him to

125 Cfr. p. 24.

exercise that authority over others, that is inbred in him, and which is his right. And since this mental attitude is not acquired, though a spiritual entity, it must in some way be physically passed from parent to child. And so their system of the transmitted Ntoro has been evolved, without, of course, our long process of reasoning.

**Conclusions.** To the cultural traits then, already mentioned in the last chapter, we have now added other more or less cogent reasons for concluding that somewhere in their development as a tribe, the Ashanti came under a strong Hebraic influence. The facts adduced include first of all the remarkable similarity of the Ashanti Nyame and the Hebrew Yahweh, not only as regards verbal signification and derivation, but especially in their attributes and their relations to the created channels of the Divine influence, according to the accepted tribal concepts. All this is supported by such parallelisms as mixed or divided service, the adoption of fetishism or its equivalent without any apostasy from monotheism; the subtle reference to a Redeemer; Ta Kora, the "son of the Supreme God"; the "altar to Nyame" preserved in the stamp patterns of Ashanti cloth; the survival of what has every appearance of being the breastplate and misnefet of the High Priest; sterility as a curse; the traditional twelve-tribe theory; the raven story of Elias and its counterpart; New Year festivals and their ceremonies; legitimate violations of a Taboo; and, reference to the Natural Law.

These customs, it is true, as well as the cultural traits previously noted, are for the most part widespread throughout the world, and may be found individually among dissociated tribes. But it is the present contention that it would be unreasonable to ascribe to mere coincidence the entire congeries, especially if we can establish the probability of historical contact between the parent-stock of the Ashanti and the ancient Hebrews.

## *Chapter IV*

## OTHER HEBREWISMS IN WEST AFRICA

**Purport.**

It is now time to consider the Hebrewisms found in West Africa outside the Ashanti. In tracing these Hebrewisms, however, it should be kept in mind that it would be a serious mistake to expect to find in any one locality sufficient evidence to prove conclusively direct Hebraic descent from the Children of Israel. All ethnologists agree that the Negro tribes are essentially a conglomeration of stocks, good, bad and indifferent. E. D. Morel illustrates this well, when he speaks of that portion of Western Central Africa, now known as Northern Nigeria, as follows: "In the course of ages, through the influence of Moorish, Semitic, and probably pre-Semitic Egyptian culture, fused in later times with Mohammedan law, learning and religion, there has been evolved in this region a civilization combining a curious mixture of Africa and the East." [1] And again, speaking of Kano, between Bornu and Sokoto, he calls it, "the most interesting region in all the Dark Continent, where divers races have ceaselessly intermingled, attracted thither by its fertile soil and abundant pastures; Libyan and Berber, Egyptian and Semite, and the mysterious Fulani." [2]

**Racial Deterioration.**

The most that we can hope to establish then, is a strong infiltration of Hebrew stock in certain tribes or areas, with a possible explanation of the source of influence. Even those colonies of Jews which are of comparatively recent foundation in Africa have for the most part deteriorated completely from the ideals of their race and their religion. Thus, for example, in his *"Itineraires au Maroc,"* under date of July 7, 1883, Charles de Foucauld records: "In Morocco, has a Jew ever been seen writing on the Sabbath? It is forbidden

[1] Edmond D. Morel, *Nigeria: Its Peoples and its Problems,* London, 1911, p. 103.
[2] Idem, p. 232.

just like travelling, lighting a fire, selling, counting money, talking business, and what not? And all these precepts are observed with equal care! For the Jews of Morocco, all religion consists in that: moral precepts they deny. The ten commandments are bygone tales, at most good for children; but as for the three daily prayers and lengthy graces before and after meals, keeping the Sabbath and feasts, I believe nothing in the world would make them miss them. Endowed with a very lively faith, they scrupulously fulfil their duties towards God, and indemnify themselves at the expense of His creatures." [3] Nahum Slouschz strongly resents De Foucauld's "savage and prejudiced criticism of the Jews of Morocco," [4] and yet he himself admits, when speaking of the Jews in the interior of Morocco: "Their beliefs have often a polytheistic character which approaches fetichism. There are still some who worship grottoes, rocks and streams under the guise of saints. Even in the parts where there are still Spanish Jews, as in Tetuan where the Spanish rabbis still dominate the life of the community, the life of the Jew is bound up with all sorts of ancient beliefs and superstitions, which he has taken over from the Berbers and Arabs, and which have become an essential part of his existence." [5]

**Cult of the Dead.**

In the city of Morocco Slouschz found: "The strangest superstitions and customs are prevalent among the Jews of Mellah. Those connected with the cult of the dead are particularly astounding." [6] Of his experience in the Atlas Mountains, he writes: "The mountain Jews of Glawi have been in the country from ancient times, as I have proofs to show. . . . The cult of the dead plays an important part

[3] René Bazin, *Charles de Foucauld Hermit and Explorer,* London, 1923, p. 40.
[4] Nahum Slouschz, *Travels in North Africa,* Philadelphia, 1927, p. 424.
[5] Idem, p. 430.
[6] Slouschz, *Travels in North Africa,* p. 442. Note:—Of Morocco in general Slouschz writes: "There are many ceremonials in connection with the dead. In the Atlas there survives the ancient custom of placing cruses of water in the tomb. In all parts of Morocco there are to be found professional wailing women who, as in biblical times, are called in to weep for the dead; frequently these women rend their faces and their bodies in their exaltation. If two men die in the same house in the same year, a rooster is slaughtered near the door of the house in order to propitiate the angel of death. Sorcery, the weirdest medical practices, soothsaying, spells against the evil eye, magic and cabalistic formulas, all that speaks of ignorance and superstition, has a large part in the life of the Jew of Morocco. In addition to the Baale Shem, there exist sorcerers, both male and female, who go in for the most savage practices, survivals of paganism."—1. c. p. 438.

in their social life. At Teluet I saw for the first time among Jews the practice of placing a cruse of water in the tomb of a relative, after the ancient Phoenician fashion, while elsewhere they merely burn oil in a hole scooped out of the tombstone." [7] Again, he writes: "Two hours and a half from Teluet is the village of Unila. . . . The local saint of Unila is called Sidi Felful; he is in reality the genius of the river Felful, a survival of religion of fetichism, but this does not prevent the Jews from worshipping him as their own saint." [8]

**Demons' Feast.** All this is in keeping with the account of the "repast offered to the demons among the Jews of Fez," as recorded by Biarney, and which goes to show how the race deteriorated amid the hardships of the Mussulman domination. According to Biarney, if a sick Jew fails to respond to the ordinary treatment, it is concluded that he must be the victim of the demon's wiles, and a suitable propitiatory repast is accordingly prepared to placate the tormentor.[9]

So far from denying this custom, Slouschz furnishes us with some rather startling details, as follows: "If a girl is 'possessed' (ill) the sorceress bids her lay kerme (rouge) on her hands and feet, and paint her cheeks and lips, put kokul on her eyebrows, put on a green coat and yellow balush (slippers), wrap a scarlet silk kerchief round her head, and then join her eyebrows with a single thin, bright line. (We may note with M. Vassel that this kind of toilette has been found in the tombs of ancient Carthage). In this festive garb the girl must appear before the evil spirits which she seeks to placate. A midnight repast is arranged, and the spirits are invited. To this ball, called rebayboyya, men are not admitted. On the table are placed almonds, nuts and sweetmeats for the spirit-guests. Blind musicians are called in to play, for no man must see what takes place in the chamber. . . . While the melancholy music plays, the women, including the one who is sick, perform the danse du ventre, one after the other. The women then address the sick dancer as follows: 'Tell me who my representative is among the spirits?' She replies: 'It is so and so,' or 'It is the Prince of such and such a country.' Thus it is in a state of ecstasy and frenzy that

[7] Idem, p. 469.
[8] Idem, p. 472.
[9] S. Biarnay, *Notes d'Ethnographie et de Linguistique Nord-Africaines*, Paris, 1924, p. 57.

the sorceress prescribes the cures for the sick woman. The Pythoness (the votary of the Ob of the Bible) is still to be found among the Jews of Tunis. She is called the Deraia. She burns perfumes on a chafing dish, and, holding her head over the fumes, works herself into a delirium and begins to prophesy. There are certain nocturnal assemblies called stambali, where women make rendezvous with spirits, and dance with them." [10] And all this by Jews along the shore of the Mediterranean and not by savages in the heart of so-called "Darkest Africa!" In comparison, our observations among the tribes of West Africa will seem tame indeed!

**Floggings.** Mungo Park observed in 1795, in connection with a legal flogging among the pagan Blacks at Teesee, in Kassob: "It is worthy of remark that the number of stripes was precisely the same as are enjoined by the Mosaic Law, forty, save one." [11] This, too, was in the case of a tribe which had up to that time successfully withstood the encroachments of Mohammedanism.

**New Moon.** Later, Park calls attention to the resemblance that certain native marriage rites bear to "the manners of the ancient Hebrews," [12] and further describes at some length the native's veneration of the New Moon.[13] He says in part: "The moon, by varying her form has more attracted their attention (than the sun). On the first appearance of the new moon, which they look upon as being newly created, the pagan natives, as well as the Mohammedans, say a short prayer; and this seems to be the only visible adoration which the Kafirs (Pagans) offer up to the Supreme Being. This prayer is pronounced in a whisper; the party holding up his hands before his face: its purport (as I have been assured by many different people) is to return thanks to God for his kindness through the existence of the past moon, and to solicit a continuation of his favour during that of the new moon. At the conclusion, they spit upon their hands, and rub them over their

[10] Slouschz, *Travels in North Africa,* p. 283 f.

[11] Mungo Park, *Travels in the Interior Districts of Africa,* London, 1810, p. 116.

[12] Idem, p. 399. Note:—According to Wallis: "The Ashanti show respect for the moon, and Ellis believes, on linguistic evidence, that the moon was once an object of worship on the Gold Coast."—Cfr. Wilson D. Wallis, *An Introduction to Anthropology,* New York, 1926, p. 234.

[13] Cfr. Num. x, 10; xxviii, 11. Note:—As the Jews followed the Lunar Month, the 'first day of the month' marks the new moon.

faces. This seems to be nearly the same ceremony, which prevailed among the Hebrews in the days of Job." [14]

Park further remarks: "If they are asked, for what reason then do they offer up a prayer on the appearance of the new moon; the answer is, that custom has made it necessary: they do it, because their fathers did it before them." [15]

**Writing.** Richard Jobson who spent part of the years 1620 and 1621 trading on the Gambia River, under the caption "The discourse of the Maribucks or religious men," says of their writing: "The character they use, being much like Hebrewe, which in regard I understood not, I caused my Marybucke to write in paper, some part of their law, which I brought home with me, that some of our learned Schollars might peruse, if wee might by that means come to any better knowledge, then the small practise wee have hitherto had, and by men of our capacities cannot so easily be attained, onely this much wee descerne, that the religion and law they teech, is not writ in the same tongue, they publickly speake, and moreover, that none of the temporall people, of what dignity soever, are traded up to write, or reade, or have any use of bookes or letters amongst them." [16] The characters referred to are unquestionably Arabic, still the reflexion of Jobson seems worth recording.[17]

**Oath-Drink.** A century later, William Bosman is more specific. "If you ask," he writes, "what opinion the negroes have of those who falsify their Obligations confirmed by the Oath-

[14] Park, l. c. p. 406. Note:—The reference is to Job, xxxi, 26 ff. "If I beheld the sun when it shined, and the moon going into brightness: and my heart in secret hath rejoiced, and I have kissed my hand with my mouth: which is a very great iniquity, and a denial against the most high God."

[15] Park, l. c. p. 408. Note:—Rabbi Kaufmann Köhler maintains: "The period of the New Moon was, in pre-exilic times, celebrated by cessation of labor; it was superior even to the Sabbath-day, which formed but a part of it; but it lost its importance during the Exile. . . . In the Temple, New Moon was celebrated by special sacrifices and by the blowing of the trumpet."—Cfr. *Jewish Encyclopedia,* Vol. IX, Article: NEW MOON, p. 243.

[16] Richard Jobson, *The Golden Trade,* London, 1623.

[17] Note:—Another fact to be noted, even if not strictly a Hebrewism, is recorded by A. L. Kroeber as follows: "The Negroes of the west coast of Africa make gold finger rings ornamented with the twelve zodiacal symbols in their proper sequence. They seem ignorant of the meaning, in fact do not possess sufficient astronomical knowledge to be able to understand the use of the signs. It also remains uncertain whether they learned the set of symbols from European navigators or from the Arabs that have penetrated the northern half of Africa. Nevertheless it is the true zodiac which they portray, even though only as a decorative pattern."—*Anthropology,* New York, 1923, p. 205.

drink; they believe the perjured person shall be swelled by that liquor till he bursts; or if that doth not happen, that he shall shortly die of a languishing sickness. The first punishment they imagine more particular to Women who take this draught to acquit themselves of any accusation of adultery; and if I may be allowed to make a comparison, this drink seems very like the bitter water administered to the women in the Old Testament by way or purgation from the charge of adultery." [18] And again: "The Negroes still retain several laws and customs which savour of Judaism, as last mentioned, their marrying of their Brother's Wife, and several more, which seem the same in effect, as well as the names, of which here are several which occur in the Old Testament." [19] In this matter Bosman himself is somewhat of a sceptic, and he would attribute all to Mohammedan influences, which attitude in itself adds weight to his testimony and admission of facts.

**Messias.** Another pronounced sceptic, Adolphe Louis Cureau, who can find no real worship in Negro religion, makes the admission: "It is a remarkable fact that White Men enter into the legends of certain peoples before Europeans made their appearance, and that such beings, who were unknown at the time, were thought to be of a superior and almost divine nature, and were awaited by some tribes in the form of a sort of Messiah." [20]

**Black Jews.** Writing of this same district, John Clarke, a missionary, says of the extreme south of French Equatorial Africa: "Oldendorp speaks of black Jews being in this part of Africa; but no confirmation of this has been met with. The practices common in many parts of Africa are those of sacrificing goats and sheep, making cuttings for the dead, circumcising, and the trial drink; but these do not particularly belong to the customs of the Jews." [21] Here again, the statement of fact is useful, as it is not written to bolster up a theory.

Friedrich Ratzel, too, refers to the "Mavumba, renowned as

[18] Bosman, *Description of the Coast of Guinea,* p. 125.
[19] Idem, p. 180.
[20] Adolph Louis Cureau, *Savage Man in Central Africa,* trans. E. Andrews, London, 1915, p. 300.
[21] John Clarke, *Specimens of Dialects: Short Vocabularies of Languages: and Notes of Countries and Customs in Africa,* Berwick-upon-Tweed, 1848, p. 91.

potters and smiths, to whom some assign a Jewish origin," [22] and probably with reason, in this instance, attributes the Jewish influence to the Portuguese Jews who at their expulsion from Europe were forcibly colonized at St. Thomas.

**Wilson's Observations.**

J. Leighton Wilson who for eighteen years was a missionary in Africa and subsequently one of the secretaries of the American Presbyterian Board of Foreign Missions, gave to the public the fruit of his experience, and after making due acknowledgement in his Preface, of the works he had consulted, adds: "But the great body of the book is the result of the writer's own observations and knowledge, and it is presented to the public as such." [23] Peculiar value then, must be attached to the following "observations": "Whether the natives of the country have the Jewish distinction between diaboli and daemonia in Northern Guinea is not certainly known, but the inhabitants of Southern Guinea undoubtedly have." [24] And a few pages later: "Mixed up with these pagan notions and customs there are many obvious traces of Judaism, both in Northern and Southern Guinea; and in the latter, some undoubted traces of a corrupt form of Christianity, which have probably travelled across the continent from ancient Ethiopia, where Christianity was once firmly established.

**Diaboli and Daemonia.**

"The African race have a wonderful capacity for conforming themselves to any circumstances in which they are placed, and they can adopt almost any number of religious creeds without being disturbed by their incongruity, or the direct antagonistic character which may exist in them. The religion of Senegambia is a complete medley of paganism, Judaism, and Mahommedanism; and it is difficult to say which of the three occupies the most prominent place, or exerts the greatest influence upon the character of the people. The prevailing philosophy on the subject is, that by combining the three they are sure to secure the aggregate good of the whole. In Northern Guinea, paganism and Judaism are united; and in Southern Guinea, paganism, Judaism, and some imperfect

[22] Ratzel, *History of Mankind,* Vol. III, p. 134.
[23] J. Leighton Wilson, *Western Africa: Its History, Condition, and Prospects,* London, 1856, Preface, p. iv.
[24] Idem, p. 216.

traces of a corrupt form of Christianity. In the former region of the country Judaism is more prominently developed; some of the leading features of which are circumcision, the division of tribes into separate families, and very frequently into the number twelve; the rigid interdiction of marriage between families too nearly related; bloody sacrifices, with the sprinkling of blood upon the altars and door-posts;[25] a specified time for mourning the dead, during which they shave their heads, and wear soiled and tattered clothes; demoniacal possessions, purifications and various other usages, probably of a Jewish origin. Some of these usages, especially the rite of circumcision, might be supposed to have been of Mohammedan origin, if it were not for the entire absence of all other traces of the religion among the pagan tribes of both Guineas.

**Circumcision.** **Duodecimal Tribal Division.** **Exogamy.** **Blood Sprinkling.** **Mourning Customs.** **Obsessions.**

**Traditional Practices.**

"Although the natives of Africa retain these outward rites and ceremonies with the utmost tenacity, they have little or no knowledge of their origin, or the particular object which they are intended to commemorate. Many of them are performed to shield themselves from some threatened evil, or to secure some coveted good. But in the great majority of cases they are attended to merely as a matter of habit; and the only reason assigned for observing them, is that their ancestors did the same before them."[26]

**Other Testimonies.**

Another witness who spent seven years among the Blacks of the Slave Coast is equally positive in his assertion. After remarking that D'Anville's map states that the country of the Nagos was formerly inhabited by Jews, and that this view was adopted by Edrisi, an Arab traveller of the eleventh century, he briefly adds: "One finds among the blacks many Jewish customs."[27] Nor must we be any longer surprised at this. For, according to C. K. Meek: "A tradition current throughout the Sudan would seem to indicate that white 'infidels'

[25] Note:—George Buchanan Gray records: "Closer analogies to the ancient Paschal blood ritual and other analogies which are closer to the Temple ritual described by Ezechiel have been detected in modern Syria or among the modern Arabs, not to speak of customs of people more remote."—*Sacrifice in the Old Testament,* Oxford, 1925, p. 359.

[26] Wilson, l. c. p. 220 ff.

[27] Pierre Bouche, *La Côte des Esclaves et Le Dahomey,* Paris, 1885, p. 268.

held, in the early centuries of our era, the chief power in some at least of the Sudanic states, and were of Semitic origin." And then he adds, not wishing to commit himself, it would seem, "Whether these rulers were Palestinian Jews, or Semito-negroid Christians from the Nile valley, or whether they were the descendants of Carthaginians, cannot now be determined." [28]

**Priestly Garb.** The Reverend Carl Christian Reindorf, a native pastor of the Basel Mission on the Gold Coast, published a little volume, of which J. G. Christaller said: "It is the first comprehensive history of an important part of Africa written by a native from the standpoint of a native." [29] The author, as he tells us himself, belonged to the family of the national officiating high priest of Akra,[30] and in speaking of "the peculiar dress" worn by that official, he asserts: "A close inspection of the priest in his officiating garb leads to the conviction that his worship must be of foreign origin. As there is no African nation or tribe ever known to have so advanced in their religious views as the Akras, one is inclined to suppose that the Jewish system of worship in the Old Testament style has been either introduced by or imitated from the people who came out first to the coast." [31]

**Legal Defilement.** Benjamin Martin in his *System of Philology* states: "On the death of an Israelite, in any house or tent, not only all the persons who were in it, but the very furniture, contracted a pollution which continued seven days, and which was to be removed by sprinkling the persons, rooms, and furniture with water, mixed with some of the ashes of a red heifer that had been sacrificed by the High Priest. But this ceremony has not been observed since the destruction of the Temple; for the Jews no longer look upon themselves as polluted by the dead body." [32] This practice may have fallen into desuetude among the Palestinian and Babylonian Jews with the destruction of the Temple in Jerusalem, for they no longer had a sacrifice, but any one at all familiar with the "ninth-night" as practiced in the West Indies,[33] or its prototype in West Africa, and

[28] C. K. Meek, *Northern Tribes of Nigeria,* Oxford, 1925, Vol. II, p. 73.
[29] Carl Christian Reindorf, *History of the Gold Coast and Asante,* Basel, 1895, Prefatory Remarks, p. x.
[30] Idem, Preface, p. iv.
[31] Idem, p. 6.
[32] Benjamin Martin, *System of Philology,* London, 1759, Vol. I, p. 136.
[33] Williams, *Whisperings of the Caribbean,* p. 241.

observing how even the sprinkling with water is not omitted, is apt to see in this modern weird spectacle only another vestige of the Jewish custom as practiced in the days of King Manasses with whom we are trying to link up so many of the West African customs.

**Jewish Octave.** Still another valuable piece of evidence comes from rather an unexpected source. Ignaz Goldziher calls attention to the preservation of the Jewish octave among the African savages pretty much as it exists in the liturgy of the Church. He tells us: "In old Calabar on the West Coast of Africa a week of eight days occurs; most curiously, as the people cannot count beyond five.[34] A priori this would seem impossible; but it is vouched for by an observer as accurate as Bastian." [35]

**Adultery.** Further south in the Congo, Herbert Ward remarks the affinity of certain customs with ancient Hebrew law. Thus, for example, "If adultery be committed within the village, both the man and woman are considered equally guilty; outside the village boundary, however, the man only is held at fault." [36]

**Parallelisms.**

**Funeral Customs.** Professor Keller of Yale University, relying in great part on data gathered by William Graham Sumner, while treating of "Disguise and other Forms of Mourning," [37] places many West African funeral customs [38] in the same class with the ritual "sackcloth and ashes" of the Old Testament.

Later on, Professor Keller classifies the human sacrifices and disfigurements that accompanied West African funerals down to quite recent date,[39] in the same category with the fact that "the Jews had to be warned repeatedly not to cut hair or beard or gash themselves for the dead." [40]Again he finds the Yoruba ako-ojo (first-day) and similar days of rest in other West African tribes analogous to the Hebraic Sabbath

**Sabbath Rest.**

[34] Cfr. Theodor Waitz, *Anthropologie der Naturvolker,* Vol. II, p. 224, compared with Bastian, *Geographische und ethnologische Bilder,* Jena, 1874, pp. 144; 155.

[35] Ignaz Goldziher, *Mythology among the Hebrews and Its Historical Development,* trans. Russell Martineau, London, 1877, p. 66.

[36] Herbert Ward, *A Voice from the Congo,* London, 1910, p. 252.

[37] Sumner, Keller and Davie, *The Science of Society,* New Haven, 1927, Vol. II, p. 868.

[38] Idem, p. 870.

[39] Idem, p. 899.

[40] Idem, p. 907.

with its death-penalty for violators.[41] In connection with human sacrifice, he remarks that "even Israelites, differ, in this matter, from the negroes of our own times, in nothing save the object they assign to this kind of sacrifice." [42] Further he quotes Barton to show that "temple harlotry" as found in West Africa [43] and elsewhere "goes back to primitive Semitic times," [44] and finds a parallelism to the Levirate of the Jews [45] in West African Marriage customs.[46] In all this, it is true, he is not explicitly connecting the West African with the Jews, but his observations are none the less valuable to our present purpose.[47]

**Human Sacrifice.**

**Levirate Marriages.**

**Vestiges.**

P. Amaury Talbot, of the Nigerian Political Service, after five years among the Nigerian Tribes, saw in the tribal worship of the Ekoi a vestige of "the oldest known Minoan civilization." [48] But in a more recent work, he ascribes the principal foreign influence in West Africa to Egypt, and observes: "The Nupe may have brought over with them their art of making glass, so highly prized in Egypt. The statues, which reached their greatest development in the Mbari temples of the Ibo, though in clay, and most primitive, are similar in feeling and design to some found in Tutoukhamem's tomb; a likeness specially noticeable in the animals supporting the couches." [49]

**Glass Making.**

In her turn, the last author's wife, D. Amaury Talbot, who had many opportunities of observation seldom granted to others, as she had accompanied her husband through parts hitherto unvisited

[41] Idem, p. 1112.
[42] Idem, p. 1251.
[43] Idem, p. 1272.
[44] Idem, p. 1273.
[45] Idem, Vol. III, p. 1901.
[46] Idem, p. 1903.
[47] Note:—In passing it might be remarked that according to some even the Medicine-man or Witch-doctor of West Africa seems not entirely inconsistent with Jewish tradition. For we read: "In ancient Israel, the theory was that sickness was due to a demon, to Yahweh, or to his angel; the healer was therefore a man of God, a magician, or a priest; and the methods fo healing were plainly of a magical type. (II Kings, v, 11; xx, 7.) There was nothing of the nature of scientific research or scientific treatment, but no doubt, much experimental knowledge was gradually accumulated."—Blunt, *Israel before Christ,* p. 124.
[48] P. Amaury Talbot, *In the Shadow of the Bush,* London, 1912, p. 13.
[49] Talbot, *Peoples of Southern Nigeria,* Vol. I, p. 21.

by white women, also published a little volume. It is her conclusion, that "fragments of legend and half-forgotten ritual survive to tell of times shrouded in the mists of antiquity, when the despised Ibibio of to-day was a different being dwelling not amid the fog and swamp of fetishism, but upon the sunlit heights of a religious culture hardly less highly evolved perhaps than that of ancient Egypt.[50]

**Magic Lore.** "Indeed," she adds, "if, as is held by so great an authority as Dr. Wallis Budge, much of the magic lore of Egypt may have originally come from the West, it is most probable that these Ibibios formed a link in the long chain by which such knowledge passed across the continent. In this case, the likeness in ritual and legend still occasionally to be traced between those present-day West African tribes and of ancient Egypt would not appear to have been borrowed from the latter and borne across the continent from east to west, but rather contrariwise, from Niger to the Nile. In any case, the Ibibios would seem to be a people of hoar antiquity, and so long have they dwelt in this region, that no legend of an earlier home can be traced among them." [51] But contrary to Mrs. Talbot's suggestion, the general trend of influence in Africa has been from the east to the west, and there is no sufficient indication here of any reversal of direction.[52]

**Egyptian Influence.** Far more reasonable appears the position of Professor Rawlinson. "It is quite possible," he says, "that the Phoenicians of Memphis designed and organized the caravans which proceeding from Egyptian Thebes,

[50] Note:—G. T. Basden who was for many years a missionary in Nigeria states: "Amongst the Ibo people there is a distinct recognition of a Supreme Being beneficent in character—who is above every other spirit, good or evil. He is believed to control all things in heaven and earth, and dispenses rewards and punishments according to merit."—*Among the Ibo of Nigeria,* Philadelphia, 1921, p. 215.

[51] D. Amaury Talbot, *Woman's Mysteries of a Primitive People,* London, 1915, p. 4 f. Note:—On the other hand, Basden asserts: "The Ibo country lies within the recognised negro belt, and the people bear the main characteristics of that stock. . . . There are certain customs which rather point to Levitic influence at a more or less remote period. This is suggested in the underlying ideas concerning sacrifice and in the practice of circumcision. The language also bears several interesting parallels with Hebrew idiom."—*Among the Ibos of Nigeria,* p. 31.

[52] Note:—It must be noticed, however, that Clark Wissler records: "Some students believe that the Negro peoples of Africa were the originators of iron culture, passing it on to Egypt."—*Man and Culture,* New York, 1923, p. 36.

traversed Africa from east to west along the line of the 'Salt Hills' by way of Ammon, Augila, Fezzan, and the Tuarick Country to Mount Atlas.[53] We can scarcely imagine the Egyptians showing so much enterprise. But these lines of traffic can be ascribed to the Phoenicians only by conjecture, history being silent on the subject." [54]

C. K. Meek asserts: "Egyptian goods had penetrated to Nubia and Kordofan as early as 3000 B. C., and from what we know of subsequent relations of Egypt and Bornu we may assume that, if there were then any tribes capable of carrying on trade, their trade was done with Egypt. There are many indications of Egyptian influence on the culture of Nigeria." [55] And in his "Ethnological Conclusions," he adds: "The bronze vessels reported from Baule on the Ivory Coast, together with the native traditions, indicate that Egyptians in those early times (5th century B. C.) penetrated West Africa in the search for gold. The Aro-Chuku culture is regarded by many as having its source in Egypt, and it would appear that certain features of the Jukun culture have a similar origin." [56] We hope to show later that the Jukun and Ashanti are probably kindred tribes.

**Long-horned Cattle.**

In speaking of the long-horned cattle of the Fulani, Sir Harry Johnston states: "The usual type of cattle belonging to the Fula is practically identical with that of ancient Egypt and modern Galaland and equatorial Africa. It is certain, however, that a considerable element of Egyptian culture entered Negroid Africa by way of Darfur, Wadai, Lake Chad, and thence to the Upper Niger; and along this route the dominant type of long-horned cattle may have reached the Fula of West Africa." [57]

**Yorubas.**

All this will explain what Morel reports: "The Yorubas profess to trace their descent from Egypt." [58] Dennett would look even further to the East for an explanation of many of the characteristics of this same people, when he quotes approvingly from an article in the *Nigerian*

[53] Herodotus, IV, 181–184. Compare Heeren, *African Nations,* Oxford, 1832, Vol. II, p. 202–235.
[54] George Rawlinson, *History of Phœnicia,* London, 1889, p. 297.
[55] Meek, *Northern Tribes of Nigeria,* Vol. I, p. 59.
[56] Idem, Vol. II, p. 162.
[57] Johnston, *British Empire in Africa,* p. 332.
[58] Morel, *Nigeria,* p. 81.

*Chronicle* as follows: "There can be little doubt that the Yoruba people are at least intimately connected with the Orientals. Their customs bear a remarkable resemblance to those of the races of Asia. Their vocabulary teems with words derived from some of the Semitic languages; and there are many natives of Yoruba-land to be found having features very much like those of Syrians and Arabians." Dennett adds: "Most natives I have talked to on this subject are conscious of this origin from a superior race, and the marked superiority of the Yoruba people to their neighbours certainly points to something of the sort." [59]

**Hausa**

The Hausa, too, are supposed by some to have derived their origin from Upper Egypt.[60] Others, including Meek, believe that they "had some connection with the Copts or tribes of the Nile valley." [61] Meek says of them: "The Hausa are not a race at all. They have no racial history, and they are in fact a hotch-potch of peoples of various origins, speaking a Hamitoid language." [62] However, he admits that there are "Semitic and pre-Semitic elements found in the Hausa language, which are too fundamental to be ascribed solely to the influence of Islam." [63]

Hausa folk-lore, it is true, directly contradicts both these views. For, according to their own traditions; "If a questioner asks you: 'Where did the Hausa people have their origin?' Say: 'Truly their origin was the Barebari and Northerners.' " [64] This, however, is a patent effort of a negro tribe to claim Berber origin and as such must to a certain extent be discounted. Nevertheless, it would seem to indicate at least the probability of a Berber element in their ethnic complex.

Morel speaks of the Hausa as invaders "out of the east." [65] And Lieutenant Jean asserts that the traditions of Aïr show that they dwelt for several centuries in that district after their arrival from the South-east. He also notes that the southern part of Aïr

[59] R. E. Dennett, *Nigerian Studies,* London, 1910, p. 11.
[60] Talbot, *Peoples of Southern Nigeria,* Vol. I, p. 30.
[61] Meek, *Northern Tribes of Nigeria,* Vol. II, p. 168.
[62] Idem, Vol. I, p. 27.
[63] Idem, Vol. I, p. 62 f.
[64] R. Sutherland Rattray, *Hausa Folk-lore,* Oxford, 1913, Vol. I, p. 2. Note:—Cfr. also A. C. Haddon, *Races of Man and Their Distribution,* New York, 1925, p. 50: "The Hausa of Northern Nigeria may be regarded as a Negro-Hamitic blend in which the former predominates."
[65] Morel, *Nigeria,* p. 98.

or Asben was a flourishing province of the Songhois and further that the people of Upper Egypt appear to have contributed to this Songhois Empire.[66] Here we have a possible connection between the Songhois and the Hausa. They may perhaps be offshoots from the same migration.

**Ancient Manufactures.** Lieutenant Desplagnes,[67] speaking of the traces of Mediterranean civilization to be found in West Africa, notes that M. P. Standinger published in 1906,[68] "an interesting study which shows the conformity and identifies the ancient manufactured glass in Palestine with certain glass objects still made at Nupe or Nufé in the West Soudan, where this industry had been carried on, as tradition declares by Jewish colonies." [69]

**Window Shutters.** Desplagnes also reproduces some window shutters carved with figures that are distinctively Semitic in their appearance. In one instance the figures are crowned with mitres, which he declares "represent the divine Triad." [70] They are not unlike the mitre of the High Priest of the Hebrews, as described by Josephus. Above the miznefet of the other priests,[71] "there was another, with swathes of blue embroidered, and round it was a golden crown polished of three rows, one above another; out of which arose a cup of gold." [72] Is all this, again, mere coincidence?

**Summary.** Briefly then, as supporting the theory of the Hebrewisms of the Ashanti, we have found the following indications of an infiltration of Hebraic culture among the distinctively Negro tribes of Africa. In floggings, the traditional number of strokes, "forty less one"; New-Moon festivals; the Oath-Drink akin to the scriptural "bitter waters"; expectation of a Messias; Jewish distinction between diaboli and daemonia; the duodecimal division of tribes into families; exogamy; bloody sacrifices with the sprinkling of blood upon altar and door-posts; mourning customs; obsessions; legal defilement; Jewish octave; law on adultery; funeral customs; Sabbath rest; Levirate mar-

[66] C. Jean, *Les Toureg du Sud-Est: L'Aïr,* Paris, 1909, p. 82.
[67] Louis Desplagnes, *Le Plateau Central Nigérien,* Paris, 1907, p. 135.
[68] *Zeitschrifft fur Ethnologie,* XXXVIII, p. 231.
[69] Cfr. *L'Anthropologie,* XVII (1906), p. 469.
[70] Desplagnes, l. c. p. 170 bis.
[71] Cfr. p. 82.
[72] Josephus, Bk. III, Chap. VII, # 6.

riages; glass making; besides other traits that might as well have Mohammedan or Christian origin, such as circumcision on the one hand, and priestly garb on the other. How then, are we to explain all these parallelisms? Has Hebrew culture really found its way into the heart of Negro land?

**Tribal Culture.**

Roland Dixon, Professor of Anthropology at Harvard University, has said: "The term culture has come to be used by anthropologists, sociologists, and others as a designation of that totality of a people's products and activities, social and religious order, customs and beliefs which, in the case of the more advanced, we have been accustomed to call their civilization. . . . The culture of any people comprises the sum of all their activities, customs, and beliefs. These fall rather naturally into three main categories—the physical, the social, and religious." [73] In our present quest we shall be dealing with all three sorts, or categories, of culture.

In connection with tribal culture, however, it is well to keep in mind a definition suggested by Clark Wissler: "A unit of tribal culture is spoken of as a trait. This term is also applied to mannerisms and to concepts of whatever kind. Thus the custom of a man marrying his wife's sister may be observed and, if so, is set down as a trait of the tribal culture. It follows then, that a tribal culture is characterized by the enumeration of its observable traits and that the culture of one tribe is distinguished from that of another by differences in these traits." [74] Wissler further states: "In a scientific inquiry into the nature and behaviour of culture, the theories of convergence, diffusion, and independent invention can do no more than state the different ways by which cultures may have come to be similar." [75] This marks out for us the scope of our research in trying to explain the parallelisms between the culture of the ancient Hebrews and that of the West African "bush" in general, and of the Ashanti in particular.

**Culture Parallels.**

Professor Dixon has well said: "By culture parallels is meant the phenomenon of the existence in two more or less widely separated areas, between

[73] Roland B. Dixon, *Building of Cultures,* New York, 1928, Introd. p. 3.

[74] Wissler, *Man and Culture,* p. 50. Note:—Wissler further remarks: "When a trait includes a chain of activities it is usually called a trait-complex."—l. c. p. 52.

[75] Idem, p. 108.

which there has been no known historical contact, of cultural traits or trait-complexes which seem to be similar or even identical. If in Africa, in Melanasia, and in North America, for example, we find a trait or trait-complex which seems in all three cases to be alike, how shall we explain the similarity? There are two alternatives which at once suggest themselves: either the similarity is due to diffusion which has carried the trait in some unknown way from one area to the others, or the similarity is due merely to chance and the basic unity of the human mind, which confronted with similar conditions, has reacted to them in a similar way." [76] Later Professor Dixon speaks more in detail as follows:

**Explanations.** "Parallelism or similarity of culture traits in widely separated and disconnected areas may be due to various causes. The parallelism may be real and complete and explainable as an instance of wholly independent invention; it may be real and traceable to continuous diffusion, with subsequent disappearance in a portion of the area, or to normal discontinuous diffusion; it may be real, but in a strictly limited degree, and due to convergent evolution from originally quite discrete beginnings; or, lastly, it may be specious, in that the only actual parallelism present lies in such broad and basic features that they cease to have real significance, since they are the natural or inevitable outcome of ordinary human experience. The determination of the proper category for each case that arises is not always easy, the difficulty lying usually in the inadequacy of the available historical data, a lack almost inevitable for all savage and barbarous peoples. . . . That diffusion is responsible for a large number of apparently disconnected similar traits is probable, but there remains a considerable residuum for which independent origin is the only rational explanation." [77]

**Diffusion.** Now there are, as indicated above, various systems for the explanation of parallelisms in culture. Some find in diffusion the solution of practically every question of similarity in traits between the most dissociated areas. Professor Elliot Smith and his disciple W. J. Perry may be mentioned as leading defenders of this system.

[76] Dixon, *Building of Cultures,* p. 182.
[77] Idem, p. 223.

**Environment.** Others go the opposite extreme and make environment the sole requisite need. Thus Ibn Khaldun, the Arabic philosopher and historian, we are told, "sought to explain all history and the development of civilization through environmental effects." [78]

**Convergent Evolution.** A modified form of evolution, however, is thus explained by Clark Wissler: "Since in all matters of invention one step leads to another, we may suspect that trait-complexes evolve from simple beginnings. So it is conceived that in the course of time two or more quite different traits, originating in widely separate cultures, may come to be similar. Convergence and convergent evolution are terms used to designate this method of explaining similarities in culture." [79]

Many cultural parallelisms, without a doubt, are to be explained by convergent evolution, but it is a serious mistake to overstress the point. Convergence at best is a generic explanation, and in general the great majority of cases may be accounted for in this manner. But in specific instances, there is the danger of assuming as untrue the very condition it sets out to disprove, viz., that here and now, this is not a case of diffusion. And it tends to argue from the fact that since convergent evolution may possibly explain the parallelism, therefore convergence is the solution of the question in hand. While, on the contrary, an equally plausible explanation by diffusion has frequently much in its favor.

**Contrasts.** Thus Goldenweiser lays down the principle: "Independent development of similarities must be assumed as a general postulate in connection with civilizational interpretations, although it is, of course, true that rigorous proof of independent development as against diffusion can but seldom be furnished." [80] And again: "One factor will always favor the hypothesis of diffusion: it is its demonstrability in specific instances; whereas independent origin must at best always remain problematic." [81] Goldenweiser also warns us: "The explanation of individuality (of civilization) must be sought not in biological type, nor in physical environment, nor again in psychological traits or general historical or sociological conditions, but in the

[78] Cfr. Idem, p. 7.
[79] Wissler, *Man and Culture,* p. 105.
[80] Alexander A. Goldenweiser, *Early Civilization,* New York, 1926, p. 312.
[81] Idem, p. 310.

specific historic fates of each local culture in its particular geographical and historical setting. The explanation here is identical with historic reconstruction, and to the extent to which this is faulty or incomplete, our knowledge and understanding of the particular civilizational differences involved will be the same." [82] All this must be carefully kept in mind.

Goldenweiser further states: "The most complicated and difficult aspects of the diffusion problem arises in cases . . . where the geographical distribution of a trait is discontinuous. In some cases of discontinuous distribution the geographical facts alone may furnish an answer to the problem." [83] And finally: "The classical evolutionist was not greatly troubled over examples such as this. To him all such instances attested the similarity of the human mind and the parallelism of cultural development. But we may not share the consoling faith of the evolutionist. The universality of the phenomena of diffusion amply attested by the preceeding discussion, does not permit one to stress the theory of independent development at the expense of the alternative possibility of explaining cultural similarities through a common ultimate origin or through historic diffusion from one tribe to another." [84]

**Historic Contact.**

Kroeber, too, when speaking of the analysis of cultural phenomena, has asserted: "When independent developments have occurred, there is a basic or psychological similarity, but concrete details are markedly different. On the other hand if a differentiation from a common source has taken place, so that true historical connection exists, some specific identity of detail almost always remains as evidence. It therefore follows that if only it is possible to get the facts fully enough, there is no theoretical reason why ultimately all cultural phenomena that are still hovering doubtfully between the parallelistic and the diffusionary interpretations should not be positively explainable one way or the other." [85]

In the case then, of parallelisms between two dissociated groups, to evaluate properly the counter claims of diffusion and convergent evolution, it becomes necessary to establish the weight

[82] Idem, p. 401.
[83] Idem, p. 307.
[84] Idem, p. 310.
[85] A. L. Kroeber, *Anthropology,* New York, 1923, p. 206.

of probability for the historic contact between the groups in question.

**Dixon's Ethnologic Africa.**

Before beginning our quest of historic contact between the Hebrews and the West African Tribes, we may here briefly summarize what Professor Dixon has said of the ethnological course of African development. To quote his very words as far as possible, he says: "In the early Palaeolithic period we may, I believe, think of the African population as primarily composed of the Mongoloid (Brachycephalic, Chamaecephalic, Platyrrhine) and Proto-Astraloid (Dolichocephalic, Chamaecephalic, Platyrrhine) types and their mixtures. Perhaps somewhat sparsely settled, they probably held most of the north, including large areas in the Sahara, which at this period was certainly more humid and suitable for human occupation than it is to-day. Southward they probably extended to the edge of the forest zone, and, sweeping around it on the east, followed down the grassland plateaus toward the southern portion of the continent. The Congo basin and perhaps the Guinea coast were apparently not occupied." [86]

"The Proto-Negroid (Dolichocephalic, Hypsicephalic, Platyrrhine) type spread very widely at a very early period throughout the whole northern part of the continent and blends between this type and the somewhat older Proto-Astraloid made up a large part of the population during late Palaeolithic times." [87]

"The last of what are apparently the older types is the Palae-Alpine (Brachycephalic, Hypsicephalic, Platyrrhine), presenting in many ways the most puzzling problems of all. It is in its distribution to-day concentrated in the region of the forest belt, comprising the Congo basin and the Guinea coast, with possible outliers eastward of the great Rift Valley." [88] This is the Central African Pigmy type.

Professor Dixon continues: "In spite of faint traces of this brachycephalic, platyrrhine type to be found north of the forest zone, there seems no reason to believe that it spread as widely over the continent as the types already discussed. The great tropical forest area is in many ways a refuge region, and seems to have

[86] Roland B. Dixon, *Racial History of Man,* New York, 1923, p. 182.
[87] Idem, p. 183.
[88] Idem, p. 183.

been penetrated and colonized only relatively recently by Negro peoples, who in their spread over the continent seem first to have flowed around the forest region before they attempted to penetrate it. . . . And although the numbers of the Pigmies still surviving in a relatively pure state seem to be small, the greater part of the population of the Congo basin, to-day is very largely mixed with their blood." [89]

"Into an Africa which must thus have been in the main Negroid around a core of pigmy Negritos, with, in the northwest and especially the southeast, considerable remnants of the fusion of the older Mongoloid and Proto-Astraloid types, there came in early Neolithic times a new factor, destined to become of enormous importance in the future development of the peoples of the continent. This was the first invasion of the Caspian (Dolichocephalic, Hypsicephalic, Leptorrhine) type—tall, light-skinned, with a tendency under favorable conditions towards blondness. This new type came into Africa from the northeast by way of Arabia." [90] Groups of these Caspians who are considered by Professor Dixon as the parent-stock of Semitic folk,[91] moved southward, we are told, towards the Lakes of East Africa and beyond, "blending with the older population. . . . Among them the Bantu languages developed. . . . Further north from Nubia, which seems to have been a great reservoir of these immigrants, they passed west into the Sudan and the regions of the Sahara. . . . And so, perhaps as early as late Neolithic times, some strain of this virile group reached as far as the Atlantic shores, whose modern descendants are the Fula." [92] From another branch of this Caspian migration Professor Dixon would derive the Libyans and Berbers.[93]

"With the opening of historic times," according to Professor Dixon, "a new influence again makes itself felt in Africa; another new type appears, at first feebly but then in ever-increasing volume adding its quota to the already existing complex." [94] He calls it the Mediterranean (Dolichocephalic, Chamaecephalic, Leptor-

[89] Idem, p. 184.
[90] Idem, p. 184.
[91] Idem, p. 185.
[92] Idem, p. 185.
[93] Idem, p. 186.
[94] Idem, p. 186.

rhine) type, and notes: "It seems to be the fact that this type makes its appearance in any strength in Egypt in the course of the First Dynasty. . . . It seems to have entered the Nile Valley from the delta, and while at first forming merely the backbone of the ruling caste, as the centuries passed it contributed more and more to the mass of the population, until, by the end of the Middle Kingdom, it had attained to the dominant place among the varied racial elements in the Egyptian portion of the Nile valley, and retained that leadership in Upper Egypt without interruption down at least to Roman times and in lower Egypt to the present day." [95] Beyond Egypt this influence was felt, he tells us, only along the coast and "seems to have been in part at least sea-borne" as it is also found in the Canary Islands.[96]

Finally Professor Dixon states: "One last racial factor which has played its part, albeit but a minor one, must not be overlooked, viz., the Alpine (Brachycephalic, Hypsicephalic, Leptorrhine) type. When shortly after the beginning of the Dynastic period, the Mediterranean peoples made their first appearance in force in Egypt, the Alpine type, which previously had been absent, or present in almost negligible proportions, at least in Upper Egypt, increased nearly twofold. Later it declined again until the period of the New Empire, when it once more assumed importance and continued to be a factor of significance in Roman times." [97] This Alpine type is also found along the coastal area of Northern Africa probably "largely sea-borne," which makes Professor Dixon suggest that it may be due to "pre-Phoenician and Phoenician colonists.[98] He also adds: "Westward through the Sudan traces are to be found here and there of Alpine blood, but they seem to be, so far as present data go, very slight. Yet in Dahomey the Alpine factor is more pronounced, and further material may show its unexpected strength in parts of the Sudan." [99]

From all that Professor Dixon has said, we may gather that more than one ethnic impulse has passed from Egypt out through the continent of Africa, and we hope to show that in some way

[95] Idem, p. 187.
[96] Idem, p. 187.
[97] Idem, p. 188.
[98] Idem, p. 189.
[99] Idem, p. 190.

an influence of Hebraic culture found its way along the same lines from Egypt to the heart of Negro Land. To establish this theory, it becomes necessary to study the possible historic contacts between the Hebrews and the tribes of West Africa.

*Chapter V*

# THE "LOST TRIBES" OF ISRAEL

**A Closed Question.**

If we are to establish historical contact between the Hebrews and the parent-stock of the Ashanti, it now becomes necessary to check up every possible channel by which diffusion between the two groups was possible. At the very outset, two main lines of inquiry present themselves on account of the duality of the divided Kingdom of Israel. And yet, strictly speaking it is only with the Judeans that we have to deal, since the destruction of the Northern Tribes was definitive and complete. However, as Professor Dixon says: "A few generations ago cultural parallels between the customs and beliefs of aboriginal peoples and those of the Hebrews as recorded in the Bible, were explained in accordance with the theories of the times, as the degenerate survivals of ancient Semitic culture, diffused by the Lost Ten Tribes of Israel. Traces of these extremely elusive wanderers were found in every quarter of the globe, and Bushman and Eskimo, Australian and American Indian were alike credited with being their descendants." [1] And although Professor Dixon adds: "The ghost of the Lost Tribes has long since been laid, except perhaps for some whose judgment is ruled by their imagination," [2] it may be well to introduce here

[1] Roland B. Dixon, *Building of Cultures,* New York, 1928, p. 225.

[2] Idem, p. 225. Note:—That the question is not entirely a dead one is shown by an editorial in the Boston *Herald* for April 27, 1928, entitled "Jewish Ancestry." It runs as follows: "Jews in every part of the world, and the Jews in Palestine most of all, will be interested in that controversy, just aroused by the visit of the King and Queen of Afghanistan to England, over the so-called Jewish origin of the Afghan people. Eagerness to claim Hebrew descent has been shown during the past quarter of a century in striking ways. Here and there in China are to be found small colonies whose members do not hesitate to look back to their 'Jewish ancestry,' and only the other day it was pointed out that a 'considerable number of people are still propagating the doctrine that the English themselves are descended from the tribes of Israel. As to the Afghans quite a number of intelligent British officers well acquainted with them are said to be strong believers in the Hebrew theory. And what of the evidence in its favor? One thing which travelers sometimes tell us after investigation on the spot is that nearly all the

a short chapter on the subject, to clarify our own position and to definitively eliminate all question of any contact between the Ashanti and the Northern Kingdom of Israel.

**Professor Rawlinson.** Professor Rawlinson of Oxford, in assailing the position of those who would derive the Anglo-Saxon Race from the "Lost Tribes" of Israel, ridicules the attempt, and declares that these much lost Tribes "have been found a hundred times by a hundred different travellers, and in a hundred different localities," and goes on to endorse the statement of Kitto: "There is scarcely any human race so abject, forlorn, and dwindling, located anywhere, between the Chinese and American Indians, who have not been stated to be the Ten Tribes." [3]

**Anglo-Saxons.** Towards the middle of the last century, "Our Israelitish Origin" by John Wilson [4] revived an old controversy, in an effort to derive the Anglo-Saxon Race from

Afghan women and many of the men are 'of a distinctly Jewish cast of countenance,' and that a large number of them have Jewish-Christian names, such as Ibrahim for Abraham, Ayub for Job, Ismail for Ishmael, Ishak for Isaac, Yohia for John, Yakub for Jacob, Daoud for David and Suleiman for Solomon. The Afghans, moreover, are known to recognize a common code of unwritten law which appears to resemble the old Hebraic law, though it has been modified by Mohammedan ordinances. A further strengthening of the theory has been found in the story that 'when Nebuchadnezzar overcame the Children of Israel certain of the Jewish tribes, and perhaps all of 'the lost ten tribes,' made their way eastward into a mountainous country and settled eventually in the country of Afghara, where they founded the race, of the Afghans.' And would-be supporters of the theory—like Lord Curzon himself—are especially impressed by the fact that for centuries past, and to this day, the majority of Afghans have stoutly defended the belief in their Hebrew descent. Why, it is asked, should their historians have called them Beni-Israel, meaning in the Arabic tongue 'The People of Israel'? When it comes to chapter and verse there are serious doubts in the way. Sir Edward Denison Ross, a famous expert in oriental history and languages, comes near calling the whole theory 'a myth.' 'If the Afghans were in origin a Semitic people,' he says, 'we should expect to find some trace of that origin in their language, whereas as a matter of fact there is none. As for Jewish names, they are simply taken from the Koran, and we find them among all the Mohammedan peoples.' And as to the 'Jewish cast of countenance' noticed in the Afghans another expert reminds us that 'while as a rule the Afghan nose is long and curved, this Jewish, or, rather, Hittite, nose is very widespread, and is a characteristic of races in no way connected with the Children of Israel.' It would thus seem that the theory now under discussion must be classed as one of a number which have been devised to explain the origin of the Afghans, for they have been traced to Copts, Armenians, Albanians, Turks, Arabs and Rajputs. And eager as are the subjects of the King of Afghanistan to claim Hebrew descent there is little likelihood of them joining the Zionist movement or swelling the 20th century migration to the Holy Land."

[3] Cfr. Edward Hine, *Oxford Wrong,* New York, 1880, p. 149.

[4] Published in 1845.

the Ten Tribes of Israel, that have come to be known in history as "The Lost Tribes." The Reverend E. Beckersteth proceeded to refute the arguments advanced by the theory. During the next quarter of a century there were spasmodic attempts to popularize the idea, but it was not until early in 1871 that the interest of the general public was aroused. "Twenty-seven Identifications of the English Nation with the Lost House of Israel" by Edward Hine, followed by subsequent brochures. "Flashes of Light" and "Anglo-Saxon Riddles," drew down on the author the wrath of his kinsman, Professor George Rawlinson, of Oxford, and Canon of Canterbury. That a person of such distinction should take notice of the theory, even to assail it, gave the question the needed publicity, and the controversy was well under way.

Edward Hine, in his reply to Canon Rawlinson, denies having ever read more than "a few extracts" from the earlier book of Wilson, despite the fact that a striking similarity of treatment had been pointed out.[5] Others besides the Oxford Professor had ventured to take exceptions to his attempted Hebraization of the Anglo-Saxon Stock. Mr. Hine acknowledges the attentions of some few of them, but brushes them all aside with a single bold stroke of the pen: "Not one objection has foothold as yet, and I believe never can have. The identity of our Nation with Israel is purely God's work, and no man has power to destroy it." [6] We suspect a little humor on the part of Mr. Hine.

The discussion now became general, and the literature on the subject is extensive. Space will permit only a few random comments in passing. Thus one writer finds in this theory, facetiously we suspect, the explanation of how despite many miscalculations, the ambitions of Britain are usually crowned with success. "Why should so small a country as Britain," he asks, "possess such great influence over the world as she does, and be successful in all her wars, notwithstanding that she continually makes the most palpable blunders? We have many faults, socially, nationally, and individually, to confess and bemoan; yet, for all that, it will be admitted that we are 'a great nation'. What is the secret of Britain's greatness? If

**Humorous Aspects.**

[5] Edward Hine, *Oxford Wrong in objecting to the Anglo Saxons being Identical with Israel,* New York, 1880, p. 137.
[6] Idem, p. 142.

it is proved that the British are Israelites, the whole History of England will be understood with a right point of view; and that is, that God's dealings with her, being Israel, show forth that He is true, faithful, and 'Covenant' keeping: this is the true secret of England's greatness and not any inherent goodness that rests in her or in her people." [7]

**House of David.**

Meanwhile, as early as 1861, the Reverend F. R. A. Glover transferring his attention from the Lost Tribes to the surviving Juda, had indicated what he was pleased to call the possible descent of the Royal Family of England from the House of David.[8] Sixteen years later, a pretentious effort strove to fit in some missing links.[9] However, the chain was far from complete, and it was left for the ingenuity of the Reverend A. B. Grimaldi, to devise a full unbroken line from David to the then-reigning Queen of England, Victoria of happy memory.[10] According to his schemata, the Kings of Juda from David to Sedecias, form eighteen links in this chain. The sceptre is then passed down through the Princess Tea Tephi, who, it is asserted, married Heremon, King of Ireland, and their successors, from 578 B. C. to 487 A. D. forming fifty-five links in the chain. Thirteen links of the Royal House of Argylshire passes it on to the Sovereigns of Scotland, A. D. 834, and the chain is finally completed by the twenty-five Scottish links and the successors of James I of England. It is difficult to believe that the expounders of these schemes to Judaize the Royal Family of England really took themselves seriously. And Doctor Wild, at least, must have possessed a rare sense of humor, when he evolved his theory of the Irish Jews.[11]

**Irish Jews.**

Briefly, his position is as follows. "Two colonies settled in Ireland; the first, the Phoenicians, who were Philistines or ancient Canaanites. The second settlers were Tuath de Danan. . . . The Phoenicians were sea-faring people;

[7] H. W. J. Senior, *The British Israelites,* London, 1885, p. 1.
[8] F. R. A. Glover, *England the Remnant of Judah,* London, 1861.
[9] J. C. Stevens, Geneological Chart, Showing the Connection between the House of David and the Royal Family of Britain, Liverpool, 1877.
[10] Cfr. A. K. Robinson, *Predestination, as taught in the Bible, and verified in History,* Leeds, 1895, p. 132 ff.
[11] Joseph Wild, *The Lost Ten Tribes and 1882,* London (Ontario), 1879. Note:—Incidentally, while pastor of the Union Congregational Church in Brooklyn, N. Y. Dr. Wild took the precaution of publishing his book on the safer side of the Canadian border.

pressed by Israel, Egypt and Assyria, they finally left Canaan, and settled in Ireland." [12]

Dr. Wild would have it, that at the time of the Babylonian Captivity, after the Prophet Jeremias was carried into Egypt by the remnant of the people, he escaped thence to Northern Ireland, taking with him the ark of the Covenant, Jacob's pillow—the stone of Israel—as well as the daughter of Sedecias, through whom the royal line was to continue. "Irish histories," he tells us, "some twenty of which we find agree, say that about 585 B. C. a divine man landed in Ulster, having with him the king's daughter, stone of destiny, and ark, and many other wonderful things. The people of Ulster of Dan understood the old adventurer." In passing, the author assures us: "Now at Tara, Jeremiah buried the ark of the covenant, tables of law, etc." [13]

As to the presence of the Tribe of Dan in Ulster, the matter is easily explained, according to Doctor Wild's way of thinking. "During the persecution of Ahab, thousands of them left Palestine, settling in Denmark—this word Denmark means the circle of Dan. In course of time they crossed the sea and took possession of the north of Ireland, settling the province of Ulster." Thus we have the dual race of Irishmen—Philistines in the South and God's chosen people in the North. Consequently it is easy for Doctor Wild to explain what must appeal to him as the inferiority complex of the South, which readily fell a prey to the "allurements of Rome." [14]

Furthermore, according to Doctor Wild, Jeremias "is the real St. Patrick—simply the Patriarchal Saint, which became St. Patriarch, then St. Patrick. The Roman Church introduced St. Patrick to offset the St. Patriarch." [15] However, the Doctor admits that the individual commonly revered as the Patron of Ireland was more than a "mythical person." He gives his real name as Calpurnius, and would have him born 387 A. D. near the present city of Boulogne. Further he is satisfied that this Calpurnius was himself a Jew, belonging to the tribe of Benjamin. "For the Benjaminites began to fill in that part of France about this period."

[12] Idem, p. 267.
[13] Idem, p. 269.
[14] Idem, p. 271.
[15] Idem, p. 270.

The author adds: "This tribe were by nature missionaries. This prompted him to desire to redeem his brethren in Ireland. In Ulster he began his labors." [16]

Nevertheless, Doctor Wild is insistent that Jeremias "was the real sainted patriarch of Ireland. And by a crafty design of Rome young Calpurnius was created sainted patriarch, or St. Patrick, and by this means Rome linked the greater part of the Irish nation to herself." [17] And almost it would seem with a sigh of relief, the Doctor takes care to note: "But neither Rome nor any other power ever enslaved or conquered Ulster." [18] In conclusion it should be observed that in the Doctor's view the division of Ireland is not merely due to religion. It is essentially racial. "The people of Belfast are Danites; they of Dublin are Phoenicians." [19] So, after all, the great majority of Irishmen are not Jews, even according to Doctor Wild.

**Mythical Wanderings.**

Whatever we may think of Doctor Wild's sincerity in the matter, three years later, not to mention others, the Reverend Doctor Poole seriously undertook a study of the whole question. The Jews as we know them to-day, he regards as the descendants of the Kingdom of Juda. The Lost Tribes, he would trace as follows: "Nineveh was destroyed by the Medes and the Babylonians about 621 B. C. and the Assyrian monarchy divided between them; Israel, or a large portion of them, taking advantage of the opportunity thus afforded, asserted their independence, or escaped, and planted themselves in Armenia, to the north of Assyria. During the several irruptions caused by the conquests of Alexander the Great, and his immediate successors,[20] they resumed their nomad state, and wandered northward, and westward, to some of the quiet valleys which led them on their way westward and homeward," [21] to the British Isles as their journey's end.

[16] Idem, p. 277.
[17] Idem, p. 278.
[18] Idem, p. 279.
[19] Idem, p. 274.
[20] Note:—When the Mongol invasion reached Germany in 1241, "it was fabled that the Tatars were none other than the lost tribes shut up by Alexander the Great in the Caspian mountains."—Cfr. Margolis and Marx, *History of the Jewish People,* Philadelphia, 1927, p. 379.
[21] W. H. Poole, *Anglo-Israel,* Toronto, 1882, p. 128.

These nomads, Doctor Poole would then identify with the Saxons, and he continues: "Sharon Turner states that, 'Although the Saxon name became on the continent the appellation of a confederacy of nations, yet, at first it denoted a single state, and, it appears, they were so isolated that the Romans did not come into contact with them, though continually devastating by fire and sword, the people intervening between them and the Saxons.' How clearly the providence of God was seen in their history as they passed through the great wilderness of people." [22]

In consequence of all this, and similar studies, many wild schemes were evolved, and detailed maps were constructed, marking out the wanderings from the land of exile of these Tribes, which despite their name, absolutely refuse to stay lost. The suggested itinerary is a varied one. Skirting the southern shore of the Black Sea, the first route supposedly led across the Dardanelles, and followed the Black Forest all the way to the German Sea, and then across to England. A second migration, we are told, might have passed over the Caucasus Mountains, and after some delay in what is called the "Land of Sojourn and Increase" far up to the Baltic Sea, found its way to Denmark and thence across to England. Still a third route is suggested far around the Caspian Sea, only to turn back and strike the path through Southern Germany to the Sea.[23]

But whether the propounders of these wild theories really regarded them as fact or fictional humor, they found adherents who were as ready to accept them with the same credence and authority, as if they had been culled directly from Holy Writ. As a matter of course, these absurd suggestions should all be classified with the report of Ibn Haukal, the famous traveller of the tenth century who would, to a certain extent, reverse the Darwinian Theory, by deriving monkeys from Jews, when he records: "Ableh is a small town, well inhabited, with a little tilled and cultivated land, 'In that place were some Jews; those to whom it was forbidden to hunt on the Sabbath; and God transformed them, and caused them to become monkeys.' " [24]

[22] Idem, p. 128.

[23] Cfr. Thomas Rosling Howlett, *Anglo-Israel, The Jewish Problem and Supplement,* Philadelphia, 1894, Appendix.

[24] Cfr. *The Oriental Geography of Ebn Haukal, an Arabian Traveller of the Tenth Century,* trans. William Ouseley, London, 1800, p. 10.

**Northern Kingdom Destroyed.**

Historically the obliteration of the Northern Kingdom may be concisely told. The disintegration began when Tiglath-Pileser IV, the Assyrian monarch, in his campaign of 733–732 B. C. overthrew Damascus and invaded northern Israel.[25] In consequence of this invasion, J. M. Powis Smith [26] tells us: "Israel lost her territory east of the Jordan, the population of which was deported to Assyria." [27]

The ultimate destruction of the Northern Tribes was accomplished a few years later, when Sargon II in 722–721 B. C. completed the work that had been begun by his predecessor Shelmaneser IV, finally capturing Samaria which had held out for a three-years siege. The conqueror thus recorded his triumph: "I besieged and captured Samaria. I carried away 27,290 of its inhabitants, I collected there 50 chariots. The remains of them I permitted to retain their goods, put my governors over them, and I laid the tribute of former kings upon them." [28] In another record of the same event that has come down to us, Sargon expressly states: "I set up again and made more populous than before. People from lands which I had taken I settled there." [29]

Commenting on these cuneiform records of Sargon, Barton suggests: "Only 27,290 were transported at this time. . . . When we put together all those who were deported, however, they were but a fraction of the population. As Sargon distinctly says, the others remained there. They intermarried with the settlers whom he brought in and became the ancestors of the sect of Samaritans. The 'ten lost tribes' were not 'lost', as is often popularly supposed to be the case." [30]

**Remnants Absorbed.**

Karl Kautsky, in his turn, comes to pretty much the same conclusion, as follows: "Not the entire population of the ten northern tribes of Israel were therefore carried off, but only the most distinguished inhabitants of the cities, which were then populated with strangers, but this was quite sufficient to destroy the nation-

[25] George A. Barton, *Archæology and the Bible,* Philadelphia, 1925, p. 427.
[26] J. M. Powis Smith, *The Prophets and their Times,* Chicago, 1925, p. 74.
[27] Cfr. also Samuel A. B. Mercer, *Extra-Biblical Sources for Hebrew and Jewish History,* New York, 1913, p. 40.
[28] Idem, p. 43.
[29] Idem, p. 43.
[30] Barton, *Archæology and the Bible,* p. 428.

ality of these ten tribes; for the peasant alone is incapable of constructing a specific communal life. The Israelitic city dwellers and aristocrats who were transplanted to Assyria and Media, on the other hand, disappeared in their new environment in the course of generations, becoming fused with it." [31]

**Rehabilitation of Samaria.**

Doctor Gaster in the Schweich Lectures on Bibical Archaeology for 1923 advanced the opinion that the settlers sent by Sargon were not in reality colonists in the strict sense of the word but mere military garrisons which were subsequently replaced by Persian troops.[32] But his arguments, based as they are solely on Samaritan traditions, such as the fact that they "repudiate entirely any connection with any heathen nation," [33] are far from convincing. Doctor Gaster further states: "According to the Samaritan chronicles, a large number of exiles came back and settled in the land under the High Priest Abdael, no less than 37,000 being mentioned as having returned." [34] But he candidly admits that the number given must be an exaggeration. Besides, Powis Smith is emphatic in his assertion: "The downfall of Samaria brought about the end of the northern kingdom, which now became an Assyrian province. Natives of other parts of the Assyrian Empire were imported to take the place of the twenty-seven thousand deported citizens. The result was the rise of a mixed people in Northern Israel, who were mongrel in religion as well as in blood." [35]

Stanley A. Cook, too, is entirely in accord with this opinion. He further maintains that in 715 B. C. Sargon added to the mixture of races already located in Samaria by the introduction of Bedouin colonists from Arabia.[36] These with the other colonists from Assyria he finds intermarrying with the remnants of Israel "and their descendants might in time be regarded as truly remnants of Israel, even as the semi-Edomite clans that entered Judah were reckoned as Israelites." [37] Of the exiles from the Northern

[31] Karl Kautsky, *Foundations of Christianity;* New York, 1925, p. 222.
[32] Moses Gaster, *The Samaritans: Their History, Doctrine and Literature*, London, 1925, p. 18.
[33] Idem, p. 34.
[34] Idem, p. 31.
[35] Powis Smith, *The Prophets and their Times,* p. 80.
[36] Cfr. Cambridge *Ancient History,* Vol. III, p. 383; 385.
[37] Idem, p. 386; Cfr. also p. 405.

Kingdom, Cook concludes: "They were probably soon swallowed up in their new homes." [38]

Nothing is to be gained then, by trying to trace these Northern Tribes further at the present time.[39] Lacking the spirit of the Southern Kingdom, they quickly became assimilated and lost their identity being absorbed by the peoples with whom they dwelt.[40]

**American Indians.**

Before drawing this chapter to a close, however, a word must be said about the theory of those who would find among the American Indians evidences of descent from the ancient Hebrews. In one way the question is closely allied to that of the "Lost Tribes." And even in the case of those who postulate for the Indians a Judean origin, or at least a diffusion of Judean culture, the matter is best settled here, as it may easily becloud the treatment of our own subject if reserved until later.

**Controversy in England.**

The controversy was of Spanish origin almost immediately after the discovery of America,[41] but eventually reached England. *Jewes in Amer-*

[38] Idem, p. 385.

[39] Note:—Max L. Margolis says: "The Israelitish brethren were absorbed by the foreign environment—we speak of the 'lost ten tribes'—though some residue must have maintained its identity in the Median highlands and beyond, to be merged later with the Jewish people."—Cfr. Margolis and Marx, *History of the Jewish People,* p. 115.

[40] Note:—There is also the contrary tendency that would just as arbitrarily deny practically all originality to the Hebrew people and tend to explain even distinctively Mosaic institutions as borrowings from others. Thus we are told by Kortleiter: "There was a time when the rites of the Mosaic cult were associated with the Egyptian. Thus the vestments of the priests and of the Supreme Pontiff, the ark of the covenant, circumcision were referred to examplars of the Egyptians. And J. Spencer strove to show that nearly all the forms of the Mosaic Cult are to be sought among the Egyptians. . . . At a later date it was frequently said that not a few institutions of the Mosaic Cult were received from the Babylonians. . . . Babylonia was the fatherland of the Hebrew race. But that Abraham migrating from Ur-Kasdim took with him and passed on to his posterity various opinions, habits, customs, is so evident that there is no reason why anything further should be said on the matter. . . . Other learned men of more recent age contend again that not a few sacred rites of the religion of the Old Testament are to be traced to the Arab influence of the Minæans. . . . The similarities pertaining to religion may perhaps be so explained, that the Hebrews did not imitate the forms of the Minæan Cult, but rather the Minæans imitated the forms of the Hebrew Worship. . . . Others think the Hebrews received some sacred rites from the Canaanites. Which opinion can scarcely be proven."—F. X. Kortleitner, *Archæologia Biblica,* Innsbruck, 1917, p. 45 f.

[41] Cfr. Albert M. Hyamson, *A History of the Jews in England,* London, 1907, p. 181 ff.

*ica, or Probabilities that the Americans are of that Race,* was the title of a book written in 1648 by the Reverend T. Thorowgood who was interested in the efforts of the Reverend John Eliot to evangelize the Massachusetts Indians, and who hoped to help the work financially. Four years later, Hamon L'Estrange answered it with a little volume, *Americans no Jewes, or Improbabilities that the Americans are of that Race.* Thorowgood founded his conjecture on six arguments, which are thus summarized by L'Estrange: "1) The Acknowledgment of the Americans. 2) From Rites and Customs. 3) From Words and Speech. 4) From man-devouring. 5) From the Conversion promised to the Jews. 6) From the Calamities threatened to the Jews." [42]

Before considering these claims and refuting them in detail, L'Estrange first considers the source of the aborigines of America, and concludes: "Thus far have I offered my weak conceptions, first how America may be collected to have bin first planted, not denying the Jewes leave to goe into America, but not admitting them to be the chief or prime planters there; for I am of opinion, that the Americans originally were before the Captivity of the Ten Tribes, even from Sem's near progeny." [43]

Contemporary with L'Estrange, George Horn discusses the possible descent of the American Indians from the Israelites, a theory which he also rejects.[44]

**Manasseh Ben Israel.**

Meanwhile the question had been seriously taken up on the Continent, and popularized by one of the most brilliant Jews of the day. Manasseh Ben Israel, a native of La Rochelle, while yet a boy moved to Amsterdam with his parents, early in the seventeenth century. In due course he became one of the most distinguished orators in Holland, and established the first Hebrew printing press in that country in 1626. Through the influence of a fellow Jew, Aaron Levi, better known as Antonio de Montezinos, Manasseh became a strong advocate of the theory that the North American Indians were in fact the Lost Ten Tribes of Israel.[45] With a view of se-

[42] Hamon L'Estrange, *Americans no Jewes,* London, 1652, p. 1.
[43] Idem, p. 13.
[44] Georgius Hornius, *De Originibus Americanis,* Hagae Comitis, 1652, Praef.
[45] Note:—Montezinos had "told a weird tale of American Indians he had come across in his travels in the New World, of their religious practices, and of their tradition that they were of the tribe of Reuben."—Cfr. Margolis and Marx, *History of the Jewish People,* p. 490.

curing the readmission of the Jews into England, Manasseh published a volume entitled "Esperança de Israel."[46] Written originally in Spanish, this work was quickly translated into Latin and English, and exercised a great influence, though it failed in its original purpose of opening England to the Jews. However, at the national conference at Whitehall in December 1655, it brought out the fact that their exclusion was not sanctioned by English Law, and incidentally gained many outspoken advocates to the general theory of the Israelitic origin of the American Indians.

**Missionary Reports.**

For some time, missionaries in America, especially those in Mexico, had been sending home reports of religious customs and beliefs that savored much of Semitic origin. Thus the Jesuit Acosta reported that the Indians had an infinite number of ceremonies and usages which reminded one of the ancient Law of Moses.[47]

**Mexican Mythology.**

But it was reserved for Viscount Kingsborough, who gathered all these testimonies into a single volume, to become the real propounder of the theory, that would trace to a Semitic source those Indian customs and traditions. Thus he writes: "It is impossible on reading what Mexican mythology records of the war in Heaven and of the fall of Zontemoque and the other rebellious spirits, of the creation of light by the word of Tonacatecutli and of the division of the waters, of the sin of Yztlacohuhqui and his blindness and nakedness, of the temptation of Suchiquecal and her disobedience in gathering roses from a tree, and of the consequent misery and disgrace of herself and all her posterity, not to recognize scriptural analogies. But the Mexican tradition of the deluge is that which bears unequivocal marks of having been derived from a Hebrew source."[48] The Viscount then develops the Mexican idea

[46] Manasseh Ben Israel, *Esperança de Israel,* Amsterdam, 1649. Note:—"With full credence in the story of Montezinos and the evidence culled from Jewish and Christian writers, he arrived at the conclusion that the Israelitish tribes, scattered over many countries, had wandered from Tatary across China to the American continent, thus carrying the dispersion to the farthest parts of the globe."—Margolis and Marx, l. c. p. 490.

[47] José de Acosta, *The Natural and Moral History of the Indies,* London, 1880. A reprint of the English Translation of 1604, from the Spanish, Bk. V, Chapter xxvii, p. 369. Cfr. also Joan Fredericus Lumnius, *De Extremo Dei Judicio et Indorum Vocatione,* Venice, 1569.

[48] Lord Kingsborough, *Mexican Antiquities,* London, 1829, Vol. VI, p. 401.

of the deluge and its subsequent events, such as the Tower of Babel and the dispersion of nations, in parallel with the Bible Story.

**Defenders.** In due time, Brasseur de Bourbourg became an ardent defender of Kingborough's views.[49] Among others, too, Hubert Howe Bancroft describes in detail what he regards as authentic Hebrew relics found in what is now the United States,[50] and John T. Sharp establishes, at least to his own satisfaction, numerous analogies between Jewish and Mexican codes and customs, that are certainly striking.[51]

**Opponents.** On the contrary, De Roo, who has made a special study of the subject, after discussing the whole question at some length, and giving due credit to all authorities cited, as well as quoting many others, unreservedly rejects their claim, and concludes: "For these and similar reasons, which the reader can easily find in several other works, we are of opinion that the first Jews who ever set foot on American soil were those who, in spite of the restrictions of Ferdinand and Isabella, secretly went on board the ships which Colombus and his contemporaries steered to the New World." [52]

**Concessions.** Yet De Roo subsequently admits certain seemingly Hebraic customs among the American Aborigines. Thus, after rejecting the claims of two Hebrew practices in America, he concedes: "Other souvenirs of Jewish history and rites of the Mosaic law seem to have been real, and to have actually existed among a few of America's aboriginal nations. Thus are the Yucatecs said to have had a tradition according to which they originally came from the far East, passing through the sea which God had made dry for them." [53] And again: "We may close this chapter with the remark that the Mexicans celebrated the Jewish feast of the New Year,[54] and had their

[49] Brasseur de Bourbourg, *Histoire des Nations Civilisées et de L'Amérique-Centrale durant les Siècles Antérieurs à Christophe Colomb,* Paris, 1857.

[50] Hubert Howe Bancroft, *The Native Races of the Pacific States of North America,* New York, 1875, Vol. V, p. 93 f.

[51] John T. Sharp, *The North Americans of Antiquity,* New York, 1880, p. 463.

[52] P. De Roo, *History of America before Columbus,* Philadelphia, 1900, Vol. I, p. 199.

[53] Idem, Vol. I, p. 420, quoting Bancroft, l. c. Vol. V, p. 22.

[54] Adolphe Kastner, *Analyse des Traditions Religieuses des Peuples Indigènes de l'Amérique,* Louvain, 1845, p. 102.

festivity of the Remission of Sins and the use of sacred unctions as the Jews." [55]

De Roo further qualifies his position by the statement: "We do not, however, intend to say that the western portion of the Old World had no share at all in America's greatness before the Christian era." [56] He even admits: "Not a few writers defend the opinion that the Egyptians, who sailed around Africa and far away into the Indian and the Atlantic Ocean, left in America some architectural and linguistic vestiges of their presence," [57] and conceives the possibility of the Phoenicians, whether Tyrians or Carthaginians, having also reached the American continent.

**Peru.** Speaking of the "remarkable parallel to the Egyptian development" which "is to be found in comparatively recent times in the Inca monarchy of Peru," Professor Dawson, the Oxford Historian, observes: "If it was the result of purely independent South American development, it is one of the most remarkable examples of convergent evolution in history. According to the hypothesis of Mr. Perry [58] and Professor Elliot Smith,[59] the elements of this culture were actually derived

[55] Hornius, *De Originibus Americanis,* Lib. IV, Cap. xv, p. 278.

[56] De Roo, l. c. Vol. I, p. 192.

[57] De Roo, *History of American before Columbus,* Vol. I, p. 192. Note:—He probably has reference to the Phoenicians in the employ of Egypt.

[58] Note:—Writing in 1923, Perry makes the assertion: "My indebtedness to Professor Elliot Smith does not need emphasis. To him I owe the realization of the importance of Egypt in the history of civilization; and it is a matter of gratification to all those who agree with his views to see that opinion is slowly, but surely, coming round to his point of view, so that the ultimate justification of his courageous and outspoken attitude is assured."—W. J. Perry, *Children of the Sun,* London, 1927, Preface, p. viii. Mr. Perry further unhesitatingly adopts "the hypothesis of an early movement out from Egypt, which resulted in the translation of the civilization of the Sixth Dynasty to the uttermost parts of the world," and regards the Phoenicians as the probable "link between Egypt and the external world." l. c. p. 461.

[59] Note:—Clark Wissler insists: "Elliot Smith, in particular, is an extreme diffusionist, denying the possibility of independent invention. So wherever he observes a similarity between cultures, no matter if half the circumference of the world intervenes, he declares that diffusion is obvious and the only problem presented is to discover how the trait-complexes involved managed to leap the gap."—*Man and Culture,* p. 107. Goldenweiser is even more outspoken. He says: "Elliot Smith has achieved the questionable distinction of outdoing the dogmatism of the evolutionist by his reckless utilization of diffusion as an interpretation of widespread cultural similarities, supporting his theory by a comparative material apparently as inexhaustible in quantity and handled as uncritically as was the comparative material of the evolutionist. The value of the last-named theory cannot be examined here. The idea of a Megalithic culture originated in Egypt in the 18th.—20th dynasty, spreading thence through the Mediterranean region, over the southern areas of Asia and the

from Egypt, and were introduced into South America by the same race of megalith builders who have left traces of their presence throughout the Pacific from Easter Island to the Carolines. Now the monarchy of Japan, the rulers of which also claim to be Children of the Sun, was undoubtedly founded by megalith builders who arrived by sea, not long before the Christian era, and it is not impossible that the same influence may have reached the Pacific Coast of America. But the gap in time and space between this prehistoric Pacific culture and the historic civilization of ancient Egypt is so great that it is difficult to affirm any direct cultural influence on the part of the latter in the present state of our knowledge." [60]

**Kroeber's Conclusions.**

Finally, A. L. Kroeber, after asserting: "The American race can hardly have come from anywhere else than Asia," [61] adds: "About the end of the Palaeolithic or beginning of the Neolithic some of the protomongoloids drifted from Asia into North America. These were probably the real discoverers of the New World, which they found inhabited only by brutes." [62] He later states: "Since the early culture importation of the period of the settlement of America eight or ten thousand years ago, the influences of the Old World have always been slight as compared with the independent developments within the New World. Even within the northwestern segment of North America, the bulk of culture would seem to have been evolved on the spot. But mingled with this local growth, more or less modifying it in the nearer regions, and reaching its greatest strength among the Eskimo, has been a trickling of series of later Asiatic influences which it would be mistaken wholly to overlook." [63]

island expanses of Melanesia and Polynesia to the remote countries of Mexico and Peru; this idea, however alluring, would require a delicate technique and categorical demonstration before it could claim serious attention. The methods used by Elliot Smith are, on the contrary, so loose that the entire speculative edifice erected by him can at best be regarded as another link, in that chain of top-heavy hypotheses born of uncontrolled flights of the imagination and unchecked by either patient research or a strict method of procedure."—Goldenweiser, *Early Civilization*, p. 311.

[60] Christopher Dawson, *The Age of the Gods*, Boston, 1928, p. 163 f.

[61] Kroeber, *Anthropology*, p. 343.

[62] Idem, p. 344.

[63] Kroeber, *Anthropology*, p. 392. Note:—No reference will be made to the Mormons, as they do not claim for themselves continuity of race with the Jews, but merely subscribe to the general theory that the North American

**True Diaspora.** With this somewhat lengthy preamble, we are now ready to withdraw from the grotesque and fantastic, to take up, in the next chapter, the real question of the Diaspora, tracing in roughest outline, within the realms of reasonable probability, the wanderings of that race or people whose dispersion is regarded by some as the means chosen by Divine Providence to prepare the way for Christianity, by drawing back to the primitive monotheistic idea the pagan world that had become corrupt, and through unbridled lusts sunk deep into the polytheistic practices of sensuous idolatry.

**Spiritual Influence.** For, as Professor George Foot Moore has well observed: "Among the Oriental religions which made successful propaganda in the first century before the Christian era and the first century after it, Judaism was not the least important. The ubiquitousness of the race had its part in this; but the chief cause lay in the character of the religion. Its monotheism was of a type to which the popular philosophies all tended; indeed the synagogue, with its gathering for the study of the Law and the Prophets, seemed much more like a school of philosophy than like religious worship or the ritual of a mystery. The possession of these sacred scriptures, descended from an antiquity by the side of which the beginnings of Greek philosophy were modern, and derived from divine revelation, made a doubly profound impression upon an age which turned its eyes to the ancients for wisdom and to heaven for a truth beyond the attainment of reason. The Jewish life, with its multitudinous observances and its meticulous precautions against pollution from unclean men and things, had nothing strange or unreasonable about it when not only religious sects but philosophical schools made diet and dress and rules of intercourse an essential part of their discipline." [64]

Indians were descended from the Ten Tribes of Israel, and that an exodus of Jews from Jerusalem took place prior to the birth of Christ, and carried away the records, a part of which was the Book of Mormon. This book, it is asserted, was discovered by the Prophet Joseph Smith in the side of a hill, called Cumorrah, in Ontario County, New York.—Cfr. *Confessions of John Doyle Lee, Danite,* New York, 1905, p. 140 ff.

[64] George Foot Moore, *History of Religions,* Edinburgh, 1914, Vol. I, p. 531.

## *Chapter VI*

# THE DIASPORA

**Beginnings.** At all ages, Israelites, either individually or in small groups, must have taken up their residence in the land of strangers. In fact, George A. Barton writes: "It appears from I Kings, xx, 84 [1] that an Israelitish colony was established in Damascus in the reign of Ahab. (i. e. About 900 B. C.) Possibly the similar alliances of David and Solomon with Phoenicia had established similar colonies there." [2] And Stanley A. Cook, when speaking of the time of the Babylonian Captivity, observes: "Apart from the Judaean exiles themselves, it is not impossible that by this time Jews, whether associated with their Phoenician brethren or not, were beginning to be found scattered over the known world." [3]

With reason then, Lewis Browne, in connection with the destruction of Jerusalem, takes care to note: "The scattering of the Jews through foreign lands—the Diaspora as it is usually called—had already been in process for many centuries before the fall of Jerusalem. Perhaps as early as the days of Solomon there were little colonies of Hebrew traders in strange lands. Certainly there were many after the destruction of the Northern Kingdom in 722 B. C. and still more after the destruction of the Southern Kingdom in 586 B. C. Indeed some scholars say that from that last date on, there were always more Jews living outside the borders of Palestine than within them." [4]

[1] Douay Bible, III Kings, xx, 34.

[2] *Dictionary of the Bible,* Ed. James Hastings, New York, 1924, Article, "Dispersion," p. 193.

[3] Cfr. *Cambridge Ancient History,* New York, 1925, Vol. III, p. 407. Note: Max L. Margolis discredits the claim of the early Spanish Jews who "imagined themselves of royal Davidic blood. They told fantastic stories that Adoniram, Solomon's master of levy, had died while collecting revenue in Spain, and that his tomb had been found in that country."—Cfr. Margolis and Marx, *History of the Jewish People,* p. 303.

[4] Lewis Browne, *Stranger than Fiction,* New York, 1925, p. 160.

And Ewald, the historian, states: "The 'Exile' in this wider sense begins as early as the tenth and ninth centuries, long before the destruction of the kingdom of the Ten Tribes; for great numbers were carried away as prisoners of war and subsequently for the most part sold as slaves, and many who sank through internal commotions took to more or less voluntary flight. . . . In particular the 'Coasts of the Sea,' i. e. the numerous maritime districts and islands of the Mediterranean, are now (as in the eighth century) frequently mentioned as a residence of the Dispersion. The extensive trade of the neighboring Phoenicians had long been directed to these countries, which now appear for the first time in the history of Israel, and many who were not sold as slaves followed the example of the Phoenicians, and went thither of their own free will." [5]

**Judeans.**

While then, from an early period, there must have been scattered throughout the known world individuals and even considerable groups of the Children of Israel, from the Northern Kingdom as well as from the Southern, the term Diaspora or Dispersion is technically restricted to the tribe of Juda, from whom the modern Jew is supposed to have sprung. Barton makes this clear in stating: "The real Dispersion began with the Babylonian Exile. Nebuchadnezzar transplanted to Babylonia the choicest of the Judaean population. Probably 50,000 were transplanted, and Jewish communities were formed in Babylonia at many points, as at Tel-abib and Casephia. Here the Jewish religion was maintained; . . . and from this centre Jews radiated to many parts of the East. Thus the Jews reached Media, Persia, Cappadocia, Armenia, and the Black Sea. Only a few of these Babylonian Jews returned to Palestine. They maintained the Jewish Communities in Babylonia till about A. D. 1000." [6] It is here interesting to remark in passing, that as late as the middle of the tenth century, we find the Arabian Traveller, Ibn Haukal, describing a Jewish kingdom at Atel near the Caspian Sea, and noting: "The smallest in number of the inhabitants of this country are the Jews; the greatest in number are the Mussulmans and Christians; but the king and his chief officers are Jews." [7] With-

[5] Heinrich Ewald, *History of Israel,* London, 1878, Vol. V, p. 4.
[6] Hastings, *Dictionary of the Bible,* p. 193.
[7] Ibn Haukal, trad. Ouseley, p. 186.

out a doubt, the kingdom referred to was that of the Mongol Chazars. As we shall see later, this people was converted to Judaism in the middle of the eighth century. Consequently, they were Jews not by race, but only by adoption.

**Fall of Jerusalem.**

Of the fall of Jerusalem, Mercer records: "Nabuchadrezzar was a great builder and architect, and consequently most of his inscriptions deal with building operations. We know, however, from Biblical sources that he interfered in Judaean affairs, and this is confirmed by some of his inscriptions.

"Jehoiakim, against the advice of Jeremiah, revolted and Jerusalem was besieged in 597. Jehoiakim died in the meantime and Jehoiachin, his successor, surrendered and was taken with many other captives to Babylonia and settled in a place near the canal Kebar near Nippur. About a decade later Hophra (Apries) of Egypt induced Judah and some other small neighboring states to revolt. This called down the wrath of Nabuchadrezzar who laid siege to Jerusalem in 587, and although he was called off to defeat Hophra succeeded in returning and capturing the city in 586 B. C. Zedekiah was taken captive to Riblah, where his eyes were put out, and Gedaliah was made governor of the city." [8]

**Remnant in Juda.**

As Kautsky remarks: "Very probably the entire population was not taken away this time either; but all the population of Jerusalem was taken away. At any rate, most of the country population was left. But what was left ceased to constitute a specific Jewish community. The entire national life of the Jews was now concentrated in the city-dwellers now living in exile." [9]

**Babylonian Sojourn.**

Of the days of sojourn in Babylon, we need say little here. Harold Hunting writes: "When they reached the land of their captors they were not made slaves, but were allowed to make their home together in settlements on land set apart for them. In these colonies they probably worked as tenant-farmers on the estates of Nebuchadnezzar's nobles. In the prophetic book of Ezekiel, who was among the exiles, we read about one of these Jewish colonies by the river or canal, called Chebar (or in Babylonian Kabary), which means

[8] Mercer, *Extra-Biblical Sources*, p. 57.
[9] Kautsky, *Foundations of Christianity*, p. 226.

the Grand Canal." [10] And again: "Many Hebrews, or Jews (that is Hebrews from Judaea), became merchants. . . . The reputation of the Jews for cleverness in trade began with these experiences in Babylon when hundreds of Jewish boys obtained positions in great Babylonian stores and banks, and by and by set up for themselves as merchants. Among the Babylonian contracts on clay tablets coming down to us from this period are many Jewish names." [11]

On the other hand, the period of the Babylonian Captivity was characterized by a rejuvenation of the religious spirit of Juda, and the prophets of the Exile left a lasting impress on the Nation. No matter what their previous practices had been, idolatry never again became a national crime, although, it is true, it was still to have its devotees in private.

**Return from Exile.**

When, at length, Cyrus permitted the Exiles to return to their own country, it was principally the poorer and more fervent element apparently that availed itself of the privilege.[12] The wealthier class, for the most part, rather chose to remain in Babylonia, and established there a numerous and influential community, which was to endure for 1500 years.[13]

**Babylonian Community.**

Powis Smith clearly explains the reason for all this as follows: "There is good reason to think that the Jews in Babylonia had prospered. They had acted upon the advice given them in Jeremiah's letter,[14] and built themselves into the economic and industrial life of the Babylonian community as a whole. They had all their investments and business interests in Babylonia. The proposition to pull up stakes, sell out, and start all over again in a new and far-off location would not appeal with great force to successful Jewish merchants or farmers in Babylonia. Another difficulty in the way of the creation of great enthusiasms for the return movement lay in the

[10] Harold B. Hunting, *Hebrew Life and Times,* New York, 1921, p. 120 f.
[11] Idem, p. 122.
[12] Note:—Esdras enumerates 4289 of the priestly class (I Esdras, ii, 36–39) among the 42360 exiles who returned (ii, 64) besides the 7337 servants (ii, 65). However, Blunt thinks: "The majority of the reviving nation consisted of refugees returned from Egypt and of those who had never quitted the country at all."—*Israel before Christ.* p. 105.
[13] Cfr. C. Van den Biesen, *Catholic Encyclopedia,* Vol. IV, p. 775.
[14] Jeremias, xxix.

fact that most of the original exiles of 597 and 586 B. C. must have died before 538 B. C. Very few of the exiles of 538 B. C. had ever seen Jerusalem or Judah. Those who had once lived there had left it so early in life as to have forgotten practically all about it. They had lived in Babylonia practically all their lives and in no real sense ever thought of Judah as 'home.' They were content where they were; or if not wholly satisfied, probably thought it 'better to bear the ills they had than to fly to ills they knew not of.' It is not probable that there was any degree of homesickness among the Jewish population of 538 B. C. A still further element working against the creation of a general desire to return to Palestine was the length of the arduous journey. . . . It would appear, therefore, that there was no concerted movement to return in large numbers, but that the return movements were confined to small groups of enthusiasts or malcontents who trickled back to Judah from time to time as occasion served. These made no marked impress upon the life of the Jerusalem community, for they were too few in number, and probably also too insignificant in character and ability, to count for much in the group as a whole." [15]

**Esdras.** Cyrus had liberated the Jews in 538 B. C. but it was not for another eighty years, until the reign of Artaxerxes I, that there was anything like a migration from Babylonia to Palestine.[16] In fact it was only in 458 B. C. that Esdras led back the remnants of the people, on which he was to build up the Nation anew. And even then large numbers of Jews made their choice to remain in Babylonia and Mesopotamia,[17] unwilling to sacrifice their ease and comfort.

**Post-exilic Judea.** The subsequent history of the Jewish State in Palestine is politically an uninterrupted alternation of partial successes and reverses, and only too frequently we find her the innocent victim of circumstances, due to her position as a natural obstruction on the path that the battling nations of East and West were forced to take in their interminable conflicts for world supremacy.

**Jews Abroad.** Thus, Theodore Reinach relates: "During the wars of the third and second centuries B. C.

[15] Powis Smith, *The Prophets and their Times,* p. 193 f.
[16] Mercer, *Extra-Biblical Sources,* p. 197.
[17] Cfr. Sidney Mendelssohn, *The Jews in Asia,* London, 1920, p. 214 f.

thousands of Jews were made captive and reduced to slavery, passing from owner to owner and from land to land until their enfranchisement. This enfranchisement indeed usually occurred very soon, it being precipitated by the fact that, through their unswerving attachment to their customs, they proved indifferent servants. . . . The Jews thus freed, instead of returning to Palestine, usually remained in the land of their former slavery, and there, in conjunction with their brethren in faith, established communities." [18] And again: "Thus as early as the middle of the second century B. C. the Jewish author of the third book of the Oracula Sibyllina, addressing the chosen people says: 'Every land is full of thee and every sea,' [19] and if these words contain any exaggeration, the prophecy became true in the subsequent century. The most diverse witnesses, such as Strabo, Philo, Seneca, the author of the Acts of the Apostles, and Josephus, all bear testimony to the fact that the Jewish race was disseminated over the whole civilized world." [20]

**Jewish Merchants.**

Karl Kautsky finds another reason for the widespread infiltration of the Jews. According to his view: "The 'Diaspora,' the dispersal of the Jews throughout the world, certainly does not begin as late as the destruction of Jerusalem by the Romans, nor with the Babylonian Exile, but much earlier; it is a natural consequence of trade, a phenomenon shared by the Jews with most commercial peoples." [21]

Quoting from Franz Buhl,[22] Kautsky had previously explained: "Even before the Israelites came to Canaan, trade was highly developed in this country. In the Tell-el-Amarna Letters (of the fifteenth Century before Christ) caravans are mentioned that travelled through the country under armed protection." [23] And in a later volume, he further developed his idea of the mercantile

[18] *Jewish Encyclopedia,* Vol. IV, Article "Dispersion," p. 560.
[19] Sibyllines, III, 271; Compare I Mach. xv.
[20] *Jewish Encyclopedia,* l. c. p. 561.
[21] Kautsky, *Foundations of Christianity,* p. 212. Note:—According to Blunt: "Israel before the kings had left trading to the Canaanites. But under the monarchy began a process of commercial development which was to write its mark deep on the character of the people, and which led in later Judaism to the custom that every Jewish father should teach his son a trade. Solomon and his successors sedulously fostered commercial relations."—Blunt, *Israel before Christ,* p. 62.
[22] Franz Buhl, *Die Sozialen Verhältnisse der Israeliten,* 1899, p. 76.
[23] Kautsky, l. c. p. 196.

propensity of the Jews. He says in part: "It was too small and weak, the superior power of its neighbours too crushing, to enable Palestine to dispose of its population by settling it in conquered regions. The territory of the Phoenicians cut Palestine off from good seaports and the practice of navigation. Therefore the path of colonization beyond the seas was also closed to the Israelites. Their surplus population had no other alternative than to go abroad as merchants (sometimes as mercenaries, but these played no important part in history). In this capacity, they travelled further and further and founded a number of settlements. In many cities they became so numerous as to conduct not only trading operations, but also to employ artisans of their own; the number of their intellectuals also increased.

**Colonies.**

"Constantly crowded and congested in their homeland by the overwhelming strength of their neighbours, this little race had no other path of expansion. This path was pursued so energetically that the Israelitic population abroad finally became more numerous than the home population. The home population repeatedly loses its status as an independent nation, finally losing it forever. But before this time has come, the centre of gravity of Judaism had been shifted from its original location to a number of cities in Egypt, Syria and Mesopotamia." [24]

**Proselyting.**

These Jewish Colonies expanded, according to the same author, not only by natural increase, but also by assimilation of neophytes. Thus he explains: "Those who subjected themselves permanently to the Jewish rite might be depended on as reliable fellow-members. But every stranger was welcome who would recognise this rite—without regard to origin. Jewish exclusiveness was not an exclusiveness of race. The Jewish propaganda in all regions of the ancient world was rather calculated to stimulate tremenduously the mingling of races within Judaism." [25] And again: "A mixed race from the very start, the Jews, in the course of their migrations, have come into contact with a great succession of new races and their blood has become more and more mixed." [26]

[24] Karl Kautsky, *Are the Jews a Race?* New York, 1926, p. 111 f.

[25] Idem, p. 115.

[26] Kautsky, *Are the Jews a Race?* p. 118. Note:—Professor Dixon is clear on this point. "The questions of the racial origin and unity of the Jews have

**Yahweh's People.** It was, in fine, the religious bond, the living tradition that they were Yahweh's Chosen People, that held the Jews together amid all their infidelities, and not only preserved them in a distinct social entity, but led to the ready assimilation of the alien elements which were constantly being absorbed through infiltration from without. For, while the violations of the Mosaic exclusiveness were only too frequent even from the earliest days in Palestine, as we shall shortly see in detail, yet in the great mass of the people there was shown a remarkable fidelity in this respect, and even in the case of intermarriage, it was as a rule, the gentile who became a Jew, and not a case of perversion or formal apostasy on the part of the Israelite.

Kautsky's view of the Jew's early application to commerce, is further substantiated by an observation of G. F. Abbott, who notes: "As early as the fourth century B. C. we find the Hebrew word for 'earnest-money' domiciled in the Greek language,[27] and as early as the second century in the Latin (arrhabo)—a curious illustration of the Jew's commercial activity in the Mediterranean even in those days." [28]

**Intermarriage.** Another interesting phase of Kautsky's theory is the fact that he so fearlessly goes counter to the popular impression that Deuteronomical exclusiveness has, in the main, effectively restricted marital intercourse between Jew and

for long been fertile themes for discussion. The traditional view has always been that they were a true Semitic people, and, indeed, the term Semite has popularly come to be practically synonymous with Jew. They were regarded as a people whose purity of blood had, in spite of wide dispersion, been jealously preserved throughout the centuries. As soon, however, as detailed investigations in regard to Jewish physical types began to be available, it appeared that it was extremely doubtful whether either of these assumptions was true, for the Jews proved to be by no means uniform in their physical characteristics, and the great majority appeared to be of a different type from that found among other Semitic-speaking peoples."—Dixon, *Racial History of Man,* p. 162. Then after a careful study of all available data, Dixon come to the rather startling deduction that the Jews of to-day practically are Semites in language only.—l. c. p. 175.

[27] ἀρραβών.

[28] G. F. Abbott, *Israel in Europe,* London, 1907, Introduction, p. xvi. The author remarks in a footnote: "The oldest Greek author in whose works the term occurs is the orator Isaeus who flourished B. C. 364; the earliest Latin writer is Plautus who died B. C. 184. Of course, the word, though very good Hebrew, may have been imported into Europe by the Phœnicians. But it would be a bold man who would attempt to distinguish between Jewish and Phœnician merchants at this time of day."

Gentile, and thus preserved racially the Children of Israel unto our own day.[29]

But, as a matter of fact, the Scriptures themselves show that, not only was marriage with the Gentile commonly practiced in the early history of the Hebrew People, but that it was at times directly approved of in the Law itself.

**Early Biblical Examples.**

Of Jacob's sons, Juda certainly took a Canaanite to wife,[30] and Joseph married an Egyptian.[31] The children of Israel numbered seventy souls at the time when they came into Gessen,[32] and of these, the three sons and two grandsons of Juda;[33] Saul, the son of Simeon;[34] and the two sons of Joseph—eight in all—were without question of mixed blood. Of the other sons of Jacob, some at least, in all probability, had wedded Canaanites. For the Tell-el-Amarna Letters show that the Khabiri,[35] who are, as far as we know, the only Tribes akin to the Israelites, and even that is questionable, did not invade Canaan until the Children of Israel were in Egypt.[36] While then, individuals or small groups of kindred race may have been in contact with Jacob and his immediate family, still the presumption is that the other sons followed the example of Juda and Joseph in their choice of wives.

At the time of the Exodus, 430 years after the Israelites had

29 Doctor Haddon, too, is outspoken on this point. He says: "The Abrahamic family were a tribe of Mesopotamian Semites, probably identical with the Ibri, whom the Egyptians knew as Habiru, i. e. nomadic Semites equivalent to the Bedawin; they entered the land of Goshen during the period of the Hyksos domination and left the country at the time of the expulsion of their patrons (1575 B. C.) or shortly afterwards. On their return to Palestine they met, conquered and amalgamated with the Amorites and Hittites. The monuments, as well as philological evidence, show that the former were Semites, in appearance not to be distinguished from the Habiru. The Hittites were a people whose governing class at least were entirely different from both and are to-day represented by the Armenians. Later the Israelites, now a mixed people of Semitic and Armenoid origin, took into their midst a third stock, the Philistines, a typical Mediterranean race. The rounded Armenoid type of face is dominant to the other two. However, when an Armenoid Jew is mated with a western European the latter type is dominant."—*Races of Man and Their Distribution,* p. 107.

30 Gen. xxxviii, 2.

31 Gen. xli, 45.

32 Gen. xlvi, 27.

33 Gen. xlvi, 12.

34 Gen. xlvi, 16.

35 Note:—Professor Breasted takes it for granted that the Khabiri were Hebrews.—Cfr. James H. Breasted, *Conquest of Civilization,* New York, 1926, p. 219.

36 Mercer, *Extra-Biblical Sources,* p. 12.

taken up their residence in Gessen,[37] the original band of seventy had grown into a nation numbering 600,000 men besides children.[38] During this period there must have been constant intermarrying with the Egyptians and other outsiders. Moses' wife was a Midianite,[39] and even after the Exodus, circumcision was to make the stranger as one of the land.[40]

According to the command of God, the seven nations within the confines of the Promised Land were to be utterly exterminated,[41] and no marriage might be contracted with them.[42] But as regards the other nations outside the confines of the Promised Land, treaties might be made with them,[43] and in case of war, their children might be taken by the Israelites,[44] and be eligible as wives.[45] Nay more, children begotten of Edomites or Egyptians, in the third generation, were to gain full membership in the congregation.[46]

Despite the command to exterminate the original dwellers in the Promised Land, the Jebusites dwelt with the children of Benjamin,[47] and the other proscribed nations became tributaries to the Israelites.[48] Consequently, as might be expected, they gradually intermarried.[49] Thus, for example, Samson chose as wife a Philistine.[50]

[37] Exod. xii, 40.
[38] Exod. xii, 37.
[39] Exod. ii, 21.
[40] Exod. xii, 48.
[41] Deut. vii, 1, 2. Note:—Kortleitner asserts: "Lest the Hebrews might be seduced, the seven tribes of Canaanites were to be extirpated, and the images and sacred paraphernalia of the gods were to be utterly destroyed, so that no vestige even of the name of an idol might remain."—*De Polytheismo Universo,* p. 166. Moreover, the reason for this extermination of the Canaanites is to be found in Holy Writ itself: "For those ancient inhabitants of thy holy land, whom thou didst abhor, because they did works hateful to thee by their sorceries, and wicked sacrifices, and those merciless murderers of their own children, and eaters of men's bowels, and devourers of blood from the midst of thy consecration, and those parents sacrificing with their own hands helpless souls, it was thy will to destroy by the hands of our parents, that the land which of all is most dear to thee might receive a worthy colony of the children of God." Wisdom xii, 3–7.
[42] Deut. vii, 3.
[43] Deut. xx, 11.
[44] Deut. xx, 14.
[45] Deut. xxi, 11–13.
[46] Deut. xxiii, 7, 8.
[47] Judges i, 21.
[48] Judges i, 27–36.
[49] Judges iii, 5, 6.
[50] Judges xiv, 2 ff.

**Absorption.** Professor Moore positively asserts: "The Canaanite population had been absorbed in Israel by intermarriage," [51] and Johs Pederson, in reference to what he calls the Davidic Empire, says: "The Israelitic communities are merged in an empire which, it is true, was Israelitic and had the God of Israel as its imperial God, but this empire also included the non-Israelitic inhabitants of the country. A non-Israelitic city, Jerusalem, was made the capital of the country, and David surrounded himself with many foreigners. He was the ruler of a country and an empire, and we hear of no antagonism between Israelites and Canaanites in his empire, it can only mean that the Canaanites were merged into the Israelitic unity and thus disappeared, naturally infusing Canaanite life and culture into Israel. And so nearly every trace of the Canaanites vanishes, while at the same time Israel becomes more Canaanite." [52] Later, while speaking of marriage, Professor Pederson adds: "The demand that marriages should take place only among those of the same kin is not absolute, and there is even ample evidence that the Israelites had connubium with other peoples. Through that fusion the Israelitic empire was created." [53]

**King David.** As W. M. Flinders Petrie shows from the Tell-el-Amarna letters, especially those from Abdikhiba, King of Jerusalem, "Jerusalem was not merely a Jebusite village made into a capital by David and Solomon, but was the capital of south Palestine from early times.[54] From the accounts of the state of Palestine at the Israelite invasion it appears that the Amorites held most of the country. . . . By the time of the Israelite invasion, the Amorites were paramount in the whole of Palestine." [55]

When King David then, took many concubines and wives out of Jerusalem after its capture,[56] they must have been for the most part Jebusites or Amorites—certainly Gentiles. His favorite son

[51] George Foot Moore, *Judaism in the First Centuries of the Christian Era,* Vol. I, p. 221.

[52] Johs Pederson, *Israel: Its Life and Culture,* London, 1926, p. 22.

[53] Idem, p. 67.

[54] Note:—Christopher Dawson says: "Jerusalem itself was a sacred city long before historic times, as we see from the Hebrew tradition of the mysterious priest king, Melchisedech, who met Abraham returning from the battle of the kings. Even its name is non-Semitic and contains the Sumerian root Uru, city."—*The Age of the Gods,* p. 114.

[55] W. M. Flinders Petrie, *Syria and Egypt,* London, 1898, p. 117 f.

[56] II Kings v, 13.

Absalom was, through his mother, grandson to the King of Gessur,[57] and Solomon's mother was Bethsabee, the former wife of Urias the Hethite,[58] whom David had sent to his death.

**Solomon.** Solomon, in turn, first married the daughter of the Egyptian Pharaoh,[59] and subsequently took many wives and concubines from the very nations specifically prohibited by God,[60] and his son Roboam, who was to succeed him, had an Ammonite as his mother.[61]

In this connection Max L. Margolis writes: "Solomon was devoted to the service of the God of his fathers. Reasons of state, however, compelled him to enter into alliance with many foreign powers. His harem contained, in addition to the Egyptian princess, women of the Moabites, Ammonites, Edomites, Sidonians, and Hittites. Jerusalem was in his conception to be a city in which all these nations should feel at home. For their benefit he built chapels in which they might worship their gods. State interests clashed with a rigid interpretation of Mosaism." [62]

**Mosaic Exclusiveness.** Despite then, the sacredness of the Mosaic Law of Exclusiveness, its disregard and violation was at times fairly common. This was especially true during the period of the Babylonian Captivity, in the case of the handful of Jews who still lingered in Palestine. They naturally mingled with the hybrid population of Samaria, with whom they claimed a distant kinship, and their example was followed by some of those who first returned from Babylon, until Esdras began to firmly enforce the Law.[63]

It was this condition of affairs, perhaps, that led Doctor Krausse to assert: "In view of the undoubted fact that the Jewish inhabitants of Babylonia were of purer racial extraction than the Jews of Palestine, the former considered themselves, especially after the fall of Jerusalem, as the genuine Israel, and their differing traditions and customs as of higher authority than those of the home-country." [64]

[57] II Kings iii, 3.
[58] II Kings xii, 24.
[59] III Kings iii, 1.
[60] III Kings xi, 1–3.
[61] III Kings xiv, 31.
[62] Margolis and Marx, *History of the Jewish People,* p. 65.
[63] I Esdras ii.
[64] S. Krausse, in *Jewish Encyclopedia,* Vol. II, Article: "Babylonia," p. 404.

**Hittite Nose.** All this is further confirmed by an observation of Professor Breasted, that "the prominent aquiline nose, still considered to be the mark of the Semite, especially of the Jew, was really a feature belonging to the (non-Semitic) Hittites, who intermarried with the people of Palestine and gave them this Hittite type of face." [65]

What is the wonder then, that Nehemias should complain that the children of mixed marriages were unable to speak Hebrew? [66]

**Jews and Samaritans.** Moreover, Doctor Gaster adopts the opinion that "intermarriage had taken place between the Jews and Samaritans down to the time of Ezra and Nehemiah, not only among the lower classes but also among the highest in the land and the leaders of the Jews." [67] He finds in this fact a confirmation of his theory that the Samaritans were of pure Israelitic stock. While rejecting his theory in the matter, his admission is useful to our present purpose.

We can understand then, the remark of Max L. Margolis: "Often the language of one people is acquired by another of a totally different stock. When, therefore, we speak of Semites, we have in mind solely their speech and culture, not the form of the skull

[65] James Henry Breasted, *Ancient Times,* Boston, 1916, p. 199. Note:—According to Professor Dixon: "The brachycephalic 'nosy' immigrants from the north (Hittites) had doubtless mixed to some extent with the earliest Canaanite Semitic settlers, and the later Hebrews, coming into Palestine in the second mileenium B. C. must have absorbed not a little of this element, either by intermarriage with the Canaanites or with pure remnants of the Anatolian group, or by conversion. This result probably occurred irregularly, although the mixtures were probably more common in the north than in the south, where the mass of the Hebrews probably retained substantially unchanged the physical characteristics with which they came into Palestine. That they were predominantly dolichocephalic seems probable, yet the possibility that some round-headed factors may have been brought from southern Arabia must not be forgotten. The population of Palestine and western Syria was thus probably much mixed at the beginning of the first millenium, although not so much so as it is to-day. That some portion, at least, of the Jewish people at this period were already marked by the same peculiar type of nose which was also found among the Hittites, is shown by the representations of the Jewish prisoners in the famous Black Obelisk of Shalmaneser II, dating from the ninth century B. C.—Dixon, *Racial History of Man,* p. 173. Christopher Dawson states: The land of Hatti itself, the core of the Empire, lay in Western Cappadocia with its capital at Hattushash, the modern Boghaz Keui, east of the River Halys."—Dawson, *The Age of the Gods,* p. 301. And again: "The hypothesis of a Caucasian origin for the Hittites is perhaps favoured by the existence of the peculiar hieroglyphic script, which makes its first appearance under the Hittite Empire."— l. c. p. 308. This would imply a distant Caucasian element in the evolution of the Hebrew.

[66] II Esdras xiii, 24.

[67] Moses Gaster, *The Samaritans,* London, 1925, p. 29.

or facial expression. If at all there was a primitive Semitic stock, its earliest habitat is a matter of conjecture. Nowhere, not even in Arabia, were the people of Semitic speech indigenous to the soil. It seems probable that at divers periods in remote antiquity they had migrated from somewhere in Central Asia." [68]

**Pure Race Non-existent.**

Eugene Pittard, Professor of Anthropology at the University of Geneva, after a careful study of the subject, was led to the conclusion that such a thing as a pure race is non-existent to-day, and that even at the period commonly known as the beginning of historical times, practically every nation was already an ethnic complex. Thus he asserts, for example: "Primitive races became mixed from the time that the wanderings of humanity over the continents became intensive. Up till the Mesolithic, Western Europe knew only Dolichocephals—of different types, it is true. The arrival of the first Brachycephals profoundly disturbed this relative unity. From that day forward—and the mingling increased progressively as time goes on—it is impossible to speak of pure races as regards Europe." [69]

**Ethnic Permanency Impossible.**

Professor Dixon is quite of the same opinion. He writes: "By migration and conquest the original racial factors, whatever they were, have been so interwoven and blended that the vast majority of all living men must have a complex racial ancestry, and such a thing as a pure race can hardly be expected to live." [70] And again: "There is not a race in all history that has remained permanently unchanged, although the rate and degree of change have varied. Some races have retained their fundamental characteristics for millenia with but slight modifications, whereas others have, as a re-

[68] Margolis and Marx, *History of the Jewish People,* p. 3.

[69] Eugene Pittard, *Race and History,* London, 1926, p. 17. Note:—Dawson makes the observation: "The pure race is at best a scientific abstraction, and the generalisations, in which many anthropologists still indulge, regarding the fixed types of racial psychology, which lie at the root of all historical cultures, are mere speculations, often influenced by modern national prejudices. From the first we have to deal, not with pure races, but with regional types which are the products of social and cultural influences."—*The Age of the Gods,* p. 21 f.

[70] Dixon, *Racial History of Man,* Introduction, p. 4. Note:—Professor Dixon thus defines his terms. "From the standpoint of the anthropologist . . . a race is a biological group, based on community of physical characters." For groups characterized on the one hand by linguistic, or on the other hand by cultural, historical, or political unity, he employs the terms "stock" and "nation."—l. c. p. 3.

sult of the incorporation of new factors, ceased to exist, because by virtue of such amalgamation they have become something else." [71]

**Jewish People.**

Concerning the Jews, Professor Pittard expresses this view: "I do not know what specialists think about the influence that may be attributed to the Jewish people in the general history of the Oriental peoples. It seems to me that if we take into consideration the two kingdoms of Judah and Israel only, the influence would appear to be a small one. Can we not say that it is thanks to their very dispersion that the Jews, in certain circumstances, have been more or less important factors in History as a whole? It has developed upon individuals and groups and not on the nation to exercise a frequently decisive influence. For anthropologists, though they may consider certain Jews to be inspired by the Israelitish racial idea, all Jews are very far from belonging to the 'Jewish race.' There is no such thing, said Renan, as a Jewish type—there are Jewish types. Nothing would be more true. We cannot consider the Jews to-day —not even in Palestine, because the Sionist movement has imported all kinds and conditions of Israelites—as constituting a homogeneous ethnic group. The Jews belong to a religious and social community to which, in every period, individuals of different races have attached themselves. These Judaized people have come from every kind of ethnic stratum, such as the Falashas of Abyssinia and the Germans of Germanic type; or the Tamils—Black Jews—of India, and the Khazars, who are supposed to be of Turki race." [72]

**Ethnic Complex.**

A little later the same author ascribes the large number of Jews scattered throughout the world at present not merely to "a natural excess of births over deaths during historic times," but rather to "the incorporation of other more or less large populations," and adds: "On many occasions entire groups have become Judaized and thus contributed their numbers and their eugenic qualities to the Israelite contingent." [73]

[71] Idem, p. 503.

[72] Pittard, *Race and History*, p. 337.

[73] Idem, p. 339. Note:—Friedrich Hertz insists: "A most remarkable instance of racial compound is the Jews. . . . Besides Semites and Hittites, the Amorites, who probably were Aryans, formed a component part of the Jewish stock.

**Converts to Judaism.** This is precisely Kautsky's opinion also. He tells us: "As early as 139 B. C. Jews were deported from Rome because they had made proselytes in Italy. It is reported from Antioch that the majority of the Jewish congregation in that town consisted of converted Jews, not of Jews by birth. Conditions must have been similar in many other places. This fact alone shows the absurdity of the effort to explain the traits of the Jews on the basis of their race." [74]

**Community: not Race.** Finally, after a careful comparison of data gathered from the various Jewish groups throughout the world, Professor Pittard concludes: "It seems to us that the least informed reader will come to the conclusion that no Jewish race, in the zoological sense of the word, exists. The Israelites constitute a religious and social community, certainly very strong and very coherent; but its elements are heterogeneous in the extreme. In face of certain ethnic analyses, we may even ask ourselves to what extent this and that Jewish group includes any typical Jews—those who, in the neighbourhood of the Dead Sea, constituted that zealous people so familiar to us—the Chosen People." [75]

Griffith Taylor, in his turn, comes to pretty much the same conclusion.[76] He writes: "There is of course little relationship between the original Semitic Jews of Syria and the Russian Jew of Poland and the vicinity. Ripley explains this diversity mainly by an extensive proselytising movement among the Southern Russians in the early centuries of our era. Indeed he affirms that the 'Jews are not a race, but only a people. . . . In long-headed Africa they were dolichocephals, in brachycephalic Piedmont they

The vulgar notion of the Indogermans and Semites being in radical contrast to one another is at any rate quite untenable. The close physical kinship of these two racial groups has, on the contrary, been established beyond dispute by anthropological research, and the more information we get on the prehistoric cultures of Western Asia, the more it becomes evident that numerous contacts and crossings must have taken place. The Jews then, during the whole course of their history, always absorbed appreciable infiltrations of foreign blood, a fact which partly explains the variegations of types one meets among them, and also their partial assimilation to the physical types of the nations they live among."—Friedrich Hertz, *Race and Civilization,* trans. Levetus and Entz, London, 1928, p. 133.

[74] Kautsky, *Foundations of Christianity,* p. 261 f.

[75] Pittard, *Race and History,* p. 350 f.

[76] Griffith Taylor, *Environment and Race,* Oxford, 1927, p. 184 f.

were quite like the Italians of Turin, and all over Slavic Europe no distinction between Jew and Christian existed.' "[77]

**Protection of Ghetto.**

Well, then, does Kautsky argue: "It is only in the ghetto, in a condition of compulsory exclusion from their environment, and under political pressure, deprived of their rights and surrounded by hostility, that the Jews can maintain themselves among other peoples. They will dissolve, unite with their environment and disappear where the Jew is regarded and treated as a free man and as an equal."[78] And once more: "When the artificial exclusiveness of the Jews is terminated, when the ghetto ceases to exist, their assimilation will become everywhere inevitable."[79] The very hardships of the Ghetto thus find their own reward.

**Foreign Influences.**

This apparently was already, to a certain extent, becoming the condition of things in the early days of the Christian era, when, as Reinach assures us: "The great Jewish insurrections under Vespasion, Trajan, and Hadrian, terminating, as they did so disastrously, threw upon the market myriads of Jewish captives. Transported to the West, they became the nuclei of communities in Italy, Spain, Gaul, etc. Amongst these captives was the historian of the Jewish people,

[77] Ripley, *Races of Europe*, p. 397. Note:—Professor Dixon, too, is in agreement with this point of view. He writes: "One of the main causes which has been suggested as responsible for the variation in the physical type of the Jews is that of intermarriage with the Gentile population among which they live, and it has frequently been pointed out that the Jew thus generally approximates the character of the surrounding peoples, whatever this may be. That such intermarriage does indeed occur and has occurred throughout the past, can be demonstrated, although the extent of the practice is very hard to determine. The belief that the Jew merely reflects the physical type of the Gentile population among which he lives we shall find to be borne out in general by the facts."—*Racial History of Man*, p. 164.

[78] Kautsky, *Are the Jews a Race?* p. 156.

[79] Idem, p. 216. Note:—Doctor Haddon assures us: "The Jewish people today are grouped into two stocks, the Ashkenazic and the Sephadic. The first comprises the Jews of Russia, Central Europe, Western Europe, and England, the latter is made up of the Spanish and Portuguese Jews, and the Jews in Asia Minor, Egypt and Arabia. Both groups derive directly from the common source in Palestine and Mesopotamia, and, taking different paths in the Diaspora, met with different fates, but they both exhibit the peculiar Jewish expression, though the latter resemble more closely the southern European peoples and they are known to have absorbed Moorish and Iberian blood, whereas the Ashkenazim can show a far clearer bill."—Haddon, *Races of Men and their Distribution*, p. 107. Professor Dixon, on the contrary, asserts: "The Sephardim generally regard themselves as a sort of aristocracy, holding more or less aloof from the other Jews, and claiming to represent the purest survivors of the original Hebrews."—Dixon, *Racial History of Man*, p. 163.

Flavius Josephus." [80] And this same Flavius Josephus, who must ever be regarded among the Jews as a renegade, is but an example of what foreign influence in his time was effecting everywhere throughout the Dispersion.

**Language Difficulties.**

Then, too, the whole language question afforded another means of ultimately destroying racial exclusiveness, at least among the Jews scattered abroad. Again Kautsky may be quoted to advantage. "The Jews living abroad had to speak the foreign tongue, and if several generations had already been living abroad, the younger generations finally would be able to speak only the language of their native country, forgetting their mother tongue. Greek particularly became very popular among them. Already in the Third Century B. C. the sacred writings of the Jews were translated into Greek, probably for the reason that but few Alexandrian Jews still understood Hebrew and possibly also for purposes of propaganda among the Greeks. Greek became the language of the new Jewish literature, and even the language of the Jewish people living in Italy. 'The different (Jewish) communities in Rome had burial grounds in common, five of which are known. The inscriptions are *mainly in Greek,* some written in an almost unintelligible jargon; some are in Latin, none in Hebrew.' [81] The Jews were not able to maintain the use of Hebrew even in Palestine, where they adopted the language of the population surrounding them, which was Aramaic. Several centuries before the destruction of Jerusalem by the Romans, Hebrew already ceased to be a living tongue. It no longer served as a means of communication between the members of the nation, but only as a means of access to the sacred writings of antiquity." [82]

**Weakenings.**

So, too, Van den Bissen remarks: "In Mesopotamia the Jews read and studied the Bible in Hebrew. This was comparatively easy for them since Chaldee, their vernacular, was kindred to the Hebrew. The Jews in Egypt, and throughout Europe, commonly called Hellenistic Jews, soon forgot Hebrew. A Greek version of the Bible, the Septuagint, was made for them. The consequence was that they were less ardent

[80] Theodore Reinach, *Jewish Encyclopedia,* Vol. IV, p. 561.

[81] Cfr. Friedlander, *Roman Life and Manners under the Early Empire,* Vol. III, p. 178.

[82] Kautsky, *Foundations of Christianity,* p. 257 f.

in the punctilious observance of their Law. Like the Samaritans they showed a schismatic tendency by erecting a rival temple to that in Jerusalem. . . . It is a curious fact that whereas Hellenistic Judaism became the soil in which Christianity took root and waxed strong, the colony in Babylonia remained a stronghold of orthodox Judaism and produced its famous Talmud." [83]

**Black Jews of India.**

In any case, the diffusion of the Jews throughout the world greatly increased after the final destruction of Jerusalem. Sidney Mendelssohn sought to trace these various migrations both in Asia,[84] and in Africa.[85] In due course we shall study Africa in detail, but space will permit only a passing reference here to a few of the Asiatic colonies. Of these, perhaps the most famous are the Black Jews of Cochin and the Beni Israel of India.[86] While the extreme claim of the latter is a lineal descent from the exiles of the Ten Tribes, the former are even more pretentious in their demands, which are thus set forth by the *JEWISH WORLD,* under the caption "The Black Jews in India." "The majority are natives of the Malabar coast, where, especially in the city of Kotschin, they reside in considerable numbers. It is said they are the descendants of the Jews who were sent to India by King Solomon to capture elephants for his use and to work in the gold mines; and that their skins in the course of three thousand years have entirely changed color, so as to make it almost impossible to distinguish them from the rest of the natives." [87]

According to Julius Kernan, "A unique group of Jews are the Beni Israel—the Black Jews of India. They know very little of their own history. Most of them, 8,000 in number, live in Bombay. In Dahomey, they have a temple where they still offer sacrifices. They observe the Sabbath scrupulously. They know the books of Moses, but no other literature." [88]

As a matter of fact, the probability is that these Jews in India came originally from Minorca whither they had fled from Jerusa-

[83] *Catholic Encyclopedia,* Vol. IV, p. 776.
[84] Sidney Mendelssohn, *The Jews in Asia,* London, 1920.
[85] Sidney Mendelssohn, *The Jews in Africa,* London, 1920.
[86] Mendelssohn, *Jews of Asia,* Chapters VII & VIII.
[87] Quoted by Poole, *Anglo-Israel,* p. 52 f.
[88] Cfr. *Jewish Encyclopedia,* Article: "Cochin."

lem in the time of Titus.[89] Their color, etc., may be accounted for by inbreeding with the natives. Here is another instance of the steady assimilation of the race.

**Jews of China.** Of almost equal interest are the Jews of China with a well-organized synagogue dating back to obscurity.[90] Some would trace this portion of the Diaspora back to travellers through Persia in the time of Antiochus the Great (sixth century B. C.), but seemingly with more reason others ascribe the origin to Talmudist Jews of Babylonia. However Kaufman Köhler believes that "their celebration of the New Moon as a festival is proof of pre-Talmudistic tradition," [91] and it is not without reason that he concludes: [92] "It is as hazardous to connect the first Jewish settlement in China with the Lost Ten Tribes [93] as it is unwarranted scepticism to doubt the correctness of the Chinese Jews themselves, which traces the first immigration back to the Han dynasty between 206 B. C. and 221 C. E. and more exactly to the time of the emperor Ming-ti." [94]

**Their Discovery.** Henri Cordier thus describes the discovery of these Jews in China: "At the beginning of the seventeenth century, the celebrated Father Mat-

[89] Cfr. *B'nai B'rith Manual,* ed. Samual S. Cohon, Cincinnati, 1926, p. 157 f. Note:—Deniker observes: "It has been said and frequently repeated that the Jews who migrated to Cochin (India), after the destruction of Jerusalem by Titus, had become as black as the native Tamils in the midst of whom they lived. The assertion is so contrary to fact that they give in the country the name of 'White Jews' to the descendants of true Jews (and who are white in reality), to distinguish them from the 'Black Jews' or Tamils converted to Judaism."— Deniker, *Les Races et les Peuples de la Terre,* Paris, 1926, p. 137.

[90] *Recueil d'Obervations Curieuses,* Tome II, Chap. VII.

[91] *Jewish Encyclopedia,* Vol. IV, Article: "China," p. 37. Note:—Köhler further asserts that the majority of Bible Commentators identify China with "the land of Sinim" (Cfr. Is. xlix, 12—מֵאֶרֶץ סִינִים) which is translated in the Vulgate as "the south country," whence the deported sons of Israel shall return to their land.—l. c., p. 33. If his reference is restricted to rabbinical commentators the remark perhaps may be allowed to pass unchallenged.

[92] Idem, p. 33.

[93] *Jewish Quarterly Review,* XIII, 23.

[94] Han Ming-ti reigned 58–76 A. D. Note:—Cordier records: "According to their tradition these Jews arrived in China by way of Persia, after the seizure of Jerusalem by Titus, in the first century of our era, during the Han dynasty and under the Emperor Ming Ti. However it would appear from an inscription of 1489 preserved in their synagogue or Li Pai Seu, that they had arrived by sea at the Court of the Soung, then at Lin Ngan or Hang Tcheou."—Henri Cordier, *La Chine,* Paris, 1921, p. 40. J. H. Denison, however, would have it that the first Jews arrived in China "about 200 B. C."—*Emotions as a Basis of Civilization,* New York, 1928, p. 117.

thew Ricci, the founder of the missions of the Jesuits at Pekin, received the visit of a young Jew; who declared to him that he adored only a single God. He mistook at the mission the image of the Virgin with the Infant Jesus for that of Rebecca with Esau or Jacob, and said that he came from Kai-foung-fou, in the province of Honan, where there sojourned ten or twelve families of his religion, having their synagogue, in which they had preserved books written in a language similar to that of a Bible which Ricci showed to him: this last was in Hebrew." [95]

**Renegades.**

Frequent reference is made to this curious people by the early Jesuit Missionaries in China, such as Matthew Ricci, who arrived in China about 1581 to found the Pekin Mission. Gonzani, Brotier, and others, also often mention them and conjecture concerning their origin. But here again, we have evidence of intermarriage and general adaption to environment noticed among similar Jewish colonies elsewhere. Thus James Finn [96] states that these Chinese Jews "were not particular in regard to eating forbidden animals," and Henri Cordier makes it clear that by the middle of the last century they were Jewish in name only, and that they had "intermarried outside the faith and preserved only a few ceremonies and names of holy days." [97] Cordier had become acquainted at Shanghai with some of the descendants of the original colony, and he further tells us: "Two of them have become Mandarins, professing Confusianism, at least in form; and another is a Bhuddist priest." [98]

**Mongol Chazars.**

Still another group, that have been already referred to, are the Mongol Chazars of whom Madison Grant writes in his Introduction to Doctor Stoddard's work, "The Rising Tide of Color against White World-Supremacy": "Other Tatar and Mongoloid tribes settled in south-eastern and eastern Russia. Chief amongst these were the

[95] Henri Cordier, *Les Juifs en Chine—L'Anthropologie,* Paris, Tome I (1890), p. 547. Note:—Cordier adds elsewhere: "Ricci detained at Pe King by age and the needs of the mission, was unable to go to Kai Foung, but he sent thither in his place a Chinese Jesuit; in the manuscript of the Penteteuch in the possession of the Jewish colony all the sections were found, after the examination from beginning to end 'in perfect agreement with the Hebrew Bible of Plantin, except that they have not the vowel points in the Chinese copy.'"—Cordier, *La Chine,* p. 40.

[96] James Finn, *The Jews in China,* London, 1843, p. 7.

[97] *Jewish Encyclopedia,* Vol. IV, p. 35.

[98] Cordier, *Les Juifs en Chine,* p. 550.

Mongol Chazars who founded an extensive and powerful empire in southern and south-eastern Russia as early as the eighth century. It is interesting to note that they accepted Judaism and became the ancestors of the majority of the Jews of Eastern Europe, the round-headed Ashkenazim." [99]

**Jewish Battalions.** Of the Jewish battalions in the Persian Armies, we need say little here.[100] Let it suffice to note, that in all probability there were many Jews with Datis and Artaphernes at Marathon in 490 B. C. and with Mardonius at Plataea in 479 B. C. and that prisoners there taken

[99] Lothrop Stoddard, *The Rising Tide of Color against White World-Supremacy,* New York, 1921, Introduction, p. xxii. Note:—The Chazar State was located between the Caucasus, the Volga, and the Don. Its khakan, Bulan, was converted to Judaism about 740 A. D. From Obadiah until the last Chazar ruler, Joseph, "none but a Jew in religion was permitted to ascend the throne." For fifty years after the fall of its capital, Itel, in 969, vestiges of the nation struggled on in the Crimea, only to be utterly annihilated in the end.—Cfr. Margolis and Marx, *History of the Jewish People,* p. 525 f. Professor Dixon, also, says of what he styles "the somewhat mysterious Khazars": "The Khazar being converted to Judaism in the eighth century, thereafter seem to have spread far and wide to the west and northwest, their modern descendants probably forming the preponderant element among the east European Jews."—*Racial History of Man,* p. 37. And again: "This people, whose early history is still obscure, were perhaps a branch of the inner Asiatic Turkish-speaking folk, who by the opening of the Christian era were beginning to penetrate into eastern Europe; perhaps in part derived from some of the ancient population of the Caucasus. They had for five or six centuries held much of the region north of the Caucasus and between the Caspian and the Black Seas. A city-building, strongly commercial people, with well-organized government, they built up a powerful empire whose influence spread far into the heart of Russia, into which the Slav had as yet hardly come. Great numbers of Jews are known to have settled among the Khazars, and their conversion to Judaism followed. In the tenth century, however, the Khazars were crushed by the rising power of the Slavs and scattered far and wide. In these widely dispersed, strongly commercial peoples converted to the Jewish faith, and in the great numbers of Jews from the Caucasus and the northern borders of Asia Minor, who had there been brachycephalized through centuries of contact with the surrounding population, we may in all probability see the origin of the great mass of the East European Jews of to-day."—l. c. p. 174. Professor Dixon further tells us: "The Jews of the Caucasus are divided into two groups, the Gruzinian living in the southeast near the Black Sea, and the Mountain Jews, so called, of Daghestan and Baku, at the Caspian end of the range. The latter group, at least, are very ancient residents of the Caucasus, being traceable at least as far back as the beginning of the Christian era, and with little less certainty for several centuries more."—l. c., p. 166.

[100] Note:—Julius Kernan says: "The Jews of Persia proper, Kurdistan, Bokkara, and Daghestan have a tradition that they are descendants of the ten tribes who were exiled from Palestine by the Assyrian kings in 735 B. C. E. and in the following years. We know that in the sixth century many Jews lived in Susa, the ancient Persian capital, and in the third century of the common era, King Shapur I transferred to Susa many Jews from Armenia."—Cfr. *B'nai B'rith Manual,* p. 151.

by the Greeks may well have formed the first real contact between Jew and Greek. True it is, that slavery had previously brought many of the Children of Israel to the Grecian States. For, even in pre-exilic days the Prophet Joel had reproached Tyre and Sidon [101] as follows: "And the children of Juda, and the children of Jerusalem you have sold to the children of the Greeks, that you might remove them far off from their own country." [102] But these struggling exiles may be disregarded as they left no abiding influence, as far as we know, on their environments. In fact, Max Radin, in connection with the Greeks and Romans, assumes it as a first principle, that "Jews of to-day are lineal descendants of the community organized by Ezra," [103] and consequently post-exilic.

**Greece and Rome.**

As regards Rome, Philo is explicit,[104] that the Jewish community there had its origin in released prisoners of war.[105] And the relation of Jew and Gentile in the national stories of Greece and Rome is altogether too extensive to be noticed here even in summary. Those who are interested will find the detailed account of Radin well worth their perusal.[106]

[101] Note:—Doctor Contenau remarks how the Phoenicians enjoyed an unenviable reputation as unscrupulous merchants and at times descended to piracy. It was a common practice of theirs, he says, when about to set sail, to entice on board children and young people, whom they would forthwith sell as slaves in a distant country. In this connection, he adds, Homer's *Odyssey,* XV, 493 ff is suggestive.—Cfr. G. Contenau, *La Civilisation Phénicienne,* Paris, 1926, p. 300.

[102] Joel iii, 6.

[103] Max Radin, *The Jews amongst the Greeks and Romans,* Philadelphia, 1915, p. 15.

[104] Pegat. ad Caium, # 23.

[105] Cfr. *Jewish Encyclopedia,* Vol. IV, p. 561.

[106] Note:—J. P. Arendzen has remarked: "The extension of the Jewish diaspora is well portrayed by St. Luke in the Acts. On Pentecost there were present in Jerusalem Jews from Parthia, Media, Elam, Mesopotamia, Cappadocia, Pontus, Asia, Phrygia, Pamphilia, Egypt, Libya, Cyrene, Crete, Arabia and Rome, with others from the whole Orient and Italy. Gaul, Africa and Spain are indeed not mentioned, but this need not imply that there were no Jews in those parts, because Greece is not mentioned either, and yet it contained many Jewish communities. The enumeration of localities is evidently based on the difference of languages or dialects. On the other hand, mere distance must have made the attendance of Jews from Gaul, Africa and Spain somewhat rare at Whitsuntide, even if they came for Passover."—J. P. Arendzen. *Men and Manners in the days of Christ,* London, 1928, p. 95. Cfr. Acts, II, 9-11.

**"Killing" of Crockery.** Professor Flinders Petrie, reviewing "Archaeology of the Lower Mimbres Valley, New Mexico," by Walter Fewkes,[107] declares: "This account refers to a region scarcely touched yet by research, but evidently containing remains of a considerable civilization. A few parallels to Egyptian subjects should be noted. The contracted burials are seated, as the Peruvian, not recumbent; usually a 'killed' bowl with a hole knocked in the bottom is placed over the head.[108] This custom is explained thus: 'Ceremonially every piece of pottery is supposed by the Hopi (tribe) to be a living being, and when placed in the grave of the owner, it was broken or killed to let the spirit escape to join the spirit of the dead in its future home.' As we have no record of the Egyptian motive for 'killing' pottery, furniture, etc., any clear statement like this is of value. Some animal figures are much like the prehistoric Egyptian hippopotomi. Hooked sticks, like those in the tomb painting in Hierakonpolis, LXXVI, are shown as carried by hunters; and parallels are given for such being throwing sticks used in hunting. Later they became sacred emblems among the Hopi. These similarities may serve to explain Egyptian usages, without any suggestion of actual derivation." [109]

**Present Quest.** After all this, it must be apparent how ill-judged it is to stress too much similarities in manners and customs between two peoples widely separated by time and dis-

[107] Walter Fewkes, *Archæology of the Lower Mimbres Valley, New Mexico,* Washington, 1914.

[108] Note:—In passing attention might be called to the fact that this same custom so common in Egypt, is also prevalent among the Negroes both of Africa and the South, as well as in the West Indies. E. J. Grave explains the "killing" of crockery on the Negro graves, as a precaution against theft.—Cfr. E. J. Grave, "Fetishism in Congo Land," *Century Magazine,* New York, Vol. XIX (1891), p. 825. Newbell Niles Puckett comes to pretty much the same conclusion, but records the opinion of a Louisiana Negro that "Probably the original remote African idea was to free the spirit from the article and let it go on to the next world to serve the dead owner."—Cfr. Newbell Niles Puckett, *Folk Beliefs of the Southern Negro,* p. 106. General Barrows in turn, reports from Africa: "Near the Mossi town of Lay, I observed a rather singular burial place which they told me was called 'yawgo.' There were about 100 interments and these were made in great jars called 'singga." The remains are either placed in these jars and covered over with earth or buried beneath them. There was a hole broken in each urn. The chief informed me that only important people are buried in this way."—Cfr. David Prescott Barrows, *Berbers and Blacks,* New York, 1927, p. 172.

[109] *Ancient Egypt,* 1915, Part IV, p. 189.

tance. With a certain amount of sceptical reserve then, we may now approach the study of the Jews in Africa. Nevertheless, it would be a great mistake at the very outset, to look anywhere for a clearly defined ethnic group.[110] The present chapter shows that in their Dispersion, the Jews not only ceased to be a homogeneous people, but partly by absorption where their numbers were comparatively small, and partly by proselytism where they constituted an appreciable element in the community, they have tended in the course of centuries, to build up an entirely new Ethnic Complex, or rather a widely scattered series of Ethnic Complexes, all differing one from another, and one and all essentially divergent in race and language from what they are pleased to regard as their parent-stock, the family of Abraham. And yet they are still in their own estimation, as well as in the regard of the world, the Children of Israel.

**Jewish Types.** After showing that there is no such thing as a Jewish race, Professor Pittard makes the comment: "It is possible that, in all large communities there exist a certain number of individuals representing the genuine original Jew who is probably the Assyroid dolichocephalic type.[111] But in the central and east European countries (Germany, Austria and Russia) this type appears to be in a minority. Maybe as a group, the Spaniols represent it better than other groups." [112]

[110] Note:—After careful consideration of the subject, Professor Dixon draws this conclusion: "If, as is possible, the northern Arabs or Bedouin of to-day are to be regarded as the best modern representatives, from the racial point of view, of the very early Semitic-speaking peoples of whom the original Hebrews were a part, then the great majority of all the Jews to-day are 'Semites' only in speech, and their true ancestry goes back not so much to Palestine and Arabia as to the uplands of Anatolia and Armenia, the Caucasus and the steppes of Central Asia, and their nearest relatives are still to be found in these areas to-day."—*Racial History of Man*, p. 175.

[111] Note:—Maspero thus describes the Hebrews of the days of Solomon: "They are distinguished by an aquiline nose, projecting cheek bones, and curly hair and beard. They were vigorous, hardy, and inured to fatigue, but though they lacked those qualities of discipline and obedience which are characteristic of true warrior races, David had not hesitated to employ them in war."—*History of Egypt*, Vol. VI, p. 387.

[112] Pittard, *Race and History*, p. 351. Note:—According to Friedrich Hertz: "Fischburg, after an intensive study of the racial features of the living generation of Jews, came to the conclusion that there exists no such thing as one homogeneous Jewish type, but that there is a multitude of Jewish types, according to the nations among whom the Jews live and to whom, to a higher or less degree, they have assimilated."—Hertz, *Race and Religion*, p. 134. For as Fischburg reasons: "The Jews, unquestionably, are the product of manifold crossings."—l. c., p. 135.

Cephalic indices then, will aid us little in our African quest, and that tenacity to the religious traditions, that so long characterized the Jew of the Ghetto, has too frequently yielded before the enervating influence of prosperity on the one hand, and the devitalizing tendency of Mohammedanism on the other.

**What Constitutes the Jew?**

Yet, there remains that mysterious something deep ingrained in his very being, that effectively segregates the Jew from the rest of humanity, if not racially, at least socially. For, while strictly speaking, the Jews are not a race but "a social and religious community," as we have seen,[113] still in everyday life, when even the religious element has been eliminated, the renegade must still be classified as a Jew and nothing else. As a consequence, although a Jew may be a perfect gentleman in every way, endowed with wealth, and a man of education and refinement, the fact that he is a Jew is ever uppermost in the minds of men, and too often, the high esteem that is his due, is tempered by disgraceful prejudice. Nay more, if in time he comes to neglect the Sabbath rest and ignores the fasts of precept; if he utterly disregards all dietary restrictions, and openly scoffs at the Law and the Prophets; if, finally, he casts all religion aside and becomes an avowed atheist or Bolshevist—in a word, if he proves himself faithless to the most sacred traditions of his religion and his people—it makes no difference in the eyes of the world, he is still a Jew; and according to the consensus of public opinion, nothing he can do will make him less a Jew.

Let him, on the other hand, go so far as to become a Christian, it matters not. Among the Christians themselves he must now be pointed out as a convert-Jew. And the term, let it be understood, is not used in any derogatory sense, or as implying the slightest opprobium. Christ was a Jew! The nucleus of the Church was Jews! And his fellow Christians, for the most part, hold him in high esteem precisely for his antecedents and the sacrifices that

[113] Cfr. page 147. Note:—This view is also supported by Kroeber who maintains: "The Jews, who were once a nationality, at present, of course, form a religious body which somewhat variably, in part from inner cohesion, and in part from outer pressure, tends also to constitute a caste. They evince little hereditary racial type, measurements indicating that in each country they approximate the physical type of the gentile population."—Kroeber, *Anthropology*, p. 57. Kroeber incidentally thus defines the term racial: "A race is a subdivision of a species and corresponds to a breed in domestic animals."—l. c., p. 56.

his conversion must have entailed. Yet even in their eyes he has not ceased entirely to be a Jew.

**Definition of Question.**

What then, practically constitutes the Jew?[114] It is not race. The Jews form not a race. Racially they are as complex as many of our best Americans. It is not place of birth. No more is it a question of language. Neither, finally, is it any longer a matter of religion. What is it then? I do not mean technically, but in the broad acceptation of the word—what really differentiates the Jew from other men? The minimum requirement would seem to be a descent through at least one line of ancestors from one of the sons of Jacob, or from some individual who in the past was incorporated into the body of Jews so as to imbibe their spirit and adopt their practices. In our quest then, for the Jews in Africa, this must be the criterion of our judgment.

[114] Note:—Frank H. Hankins thus answers the question briefly and in his own way. "Judaism is essentially a culture, while the Jews are best thought of as a people, though many of them aspire also to become a nation."—Frank H. Hankins, *Racial Basis of Civilization,* New York, 1926, p. 84. He also states: "It has been statistically shown that Jewish-Gentile intermarriages have in recent times been less frequent in eastern Europe than in western, reaching the proportion of one-third of all the Jewish communities of England and the United States."—l. c., p. 84.

## *Chapter VII*

# THE LION OF THE TRIBE OF JUDA

**Mode of Inquiry.**

By two routes Hebraic culture may have penetrated to West Africa. From the north, across the desert wastes; and from the east, along the general line of traffic that skirts the great tropical forests. The possibility of its introduction by sea is so remote that it may for the present at least be disregarded.

That Hebraic influence did penetrate to the very heart of Negro Land by both routes indicated, will be shown in due course. And in the detailed study of the question, the obvious order of treatment would be the chronological one, if we could precisely determine the inception of each cultural advance. As it is, the logical sequence seems to demand that we first investigate the more or less mythical antecedents of the present Falashas of Abyssinia, since to-day they constitute by far the largest and most influential individual group in Africa which has distinctively Jewish descent. Next in order, we shall search out the origin of those Jewish colonies that have clustered along the southern shore of the Mediterranean almost from time immemorial, and have unquestionably had at least commercial contact with the interior of the Dark Continent. Finally, we propose to trace the historical relation between the Jews and Egypt, and the far-reaching consequences produced by the steady advance of Hebraic cultural influence up the Nile and into the heart of Africa.

**Queen of Sheba.**

James Bruce, in the well-known account of his travels in quest of the source of the Nile, says in reference to the Queen of Sheba whose visit to King Solomon is recorded in Holy Writ:[1] "The Abyssinians, both Jews and Christians, believe the XLVth psalm to be a prophecy of this queen's voyage to Jerusalem; and that the last

[1] III Kings x, 1–13.

part of it contains a declaration of her having a son by Solomon, who was to be king over a nation of Gentiles.

**Menilek.**

"To Saba, or Azab, then, she returned with her son Menilek, whom, after keeping him some years, she sent back to his father to be instructed. Solomon did not neglect his charge; and he was anointed and crowned king of Ethiopa, in the temple of Jerusalem, and at his inauguration took the name of David. After this he returned to Azab, and brought with him a colony of Jews; among whom were many doctors of the law of Moses, particularly one of each tribe, to make judges of his kingdom, from whom the present Umbares (or supreme judges, three of whom always attend the king) are said and believed to be descended. With these came also Azarias, the son of Zadok, the priest, and brought with him a Hebrew transcript of the law, which was delivered into his custody, as he bore the title of Nesbrit, or High Priest; and this charge, though the book iself was burned with the church at Axum in the Moorish war of Adel, is still continued, as it is said, in the lineage of Azarias, who are Nesbrits, or keepers of the church at Axum, at this day. All Abyssinia was thereupon converted, and the government of the church and state modelled according to what was then in use at Jerusalem." [2]

**Abyssinian Royal Family.**

Later Bruce adds: "The Queen of Sheba died, after a long reign of forty years, in 986 before Christ, placing her son Menilek upon the throne, whose posterity, the annals of Abyssinia would teach us to believe, have ever since reigned. So far we must indeed bear witness to them, that this is no new doctrine, but has been steadfastly and uniformly maintained from the earliest account of time; first, when Jews; then, in later days, after they had embraced Christianity.We may further add, that the testimony of all the neighbouring nations is with them upon this subject, whether friends or enemies. They only differ in the name of the queen, or in giving her two names." [3] And again, the same author remarks: "All the inhabitants of Arabia Felix, especially those of the coast opposite to Saba, were reputed Abyssinians, and their country part

[2] James Bruce, *Travels to Discover the Source of the Nile,* Edinburgh, 1804, Bk. II, Chapter VI, p. 399.
[3] Idem, p. 401.

of Abyssinia, from the earliest ages, till after the Mahometan conquest. They were her subjects; first Sabean Pagans like herself; then converted (as tradition says) to Judaism, during the time of the building of the Temple; and Jews from that time to the year 622 after Christ, when they became Mahometans." [4]

**Lion of Juda.**

Bruce refers to the kings of Abyssinia as "Kings of the race of Solomon, descended from the queen of Sheba, whose device is a lion passant,[5] proper, upon a field gules, and their motto, 'Mo Anbasa am Nizilet Solomon am Negade Juda'; which signifies, 'the lion of the race of Solomon and tribe of Judah hath overcome.' " [6]

**Falashas.**

In conclusion Bruce observes: "As we are about to take leave of the Jewish religion and government, in the line of Solomon, it is here the proper place where I should add what we have to say of the Falasha, . . . who are reported to have come originally from Palestine. I did not spare my utmost pains in inquiring into the history of this curious people, and lived in friendship with several, esteemed the most knowing and learned among them, if any of them deserve to be so called; and I am persuaded, as far as they knew, they told me the truth.

**Traditional Origin.**

"The account they gave of themselves, which is supported only by tradition, is, that they came with Menilek from Jerusalem, so that they perfectly agree with the Abyssinians in the story of the queen of Saba, who, they say, was a Jewess, and her nation Jews, before the time of Solomon; that she lived at Saba, or Azaba, the myrrh and frankincense country upon the Arabian Gulf. They say further, that she went to Jerusalem, under protection of Hiram, king of Tyre, whose daughter is said, in the XLVth psalm, to have attended her thither; that she went not in ships, nor through Arabia, for fear of the Ishmaelites, but from Azab round by Masuah and Suakem, and was escorted by the Shepherds, her own subjects, to Jerusalem, and back again, making use of her own country vehicle, the camel; and that hers was a white one, of prodigious size, and exquisite beauty.

[4] Idem, p. 401.

[5] Note:—It is worth while remarking that the highest official among the Babylonian Jews was the exilarch, Resh Galutha, 'Head of Captivity,' whose seal was originally "adorned with the design of a lion, the lion of Judah."—Cfr. Margolis and Marx, *History of the Jewish People*, p. 235.

[6] Bruce, *Travels to Discover the Source of the Nile*, Bk. II, p. 402.

"They agree also, in every particular, with the Abyssinians, about the remaining part of the story, the birth and inauguration of Menilek, who was their first king; also the coming of Azarias, and twelve elders from the twelve tribes, and other doctors of the law, whose posterity they deny to have apostatised to Christianity, as the Abyssinians pretend they did at their conversion. They say, that, when the trade of the Red Sea fell into the hands of strangers, and all communication was shut off between them and Jerusalem, the cities were abandoned, and the inhabitants relinquished the coast; that they were the inhabitants of these cities, by trade mostly brick and tile-makers, potters, thatchers of houses, and such like mechanics, employed in them; and, finding the low country of Dembea afforded materials for exercising these trades, they carried the articles of pottery in that province to a high degree of perfection, scarcely to be imagined.

"Being very industrious, these people multiplied exceedingly, and were very powerful at the time of the conversion to Christianity, or as they term it, the apostasy under Abreha and Atszbeha. At that time they declared a prince of the tribe of Judah, and of the race of Solomon and Menilek, was their sovereign. The name of the Prince was Phineas, who refused to abandon the religion of his forefathers, and from him their (Falasha) sovereigns are lineally descended; so they have still a prince of the house of Judah, although the Abyssinians, by way of reproach, have called this family Bet Israel, intimating that they are rebels, and revolted from the family of Solomon and tribe of Judah; and there is little doubt but that some of the successors of Azarias adhered to their ancient faith also." [7]

**"Kebra Nagast."**

The principal source of Bruce's information was unquestionably a Coptic work, supposedly of the sixth century A. D., translated into Arabic in the fourteenth century and subsequently into Ethiopic, which is known to-day as the "Kebra Nagast" or "Glory of the Kings." It is held in such high esteem by the Ethiopian people, that as recently as August 10, 1872, after the two authentic copies of the work had been carried off by the British army in 1868, and presented to the British Museum, Prince Kasa, the future King John IV, wrote to Earl Granville an appealing letter, which closed with

[7] Bruce, *Travels to Discover the Source of the Nile,* Bk. II, p. 406.

these words: "I pray you will find out who has got this work, and send it to me, for in my Country my people will not obey my orders without it." [8]

When he was leaving Gondar, Bruce received as a gift a copy of the Kebra Nagast, and while he does not quote it directly in the first two editions of his Travels, in the third edition he devotes some half-dozen pages to a rough outline of its contents.[9]

**Wallis Budge's Version.**

Sir E. A. Wallis Budge says of the Kebra Nagast: "This work has been held in peculiar honour in Abyssinia for several centuries, and throughout the country it has been, and still is, venerated by the people as containing the final proof of their descent from the Hebrew Patriarchs, and of the kinship of their kings of the Solomonic line, with Christ, the Son of God." [10]

The book itself is a strange mixture of fact and fiction, and in Budge's opinion, "The principal groundwork of its early form was the traditions that were current in Syria, Palestine, Arabia and Egypt during the first four centuries of the Christian era." [11]

Not only do we have repeated with unseemly details the account of the Queen of Sheba's visit to King Solomon,[12] and the subsequent birth of Bayna-Lehkem or Menilek,[13] but a new and striking feature marks the visit of the young prince to his father Solomon. When he was about to return to his own country, Solomon decided to send with him the firstborn of the leading priests, officers and councillors, that a new Jewish kingdom might be established.[14] The list of exiles was headed by the son of Zadok, the high priest, Azaryas, who was in turn to be the high priest of the new colony.[15] To these exiles, the loss of home and of country meant nothing in comparison with the separation from the Ark of the Covenant, which they picturesquely called Lady Zion, and at the instigation of their new

**"Lady Zion."**

[8] E. A. Wallis Budge, *The Queen of Sheba and her only Son Menyelek*, Liverpool, 1922, Introduction, p. xxvii.

[9] James Bruce, *Travels to Discover the Source of the Nile*, Third Edition, Edinburgh, 1813, Vol. III, p. 411 ff.

[10] Budge, l. c. Preface, p. vii.

[11] Idem, Preface, p. viii.

[12] Kebra Nagast, Chap. XXV–XXXI; Cfr. Bydge, l. c., p. 23 ff.

[13] Idem, Chap. XXXII; Budge, p. 37 f.

[14] Idem, Chap. XXXVIII; Budge, p. 51 f.

[15] Idem, Chap. XLIII; Budge, p. 62.

high priest, they conspired to steal their Lady Zion at their departure, substituting a similarly constructed receptacle in its place.[16] The Angel of the Lord appeared to Azaryas, approved the design and helped in its execution.[17] All the way to Ethopia, the Archangel Michael led the way. They did not toil on the march, they simply floated along, camels, wagons and all, "raised above the ground to the heighth of a cubit." [18]

Wallis Budge well sums up the entire work, when he says of the scribe who translated it into Ethiopic: "He firmly believed: 1. That the lawful kings of Ethopia were descended from Solomon, King of Israel. 2. That the Tabernacle of the Law of God, i. e. the Ark of the Covenant, had been brought from Jerusalem to Aksum by Menyelek, Solomon's firstborn son, according to the Ethiopians. 3. That the God of Israel had transferred His place of abode on earth from Jerusalem to Aksum, the ecclesiastical and political capital of Ethiopia." [19]

Despite the fact that the entire narrative reads like a mythical tale or folk-lore story, and apparently has practically little historical value, still, as Wallis Budge assures us: "The Kebra Nagast, or the Book of the Glory of the Kings (of Ethiopia), has been held in the highest esteem and honoured throughout the length and breadth of Abyssinia for a thousand years at least, and even to-day it is believed by every educated man in that country to contain the true history of the origin of the Solomonic line of kings in Ethiopia, and is regarded as the final authority on the history of the conversion of the Ethiopians from the worship of the sun, moon and stars to that of the Lord God of Israel." [20] It is no wonder then, that Bruce the traveller laid so much stress on the traditional origin of the Royal Family of Abyssinia, or as it was called of old, Ethiopia.

**Abu Salih.**

Abu Salih, the Armenian, writing in the early part of the thirteenth century, reports: "All the kings of Abyssinia are priests, and celebrate the liturgy within the sanctuary, as long as they reign without slaying any man with their own hand." [21] And he only expresses the common tradition

[16] Idem, Chap. XLV; Budge, p. 66 f.
[17] Idem, Chap. XLVI; Budge, p. 68 f.
[18] Idem, Chap. LII; Budge, p. 76 f.
[19] Budge, *The Queen of Sheba*, Preface, p. ix.
[20] Idem, Introduction, p. xxiii.
[21] Abu Salih, the Armenian, *The Churches and Monasteries of Egypt and*

of his day, when he states: "The Abyssinians possess also the Ark of the Covenant, in which are the two tables of stone, inscribed by the finger of God with the commandments which he ordained the Children of Israel. The Ark of the Covenant is placed upon the altar; it is as high as the knee of a man, and is overlaid with gold." [22] And again: "The liturgy is celebrated upon the Ark four times in the year, within the palace of the king: . . . And the Ark is attended and carried by a large number of Israelites descended from the family of the prophet David,[23] who are white and red in complexion, with red hair." [24]

**Stern's Report.**

More than half a century after Bruce's account, the Reverend Henry A. Stern, a converted Jew,[25] visited Abyssinia, and as he declares himself, the special object of his visit to that country was "the evangelization of that remnant of Israel, known by the name of Falashas." [26] As regards the antecedents of these Falashas, he is more than sceptical about accepting the popular version. For after repeating the traditional story of Menilek, he takes care to state: "From these vague traditions in which truth and fiction are inextricably jumbled together, the inquirer does not gain much trustworthy information on the history of Ethiopia, and the settlement of the Jews in that country. The most probable conjecture is, that at a very early period—perhaps when Solomon's fleet navigated the Red Sea—some adventurous Jews, impelled by love of gain, settled among the pleasant hills of Arabia Felix; whilst others of a more daring and enterprising spirit were induced to try their fortunes in the more remote, though not less salubrious, mountain scenes of Ethiopia. The Queen of Sheba's visit to Solomon, whether she reigned over both or only one of these countries, is an incontestable proof that the wise king's fame had spread far beyond his own empire. To subjects of a monarch so renowned for

*Some Neighbouring Countries,* trad. B. T. A. Evetts, Oxford, 1895, p. 286, Fol. 105b

[22] Idem, p. 287. Fol. 105b.

[23] "i. e. The Royal Family who, as descended from Menelek David, son of Solomon, are descended from King David his father."—Note by Alfred J. Butler, Idem, p. 288 Note.

[24] Idem, p. 288, Fol. 106a.

[25] Cfr. Mendelssohn, *Jews in Africa,* p. 27.

[26] Henry A. Stern, *Wanderings among the Falashas in Abyssinia,* London, 1862, Preface, p. iii.

wisdom, wealth and power, a gracious reception was, no doubt, everywhere accorded, and the new settlers, in their prosperity abroad, probably soon forgot the attractions of their home in Judea. Subsequent troubles in Palestine and the final overthrow of the Jewish monarchy by Nebuchadnezzar, increased the number of the emigrants, and in the lapse of a few centuries the Jews formed a powerful State in Arabia, and a formidable and turbulent people in the Alpine regions between Tigre and Amhara in Ethiopia.

**Jewish Influence.**

"The legend of Menilek and the supposed descent of the Abyssinian Sovereigns from the line of Solomon, unquestionably exercised a salutary influence in favour of the Jews, and contributed more than anything else towards the spread of those Mosaical rites and ceremonies, which to this day are still so extensively engrafted on the Christianity of the country. On the promulgation of the Gospel, the Jews, who had now become scattered all over the western plains of Tschelga and Dembea, returned again to their mountain fastnesses of Semien and Bellesa, where, under their own kings and queens, called Gedeon and Judith, they maintained till the beginning of the 17th century a chequered and independent existence. With the fall of their ruler, and the capture of their strongholds, the Falashas were driven from their rocky homes, and forced to seek a refuge in the midst of their enemies, the detested Amharas. The provinces where they at present reside are Dembea, Quara, Woggera, Tschelga, and Godjam, where their settlements are strikingly distinguished from the Christian villages by the red earthen pot on the apex of their mesquid, or place of worship, which towers from the centre of the thatched huts by which it is invariably environed.

"Claiming a lineal descent from Abraham, Isaac, and Jacob, the Falashas pride themselves on the fame of their progenitors, and the purity of the blood that circulates in their own veins. Intermarriages with those of another tribe or creed are strictly interdicted, nay, even the visit to an unbeliever's house is a sin, and subjects the transgressor to the penance of a thorough lustration and a complete change of dress before he can return to his own home." [27]

[27] Idem, p. 185.

**Werner's Theory.**

Professor Werner is more specific in her statement, when she says: "Abyssinia was very early colonised by settlers from Yemen. It is not known when this migration took place, but probably it was accomplished in a series of movements extending over a considerable period. In this way the Semitic immigrants would become incorporated with the original Hamitic population; and such—with the addition of a strain of negro blood—is, in the common opinion of anthropologists, the composition of the Abyssinian people." [28]

**Mercer's Conclusions.**

This is also the opinion of Professor Samuel A. B. Mercer, who has made a special study of Ethiopic Liturgy. He writes: "The inhabitants of Abyssinia or Ethiopia belong to three distinct races, the African aborigines, the Hamites, and the Semites. The Semites came to Abyssinia from Arabia by way of the Red Sea. Whether they were Jews or pagans is not known, although there are many Jewish traces in later Abyssinian Christianity, such as the observance of the Sabbath, the distinction between clean and unclean, the idea of sexual uncleanness, the custom of circumcision, the prohibition of graven images, and other characteristics whch seem to point to Jewish influence or origin. These Semites, at all events, soon gained the upper hand in the country which they had invaded, and their Semitic language, which was later called Ethiopic, gradually became the official means of communication." [29]

**Morié Disagrees.**

Louis J. Morié, on the other hand, would accept the popular tradition concerning the paternity of Menilek,[30] and the subsequent conversion of the Abyssinian people to the Hebrew religion.[31] Further, he would derive the Falashas specifically from the tribe of Levi.[32] These Levites, in his opinion, arrived in Abyssinia, if not with the group that accompanied the Queen of Sheba, at least during the reign of Menilek, when many Jewish fugitives from the tyranny and exactions of Roboam found refuge in his country.[33]

**Mendelssohn.**

Sidney Mendelssohn tries to approach the question of the origin of the Falashas with an open

[28] A. Werner, *The Language-Families of Africa,* London, 1925, p. 132.
[29] Samuel A. B. Mercer, *The Ethiopic Liturgy,* Milwaukee, 1915, p. 81 ff.
[30] Louis J. Morié, *Histoire de l'Ethiopie,* Paris, 1904, Tom. II, p. 77 ff.
[31] Idem, p. 94.
[32] Idem, p. 94.
[33] Idem, p. 94.

mind, and he admits: "It is a difficult task to compile from legend, tradition, and such scanty documents as exist the conjectured history of the Falashas, those dark-visaged Hebrews, whose ancestors were distinguished throughout the great and distant regions which were nominally or actually under the authority of the rulers of Abyssinia and Ethiopia. As far, however, as can be surmised from such sources as are available, an independent Jewish Kingdom long existed within the confines of what was known as the Ethiopian Empire." [34]

Referring to Balthazar Tellez,[35] Mendelssohn observes: "A well-known authority states, that 'there were always Jews in Ethiopia from the beginning,' and this statement may be conjecturally justified by the proximity of Abyssinia and Ethiopia and their dependencies to the ancient homes of the Israelites in Egypt and Palestine. There are, however, several theories respecting the origin of the Jews in Abyssinia and Ethiopia, and Falashas and Abyssinians alike have always believed, and still believe, in the

**Judaic Origins.**

Judaic origin of their individual races, while many authorities are of opinion that three separate migrations of Jews into Ethiopia actually took place. The three theories chronologically arranged are as follows:

(1) That Menelik, son of King Solomon and the Queen of Sheba, had received his education in Palestine, went back to Abyssinia on the establishment of the Ethiopic Empire by his mother, bringing with him a large number of Jews, at a day somewhat anterior to that in which he ascended the Abyssinian throne (986 B. C.).

(2) That Sargon, or Sennacherib,[36] the successor of Shalmanessor III,[37] King of Assyria, having continued the war commenced by his predecessor, conquered the Kingdom of Israel, and brought the captive Jews and the King Hosea to his country (circa 722 B. C.), and from thence they actually found their way into Abyssinia and Ethiopia.[38]

(3) That after the destruction of Jerusalem by Vespasian in

34 Mendelssohn, *Jews in Africa*, p. 4.
35 F. Balthazzar Tellez, *Travels of the Jesuits in Ethiopia*, London, 1710.
36 Sargon II:—Cfr. Mercer, *Extra-Biblical Sources*, p. 41.
37 Note:—This should be Shalmaneser IV.—Cfr. Mercer, l. c., p. 41.
38 A. H. Sayce, *The Ancient Empires of the East*, London, 1884, p. 128.

70 A. D. large numbers of Jews fled or drifted into Ethiopia, Abyssinia, and the neighbouring territories." [39]

**Disagreements.**

Mendelssohn adds: "Some writers state that the descendants of the earlier emigrants who were supposed to have accompanied Menelik, treated the later arrivals as strangers, and that the latter practiced rites and observed festivals unknown to the earlier colonists, who for example, had never heard of the minor festivals of Hanucah or Purim, or of the Talmuds. If these statements are accepted they provide justification for the acceptance of the first theory with reference to their origin. How far the account of the establishment of the Empire of Ethopia by the Queen of Sheba may be considered as historical, it is probably useless to discuss to-day." [40] Nevertheless, he goes on to discuss the question for many pages, and mentions that "it has been maintained that it is quite possible that the Queen of Sheba and her people professed the Jewish Religion even before the reign of King Solomon,[41] and closes by quoting at some length from Walter Chicele Plowden,[42] at one time British Consul in Abyssinia, who after reviewing the national traditions, maintains: "Two things are certain—that at a far later period, six sovereigns of pure Jewish race and faith reigned at Gondar, and that to this day numerous Jews are found throughout Abyssinia. I think it also highly probable, that (at whatever epoch it may be placed) the whole of Abyssinia was of the Jewish persuasion previous to its conversion; as even those who have adopted the Christian creed still maintain . . . numerous Jewish forms and observances. Their conversion to Christianity occurred about three centuries after Christ." [43]

**Sheba's Residence.**

This more or less mythological derivation of the Royal House of Abyssinia from King Solomon rests on such uncertain grounds, that it is very much controverted as to whether or not the Queen of Sheba really had her residence in Abyssinia at all. Arabia Felix, or as we know

[39] Mendelssohn, *Jews in Africa,* p. 5 f.
[40] Idem, p. 6.
[41] Idem, p. 7.
[42] Walter Chicele Plowden, *Travels in Abyssinia and the Galla Country,* London, 1868.
[43] Mendelssohn, *Jews in Africa,* p. 32.

it to-day Yemen, certainly has as strong a claim to the distinction.[44] And there are those who would connect her domicile with the mysterious ruins of Zimbabwe in Rhodesia which they also would identify with the Ophir of the Scriptures, picturesquely naming the old gold-diggings in the vicinity, King Solomon's Mines.

**"King Solomon's Mines."**

Thus the *London Daily Despatch* of February 19, 1923, under the very caption, "King Solomon's Mines," furnishes the following item: "The rich gold embellishments of the tomb of a Pharao again raise the question, Where was this ancient gold obtained? It is supposed that the Land of Ophir, from which the Queen of Sheba obtained the gold that enriched Solomon's Temple, was Rhodesia. There are many 'old workings' there, from which all the gold has been extracted, not by savages, but by skilled miners of a long-past age."[45]

**Land of Ophir.**

It would be well to remember that in the Middle Ages at least the whole of Eastern Africa, from the Cape of Good Hope to the confines of Egypt, was considered as a part of Ethiopia.[46] In passing, too, it might be of interest to note, that Milton only repeated the accepted opinion of his own day, when in Paradise Lost he refers to Sofala as the land of Ophir.[47] However, one of the earliest to express a decided opinion of the ancient Rhodesian ruins, the very existence of which was unsuspected by the Blind Bard, was Thomas Baines, subsequently a Fellow of the Royal Geographical Society, but who first came out to Cape Colony as an artist in 1842. He accompanied for a time the Livingston Zambesi Expedition of 1855, and later joined the Chapman Expedition of 1861. The results of his observations were published after his death under the title "The Gold Coast Regions of South Eastern Africa." In the Preface to the book, we read: "The Seaboard or Coast Region was known under the name it still bears of 'Sofala,' which signifies in Arabic a plain or low country. Sabia lies more inland behind Sofala, and is supposed by some authorities including Josephus, and no less a personage than the author of the Koran, to be the ancient

[44] Cfr. Rawlinson, *Herodotus,* Vol. II, p. 43 Note 2.
[45] Cfr. Fred A. Donnithorne, *Wonderful Africa,* London, 1924, p. 170.
[46] Cfr. Ioas dos Santos, *Ethiopia Oriental,* Evora, 1609, Fol. 4 f.
[47] John Milton, *Paradise Lost,* Bk. IX, v. 400.

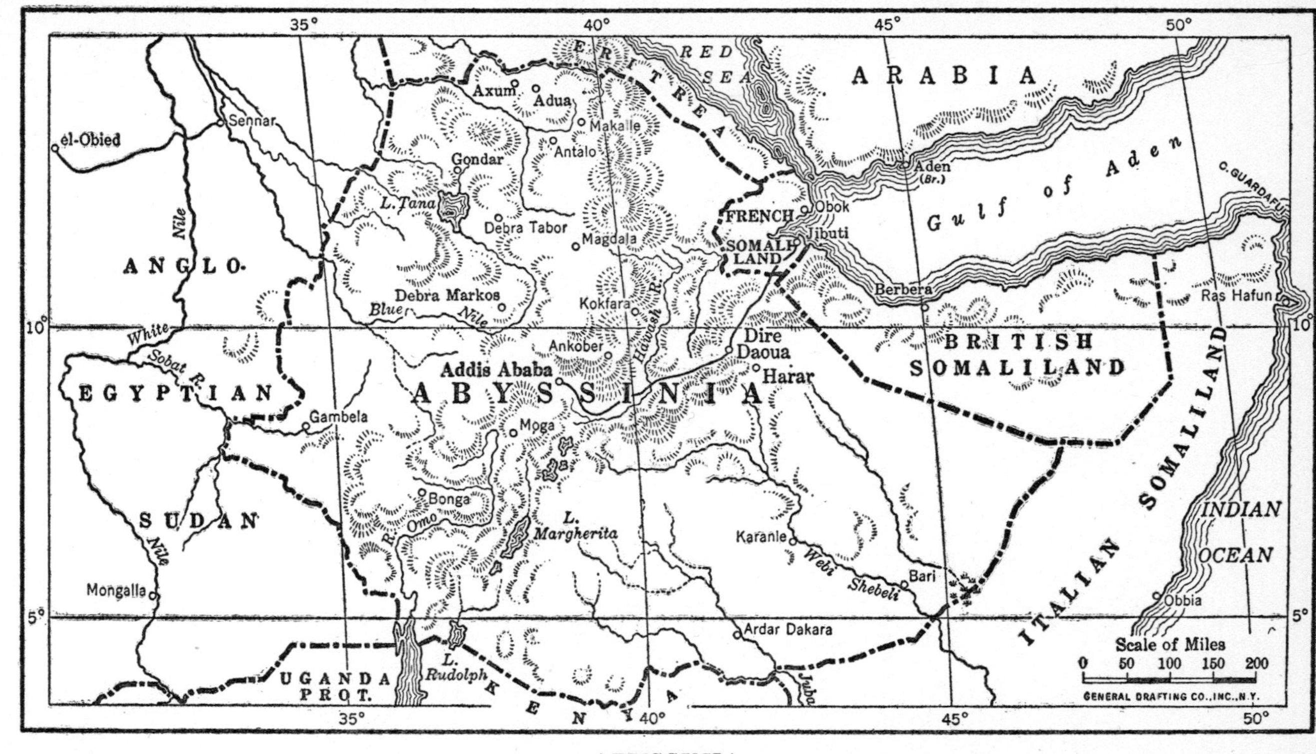
35°
40°
45°
50°
10°
5°
ERITREA
RED SEA
ARABIA
Axum
Adua
Makalle
Antalo
Gondar
L. Tana
Debra Tabor
Magdala
el-Obied
Sennar
Nile
ANGLO-EGYPTIAN SUDAN
Debra Markos
Blue Nile
White
Sobat R.
Kokfara
Hawash R.
Ankober
Addis Ababa
ABYSSINIA
Dire Daoua
Harar
FRENCH SOMALILAND
Obok
Jibuti
Aden (Br.)
Gulf of Aden
C. GUARDAFUI
Berbera
Ras Hafun
BRITISH SOMALILAND
ITALIAN SOMALILAND
INDIAN OCEAN
Obbia
Gambela
Moga
Bonga
R. Omo
L. Margherita
Karanle
Webi Shebeli
Bari
Mongalla
Ardar Dakara
Juba
L. Rudolph
UGANDA PROT.
KENYA
Scale of Miles
0 50 100 150 200
GENERAL DRAFTING CO., INC., N.Y.

ABYSSINIA

kingdom of the love-sick Queen, who visited Solomon when in all his glory, and of whom Mahommedan, Abyssinian, and Jewish writers relate such innumerable traditions. Several ruins of ancient buildings are found still in this region, which is drained by a river disemboguing on the east coast, still called 'Sabia'. . . . The memory of the Queen of Sheba is still preserved among the Arabs of Sofala, as well as among the Habesh of Gondar in their scandalous chronicles." [48] In a footnote, the information is added, that the Transvaal Boers, although not a very literary people, yet like their Colonial brethren, great readers of the Bible, especially the Old Testament, are firm believers in the realm of Sheba and Ophir, as bordering on the Republic." [49]

**Zimbabwe Ruins.**

Of the Rhodesian ruins themselves, Baines reports: "The country according to the early historian, abounded in gold, which in great quantities was extracted from veins in many of the provinces, especially in the kingdom of Torva, where also remained the ruins of ancient stone buildings, which for splendour and magnificence were reported to bear comparison with those of ancient Rome. The largest of these was traditionally supposed to have been the Queen of Sheba's palace, and the Moors of Sofala were said to have written testimony that Solomon derived his gold from the Torvan mines." [50]

**Krapf's Opinion.**

Baines, who certainly exaggerated the magnificence of the ruins, evidently was not familiar with the previous report of the Reverend J. Lewis Krapf, who after eighteen years as a missionary in Eastern Africa became Secretary of the Christian Institute at Basel, and published an account of his African experiences. Doctor Krapf writes as follows: "Among the most important phenomena in the early history of Eastern Africa must have been the intercourse kept up with it by the inhabitants of the Arabian seaboard. The southern coast of Arabia must, from the earliest period, have been necessarily connected with Eastern Africa by the wants of its inhabitants. From Eastern Africa the Arab of the coast derived his corn, his rice, his Durra, his wool, his ivory, and especially his slaves. It

[48] Thomas Baines, *Gold Coast Regions of South Eastern Africa,* London, 1877, Preface, p. v f.
[49] Idem, p. vi, Note.
[50] Idem, p. 2.

is so to-day, and it must have been so from immemorial antiquity. Such being the case, it is extremely probable that when the Hamiaritic kings and the Arabs had thus recognised their dependence on it, and had once established commercial relations with Eastern Africa, and obtained a footing on its coast, they would desire to exclude all other nations, especially the Egyptians, from a share in this commerce; and that with this design, more especially to keep the power of Egypt in check, these South Arabs would be disposed to form a close connection with the greatest ruler of Western Asia, King Solomon. According to this theory, it may have been in part a political connnection which was formed between Solomon and the Queen of Sheba, who was at once a South-Arab potentate and sovereign of Abyssinia, and ruler of the coast of Eastern Africa lying southward. The policy of the King of commercial Phoenicia would naturally coincide with that of these two great sovereigns. The Phoenicians had probably attempted to establish a direct intercourse with the Red Sea and the Arabs by means of Egypt; but the Egyptians were not fond of the sea; their monarchs were too haughty, self-seeking, and exclusive; nor had it been otherwise, would the Arabs have been disposed to allow the energetic Phoenicians to compete with them on the seas of the south. All the more welcome then to the Phoenicians must have been the alliance which Solomon contracted with their King Hiram, in accordance with which they received a port in Idumea on the Red Sea, apparently, amongst other things for the purpose of teaching the Israelites both shipbuilding and navigation." [51]

**Margolis and Du Toit.**

Max L. Margolis in his recent History of the Jewish People, accepts the location of Ophir as "on the coast of Southern Arabia or of Eastern Africa." [52] So, too, Du Toit, organizer of the Afrikander Bund, and who was representative of the Transvaal to the London Convention of 1883–84, subsequently wrote from Pearl River, August 27, 1894, and describing his journey through the gold fields, adds: "I shall wait with a description of this part of our journey, so rich in adventures, till I am safely back, when I shall try and write a

[51] J. Lewis Krapf, *Travels, Researches, and Missionary Labors, during an Eighteen Years' Residence in Eastern Africa,* Boston, 1860, p. 418.
[52] Margolis and Marx, *History of the Jewish People,* p. 63.

romance about the working of these old mines in the time of Solomon, when the Queen of Sheba reigned here."[53]

**Peters' Findings.**

Doctor Carl Peters, the founder of what was once known as German East Africa, was actively engaged in that field from 1884 until 1896, when he was forced to resign from the German Imperial Service as a result of charges of cruelty that had been laid against him. Retiring into British South Africa, he devoted six years to a special study of the ruins of East Africa. He tells us the purpose of his work in the opening words of the Introduction to his printed report. "In publishing this detailed account of explorations and researches which have occupied me from 1896 till 1902, I intend to prove that the most ancient nations of history obtained their gold, ivory, and other precious goods from South Africa. My discoveries show particularly that the 'Ophir' of the time of Solomon was the country between the Upper Zambesi and the Limpopo River, and tend to establish the fact that the Egyptian 'Punt' expeditions in search of the yellow metal, copper, frankincense, and many other things were directed to the same regions."[54]

In this preamble, Doctor Peters assures us: "All over this district we shall find many ruins of an ancient gold-mining era, and remnants of the Punic Baal-Ashera worship partly in existence up to the present day."[55] And later, while speaking of the Kingdom of Macombe, he asserts: "Under any circumstances we have here absolutely ancient Semitic religious ideas before us. The sun-god is still to-day the centre of worship and of hill sacrifices, and in his honour the perpetual fire burns in the house of Quarra Quate."[56] He is referring to the religious ideas of the people which he is describing, and then goes on to develop this idea at considerable length. Again, he insists: "Manicaland is full of relics of the ancient Semitic era,"[57] and, "Throughout Manicaland one finds ancient Phoenician gravestones,"[58] and finally declares of the

[53] S. J. Du Toit, *Rhodesia Past and Present,* London, 1897, p. 54.

[54] Carl Peters, *The Eldorado of the Ancients,* New York, 1902, p. 1. Note:—Christopher Dawson speaks of the Land of Punt as "situated at the southern end of the Red Sea, either in South Arabia or on the opposite coast of Africa."—*The Age of the Gods,* p. 152.

[55] Peters, l. c., p. 1.

[56] Idem, p. 127.

[57] Idem, p. 221.

[58] Idem, p. 222.

Zambesi: "This river was apparently a highway for the most ancient Semitic migrations to South Africa. These Semites came from South Arabia and worshipped Baal and Ashtaroth. These we can regard as established facts." [59]

**Egyptian Statuette.**

Among the exhibits gathered by Doctor Peters was a statuette which he thus describes: "I saw much of Mr. Birch, the Director of Police at Umtali, who is also an archaeologist and has also made an interesting collection, wherein he is greatly assisted by his many relations with the natives. Among other things, he shewed me the upper part of a statuette which was found 17′ S, lat., 32′ E. long., south of the Zambesi. The figure was undoubtedly Egyptian. Mr. Birch gave it to me, so as to have it examined more closely. This further examinaton which Professor Flinders Petrie made here in London proved the entire correctness of our assumption. If we find Egyptian relics south of the Zambesi, we may consider ourselves justified in inferring that direct Egyptian relations were maintained as far as these regions." [60] He later gives the official report on the statuette in full. It runs as follows. "Professor Flinders Petrie, to whom I submitted it, pronounced it a figure of Thotmes III, or one of his courtiers, and describes it as follows:—'Upper part of an Ushabte figure of pottery impressed in a mould. On the head is an elaborate wig, in each hand a scourge instead of a hoe. On the chest is the cartouche of Tahutmes III (about 1450 B. C.). Three lines of inscription remain below, so much effaced that only the title Osiris can be seen; but there is no trace of a cartouche with it. The wig and the scourges in the hands point to this being a figure of the king himself, but his name cannot be traced in the lower inscription. As to the source the figure is certainly genuinely ancient, and by its smell it has been buried in moist earth (not in an Egyptian tomb), and has not been kept long by an Arab. All this agrees with the account of its finding." [61] Doctor Peters adds: "My readers will remember that Thotmes or Tahutmes III is one of the chief figures in the Punt pictures on the temple of Deir-el-Bahri. He is the prince who offers sacrifice to Ammon. His effigy

[59] Idem, p. 356.
[60] Idem, p. 285 f.
[61] Idem, p. 393.

was found about 300 miles up-stream on the south side of the Zambesi." [62]

**Ancient Coins.**

Another valuable find reported by Doctor Peters is thus recorded: "I bring back with me thirty-four coins that were found in Inyanga, which Mr. Birch, chief of the Police in Umtali, handed to me." [63] And in an appendix to his work, he gives the report of Rudolph Frentzel, Member London Numismatic Society, on "Particulars of a find of Coins in Inyanga, Rhodesia," and included among the coins are three that antedate the Christian era; "Eukratides, 180–160 B. C.; Appollodorus, 135 B. C.; Straton, about 120 B. C." [64]

**Coins of Machabees.**

In connection with these ancient coins of Doctor Peters, the further testimony of Sir Harry Johnston should be called to mind. He unequivocally asserts: "It is a curious fact that coins of the Machabees, dating from more than a hundred years B. C. have recently been found in Natal and Zululand, an evidence possibly that Jewish indirect trade with East Africa was kept up almost down to the time of Christ." [65]

Simon Machabeus succeeding his brother Jonathan, renewed the treaty of friendship with Imperial Rome,[66] and was declared a Prince by the Jewish people. In this capacity of Prince, Simon exercised authority from 143 to 135 B. C. and, we find it recorded in the letter addressed to him by the Syrian King, Antiochus: "And I give thee leave to coin thy own money in thy country." [67] In the opinion of Gabriel Arié, he proceeded to strike off coins, which are said to be the first Jewish money.[68]

G. A. Cook, on the contrary, doubts whether Simon ever actually issued any coins. He is rather inclined to reserve the distinc-

[62] Idem, p. 393.
[63] Idem, p. 186.
[64] Idem, p. 433.
[65] Johnston, *British Empire in Africa,* p. 24.
[66] I Mach. xiv, 16–29.
[67] I Mach. xv, 6.
[68] Gabriel Arié, *Histoire Juive,* Paris, 1923, p. 5 f. Note:—Farbridge thus describes the earliest Jewish coin; "The palm as a symbol was very often exhibited on Jewish coins in post-Biblical days. One need only refer to the half-shekel of Simon Maccabeus, which had on the reverse side a palm-tree between two baskets filled with various fruits."—Maurice H. Farbridge, *Studies in Biblical and Semitic Symbolism,* London, 1923, p. 41.

tion for Simon's son and successor, John Hyrcanus (135–104 B. C.) of whom he says that he "was the first Jewish prince to issue money in his own name." [69] In connection with these Jewish coins which bore Hebrew inscriptions, Cook further tells us: "Their appearance thus marks the efforts that were made to maintain or assert the independence of the nation; and in agreement with the spirit of these movements the coins are stamped with legends in Archaic character which had long ago fallen out of use, and given way to the square character developed in Arámaic." [70] It is some of these very coins that have been found in Natal and Zululand, as recorded by Doctor Johnston.

**Johnston's Deductions.**

From the same source we learn: "Though we have not as yet absolute, definite proof in all particulars, there is a great mass of recently collected evidence which goes to show that onwards from about a thousand years before Christ, the intelligent Arabs of Southern and South-west Arabia had begun to interest themselves greatly in East Africa, more especially seeking for gold." [71] And again: "The Semites, we believe, some two thousand years before Christ (if not earlier) began to exercise a potent influence on the people and country of Egypt. Somewhere about a thousand years B. C. they had conquered the highlands of Abyssinia, and had obtained a foothold in Northern Somaliland, and this was the period, no doubt, at which they commenced their journeys of exploration from the great trading cities of Yamen, Aden and the Hadramaut along the east coast of Africa. They must have had an emporium of Zanzibar, and possibly they occupied the little island of Mozambique." [72]

[69] G. A. Cook, *North Semitic Inscriptions,* Oxford, 1903, p. 353. Note:—Edgar Rogers goes to the other extreme and asserts: "We propose in the following classification to assign the first Jewish coins (copper) to the early days of the Maccabees, the silver shekels to Simon and John Hyrcanus."—*A Handy Guide to Jewish Coins,* London, 1914, p. 20.

[70] Cook, l. c., p. 352 f. Note:—An illustration of the coins of John Hyrcanus may be found in Fillion, *Histoire d'Israel,* Paris, Vol. III (1928), p. 295, Fig. 105; "Coin of John Hyrcanus. Double cornucopia; in the middle, a head of poppy. Reverse 'Iokhanan the high priest and the community of the Jews.'" See also Rogers, *Handy Guide to Jewish Coins,* p. 21 ff for detailed description of coins.

[71] Johnston, *British Empire in Africa,* p. 22.

[72] Idem, p. 23.

**Semitic Influences.**

To this last observation of Doctor Johnston, may be added the authority of Professor Keane who in his book "The Gold of Ophir" [73] points to ancient Punic influence in Madagascar and the survival of ancient Jewish practices still extant among the modern Hovas.

Granting this Semitic influence along the whole Eastern littoral of Africa, an influence apparently exercised from Arabia, it would naturally be expected to find a strong Hebrew element in the resultant complex. Doctor Lavine has said: "Jews probably settled in Yemen in Biblical times. The favorable position of southwestern Arabia for commercial purposes must have fairly thrust itself upon the attention of a people who in the days of Solomon pushed their way even to Spain." [74] And Sidney Mendelssohn states: "Although one tradition among the Yemenite Jews traces the earliest settlement of their ancestors back to the days of King Solomon, their most generally accepted legend is to the effect 'that their forefathers settled there forty-two years before the destruction of the first temple.' [75] It has further been stated that 'under the prophet Jeremiah 75,000 Jews, including priests and Levites, are said to have gone to Yemen.' " [76] This, however, is assuredly a gross exaggeration.

**Scepticism of Randall-Maciver.**

As regards the explanation of the Zimbabwe ruins, however, scholars are far from being in agreement. Thus, in 1905, David Randall-Maciver, Leycock Student of Egyptology at Worcester Colloge, Oxford, undertook personally to visit the site and to sift the evidence. He thus sums up his findings. "The account of exploration and excavation being finished, it remains briefly to recapitulate the main results arrived at, and to gather them into a coherent whole. Seven sites have been investigated, and from not one of them has any object been obtained by myself or by others before me which can be shown to be more ancient than the fourteenth or fifteenth century A. D. In the architecture, whether military or domestic, there is not a trace of Oriental or

[73] A. H. Keane, *The Gold of Ophir,* Chapters XII and XIII.
[74] David Lavine, *Introduction to Bustan Al-Ukal by Nathanael ibn al-Fayyumi,* New York, 1908, p. vii.
[75] *Jewish Encyclopedia,* Vol. XII, p. 592.
[76] Mendelssohn, *Jews in Africa,* p. 164 f.

European style of any period whatever. Not a single inscription has ever been found in the country." [77]

It is difficult to reconcile this statement with the positive claims of finds by Doctor Peters and Mr. Birch, to say nothing of the coins of the Machabees referred to by Doctor Johnston. But at the very outset of his work, Randall-Maciver makes clear his position: "My report, being wholly independent and original, may be judged upon its own merits, and it will be sufficiently clear why little or no reference has been made to various books which it is impossible to praise and would be invidious to criticise." [78]

**Doubtful Evidence.**

Again he tells us: "I reached Southern Rhodesia early in April and continued at work till the middle of September." [79] This means that, while a stranger in Africa, he devoted less than six months to his investigations, and Doctor Peters who had already lived twelve years in East Africa required another six years to cover the field. Moreover, Doctor Randall-Maciver refers to Mr. Andrews as "my esteemed colleague" and notes that "he worked alone at Umtali, while I was away at Inyanga," [80] an indication that the personnel of the expedition was certainly restricted.

Then, too, it must be remembered that Doctor Randall-Maciver's argument is purely a negative one; viz. he found nothing, and therefore it is to be presumed that all those who have reported finds must be in error. In view of all this, as well as the fact that he ignores, rather than checks up, the statements and claims of others, one cannot help questioning the reliability of Doctor Randall-Maciver's conclusions.

**Donnithorne's Observation.**

In any case, as Fred A. Donnithorne well remarks: "Mr. Maciver stated in his book that the ruins were solely the work of Kaffir races. He could not have had any experience of the African peoples, for, if he had, he would have written quite differently. No one has ever traced any architectural skill in the Kaffir races. Had they possessed such knowledge they would have developed it, with the result that many of our famous African explorers would have come across stone-built houses and kraals all over Africa in place of

[77] David Randall-Maciver, *Mediæval Rhodesia,* London, 1906, p. 83.
[78] Idem, Preface, p. viii.
[79] Idem, p. vii.
[80] Idem, p. ix.

those which are actually met with—grass and mud huts—with not the remotest pretense at skilful or architectural design."[81]

Donnithorne expresses his own view thus: "In my opinion, these walls were built under the lash of slavery, probably by the Egyptians, and enough of them and their crude ornamentations were built in this part of Africa to warrant the natives understanding the placing or carving of the chevron-pattern ornamentation, which can be traced to all the tribes within 1000 miles of the district."[82]

**Burkitt's View.** Of the latest writers on the subject, we may quote for one extreme Professor Burkitt of Cambridge University who "holds strongly to the view" that the Zimbabwe ruins belong to a relatively recent date and "that they were only developed a comparatively short time before the Portuguese first set foot on the shore at Capetown, if not later still."[83] He would have their origin subsequent to the arrival of the Bantu who, he argues, were not in Southern Rhodesia much before 900 A. D. and thinks it "reasonable to suggest some date lying between 1000 A. D. and 1200 A. D. for their construction and use."[84] He further ascribes them to Kaffir labor enforced and directed by some foreign influence that had invaded the country in quest of gold and adds: "The chain of forts that are found in Southern Rhodesia, of which Zimbabwe is the greatest, must have been essential to ensure the safe storing, smelting and perhaps exporting of the precious metal."[85] Professor Burkitt, however, is very vague as to the source of this foreign influence.[86]

**Walker's Conclusions.** On the other hand, Professor Eric A. Walker of the University of Capetown, finds Zimbabwe the work of different peoples, at different times. "The main mass," he says, "is well built, but the western wall was rebuilt later and much more rudely on a foundation of ash, slag

[81] Donnithorne, *Wonderful Africa*, p. 175.
[82] Idem, p. 177.
[83] M. C. Burkitt, *South Africa's Past in Stone and Paint*, Cambridge, 1928, p. 160.
[84] Idem, p. 163.
[85] Idem, p. 163.
[86] Idem, p. 164. Note:—J. F. Schofield goes even further and would credit the Zimbabwe ruins to the Barotse and would make the date of construction subsequent to the arrival of the Portuguese.—Cfr. "Zimbabwe: A Critical Examination of the Building Methods Employed"—South Africa *Journal of Science*, Vol. XXIII (1926).

and earth left by gold-smelters; later still, Bantu Makalanga occupied the ruins and roughly repaired the breaches." [87] While admitting that the Bantu made use of the ruins in mediaeval times, he requires an ancient origin and rather hesitates between the Sabaean theory and that which would ultimately ascribe the workmanship to Dravidian Indians.[88]

**Unsolved Mystery.**

We need delay no longer on the possible explanation of these Rhodesian ruins. In any case, the question scarcely falls within the real scope of the present work. Suffice it to say that their origin is scarcely less mystifying and baffling to research than is the task of tracing and explaining the predominant Jewish blood in the Falashas of Abyssinia. Certainly in their case, cold reason shrinks from the ingenious myth of the Lion of the Tribe of Juda!

**Jewish Refugees.**

While then, not agreeing with Sir Harry Johnston in as far as he questions the "real historical existence" of the Queen of Sheba,[89] we must subscribe to his other conclusion: "After the smashing of the Hebrew State by the Assyrians there are good reasons for assuming that a number of the dispersed Israelites migrated to Abyssinia, as no doubt they did to other parts of the Sabaean Empire." [90] Johnston further describes the Ethiopian kings of the days of the Ptolemies as "Gala dashed with Arab and Jew." [91]

**Falasha Means Exiles.**

The word Falasha itself means Exiles, according to Job Leutholf, who calls them Falasjan.[92] And many with reason derive them from exiles, possibly after the destruction of the Northern Kingdom, but more probably exiles from Judea, after the destruction of Jerusalem by the Romans.[93]

**Himyarites?**

Others with J. D. Perruchon in the Jewish Encyclopedia, accept as most probable the explanation

[87] Eric A. Walker, *History of South Africa,* London, 1928, p. 3 f.
[88] Idem, p. 4 ff.
[89] Cfr. Harry Johnston, *The Nile Quest,* New York, 1903, p. 32; "The Queen of Saba (Sheba) is no doubt in many respects a legendary personage, but if she had any real historical existence she is another instance of an Arab ruler who governed both Abyssinia and Yaman."
[90] Idem, p. 32.
[91] Idem, p. 30.
[92] Jobi Ludolphi *Historia Aethiopica, Frankfurt,* 1681, Vol. I, Cap. XIV, # 46.
[93] *Jewish Encyclopedia,* Vol. V, p. 327.

of "Joseph Halevy, who visited them in 1868, and who thinks that the Jewish element of the Falashas proceeds especially from the Himyarites captured in Ethiopia by the king Kaleb, conqueror of Dhu-Nuwas.[94] Taking refuge in the mountains beyond the Takuzze, they converted a part of the Agaus, and through intermixture with them produced the Falasha type." [95]

**Egyptian Jews?**

Julius Kernan, on the other hand, adopts a somewhat different view, when he writes: "How the Falashas came into Abyssinia is surrounded by legends. An opinion which appears to be historical is that the Falashas are descendants of Jews who settled in Egypt after the first exile (587 B. C. E.) whence they penetrated into the Soudan and into the interior parts of Abyssinia. In the fifth century of the present era, their number was augmented by captive Jews that were led away from southern Arabia following the Abyssinian wars in that peninsula. The new arrivals, together with many converts to Judaism, and the old residents fused into one community and, forming a small state, led an independent existence for many centuries." [96]

**Falasha Religion.**

But whatever the real explanation of their origin may be, this much is certain, that even anthropologists unequivocally classify them as Jews.[97] And Perruchon expresses the opinion that the "religion of the Falashas is pure Mosaism, based upon the Ethiopic version of the Pentateuch, but modified by the fact that they are ignorant of the Hebrew language. Indeed, they appear never to have known the Hebrew text of the Bible. They have no Hebrew books at all, despite the exaggerated reports of some scholars." [98]

One of the scholars thus discredited, and seemingly with good

[94] Note:—Margolis writes: "Long before the advent of Mohammed Jews had settled in Arabia, a remnant broken off from the main body and carried thither in the wave of dispersion which set in after the legions of Rome had laid waste the Holy City. . . . They instigated the native Himyarites to repel the invasion from the Christian Abyssinians. . . . In the fifth century there arose a new kingdom, half Jewish, half Sabean, whose most illustrious ruler, Dhu-Nuwas, became converted to Judaism and took the name of Joseph. But a renewed attack of the Abyssinians, supported by the Byzantine emperor, made an end of the kingdom in 523."—Cfr. Margolis and Marx, *History of the Jewish People,* p. 248.

[95] *Jewish Encyclopedia,* Vol. V, p. 327.

[96] Cfr. *B'nai B'rith Manual,* p. 167.

[97] Pittard, *Race and History,* p. 337.

[98] *Jewish Encyclopedia,* Vol. V, p. 327 f.

reason, is Job Leutholf who in 1681 had boldly asserted: "Most of them have their synagogues and their Hebrew Bibles, and among themselves they use a dialect with Talmudic corruptions." [99] But if there were any truth in the statement, surely some few at least of these supposedly Hebrew Bibles would have survived to our own day.

**Conclusions.** While classifying, then, the "Lion of the Tribe of Juda" as a mythological invention, the Falashas themselves we may accept as bona fide Jews within the scope of our quest, and all the arguments of Bowditch to establish a connection between the Ashanti and Abyssinia only tend to strengthen the supposition of a Jewish influence over the Gold Coast tribe, at some period in the past. However, we do not think that this influence is of a character to explain the Hebrewisms recorded in our early chapters which for the most part require an older and purer Hebraic culture than that furnished by the Falashas.[100]

[99] "Plerique suas synagogas, suaque Biblia Hebraica adhuc habent, ac dialecto Talmudica corrupta inter se utuntur."—Jobi Ludolfi *Historia Aethiopica,* Lib. I, Cap. XIV, # 46.

[100] Note:—There can be little doubt but that somewhere in the dim past, probably by way of Abyssinia, a wave of Hebraic culture penetrated to the Lake District of East Africa, if we may credit the following citations:—

Speaking of Uganda to the west of Lake Victoria and north-east of the Belgian Congo; "It has an organized native government, with a tradition of thirty-three kings, and a legendary line that traces back to King David. It is a proud history. The legends tell of the Uganda people crossing the Nile centuries upon centuries ago, and subduing all tribes whose country they traversed. They claim the highest native civilization in Africa."—Hermann Norden, *White and Black in East Africa,* Boston, 1924, p. 248.

Mary Hastings Bradley, during a journey through Tanganyika, speaks of "the sophisticated Watusi of Ruanda, . . . who have a precise theology and an elaborate account of the creation of the world, the fall of man—through the sin of woman disclosing a secret she had promised her Creator to guard!—the subsequent punishment, and the sending of a Friend, or Mediator. The stories came down from the north with these tribes of pronounced Hamitic and Semitic origins."—*Caravans and Cannibals,* New York, 1926, p. 65. "Ruanda is a fascinating place. It is the last great native kingdom, the kingdom of the Sultan Musinga, who keeps his court at Nyanza, lord over four million people, the Wahutu, who with the dwarf Batwa were here before the conquerors came, and the conquerors, the Watusi, who at some undated time came down from the north bringing their fine herds of long-horned cattle with them. The Watusi are born aristocrats, tall and slender as wands—some of the men are seven feet and over—bronze skinned, with finely modeled hands and feet, and oval, clear-cut features, of an Egyptian cast."—l. c., p. 281.

T. Broadway Johnson, writing of Ankole, southeast of Lake Albert Edward Nyanza: "The Banyankole, as the people of Ankole are called, are an exceedingly interesting race, the purest, least mixed branch of the great Baima stock, which constitutes the ruling caste in all the kingdoms around. In figure they are tall and lithe, and, their long, thin faces, with a very Jewish nose and lips, forcibly suggest a Semitic origin, and strongly mark off their features from the bullet head, flat nose, and thick lips of their neighbours. Captain Speke, who was the first European to travel amongst them, reasonably assumes, from their own traditions and his own wider observations, that the whole race are closely allied to the pastoral Gallas, who came from Abyssinia. Centuries perhaps before the Christian era, some roving Asiatic race with long-horned cattle came streaming in from Arabia on the east and Palestine on the north, and settled themselves in the mountain fastnesses of Abyssinia. Mixing with the agricultural Hamite negroes dwelling there, they still retained their Semitic features, their pastoral habits, and their fine breed of cattle. The fact that on some of the ancient Egyptian tombs may be found sculptures of men bearing exactly similar features and with like long-horned cattle is significant. Thence, within recent centuries, a further migration was made, and the race, by their greater forcefulness and pride, subjugated the people in their path and, though aliens and few in number, became, like the Manchus in China, the ruling caste. In other countries such as Uganda, Unyoro, and Toro (all situated to the north of Ankole and filling up the territory bounded by Lake Victoria Nyanza, the Victoria Nile, Lake Albert and Lake Albert Edward Nyanza), they have become assimilated much more closely to the indigenous races, but in Ankole they have remained very definitely distinct from the original agricultural inhabitants who rank with them as mere 'Bairu,' (Slaves)."—*Tramps round the Mountains of the Moon,* Boston, 1909, p. 184 f.

## *Chapter VIII*

## VANISHED GLORIES OF THE NORTH

**North African Jews.**

Professor Dixon states conservatively: "The Jews of the North African coast, from Tunis to Morocco, although not as ancient residents as those in Egypt, have nevertheless been settled in the country at least since the second century A. D. By the fifth century they were numerous, and had converted to Judaism several Berber tribes, who offered vigorous opposition to the advance of the Moslem conquerors a century or two later." [1]

That there were many Jews, however, in Northern Africa long before the second century, there can be little question. In fact, as we shall see, the destruction of the Temple in Jerusalem by Titus undoubtdly found numerous well-established and influential Jewish colonies located there, to which refugees from the fallen city fled for asylum. Nay more, we hope to show that almost from the earliest days of Phoenician adventure, the Jews, at first as individuals, and then in small groups, identified themselves with the commercial enterprises of Tyre and Sidon.

At the very outset of this chapter then, it may be well to outline briefly the remarkable story of this energetic nation of merchants and mariners.

**Phoenicians.**

The latest archaeological researches indicate that the Phoenicians were not autochthonous to the districts occupied by them in Biblical times. The original settlers of the eastern littoral of the Mediterranean, it would appear, were closely related to the Egyptians.[2] The Phoenicians themselves were in all probability a Semitic tribe closely akin to the Akkadians of Amurru who, under Sargon I, overthrew the Sumerians and established the first Semitic Dynasty of Babylon in the 28th

[1] Dixon, *Racial History of Man,* p. 169.
[2] Contenau, *La Civilisation Phénicienne,* p. 351.

century B. C.[3] This would agree approximately with the account as told by Herodotus concerning the founding of Tyre.[4] Doctor Contenau comes to the conclusion that the Phoenicians as a matter of fact were an ethnic complex, Egyptians, Semites, Hittites and Aegeans all contributing an influx, "to say nothing of the aborigines (autochthones) whom it may be necessary to connect with one or other of the aforementioned groups." [5]

**Origin.** Sir Harry Johnston is of opinion that "the Phoenicians were a Semite tribe, closely allied to the Hebrew stock, which originated in the vicinity of the Persian Gulf, and spread across Arabia to the Syrian coast, halting traditionally for some time on the Dead Sea and the Gulf of Akabah. Their head quarters were at Tyre and Sidon. The Greeks called them Phoenikoi; the Romans, Phoeni or Punici. The Greek word means the 'red' people.[6] Their own name seems to have been Khna or Kina'an (Canaan)." [7] We shall have occasion before long to refer back to these 'red' people.

[3] Breasted, *Conquest of Civilization,* p. 139. Note:—Contrary to the general theory of Semitic origins, and with good reason, Christopher Dawson states: "The original habitat of the Sumerians was probably in the mountainous region to the east." (Elam.) At their entrance into Mesopotamia, he says, that they found "the Semitic peoples who occupied the great lowland region of Western Asia, and by whom they were ultimately absorbed in Mesopotamia itself." He adds: "The evidence of recent discoveries has proved the co-existence of two completely different racial elements in Mesopotamia in very early times, a broad-headed minority and a majority with extremely long and narrow skulls. The latter would seem to represent the Semitic or Mediterranean aborigines, and the former the dominant Sumerian element."—Dawson, *The Age of the Gods,* p. 61. Dawson goes on to say: "Thus the disappearance of the Sumerian people and language in the latter part of the third millenium would seem to be due, not to a wave of Semitic migration from the desert, but to the gradual absorption of a foreign minority by the mass of the native population. This process was no doubt accomplished even more rapidly . . . in the region of the Upper Euphrates and Northern Syria, and it was from this direction—the land of Amurru—that the returning wave of Semitization first spread into Mesopotamia itself."—l. c., p. 82. Finally Dawson adds: "The conquests of the dynasty of Agade were in no sense barbarian invasions of the civilized Sumerian cities by warlike Semitic nomads. Semites and Sumerians were already indistinguishable from the point of view of culture, and the empire of Sargon and Naram Sin was a work of consolidation rather than of destruction."—l. c., p. 119.

[4] Contenau, l. c., p. 44.

[5] Idem, p. 363.

[6] Note:—Major Powell, would translate the word as "the Land of Purple—so called, no doubt, from the purple dyes for which the Tyrians were famous."—Cfr. E. Alexander Powell, *In Barbary, Tunisia, Morocco and the Sahara,* London, 1927, p. 57.

[7] Johnston, *History and Description of the British Empire in Africa,* p. 31.

**National Development.**

Professor Rawlinson explains concisely the position of this great sea-faring nation. "The narrowness of the territory which the Phoenicians occupied, the military strength of their neighbors towards the north and towards the south, and their own preference for maritime over agricultural pursuits, combined to force them as they began to increase and multiply, to find a vent for their superfluous population in colonies." [8]

**Colonization.**

Utica is said to have been their first North African settlement, and nearly three centuries later, Carthage, the most important Phoenician colony, was founded not far from the present city of Tunis. The date usually assigned for the last foundation was the middle of the ninth century B. C.[9] which is sufficiently accurate for the present discussion.

**Hebraic Participation.**

Stanley A. Cook has come to the conclusion that "although direct evidence is wanting and hints are few, it is probable that during the great changes" at the end of the eighth century B. C. "and amid the contemporary movements in the Mediterranean, 'Hebrews' participated in the trading and colonizing activities of the Phoenicians with whom . . . they were closely united." [10]

**Jews of Carthage.**

From Sidney Mendelssohn we learn: "There is an old tradition among the nomadic tribes of Tunisia, that the Jews settled in the country before the destruction of the First Temple, and although this statement has been sometimes regarded as unfounded, [11] there can be little doubt that a colony of Jews existed in Carthage soon after the building of the city." [12] And Casserly is even more specific when he says of the Phoenicians: "They founded mercantile depots along the North African shores, generally placed in charge of Jews—then as now distinguished by their commercial aptitude. Thus were established among others on the Tunisial coast colonies at Lamta, Souca, Tunis, Carthage and Benzert." [13]

[8] George Rawlinson, *History of Phœnicia,* London, 1889, p. 58.
[9] Idem, p. 105 f.
[10] *Cambridge Ancient History,* Vol. III, p. 387, Note 1.
[11] *Jewish Encyclopedia,* Vol. XII, p. 271.
[12] Mendelssohn, *Jews in Africa,* p. 80.
[13] Casserly, *Africa To-Day,* p. 64.

It is not surprising then, to find Nahum Slouschz claiming: "There are indications in the Bible, as well as in the works of ancient writers and in Phoenician inscriptions discovered from time to time, that numbers of Hebrew settlers, or slaves, followed the Phoenicians in the excursions across the Mediterranean." [14] And again: "Inscriptions indicate that certain tribes of Asher and of Zabulun lived in Carthage ever since the foundation of the city." [15] And finally. "We have seen that in all probability there were in Carthage and its dependencies large numbers of Jews, who followed the Phoenicians into Africa. In this local tradition is in agreement with certain historical indications, while the manners and customs of the Jews of Tunis still give evidence of their ancient origin. There is not the slightest doubt that the Jew has persisted in these parts from the Roman epoch to our own times." [16]

**Language of Carthage.**

Nay more, Slouschz goes so far as to make the language of Carthage nothing more nor less than a Hebrew dialect. He states: "Nearly four thousand inscriptions in the ancient tongue of Canaan have been unearthed in the city of Carthage, dating from the days of Nehemiah, of Simon the Just, of Hannibal, of Hasdrubal. . . . And most valuable of all, we have found again the ancient language and writing of Canaan, the rich, idiomatic speech of a city which once counted seven hundred thousand inhabitants. And we Hebrew writers, we who write and feel in our biblical tongue, have recognized at once that this so-called Phoenician language is nothing more nor less than Hebrew—a pure Hebrew dialect, nearly the same as was spoken in the country of Israel in the days before the Aramaic, and before the Masora came to fix its orthographic rules artificially." [17] The script too, he declares to be Hebrew, "with a few minor differences" as used in the time of David and the Prophets, as opposed to the Assyrian square script which was introduced at the period of the Machabees. He concludes: "This language and script show us that the Phoenician is for us Hebraists nothing but Hebrew. The population of Carthage was Palestinian in

[14] Slouschz, *Travels in North Africa,* p. 211.
[15] Idem, p. 230.
[16] Idem, p. 271.
[17] Idem, p. 227 f.

origin and Hebraic in civilization, and if, instead of succumbing, the city of Hannibal had triumphed over Rome, it is probable—nay almost certain—that Hebrew, and not Latin, would have become the dominant language of the Mediterranean countries." [18] All this, of course, is the extreme view of an enthusiast. Still it is not entirely without foundation.

**Testimony of the Tombs.**

The Jewish Encyclopedia, always conservative in such matters, states briefly: "CARTHAGE: Ancient city and republic in Northern Africa; of especial interest to the Jews on account of the Phenico-Semitic origin of its inhabitants, its government under the suffetes, recalling the 'shofetim' (judges) among the Hebrews, and on account of the religion of the inhabitants." [19] and later observes: "In Africa the first Jewish graveyards to be noted are those of Carthage, in which Jewish Catacombs are recognized. [20] The Necropolis lies to the north of the city, on moderately high hills near the hill Gamart. It contains about 200 tombs, that resemble the Palestinian hypogea, although the loculi give it the character of catacombs. It has been found that the Talmudic regulations regarding the rocktombs have been implicitly observed in this necropolis; and the fact that it is Jewish is fully determined by fragments of Hebrew inscriptions that have been found and the frequent representation of the seven-branched candlestick, although most of the inscriptions are in Latin. The tombs contain no vessels except the lamps; but the walls were richly decorated in relief and frescoes, indicating a certain degree of wealth among the Jews of Carthage." [21]

While these tombs would appear to belong to the Roman period of Carthage, Mendelssohn finds in them a confirmation of his own views, and argues: "The early advent of the Jews in the country now known as Tunisia was conclusively proved by the discovery of the ancient Israelite cemetery in the Gamart

[18] Slouschz, *Travels in North Africa,* p. 228. Note:—A few pages later Slouschz repeats: "I still firmly believe that there never was a language of Canaan, and that it was merely a dialect of the language of the Hebrews."—l. c., p. 231.

[19] *Jewish Encyclopedia,* Vol. III, p. 594.

[20] Cfr. Delattre in *Revue Archéologique,* Paris, Vol. XIII (1889), p. 178.

[21] *Revue d'Études Juives,* Vol. XLIV, p. 14.—*Jewish Encyclopedia,* Vol. III, p. 617.

Hills in the vicinity of the city of Tunis, in close proximity to the site of Carthage." [22]

In any case, while the date of their advent may well be disputed, this much is certain, that a strong and influential colony of Jews was established at Carthage long before the city had risen to the height of its glory.

**Soloman and Hiram.**

Isaac M. Wise wrote in his History of the Israelitish Nation, only the first volume of which was ever published: "The connection of the Israelites with Phoenicians, Egyptians, and especially Tyrians, improved the industry of the nation. . . . Solomon favored this state of things by entering into a closer connection with the maritime enterprises of Hyram. The Israelites were unacquainted with ship construction and navigation, wherefore a commercial fleet was constructed, most likely at Joppa, which manned by Tyrians and Israelites, went to Tarshish, [23] which was probably the name for all the known coasts of Africa and Europe, because ships sailed for Tarshish from Joppa and Eziongaber. . . . This much is sure, that the Israelites took an active part in the Mediterranean trade, which poured additional wealth into the coffers of the king, but also into the nation." [24]

**Tarshish.**

Doctor Davis, in his turn, begins his work on Carthage by endeavoring to establish his claim that Carthage was in reality the Tarshish of the Sacred Writers, and urges in support of his theory: "The Chaldee paraphrase of the Scripture, supposed to have been written about the time of our Saviour, renders the word Tarshish by Africa." [25] This view is supported by the Jewish Encyclopedia, where we read: "Modern scholars are inclined to identify the Bibical Tarshish with Carthage, since it is thus translated in the Septuagint, the Targum, and the Vulgate." [26]

Professor Rawlinson, subscribing to the view of Dean Stan-

[22] Mendelssohn, *Jews in Africa,* p. 90.

[23] Note:—Doctor Contenau thinks that Tarshish meant to the Phoenicians the "extreme West," especially referring to Spain and the Scilly Islands.—Cfr. Contenau, *La Civilisation Phénicienne,* p. 92.

[24] Isaac M. Wise, *History of the Israelitish Nation,* Albany, 1854, p. 376.

[25] N. Davis, *Carthage and her Remains,* London, 1861, p. 24.

[26] *Jewish Encyclopedia,* Vol. III, p. 594.

ley [27] and the Reverend J. Hammond,[28] insists on a clear distinction between the navy of Tarshish, and the one which brought gold from Ophir.[29] Consequently he maintains: "It was the ambition of Solomon to make the Israelites a nautical people, and to participate in the advantages which he had perceived to have accrued to Phoenicia from her commercial enterprises. Besides sharing with the Phoenicians in the trade of the Mediterranean, he constructed with her help a fleet at Ezion-Geber upon the Red Sea, and the two allies conjointly made voyages to the region, or country, called Ophir." [30]

**Continued Alliance.**

Again Rawlinson comments: "Hiram's friendly dealings with David and Solomon are well known; but the continued alliance between the Phoenicians and the Israelites has attracted less attention." [31] Wise also shows in detail that the maritime trade of the Israelites continued certainly up to the days of Isaias, if not longer.[32]

**United Navies.**

Now Herodotus, in speaking of Xerxes' expedition against Greece in 480 B. C. says of the naval equipment, that of the twelve hundred and seven triremes, "The Phoenicians with the Syrians of Palestine, furnished three hundred vessels." [33] As Josephus shows, when Herodotus makes mention of the Syrians of Palestine, he really means the Jews. For he speaks of them as being circumcised,[34] and Josephus is careful to point out: "There are no inhabitants in Palestine that are circumcised excepting the Jews." [35] Furthermore, Josephus strengthens his position by the following statement: "Cherilius also, a still ancienter (than Herodotus) writer, and a poet, makes mention of all those nations, he last of all inserts us among the rest." [36]

"Rawlinson, it is true, in his translation of Herodotus, takes exception to this view of Josephus, as he regards the Jews as an

[27] Dean Stanley, *Lectures on the Jewish Church,* London, 1863–1876, Vol. II, p. 156.
[28] J. Hammond, *Pulpit Commentary,* London, 1883, p. 213.
[29] Rawlinson, *History of Phœnicia,* p. 430.
[30] Idem, p. 307.
[31] Idem, p. 58.
[32] Wise, *History of the Israelitish Nation,* p. 498 ff.
[33] *History of Herodotus,* Bk. VII, # 89.
[34] Idem, Bk. II, # 104.
[35] Flavius Josephus, *Against Apion,* Bk. I, # 22.
[36] Idem, Bk. I, # 22.

inland people.[37] But, on the other hand, William Whiston, the translator of Josephus, expressly places unlimited reliance on the judgment of the renegade Jew.[38] If then, the Jews actually did take part in the Xerxes' expedition as seamen, in conjunction with the Phoenicians, it would indicate that the two nations were still closely associated in maritime commerce nearly four centuries after the founding of Carthage.

**Carthaginian Hebrewisms.**

This would explain the close similarity between Hebrew and Carthaginian legal and religious practices. Thus, comparing a Carthaginian law concerning sacrifices,[39] Professor Barton draws attention to alleged parallelism with the Levitical law, and remarks: "This document is not earlier than the fourth or fifth century B. C. The Carthaginians, from whom it comes, were an offshoot of the Phoenicians, who were, in turn, descended from the Canaanites. They were accordingly of kindred race to the Hebrews. One can, therefore, see from this document something of how the Levitical institutions of Israel resembled and how they differed from those of their kinsmen. It will be seen that the main sacrifices bore the same names among both peoples. We find the 'whole burnt-offering,' the 'peace-offering,' and the 'meal-offering.' The Carthaginians had no 'sin-offering,' while among the Hebrews we find no 'prayer-offering.' The Hebrews had no such tariff of priests' dues as the Carthaginians, but parts of certain offerings and all of others belonged to them." [40] Might not the presence of the Jews in Carthage more easily explain all the conditions cited? [41]

"It is interesting, too, to notice that Max L. Margolis finds in the Hebrew "title of 'Judges,' the name given to the chief magistrates by the Carthaginians, the Canaanite (Phoenician) outposts on the North African Coast." [42]

[37] Rawlinson, *Translation of Herodotus,* Vol. II, p. 404, Note 8.
[38] William Whiston, *Translation of Josephus,* Vol. III, p. 616, Appendix.
[39] *Corpus Inscriptionum Semiticarum,* Vol. I, # 165.
[40] George A. Barton, *Archæology and the Bible,* p. 400.
[41] Note:—In reference to the religion of Carthage, Slouschz says: "A hereditary high priesthood presided over this cult, and—judging from an inscription recently unearthed—the priests seem to have been descendants of Hiram, King of Tyre, while the ritual and sacrifices are almost adaptations from the book of Leviticus, and from the formulas of prayers and vows which are still in use in our synagogues."—*Travels in North Africa,* p. 229.
[42] Margolis and Marx, *History of the Jewish People,* p. 29.

**Development of Carthage.**

In any case, Professor Pittard is of opinion: "We would only be deceiving ourselves were we to think we could easily find the ethnic features of the conquerors even in those places where they built flourishing cities or a metropolis such as Carthage. There, too, the Phoenicians themselves were but a handful of men. They could never have peopled these territories by their own unaided efforts. They occupied them and imposed on them their tongue and their customs. The trading centre, once created, was protected by a fortress. Then the native families, attracted by trade, more or less quickly settled in groups in its neighbourhood, the more quickly as the benefits of all kinds to be had, material and moral, were the greater. First the village, then the town, was built up of inhabitants who were not Phoenicians. In the eyes of the world at large this town was Phoenician (and we to-day look upon it in exactly the same way): it has remained Phoenician for suceeding generations of historians. But it has this ethnic quality in appearance only." [43] And again: "It is certain that a great portion of the Carthaginian population was not Phoenician. It merely bore the Phoenician label." [44]

**Absorption of Tribes.**

This is in keeping with the statement of Professor Rawlinson who says: "Unlike the other Phoenician colonies, and unlike the Phoenician cities of the Asiatic mainland themselves, Carthage aimed from the first at uniting a land with a sea dominion. The native tribes in the neighbourhood of the city, originally nomads, were early won to agricultural occupations; Carthaginian colonies were thickly planted among them; intermarriages between the colonists and the native races were encouraged; and a mixed people grew up in the fertile territory south and south-west of Carthage, known as Liby-Phoenicians, who adopted the language and habits of the immigrants, and readily took up the position of faithful and attached subjects." [45] And once more: "To effect her conquests the great trading city had, almost of necessity, recourse to mercenaries. Mercenaries had been employed by the Egyptian

[43] Pittard, *Race and History*, p. 331.
[44] Idem, p. 334.
[45] George Rawlinson, *Ancient History from the Earliest Times to the Fall of the Western Empire*, New York, 1899, p. 66.

monarchs as early as the times of Psammeticus (B. C. 664), and were known to Homer about two centuries previously. Besides the nucleus of a disciplined force which Carthage obtained from her own native citizens and from the mixed race of Liby-Phoenicians, and besides the irregulars which she drew from her other subjects, it was her practice to maintain large bodies of hired troops." [46] We shall see shortly that numbers of Jews were serving as mercenaries in the armies of Egypt. What would be more natural than that they should also be found in a like capacity at Carthage?

**Jewish Influx.** In whatever way their presence may be explained, Paul Monceaux, the historian of Christian Africa, observes: "Of all these Jewish colonies of Africa, the most flourishing was probably that of Carthage." [47] And he incidentally infers from the fact that "among the Jewish sepulchres of Gamart, one finds tombs and inscriptions of Christians," [48] that for some time the children of the New Faith must have lived on friendly terms with their Jewish brethren in Carthage. In fact, he remarks: "In North Africa as elsewhere, it was through the Jewish communities that the preaching of the Gospel appears to have commenced." [49] All this would indicate that the Jewish communities were well established long before the Christian era, and as a consequence independent of the second destruction of the Temple of Jerusalem.

**Carthage in its Prime.** We may form some idea of what Carthage itself must have been in the day of its prime when we remember that recent excavations go to show that at the time of its destruction by the Romans in 146 B. C. houses of seven storeys were common in the city,[50] and that the circus had accommodations for 300,000 spectators.[51]

**Tripoli.** But now, leaving Carthage for the time, let us turn our eyes to the East. A. H. Keane, speaking of Tripoli, states: "Some of the Jews appear to be direct descendants, not, as has been said, of the lost tribes, but at all

[46] Idem, p. 67.
[47] Paul Monceaux, *Histoire Littéraire de l'Afrique Crétienne depuis les Origines jusqu'á l'Envasion Arabe,* Paris, 1901, Vol. I, p. 9.
[48] Idem, p. 9.
[49] Idem, p. 8.
[50] Prorok, *Digging for Lost African Gods,* p. 106.
[51] Idem, p. 120.

events of immigrants settled in the country since the Ptolemaic dynasty." [52] And Lt. Col. Casserly asserts: "Thousands of Jews expelled from Palestine in the fourth century B. C. and others driven in the second century A. D. from Cyrenaica, where they had sought refuge after the fall of Jerusalem, had swelled the number of the comparatively few descendants of those Israelites who had come to Africa as the Phoenicians' commercial agents." [53]

**Early Hebrews.**

Nahum Slouschz is more explicit. In a chapter on "The Cave Dwellers Beni Abbes," referring to the beginning of his investigations in North Africa, he tells us: "My knowledge of the interior of Libya was confined to the information brought back by writers of antiquity and to the allusions occurring in Jewish literature. I knew that at one time there was a people dwelling in these caves—as the Greek authors tell us; that in the days of Flavius Josephus this people claimed descent from Apher, son of Abraham; that elsewhere, several groups of cave-dwelling or mountain Jews, lost sight of amongst the Berbers, still maintain their existence—the remnants of a once numerous people, leading here a most primitive life, but still clinging to their ancient traditions." [54] It is interesting, then, to find the same author, after ten years of research and personal investigation, positively asserting: "There have been Jews in the town of Tripoli from the earliest times, perhaps from the period of Phoenician colonization." [55]

**Tenacity to Traditions.**

Of the present-day Tripolitan Jews Slouschz declares: "They are certainly descendants of Jews who came to this Country from Palestine, but there is undoubtedly in them a strain of Berber and Arab blood." [56] In fact the same may be said of all the Jewish colonies in North Africa who still claim Palestinian descent, and who tenaciously cling to the most ancient customs and traditions. Thus, for example, visitors to Algeria assure us that "upon returning to the White Village the traveller will find that in addition to the main road by which he has passed, it possesses a

[52] A. H. Keane, *Africa,* London, 1895, Vol. I, p. 165.
[53] Casserly, *Africa To-Day,* p. 69.
[54] Slouschz, *Travels in North Africa,* p. 115 f.
[55] Idem, p. 11.
[56] Idem, p. 202.

veritable maze of narrow tortuous lanes between houses built of the same mud and straw bricks which occupied the attention of the Children of Israel in Egypt some thousands of years ago." [57]

**Favored by Alexander.**

Flavius Josephus in his reply to Apion relates: "Hecateus says concerning us, 'Alexander honored our nation to such a degree that, for the equity and fidelity which the Jews had exhibited to him, he permitted them to hold the country of Samaria free from tribute. Of the same mind also was Ptolemy the son of Largus, as to those Jews who dwelt at Alexandria.' For he intrusted the fortresses of Egypt into their hands, as believing they would keep them faithfully and valiantly for him. and when he was desirous to secure the government of Cyrene, and the other cities of Libya to himself, he sent a party of Jews to inhabit them. And for his successor Ptolemy, who was called Philadelphus, he did not only set all those of our nation free, who were captive under him, but did frequently give money for their ransom." [58] And again. "As for Ptolemy Philometer and his wife Cleopatra, they committed their whole kingdom to Jews, when Onias and Dositheus, both Jews, whose names are laughed at by Apion, were the generals of their whole army." [59]

**And the Ptolemies.**

**Cyrenaica.**

Of the Jews of Cyrenaica, James Hamilton tells us: "Ptolemy who had succeeded to Alexander in Egypt, sent a fleet and troops and reestablished tranquillity, B. C. 322—a service which he turned to his own profit, so that Cyrene became thereafter for many years a province of Egypt, under the name of Pentapolis." [60] He then goes on to narrate: "It was about the time that the first Jewish colonies were introduced, in conformity with the general policy of Ptolemy; and they soon became so numerous here, that, at length no other country besides Palestine, contained so many individuals of their nation. Enjoying equal rights with the Greeks and the special favor of the king, they formed in the end a fourth order in the

[57] M. W. Hilton-Simpson, *Among the Hill-Folk of Algeria,* New York, 1921, p. 20.

[58] Josephus, *Against Apion,* Bk. II, # 4.

[59] Idem, Bk. II, # 5.

[60] James Hamilton, *Wanderings in North Africa,* London, 1856, Introduction, p. xvi.

State, and were governed by municipal magistrates of their own. That they had a separate synagogue at Jerusalem, we learn from the Acts of the Apostles;[61] and their frequent mention in the New Testament proves how important a part of the Jewish nation they constituted."[62]

**Pioneer Hebrews.**

Nahum Slouschz adds some interesting details as follows. "Cyrenaica is a peninsula facing Greece on the north and Palestine on the east, a plateau some twenty-five thousand square kilometers between Libya and Egypt. The Phoenicians, and without doubt the Jews also, knew of its existence and perhaps even colonized it in very early times. This region can be identified with the Sepharad or Hesperides of the Prophet Obadiah. By a piece of good fortune, there was unearthed a seal that must have belonged to an ancient Israelite: it bore, in ancient Hebrew characters of the classical epoch, the same name as the prophet just mentioned: 'To Obadiah, son of Yashub'."[63] According to Slouschz, too, "From the period of the Ptolemies, the Jews were attracted in such numbers to the district, which went by the name of Pentapolis, 'the five cities,' that Josephus looked upon it as 'the continuation of Judea beyond Egypt.' From its very beginning this colonization was of a military character. In 320 B. C. E. Ptolemy Soter, the founder of the dynasty, established a number of military colonies composed of Palestinian Semites, in order to keep a firmer hold on the Greek population. From among the Jews the Samaritans whom he led into captivity, he chose thirty thousand able-bodied men and sent them to guard the fortresses of Libya and of Nubia. These military colonies were no doubt the cause of the ascendancy of Hellenic Judaism of Alexandria. With the beginning of the second century, the arrival of large numbers of fugitives from the prosecution of Antiochus in Palestine, rekindled the spark of religious and national fervor in the Jews of Libya."[64] Inci-

**Military Colonies.**

**Renewal of Fervor.**

[61] Acts of the Apostles vi, 9.
[62] Hamilton, l. c. Introduction, p. xvii.
[63] Slouschz, *Travels in North Africa,* p. 69.
[64] Idem, p. 69 f.

dentally, Slouschz remarks concerning the Jews of Cyrenaica: "They proselytized not only amongst the Greeks but also from amongst the Libyans, even though the latter were looked upon as Egyptians by the learned men of Palestine." [65]

**Palestinian Exiles.**

With the destruction of the Second Temple in Jerusalem the Jewish centers of Africa were strengthened by the arrival of many fugitives, voluntary exiles as well as unfortunate slaves.[66] According to Slouschz: "There is a tradition common to all the Jews of Tripoli that they are the direct descendants of captive Jews from Palestine. One of the generals of Titus, called Phanagorus in the Midrash, is said to have transported some thirty thousand Jews into the mountains, and there established them as tillers of the soil. This is said to be the origin of the present Jewish population. . . . Abraham Halfon, an author of the early nineteenth century, speaks as follows in this connection. 'Among the older people I found a tradition, handed down to them from their ancestors, that at the time of the destruction of Jerusalem, one of the generals of Titus, Phanagorus, King of the Arabs, led a number of captive Jews into the mountains, two days distant from Tripoli, and there handed them over to the Arabs. From these mountains they came to Tripoli.' " [67]

**Jewish Rebellion.**

Of the part played by the Jews of Cyrenaica in the insurrection of 115–116 A. D. Slouschz writes: "In 115 they threw themselves on their Greek neighbours, massacring, it is said, some 220,000 of them, after which they endeavoured to join forces with their brothers who had risen in Egypt and in Cyprus. . . . The war lasted three years and the rebellion was mercilessly suppressed. The Roman legions surrounded the rebels and put them to the sword; even the women were not spared. Cyrene was devastated, and almost depopulated of Greek and Jews alike. To cut off the retreat of the rebels, the Romans turned the whole country into a desert. These means, however, only succeeded in drawing a large num-

[65] Idem, p. 72.

[66] Note:—Barrow is of opinion that most of the prisoners taken by Titus "were sent to the mines of Egypt."—Cfr. R. H. Barrow, *Slavery in the Roman Empire,* New York, 1928, p. 8.

[67] Slouschz, *Travels in North Africa,* p. 154.

**Survivors.** ber of Jews further into the Syrte and towards the Atlas mountains." [68] Later Slouschz returns to the same subject. "But can we be sure," he asks, "that these settlements were entirely wiped out? Did not their ascendancy amongst the Libyans render it possible for at least a remnant of them to take refuge among the Berbers, there to continue in the exercise of Political Power? Were this established as a fact, it would be the solution of a problem which has occupied me for many years. This is the situation: on the outskirts of Pentapolis, close to Bengazi, there still existed in the times of Procopius, in the sixth century, a town called Barion, not far from this town there used to be an independent Jewish colony which claimed King Solomon as its founder—to which period they attributed also their synagogue." [69] Elsewhere Slouschz expresses his personal conviction that after the destruction of the Libyan colonies, "the neighbouring countries continued in the possession of Jewish colonies." [70]

**Judeo-Berbers.** Stephen Gsell is pretty much in agreement when he says of the Jews in North Africa: "They were already fairly numerous in the Roman period and it is believed that the greater part of them were real Hebrews, connected perhaps with those who under the Ptolemies migrated to Cyrenaica. . . . However, there is reason to suppose that towards the end of ancient times, the Israelitish religion was propagated in certain native tribes: perhaps the descendants of these converts find themselves to-day confused with those of the Jews of foreign origin." [71] Gsell also notes: "Ibn Khaldoun [72] indi-

[68] Idem, p. 73 f.

[69] Idem, p. 93 f.

[70] Idem, p. 74. Note:—Treating of the "Three Jebels of the Sahara," Slouschz writes: "The Jewish population of Iffren, . . . appeared to me to be a remnant of ancient Judea. . . . The Jews of Iffren have preserved customs and traditions and even a kind of Hebrew dialect which brings them singularly close to the Jews of the biblical period."—l. c., p. 158. And: "The Jebel Iffren possesses exceedingly ancient Jewish memorials. . . . There is not the slightest doubt in my mind that these Jews are the descendants of the captive Jews carried off by Titus into Libya. . . . The Jews themselves are firmly convinced of their direct Palestinian origin. They even relate that thirty years ago a stone was found near the ruined synagogue Zlat-es-Sqaq (the market-place synagogue) with Hebrew inscriptions dating back to the first century after the destruction of Jerusalem." l. c., p. 161 f.

[71] Gsell, *Histoire Ancienne de l'Afrique du Nord,* Vol. I, p. 280 f.

[72] Ibn Khaldoun, *Histoire des Berbères,* trad. De Slane, Alger, 1852–1856, Vol. I, p. 208 f.

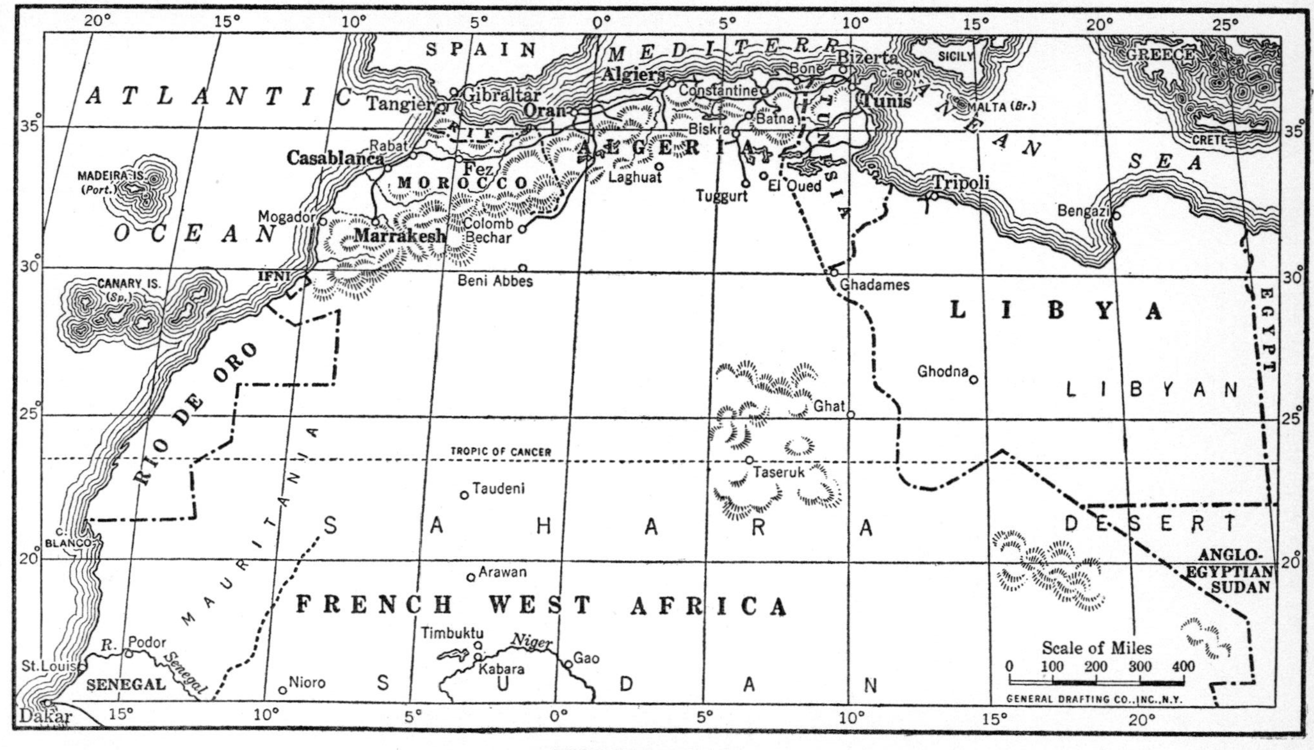


NORTH AFRICA

cates several Berber tribes professing Judaism. The question is very obscure. The Jewish groups which one actually finds in the country believe in their Palestinian origin, and certain indications can lead one to think that they are not always wrong." [73]

**Jewish Sanctuaries.** In connection with this reference to Ibn Khaldoun, Nahum Slouschz has made a special study of the Jewish Berber tribes in North Africa, and after going over the ground carefully unreservedly comes to this conclusion. "At the time of the Arab invasion, there existed in Africa numerous Jewish sanctuaries, kept up by clans of priests of Aaronide origin, who dominated the primitive Jews and the Berbers themselves. The prototype of these cults should be sought in the temple of Onias in Egypt. Of Zadokite origin, did not this last succeed in founding a rival temple in Egypt, in placing himself at the head of the Jewish military colonies of Egypt, and even had himself invested with the title of Alabarch, that is to say Prince of the nomads of the desert and the Red Sea? . . . They say in fact, that similar military colonies have all the time existed in Libya. Would it not be logical to suppose, with many African authors, that at the close of the wars in Africa at the time of the revolt of 115-118 against the Romans, the Jewish refugees of Cyrenaica, led by the descendants of Onias and even by other priestly families, penetrated with the Ethiopian Berbers to the Mountain fastnesses of Africa." [74]

**Aaronides.** Slouschz had already explained that by Aaronides he means descendants of the family of Aaron in the priestly office, "who should exercise the function of sacrifices, a prerogative which the Synagogue had set aside after the abolition of the sacrificial rites and the replacement of the Cohen (priest) or sacrificer by the rabbi." [75] He thus connects with the Old Testament Jews their brethern of North Africa who at the time of the Arab invasion had preserved their "sanctuaries kept up by clans of priests of Aaronide origin." Nay more, he positively states: "I should add that the Riff is

[73] Gsell, l. c., Vol. I, p. 280.

[74] Nahum Slouschz, *Un Voyage d'Études Juives en Afrique—Mémoires présentés par divers savants à l'Académie des Inscriptions et Belles-Lettres de l'Institut de France,* Paris, 1913, Tome XII, deuxième partie, p. 507 f. Cfr. also Slouschz, *Travels in North Africa,* p. 291.

[75] Slouschz, *Un Voyage,* etc., p. 493.

rich in Jewish sanctuaries, that it possesses a tribe of Aaronides and of Jews speaking Chleuh bound to the soil," [76] thus carrying the priestly succession up to our own day. After several years of further study and personal investigation, in his latest volume Slouschz goes more fully into the whole question. In many places he had found clans of Cohanim or Priests usually claiming Zadokite origin; he had listened to their oral tradition; he had examined many ancient Hebrew inscriptions; and in consequence of all this, his conclusion stands that previous to the destruction of the Temple by the Romans, there came to North Africa "clans of Aaronides, who, like Onias in Egypt, founded Bamoth, or sanctuaries, in various places throughout the country." [77] Thus, for example, he declares: "My researches in the Jebel brought to light the following interesting facts: In a valley situated in the heart of the Iffren there is the site of an ancient synagogue, Zlat-es-Sqaq, . . . the origin of which is said to go back to the time of the destruction of the temple. A deserted village which bears the name of Cohen testifies to the existence of a clan of Aaronides, who at one time occupied a district apart, as is still the case with the Aaronides of Jerba." [78]

**Jerba.**

Of the last-named place he writes: "Jerba, the celebrated Island of Lotus-eaters of antiquity, is to-day still illustrious in African Jewish tradition. Countless legends are told of the Hara of the Island,[79] of the Ghriba, or miraculous synagogue, of its Cohanim and its rabbis. And in these legends occur again and again the shadowy figures of Joab or Esdras." [80] The island is situated in the Syrte, ten hours' sail

[76] Idem, p. 497.

[77] Slouschz, *Travels in North Africa,* p. 273.

[78] Idem, p. 191.

[79] Note:—At El Kantara on the Isle of Jerba the "mosque goes by the name of Jama-el-Hara, or the Mosque of the Jewish town," as Slouschz tells us.—l. c., p. 265. "The word Hara, or Hora—a Berber word of Greek origin, meaning segregated place."—l. c., p. 4. Now Jama can hardly be regarded as a derivative from El Yahud, the invariable word for Jews among the Arabs. It rather looks like a form of the Tetragrammaton. Hence Jama-el-Hara might well signify Yahweh's Hara.

[80] Slouschz, l. c., p. 251. Note:—According to Slouschz: "Many of the Cohanim were men of learning, true citizens of this city of Aaronides. All of them know well and cling fondly to the same traditions. The first traditions of Jerba go back to the days of David and Solomon. These men have received it from their ancestors that there was once a stone in the island which bore the following inscription: "As far as this point came Joab, the son of Zeruia, in his pursuit of the Philistines." l. c., p. 257.

from Tripoli.[81] A few pages later Slouschz adds: "The Cohanim of Jerba are divided into two families. One family, which came from Tangiers in the Middle Ages, bears the name of Tanuji, and is spread over the whole of Africa. The other family, native of Jerba and larger than the first, claims to be descended from a family of Aaronides of the race of Zadoc which seems to have migrated to Africa direct from Jerusalem at the time of the destruction of the Holy City by Nebuchadnezzar. . . . Another tradition states that Esdras, himself a Cohen, came as far as Jerba to induce the Jews to return to Jerusalem. The Cohanim, such of them as there were in the island at the time, must have been quite comfortable in their new homeland, for they refused to return. Esdras pronounced a curse against them, saying that never would a Levite set foot on the soil of Jerba. It is curious to note that a similar tradition exists among the Jews of Yemen; but still more curious is the fact that till this very day it is impossible for a Levite to live among the Jews of Jerba." [82] This curse which is attributed to Esdras sounds like an echo from the threat of Jeremias in Egypt.

**Morocco.** Of the Morocco Jews, G. A. Jackson reported more than a hundred years ago that the great influx of this people had occurred at the time of their banishment from Spain and Portugal, but adds: "The stock, however, had long before that event taken root in this quarter of the world, and in all probability was transported together with the original settlers from Phoenicia." [83]

Major Powell, taking advantage of data gathered during a series of journeys through Africa extending over the best part of a quarter of a century, and thoroughly familiar with the Moslem of Asia as well as Africa, is in a position for observations of particular value. It is interesting, then, to find him dividing the Jews of Morocco into "two different branches: those settled among the Berbers from time immemorial, speaking their language and in addition Arabic in a hideously corrupted form; and those expelled from Spain and other European countries

[81] Idem, p. 251. Note:—Jerba Island is situated on the Gulf of Gabes. Its location is about 34° N. lat.; 11° E. long.

[82] Idem, p. 257 f.

[83] G. A. Jackson, *Algiers: Being a Complete Picture of the Barbary States,* London, 1817, p. 129.

during the Middle Ages, most of whom have got little farther than the ports." [84]

Two centuries and a half earlier, Lancelot Addison, who spent several years among the Jews of Barbary, had observed: "The Jews of this Continent much resemble the Spaniard and Portugues in their stature and complexion, but are much different in their nature and disposition, as being more flexible and sequacious, especially in things whereby they may reap advantage. . . . They are not peremptory in intitling themselves to any particular Tribes, yet they generally believe that they are the remains of Judah and Benjamin, together with a few among them of the Family of Levy: whom they conceive to be wonderfully preserved, that they might not be destitute of competent persons to officiate in the Synagogues." [85] In his last statement he probably confuses the Aaronides with the Levites.

**Atlas Jews.**

Lawrence Harris, writing in 1909, in his turn reports on the Atlas Jews: "The exact period of their settlement in the country is uncertain. In an old cemetery in the Sus country, it is said, there is an inscription on a tombstone, which dates back far beyond the destruction of the Second Temple. Many times did I send a native to get a rubbing of this inscription, but superstition is so rife that they each came back with the same old tale—'Evil spirits which haunt burial grounds would not permit them to do my bidding!' No European has penetrated into the interior of Sus, and although I made many endeavours to get there, I was always forced to turn back." [86]

**Ancient Traditions.**

This is possibly the same tradition referred to by John Davidson in a letter to His Royal Highness, the Duke of Sussex, which is dated Migador, March 18, 1836. Davidson says in part: "I was accompanied on this journey by a Rabbi, from the district of Coubba or Cobba, to which place it was my intention to have proceeded. From this man I received much curious information, and have yet great hopes of reaching the people of whom he spoke, and to whom he belongs, before I return to England. He informed me that in this place, nearly as extensive as that in which the city of Mo-

[84] E. Alexander Powell, *In Barbary, Tunisia, Algeria, Morocco and the Sahara,* p. 342.
[85] Lancelot Addison, *Present State of the Jews,* p. 11.
[86] Lawrence Harris, *With Mulai Hafid at Fez,* London, 1909, p. 190.

rocco is situated, there are not less than 3,000 or 4,000 Jews living in perfect freedom, and following every variety of occupation; that they have mines and quarries which they work, possess large gardens and extensive vineyards, and cultivate more corn than they can possibly consume; that they have a form of government, and have possessed this soil from the time of Solomon, in proof of which he stated they possess a record bearing the signet and sign of Joab, who came to collect tribute from them in the time of the son of David; that the tradition of their arrival here runs thus: 'Crossing the Great Sea to avoid the land of Egypt, they came to a head of land with a river; that here they landed, and following the course of this leading westward, but going towards the south, they came to a spot where they found twelve wells and seventy palm trees. This at first led them to suppose that they had by some means got to Elim; but finding the mountains on the west, they were satisfied that they had reached a new country; finding a passage over the mountains, they crossed and took up their dwelling in this valley, first in caves, which exist in great numbers, then in others which they excavated, and after this began to build towns; that at a distant period, they were driven across the mountains by a people that would not acknowledge them, and that some remained at Diminet, Mesfywa, and other places on the western side of the range.' Looking at the map, and following this man's observations, it is perfectly easy to trace them. They must have reached the Gulf of Tremesen, and taking the River Muluwia, or Mahala, have reached Tafilelt, where, to this day, are twelve wells planted round with seventy palm trees and which many of the Jews call Elim; and from this they have taken the pass to which I attempted to get. Knowing the interest your Royal Highness takes in all that refers to the History of the Jews, I have offered this man fifty dollars to obtain a copy of the record upon a skin of the same size and pattern as that which contains it, and ten dollars for the copy of two tombstones to which the Jews make their pilgrimages, and these he promises to send to the Jew agent in Morocco in six months, provided I do not in the meantime visit Coubba." [87] However, before he was able to accomplish

[87] John Davidson, *Notes taken during Travels in Africa,* London, 1839, p. 192 f.

anything further in the matter, Davidson was murdered by the wild Arab tribes of Morocco.[88]

**Daggatouns.**

The Jews referred to may be the same as those described by Mordecai Abu Sereur, who published the results of his travels through Morocco, and speaks of a warlike tribe in the Sahara whom he calls Daggatouns, and states that they are descendants of the early Jews.[89]

**Moroccan Legends.**

Nahum Slouschz who, according to his own statement, has "devoted many years to the study of the history and ethnography of the Jews in Morocco," [90] does not hesitate to assert: "In this country, . . . the Jewish race, which settled there in earliest times, and which for long periods was isolated from the European and Asiatic diasporas, played a most significant social and historical rôle. This rôle began with the Roman history of the country, but there was a strong Jewish influence at work even in prehistoric times; till this day the native population bears the indelible stamp of this influence." [91] Again: "There are no monuments of the presence of Jews in Morocco in the Carthaginian period, but there are widespread oral traditions which seem to establish this as a fact. Thus in the Atlas and in the Black Wed we meet with traditions relating to the wars of Joshua, David, and, above all, of Joab, who, it is said, led their troops as far as the ocean. Leo Africanus, a European author of the sixteenth century, says that in the fifteenth century there were tribes in the Atlas which claimed descent from the warriors of David. Again, certain customs and superstitions of the country are of very ancient origin. It is certain that there were Jews not only in the maritime cities but also in the Roman colony of Volubilis. An inscription discovered by La Martinière and dating from the first or second century, runs as follows: Matrona, daughter of Rabbi Judah,

[88] Idem, p. 202 ff.

[89] Mordecai Abu Sereur, *Les Daggatouns, Tribu d'Origine Juive demeurant dans le Désert de Sahara,* trad. J. Loeb, Paris, 1881. Note:—Slouschz calls them "the great tribe of the Daggatouns, who dominate the routes to the Soudan, and even further. Non-Jewish by faith, but conscious of their ethnic origin, they are particularly cordial to the Jewish merchants."—*Travels in North Africa,* p. 111.

[90] Slouschz, l. c., p. 363.

[91] Idem, p. 362 f.

rests.[92] This inscription is followed by three others in Greek, two of which are certainly of Jewish origin. Here, then, is written confirmation of the existence of a Jewish colony in Volubilis (near Mequinez) at the time of the destruction of the temple." [93]

**Mzab.**

Of the Mzab, just a word may be said in passing. Slouschz writes: "The most interesting Jewish center in Algeria is the group of Berber heretics (Abadites) who, in the tenth century, fled from the Mussulman persecution. They established themselves in the desert, and to this day they have preserved the most mysterious rites and customs." [94] Slouschz is of the opinion "that these Jews are the descendants of the Jewish group of Wargla spoken of by Ibn Ezra," [95] and remarks: "The Jews of Mzab have best preserved the customs and manners peculiar to the Jews of Africa." [96] He quotes the conclusion of Doctor Huguet: "The type of the biblical Jew has been preserved to a remarkable degree among the Jews of Mzab," and adds: "And indeed, in all the districts of the Sahara, from Tripoli to Dra'a of Morocco, the traveller could easily imagine himself transported into some ancient Judean colony—a very primitive agricultural colony, for it has neither Cohanim nor Leviim nor any written traditions. For many centuries these colonies were the counterpart of the Jewish pre-Islamic settlements of Arabia, and to-day they are a marvellous survival of the Israelite epoch of the Judges in the Wastes of the Great Desert." [97]

**Berberized Carthaginians.**

R. V. C. Bodley, as he tells us himself, spent many years in Algeria and mingled with all classes. He lived the life of the people, a business man in the city of Algiers, a sheep breeder in the Sahara, and "visiting the Arabs in such intimacy that it was possible to tell of their daily life as it is really lived." [98] In due course he re-

92 מטרונא בת רבי יהודה נח

93 Slouschz, *Travels in North Africa*, p. 363 f.

94 Idem, p. 351.

95 Idem, p. 352. Note:—Writing in the twelfth century, "Abraham Ibn Ezra speaks as follows of the heretical Jews of Wargla (Exodus 12, 2, 2nd. Commentary): 'The heretics of Wargla celebrate their Passover in the following fashion. These misled people all leave their country on the fifteenth of Nisan, to celebrate the festival in the desert as did the Israelites under Moses.'"—Slouschz, l. c., p. 346.

96 Slouschz, l. c., p. 353.

97 Idem, p. 358.

98 R. V. C. Bodley, *Algeria from Within*, Indianapolis, 1927, p. 15.

cords, but rejects, the theory that the Mzab is inhabited by descendants of the lost tribes of Israel. He rather inclines to the theory that they are of Carthaginian origin. "In the Mzab itself there are certainly things very closely connected with Carthage. The triangular decoration of the houses, the pictures of fish, or of the crescent moon, of the sun and the stars are not Arab." [99] The Mzabite, he concludes, "was a Carthaginian who became Berberised." [100]

**Persistence of the Jews.**

This brings us back to Carthage which, even at the time of the Roman conquest, was assuredly of a mixed population and the Jewish colony there was a very influential body. From that date to this, there has been in North Africa an unbroken record of the Jews who have endured all the vicissitudes of Vandal, Arab and other persecutions. In fact, it may be interesting to note in passing the statement of Lt. Col. Casserly. "The Arabs came again and swept away unstable Berber kingdoms that rose ephemerally. They welcomed into their ranks on equal terms any defeated warriors prepared to adopt Mohommedanism. A former officer of a Berber queen [101] who had fought against them, Tarik-es-Ziad, a Jewish Berber himself,[102] was made by them governor of Tangier when he became a Moslem. And this man with a Berber force, stiffened by a few Arabs, crossed into Spain, landed near Mount Calpe, since called after him Djebel-Tarik, 'The Hill of Tarik,' that is Gibraltar now, and thus began the Moorish conquest of Spain." [103]

[99] Idem, p. 196.

[100] Idem, p. 198. Note:—Of the Jews in Algeria, Bodley remarks that many of them, while speaking Arab and French fluently, use Hebrew among themselves.—Cfr. l. c., p. 39.

[101] Note:—"Cahena, the famous Queen of the Berbers who fought against the Arabs in the seventh century, professed Judaism."—Victor Picquet, *Les Civilisations de l'Afrique du Nord,* Paris, 1921, p. 384. Slouschz cannot be satisfied with this modest statement. He would have Cahena the Queen of the Jerua tribe of Jews who had "come to Africa before the destruction of the Temple,"—*Travels in North Africa,* p. 308, and maintains that she was "herself a priestess and the daughter of a Cohen."—l. c., p. 309. He also writes: "It was in the seventh century that this race of Bahuzim, or Jewish nomad warriors, rose in the desert under the leadership of the great Jewish Queen Daia, or Damia el Cahena, the priestess, celebrated for her beauty, her wisdom, and her herosim. A legendary halo has gathered round this woman, to whom French scholars have given the name 'The African Joan of Arc'; to the writer Daia el Cahena seems the greatest woman in history."—l. c., p. 231 ff.

[102] Note:—Slouschz calls him: "A Jew of the tribe of Simeon."—l. c., p. 365.

[103] Casserly, *Africa To-day,* p. 66.

It is further interesting to find Slouschz insisting: "It is certain that in the Atlas and in the south several groups of Jews maintained an independent existence for several centuries after the triumph of Islam." [104]

**Phoenician Explorers.**

Before closing this chapter, we must touch briefly on the possible influence that may have reached the coast of West Africa through the sea-faring exploits of the Carthaginians or of their parent-state.

W. Walton Claridge, speaking of the voyage of the Phoenicians around Africa, at the behest of King Necho of Egypt about 600 B. C. suggests: "If they did in fact visit the Gold Coast, it is possible that it was then that they discovered that gold was obtainable there, and founded that more or less regular trade which there is reason to suppose at one time or another existed. For similar reasons we must admit the possibility, at any rate, that the Gold Coast may have been visited by others of the Phoenician explorers, who sailed along the West African Coast, but of whose exploits no record has been preserved." [105]

Professor Breasted states: "In the Far West as early as 500 B. C. Phoenician navigators had passed Gibralter, and turning southward had probably reached the coast of Guinea, whence they brought back marvelous stories of the hairy men whom the interpreters called 'Gorillas'." [106] And again, he is of the opinion that the Carthaginian settlements extended "southward along the Atlantic coast of Africa to the edge of the Sahara. In this direction Hanno, one of the famous captains, explored the coast of Africa as far as Guinea." [107]

[104] Slouschz, l. c., p. 366.

[105] Claridge, *History of the Gold Coast and Ashanti,* Vol. I, p. 15.

[106] Breasted, *Conquest of Civilization,* p. 470.

[107] Idem, p. 521. Note:—We may perhaps find a reference to the Carthaginians in what Ferdinand Ossendowski says of the Baga and Yola whom he met in French Guinea immediately north of Sierra Leone. He refers to them as being among "the aboriginal inhabitants of this district, its 'sons,' . . . of whom there are now comparatively few representatives left."—Ferdinand Ossendowski, *Slaves of the Sun,* New York, 1928, p. 103. Later he says: "The languages of the Baga and Yola tribes now have nothing in common with Asiatic dialects, yet, the customs, beliefs and ceremonials betray Asiatic influence. These tribes have retained their belief in a great divinity, who sent mediator-spirits to the earth. They took on material forms, sometimes with the aid of magicians, in fetishes or in natural objects, in a stone of unusual configuration, a distorted root or branch of a tree, a misshapen nut, an excrescence on a plant, and also in images of stone, clay or wood made by the magicians. Among such images one comes across stone figures reminiscent of the images

**Relics.** Claridge would attribute to Phoenician origin the Aggri beads which passed for currency among the natives of the Gold Coast and which have also been found in the tombs at Thebes. He further comments: "The remains of bronze lamps of antique design and arranged to burn a wick floating in oil have also been found in some old disused gold workings."[108] These, too, he believes may be traced to Phoenician sources. Finally, he concludes: "Though, therefore, there is no definite proof of trade or communication with the Gold Coast by the Phoenicians or any other ancient race; there are, nevertheless, a number of facts which together furnish a considerable amount of evidence in favor of such a belief."[109]

In his turn, P. Amaury Talbot considers that the various pieces of ancient bronze and copper found in the vicinity of the Cross River indicate that a trading post of the Carthaginians was established there by Hanno or possibly at a later date[110] by some of his succesors.

of the Carthaginian Astarte and bearing the name of 'Sitar,' which sounds very like Ishtar or Ashtar in the language of the Carthaginians. Is this mere coincidence, or is it the echo of bygone history, of former tribal bonds, or of the yoke of invaders? Among my collection, by the side of an image of 'Sitar' I have a stone fetish of the Yolas, representing the bust of a bearded Semite wearing a cap like those worn by the Carthaginians and Egyptians. The Negroes say that this is the fetish in which settled the spirit of the ancestor of their tribe—a white man—the son of God, the sower of millet, the grain of the Asiatics. Again one is arrested by the question: Are these fetishes the remote reverberation of still more remote events, lost in the dusk of thousands of years of history, or are they only archæological excavations, the remains of an Arayan or Semitic race which in the twilight of history existed on this very soil of the African continent? Does the blood of these white races still flow in the veins of the very primitive and enigmatic 'sons of the soil'? Do not the eagle noses, the thin lips and the luxuriant beards of the Yola tribe witness to that blood? Or those of the Baga-Flora: those daring hunters and warriors who spread terror among the tribes coming from the north and south. The Yolas and the forest tribes have defended their land from strangers, and in their inaccessible jungle have preserved the primordial traditions of the primitive Negroes. Scientists are attempting to prove that these tribes were driven into the forest simultaneously with the pygmies of central South Africa by invaders belonging to white and red races, and later by tribes arising from crossing the Negroes with the new-comers. The 'sons of the soil' have almost no cognisance of their neighbours; they have retained the independent traits of their character and the vestiges of a matriarchate maintained by active, strong and courageous women."—l. c., p. 104 f. Personally we are inclined to ascribe these characteristics to an influx of Carthaginian culture. Possibly, too, they may have had their origin in the Kingdom of Ghana which will be spoken of in the following chapter.

108 Claridge, *History of the Gold Coast and Ashanti,* Vol. I, p. 27.

109 Idem, Vol. I, p. 29.

110 Talbot, *Peoples of Southern Nigeria,* Vol. I, p. 25.

**Colonies.** As a matter of fact, Stephen Gsell now considers it as proven that Hanno and his Carthaginian expedition along the West Coast of Africa [111] actually passed the Coast of Guinea.[112] He also regards it as plausible that Hanno extended his exploration almost as far as the equator.[113] In this case, there may well have been Phoenician colonies established along the Guinea coast,[114] and possibly not a few Hebrews may have joined in these enterprises.

**"Dumb" Commerce.** In this connection it is worth while calling attention to the so-called "dumb" commerce of Africa as described by Herodotus, where he says: "The Carthaginians also relate the following:—There is a country in Libya, and a nation beyond the Pillars of Hercules, which they are wont to visit, where they no sooner arrive but forthwith they unlade their wares, and having disposed them after an orderly fashion along the beach, leave them, and, returning aboard their ships, raise a great smoke. The natives, when they see the smoke, come down to the shore, and, laying out to view so much gold as they think the worth of the wares, withdraw to a distance. The Carthaginians upon this come ashore and look. If they think the gold enough, they take it and go their way; but if it does not seem to them sufficient, they go aboard the ship once more and wait patiently. Then the others approach and add to their gold, till the Carthaginians are content. Neither party deals unfairly by the other; for they themselves never touch the gold till it comes up to the worth of the goods, nor do the natives ever carry off the goods till the gold is taken away." [115]

Professor Rawlinson remarks in this connection: "The 'dumb' commerce of the African nations is now a matter of notoriety. It

[111] Cfr. Thomas Falconer, *The Voyage of Hanno,* London, 1797.

[112] Gsell, *Histoire Ancienne de l'Afrique du Nord,* Vol. I, p. 503

[113] Idem, Vol. I, p. 507.

[114] Note:—A brachycephalic, leptorrhine type which Professor Dixon suggests may be due to "pre-Phœnician or Phœnician colonists" and fairly common in Egypt and along the northern littoral of Africa shows only traces in the Sudan. Yet in Dahomey, he tells us, it is a very pronounced factor. Cfr. Dixon, *Racial History of Man,* p. 189 f. This last-mentioned fact might be explained by Phoenician and Carthaginian commerce with the West Coast, despite the previous remark of Professor Dixon: "The Carthaginian trade with the West African Coast, which appears to have gone on for some time, left no noticeable traits among the Negro peoples of the area."—l. c., p. 153.

[115] *Herodotus,* Bk. IV, # 196.

exists not only upon the western coast, but also to a considerable extent in the interior." [116] He cites several instances in confirmation of the fact. It is further recorded by recent travellers that the "dumb" commerce is still practiced in the Belgian Congo between the Pigmies and the native Blacks.[117]

It is also interesting to find an experienced missionary reporting an exactly similar scheme of barter existing on the Slave Coast about sixty years ago. Provisions are regularly deposited, he tells us, along the road that travellers may refresh themselves. There is no one in attendance, but those who wish to avail themselves of the opportunity, select what they please and leave in exchange whatever price they consider fair. The astonishing part of the transaction is that absolute honesty prevails and full value is paid.[118]

**Gold Coast and Tarshish.**

Some would even see the Gold Coast of West Africa as included in the Tarshish of King Solomon's fleets. "For the king's navy, once in three years, went with the navy of Hiram by sea to Tharsis, and brought from thence gold, and silver, and elephants' teeth, and apes, and peacocks." [119] Nowhere else do we have so conveniently the combination of gold, ivory and apes. As regards the present absence of peacocks from the coast, the difficulty is met by a record of the seventeenth century, where speaking of Guinea, the assertion is made: "They worship a certain bird which hath feathers like stars, and a voice like a bull." [120] Could there be any more distinctive description of the peacock? Josephus in his account of the fleet "upon the Sea of Tarsus," which he distinguishes from the ships of Ezion-geber that sailed to Ophir, enumerates as the fruit of trade, besides silver and gold, "a great quantity of ivory, Ethiopians, and apes,[121] and adds: "And they finished their voyage, going and coming, in three years." [122] The presence of Ethiopians might further strengthen the claim of the Gold Coast to be included in the Tarshish of Solomon, and the words of Josephus, "they finished the voyage, going and coming, in three years," may

[116] Rawlinson, *Herodotus,* p. 171, Note 7.
[117] Haardt and Audouin-Dubreuil, *The Black Journey,* New York, 1927, p. 178.
[118] Pierre Bouche, *La Côte des Esclaves et le Dahomey,* p. 74.
[119] III Kings x, 22.
[120] Alexander Ross, *Panseibia,* Little London, 1672, p. 98.
[121] Josephus, *Antiquities,* Bk. VII, # 2.
[122] III Kings x, 22.

clarify the meaning of the Scriptural "once in three years," of our English text. The "semel per tres annos ibat" of the Latin version, as well as the Septuagint Greek,[123] might even seem to favor the rendition of Josephus, that it took three years for the voyage.

However, here again, while all is conjecture, it does not seem at all likely that Hebrews could have been in sufficient numbers to have left a lasting impression on language and customs.

**Conclusions.** In the present chapter, then, we have shown that the Jews certainly from a very early period found their way in ever increasing numbers along the southern shore of the Mediterranean, and that they exerted no small influence on the commercial world of Northern Africa. At first perhaps in the employ of the Phoenicians, they soon asserted their independence and gradually superseded their former masters in the control of the commerce of many a trading post and center along the entire northern littoral of Africa, and for some distance inland.

At Carthage, they were well established by the time of Hannibal, and the tombs near the Gamart Hill give evidence of the fact that during the Roman period at least they held a position of affuence in the city. So true is this, that Carthaginian culture gives every indication of a strong Hebraic influence both in language and in customs.

Long before the Christian era, and consequently independent of the destruction of Jerusalem by Titus, we find not only at Carthage but also in Morocco as well as Tripoli, Cyrenaica and above all at Alexandria, flourishing and influential Jewish communities which must have sent out countless colonies into all the adjacent districts.

Almost from the beginning, there were inevitably commercial contacts with the hinterland, and with the advent of persecution, large numbers of Jews withdrew to the mountain fastnesses of the interior. But even before this had happened, proselytizing had converted many Berber tribes to Judaism, and it becomes practically impossible to distinguish these Judaized Berbers from the real Jewish colonists with whom they gradually amalgamated.

Jewish sanctuaries, too, were early established at many points, and there is strong evidence of colonies of Cohanim, of real or feigned Aaronide origin. But here again it is impossible to differ-

[123] διά τριῶν ἐτῶν ἤρχετο.

entiate the Jews from the Berbers who had embraced the Jewish religion and form of worship. In all probability no such distinction was long preserved among the Tribes themselves. For unquestionably intermarriage quickly obliterated all ethnic differences.

Whether, or not, there were any Jews with the Carthaginian commercial ventures which reached West Africa by sea and established there trading posts, need not concern us here. For, even if some individual Jews or at best small groups of them, were actually associated with the enterprise, their influence would have been insufficient to account for the many Hebrewisms which we are trying to explain in the present volume.

How far, on the other hand, the influence from the Jewish communities of Northern Africa penetrated to the interior of the Continent, and filtered across the Sahara to the very heart of Negro Land, we hope to show in the next chapter.

## *Chapter IX*

## MYSTERIES OF THE DESERT

**Tuaregs.**

Charles de la Roncière, custodian of documents at the National Library of Paris, quite recently published under the auspices of the Société Royale de Géographie d'Egypte a scholarly work, wherein he reproduced all the early maps of Africa that he had been able to discover. Incidentally he quoted a Latin document, apparently written at Tamentit, the old capital of Tuat, in 1447, by Anthony Malfont, who speaks of the large number of Jews at Tuat and further refers to the Tuaregs as "Phylistey" and represents them as the greates enemies of the Jews.[1]

**Divergent Theories.**

Harold N. Denny regards the Tuaregs as "a white people with a heritage, but without a history. Three thousand years ago," he says, "they were known to the ancients. Phoenician, Carthaginian and Roman traded with these people. Then came the Dark Ages, and the Tuaregs were forgotten until, in the latter half of the nineteenth century, they were rediscovered." [2]

Dugald Campbell at one time expresses the opinion of the Tuareg: "They once occupied Tripoli, and were driven out by the Romans in the early Christian era." [3] And again: "The Sanhahja, of whom much was heard in the recent Riff struggle, are the actual ancestors from whom the present-day Tuaregs are believed to have sprung." [4] But finally he admits: "His origin presents an insoluble riddle. . . . Some say they are the remnants of crusader armies that lost their way in the desert while returning from (sic) Europe after the crusades." [5]

[1] Charles de la Roncière, *La Découverte de l'Afrique au Moyen Age,* Cairo, 1925–1927, Vol. I, p. 152 f.
[2] *New York Times Magazine,* Jan. 17, 1926, p. 11.
[3] Dugald Campbell, *On the Trail of the Veiled Tuareg,* Philadelphia, 1928, p. 20.
[4] Idem, p. 21.
[5] Idem, p. 254.

E. D. Morel unhesitatingly speaks of the Tuaregs as "descendants of the Iberian," [6] while Byron Kuhn de Prorok, on the contrary, says of them: "Père de Foucauld, the Hermit of the Sahara, decided after long study of them that they were closely allied to the Egyptians and other very ancient peoples. Emile Gautier, one of the most notable explorers of the Hoggar, believes that they are the last survivors of the Libyans, and there is another theory which identifies them with the Berbers, a race with traces of distinguished lineage." [7]

The author of the *Tarikh es-Soudan,* usually referred to as Abderrahman es-Sadi, was a native of Timbuktu, and the chief purpose of his writings would seem to have been to glorify his native city.[8] Raised in the very heart of Africa and living at the beginning of the seventeenth century of our era,[9] he ascribed to the Tuaregs the founding of that "mysterious" metropolis of the desert, and then maintains that the Tuaregs themselves ultimately derived their origin from Yemen, but that by long residence among and intermarriage with the Berbers, had gradually adopted much of their language and customs.[10]

**Semitic Strain.**

Captain Angus Buchanan, as he tells us himself, "after his strenuous labors in the war in East Africa," [11] in 1920, visited the district of Aïr in the interests of the Twing Museum. His personal study of the Tuaregs led him to style them "an Arab-like Semitic race." [12] And Gordon Casserly is as positive in his statement: "It is generally agreed that all Tuaregs are of Berber origin," [13] while according to some, "the Berbers are said to have been at one time Jews,[14] or at least a Semitic tribe that invaded Africa from the East fully a thousand years before the Christian era, and which consisted of an ethnic complex with a strong Jewish blend." [15]

[6] E. D. Morel, *Nigeria: Its Peoples and Its Problems,* London, 1911, p. 232.
[7] Prorok, *Digging for Lost African Gods,* p. 330 f.
[8] Abderrahman es-Sadi, *Tarikh es-Soudan,* trad. O. Houdas, Paris, 1900, Vol. II, Introduction, p. i.
[9] Idem, Vol, II, Introduction, p. iv.
[10] Es-Sadi, *Tarikh es-Soudan,* Vol. II, Chapter VII, p. 42 ff.
[11] Angus Buchanan, *Exploration of Aïr Out of the World North of Nigeria,* London, 1921, Introduction, p. xxi.
[12] Idem, p. 233.
[13] Casserly, *Africa To-Day,* p. 230.
[14] Cfr. *Jewish Quarterly Review,* IV, p. 375.
[15] Paul Odinot, *Les Berbères.—La Géographie,* Tome XLI (1924), Paris, p. 137 ff.

It is interesting, then, to note that Doctor Vermale who was killed by the Tuaregs in the battle of Ain-el-Hajaj, on February 13, 1917, left in his notes which he had entitled "Au Sahara pendant le guerre européene" this observation, that the family tent of the Tuaregs was "fixed by cords to twelve stakes." [16] The number twelve might strike one as significant!

**People of the Veil.**

Francis Rennell Rodd, one of the most recent scholars to study the People of the Veil, as the Tuaregs are frequently called, at first expresses a doubt "whether the Tuareg are Berbers at all." [17] Then, as he begins to evolve his own theory, he ventures to remark: "There is, I think, no justification for considering the People of the Veil a large tribal group of the Berbers in North Africa; they are a separate race with marked peculiarities, distinct from other sections of the latter, and as I believe, of a different origin." [18] This idea he develops at considerable length, and incidentally remarks:

**Christian Influence.**

"There are certain incontrovertible facts which demonstrate the influence, at least, of Christianity among the People of the Veil. Much has been written of their use of the cross in ornament, nor can its so frequent occurrence be entirely fortuitous." [19] After confirming this last assertion with many instances drawn for the most part from

[16] René Bazin, *Charles de Foucauld Hermit and Explorer,* London, 1923, p. 237.

[17] Francis Rennell Rodd, *People of the Veil,* London, 1926, p. 7.

[18] Idem, p. 16.

[19] Idem, p. 275. Note:—Dugald Campbell is entirely in agreement with this view. He says: "I found the remains of mosques and Moslem monasteries still standing. Inside some of these lay ancient manuscripts, and books dating back to early Arab occupations. But for the veneration borne by the Moslem for writing these would have been destroyed long ago, or else stolen. Other evidence abounded on every hand, proving that in pre-Islamic times the ancestors of the present day Tuaregs were Christians."—*On the Trail of the Veiled Tuareg,* p. 17. And again: "My previous references to the use of the cross as a Christian sign, or symbol, in every department of Tuareg life, and my contention that the Tuaregs were a Christian people will bear the most minute examination that will satisfy the most sceptical. The Tuaregs make prominent use of the cross on their camel saddles; besides their longswords (takouba) and their daggers (telek) are also cruciform. The cross is sewn on the camel saddlery, and is seen on spoons, sandals, and on their houses and clothes. The men tattoo the cross on their bodies, the women on their foreheads, and the latter wear a beautiful silver cross called tenaghal. The letter T of Tifinach script is also a cross, while these, and others all point to a one and only origin. Neither Arabs, Hausas, Tebus, or men of Fezzan use the cross as ornament. The cross is forbidden by Koranic teachers as Christian, but in this the Tuaregs ignore Koranic teaching, as they also do in their monogamous customs, general treatment of their women, and, in fact, in all else."—l. c., p. 259 f.

his own observations, he calls attention to certain words which "seem to be so closely associated with Christianity as to require more explanation than the suggestion that they were borrowed from the North in the course of contact with the Romans or other Mediterranean influences." [20] Thus he records: "In Aïr, God is referred to either as Mesi or as Ialla, which of course comes from Alla. But there seems to be a slight difference in the use of the two words, for when Ahodu (Tuareg chief of the Kel Tadek) and others talked of praying they spoke of Ialla, but when he said to me that they were aware there was only one God, who was mine as well as theirs, Mesi was used." [21] Rodd suggests that the derivation of Mesi may be the Hebrew word [22] rendered in English by Messiah, and which occurs in the ninth chapter of the Prophecy of Daniel,[23] and in the second Psalm,[24] and signifies literally anointed.[25] Rodd further reports that another name for God in use among the Tuaregs is Amanai, which as suggested by Duveyrier may be derived from the Hebrew Adonai,[26] signifying Lord.[27]

**Hamites.** However, Charles de Foucauld who for years lived amongst the Tuaregs and mastered their language which he declares "a very pure Berber tongue," [28] and "the old language of Africa and Palestine, which the Carthaginian spoke," [29] under date of April 3, 1906, wrote to his brother the Comte de Foucauld: "They are certainly Hamites; their language shows it clearly. When of pure type they have the physiognomy of the ancient Egyptians; . . . the Egyptians of the old sculptures." [30]

To prevent confusion, it is well to call to mind the statement of Professor Werner: "The Hamitic family once extended in an unbroken area right across North Africa. The ancient Egyp-

[20] Rodd, *People of the Veil,* p. 277.
[21] Idem, p. 278.
[22] מָשִׁיחַ
[23] Dan. ix, 25, 26.
[24] Ps. ii, 2.
[25] Rodd, l. c., p. 278.
[26] אֲדֹנָי
[27] Rodd, l. c., p. 278.
[28] Bazin, *Charles de Foucauld,* p. 223.
[29] Idem, p. 213.
[30] Idem, p. 236.

tians spoke a Hamitic tongue, as did the Libyans and Numidians, whose descendants are now known as Berbers and Kabyles." [31]

**Report of Procopius.**

How comes it, then, that Malfont could refer to these Tuaregs as Phylistey? There is an oft-quoted passage in Procopius that throws some light on the subject. Procopius, it may be remembered, as legal adviser and Secretary, accompanied the general Belisarius to North Africa in 533 A. D. and later wrote his history of the Vandal War. In the course of this narrative, he states: "When the Hebrews had withdrawn from Egypt and had come near the boundaries of Palestine, Moses, a wise man, who was their leader on the journey, died, and the leadership was passed on to Joshua, the son of Nun, who led this people into Palestine, and, by displaying a valour in war greater than that natural to a man, gained possession of the land. And after overthrowing all the nations he easily won the cities, and he seemed to be altogether invincible. Now at that time the whole country along the sea from Sidon as far as the boundaries of Egypt was called Phoenicia. And one king in ancient time held sway over it, as is agreed by all who have written the earliest accounts of the Phoenicians. In that country there dwelt very populous tribes, the Geresites and the Jebusites and some others with other names which they were called in the history of the Hebrews.[32] Now when these nations saw that the invading general

**Fugitives from Canaan.**

was an irresistible prodigy, they emigrated from their ancestral homes and made their way to Egypt, which adjoined their country. And finding there no place sufficient for them to dwell in, since there has been a great population in Egypt from ancient times, they proceeded to Libya. And they established numerous cities and took possession of the whole of Libya as far as the pillars of Heracles, and there they have lived even up to my time, using the Phoenician tongue. They also built a fortress in Numidia, where now is the city called Tigisis. In that place are two columns made of white stone near by the great spring, having Phoenician letters cut in them which say in the Phoenician tongue: 'We are they who fled from before the face of Joshua, the robber, the son of Nun.' " [33]

[31] Werner, *The Language-Families of Africa,* p. 25.
[32] Note by translator: "The Canaanites of the Old Testament."
[33] *Procopius with an English Translation* by H. B. Dewing, London, 1916, Bk. IV (Bk. II of Vandal War), Chap. X, # 13–22.

Procopius later would identify these early emigrants from Palestine with the Moors of his day.[34]

**Slouschz' Statement.**

Nahum Slouschz, after "ten years of travel amongst the Jews of Africa and much of study and research into their history and ethnography," [35] has given us the fruit of his labors in a volume entitled "Travels in North Africa," to which frequent reference has already been made. Herein he devotes an entire chapter to "Joshua ben Nun in Africa." [36] He says in part: "In this work, which is nothing more than a collection of facts and observations, we can only present evidence which supports our theory, however startling the conclusion itself. But before we deal with the legend of Joshua ben Nun, it seems best to review here a number of historic traditions which have their origins in earliest antiquity. These traditions will place the legends of Joshua ben Nun in a more interesting light, for it is certain that they are almost as old as the Phoenician colonization of Africa, and have always been known in the country.

"There is an old Hebrew tradition that at the time of the conquest of the Holy Land by the Israelites, under Joshua the son of Nun, certain Canaanite tribes migrated to Africa.

"One Tosefta,[37] quoting an older source, says that when Joshua approached Canaan, he told the inhabitants that three courses were open to them: they could either leave the country, or they could sue for peace, or they could declare war against him. The Girgashites, among others, preferred to withdraw into Africa. The Tosefta goes on to say that the Amorites, the Kadmoni, the Kenites, and the Kenizites—some of whom figure among the founders of Carthage—also went to Africa. These traditions date from a period when communication between Africa and Phoenicia was continuous. The proper names of Gergash and Kenaz are often met with in Carthaginian and Phoenician inscriptions.

"The Talmud [38] says that the Canaanites in Africa asked Alexander the Great to restore to them their country, which had been taken from their ancestors by Joshua ben Nun.

[34] Idem, # 27.
[35] Slouschz, *Travels in North Africa,* Foreword, p. v.
[36] Idem, p. 336 ff.
[37] Shabat, 18. Cfr. Slouschz, *Études dans l'Histoire des Juifs au Maroc,* p. 56.
[38] Tal. Bab. Sanhedrin 91a.

"These traditions have found a place in the Books of Jubilees [39] and of Enoch.[40] They have been ratified by the Fathers of the Church; thus Saint Jerome calls to witness the Talmud to support his statement that the Girgashites established colonies in Africa; [41] and Saint Augustine designates the natives of Africa as 'Canaanites.' " [42]

Then quoting the testimony of Procopius, Slouschz concludes: "This is the statement of antiquity on the legends of Joshua ben Nun in Africa; without entering into the historic value of this statement we may see at once that these legends have persisted since Phoenician times." [43]

**Discredited by Gsell.**

Stephen Gsell, on the other hand, after considering at length the citation from Procopius, rates it as having no real historic value. According to his view, the Liby-Phoenicians were not Phoenicians of Libya, but rather those Libyans who, under the tutelage of Carthage, adopted Punic customs and consequently in a sense may be said to have become Phoenicians. He adds: "The diffusion of Phoenician language, religion and customs in North Africa is explained by the influence which Carthaginian civilization exercised on the natives," and asserts that we can find among the Berbers no proof of any Canaanitish migration.[44]

**Accepted by Many.**

Nevertheless, the story as told by Procopius has been quoted and requoted by Christian and Arabic authors, until it has left its impress on the traditions of the peoples themselves. It finds support, too, in the earlier testimony of Saint Augustine: "When our peasants are asked what they are, answering after the Punic fashion Chenani, having corrupted the word as is usual with their kind, what else do they answer but Canaanites?" [45]

[39] IX, 1.
[40] XIII, 22.
[41] Onomastica Sacra.
[42] Slouschz, *Travels in North Africa,* p. 337 f.
[43] Idem, p. 338. Note:—Later speaking of Teluet "a veritable eagle's nest among the mountains" (Great Atlas) Slouschz writes: "There are some eight hundred Jews in the city. . . . The Berbers call them Ait Musa, the Tribe of Moses, while the Jews call the Berbers El Philistin (the people of Palestine); the Jews explain that they call the Berbers by this name because tradition has it that they came to the Atlas region from Palestine at the time of the destruction of the Temple."—l. c., p. 464.
[44] Gsell, *Historie Ancienne de l'Afrique du Nord,* Vol. I, p. 341 ff.
[45] Migne, *Patres Latini,* Vol. XXXIV–V, p. 2096.

Francis Pulsky in the middle of the last century wrote: "Leo Africanus, a learned Moorish author, converted to Christianity, who lived in the sixteenth century, tells us that the Canaanites, expelled by Joshua emigrated to Africa, and settled there. The same author says that Malek Afriki, several centuries later, headed a large emigration of Sabaean Arabs to Africa; and it is singular that the Jews seem likewise to believe in a double immigration of Asiatic nations of Barbary. Up to the present day, they call the Kabyles Palestines and Philistines, identifying them with their enemies of old in Canaan; and their Rabbis believe that the Mozabites are the descendants of the Moabites, the ancient neighbours of Israel, the offspring of Moab, the son of Lot. Their language is different from that of the Kabyles, but it is said that there exists some affinity between them." [46]

**Traditional Tomb.**

According to Henri Basset, the popular tradition of the neighbourhood identifies the tomb of Sidi-Youcha, located to the East of Nemours on the North Coast of Africa, as that of Joshua son of Nun,[47] and René Basset reports that there the Hebrew leader "is still venerated in our day by Jew and Mussulman alike." [48] René Basset also cites the various Arab authors who support the view that the Berbers derive their origin from Canaanites driven from Palestine at the advent of the Chosen People.[49] A. Macallum Scott, too, has no hesitation in asserting: "The name by which the Carthaginians designated themselves for centuries after their conquest by Rome was, not Phoenicians, but Canaanites." [50]

**Cretan Refugees.**

Ibn Khaldoun, on his part, would derive the Berbers from the Philistines, the ancient enemies of the Israelites.[51] Breasted, in turn, would have the

[46] Francis Pulsky, *The Tricolor on the Atlas,* London, 1854, p. 198.
[47] Henri Basset, *Le Culte des Grottes au Maroc,* Alger, 1920, p. 28, N. 3.
[48] René Basset, *Nédromah et les Traras,* Paris, 1901, Introd. viii; p. 194.
[49] Idem, Introd. xiii ff.
[50] A. Macallum Scott, *Barbary the Romance of the Nearest East,* New York, 1921, p. 166.
[51] Ibn Khaldoun, *Histoire des Berbères,* trad. De Slane, Alger, 1852. Vol. I, p. 184. Note:—Slouschz says: "Many of the Berber tribes believe even to-day, as they did in the time of Ibn Novairi, one of the most ancient Arab writers, that they are the descendants of the Philistines who fled before David. They say that these far-off ancestors of theirs, in flight with their king Jalut (Goliath) into Africa, passed through Egypt, and there founded in the oasis a city which still bears the name of Gath, and which is to this day a famous Berber center."—*Travels in North Africa,* p. 109. And again: "The Majmuda

Philistines a Cretan tribe which sought refuge in Southern Palestine in the twelfth century B. C. when the Greek invasion overthrew the Aegean civilization which centered at Cnossus.[52] It was this same wave of Aegean fugitives which aided in the overthrow of the Egyptian Empire of Thebes. Possibly, then, other fugitives from Crete or the lesser Aegean Islands may have sought refuge in Northern Africa and developed into the parent-stock of the Berbers or Tuaregs. The linear writings of Crete, we are told,[53] has thus far defied the efforts of scholars to read them. The solution which must come in time, may show some affinity with North African dialects.

**Carthaginian Influence.**

Whatever, then, may be the origin of the Tuaregs,[54] we shall leave them now, to consider the Carthaginian influence in the interior of Africa. For the Carthaginians, if not actually the parent-stock, have from the earliest days of the colony come in close ethnic contact with the mysterious People of the Veil.

Count Prorok who has made a special study not only of the excavations of Carthage, but also of the tomb of Tin Hinan, the legendary ancestress of the Kings of Hoggar, announces that by the contents of the tomb the date was judged to be the third or fourth century B. C. as they are identical with amulets found in tombs of that period in Carthage.[55] He further observes: "The expedition has, at least, accumulated evidence which largely assures us in the belief that we have established the trade routes of the Phoenicians, and that Carthaginian influence extended into

and the Brabers of the west are part Philistine, and part Amalekite, and it is as such that they are spoken of in the writings of Ibn Ezra, etc.—l. c., p. 110. And finally: "There are others besides Philistines and Amalekites in Africa. In the Jebel Nefussa, a few days march from Tripoli, there may still be found the descendants of the congeners of Israel. They share with their co-religionists of the Isle of Jerba and of the Mozabites the honor of claiming descent from Moab and Ammon."—l. c., p. 110.

[52] James H. Breasted, *Conquest of Civilization,* New York, 1926, p. 273.

[53] Idem, p. 246.

[54] Note:—Maurice Abadie is perhaps a little too sweeping in his statement: "The Berber origin of the Tuareg is to-day admitted without discussion; it is largely proven by ethnical, linguistic and sociological reasons that it is superfluous to recall here."—Cfr. Maurice Abadie, *La Colonie du Niger,* Paris, 1927, p. 154. It is true that the weight of evidence favors the Berber origin of the Tuaregs, and the traces of Semitic and Christian elements to be found in their culture is presumably due to contact with Jewish and Christian Berber Tribes. However, in the light of present research it would still be presumptuous to summarily brush aside all other theories advanced.

[55] Prorok, *Digging for Lost African Gods,* p. 365.

the very heart of the Hoggar many centuries before Christ." [56] Resumes: "Certainly there is little room for doubt that we have worked over the route by which the Carthaginians brought their ivory, gold, gems and slaves from Central Africa, and along which merchants went to exchange beads and jewelry for the gold dust in the possession of the natives. It may have been in such trading that the personage we have exhumed obtained the wealth of Carthaginian objects found." [57]

**Ossendowski's Evidence.**

Ferdinand Ossendowiski speaks of the Phoenician influence in the heart of Africa, referring for the most part to Carthage. Thus he writes: "The African explorer, in his research in primal cults, finds many traces of other religions, either remaining as religion or lurking in tradition and custom. The Phoenicians, whose colonies ran along the northern and western coasts of Africa and whose caravans reached far back into the interior, have left their marks on the life of the black people. Among the Moslem sects in the land of Mzab, at the edge of the Sahara, there is one called Aissaua, whose witches still practise the conjuring tricks of the ancient Astarte-Tanit cult and utter invocations that begin, 'Astarte Barakat,' meaning 'Astarte, thou blessed one.' The tattoo on the forehead of the women of many tribes, showing the moon set between the horns of a bull, can also be traced back to Phoenician origin. Near Dakr, and near St. Louis, Senegal, were Carthaginian colonies in times of old. There the negroes for centuries have found earthen figures representing Astarte, and busts having distinct Semitic features. In hair-dressings, beards and head-coverings these objects resemble those that have lately been found in the excavations at Carthage and in Phoenicia. These figures have long been fetishes among the negroes. The full-moon dances and the matrimonial ceremonies found to-day in the Soosoo tribe are undoubtedly traceable to the Astarte cult." [58]

**Renegade Jews of the Desert.**

Speaking of certain tribes of the desert which "with more or less justification, claim a Jewish origin," Slouschz writes: "At one time they pro-

[56] Idem, p. 359.
[57] Idem, p. 366.
[58] Ferdinand Ossendowski, *Cruel Gods Fill the African Olympus*—the *New York Times Magazine,* May 13, 1928, p. 13.

fessed Judaism, but, as the result either of persecution or indifference, they have deserted their faith. Mussulmans though they are, they still retain customs which point to their Jewish origin, while some still marry only within the tribe. In most cases these Hebrews by race and Mussulmans by faith seek to hide their origin, which has become a burden to them. But the desert has a long memory. Ten centuries after these conversions certain tribes, nay, the inhabitants of certain sections of cities, were pointed out to us as Yahudis—Jews." [59]

**South of the Sahara.** Whatever may be thought of the more or less mythological traditions connected with the earliest Jews in North Africa, it is now practically an established fact that a Jewish nation—Jewish at least in faith, and perhaps too in origin—long held sway south of the Sahara. Maurice Delafosse [60] was the great exponent of this theory, and Charles de la Roncière [61] thus briefly summarizes his position. "Up to the seventh century, the Foulbe or Fellatah were cantoned at Touat and in the southern parts of Morocco.[62] But from the second and third centuries, there were there also Judaeo-Syrians coming from Cyrenaica. St. Augustine makes mention of them at Tazeur (Thusurus), where the Bishop himself learned Hebrew.[63] And by way of Aïr and Touat, they pushed their way as far as the country known by the name of Aoukar, to the south of the Sahara. Forty-four white kings, according

[59] Slouschz, *Travels in North Africa,* p. 111.

[60] Maurice Delafosse, *Haute-Sénégal-Niger,* Paris, 1912, Vol. I, p. 296 ff. Note:—As great stress is going to be placed on the personal views and observations of the late Maurice Delafosse, it is well to remember that the French Savant was a former Governor of French West Africa, Professor of the École des Langues Orientales Vivantes of Paris, and had shortly before his death been chosen as one of the two Directors for the guidance of the International Institute of African Languages and Cultures. Sir Frederick Lugard, Chairman of the Executive Council of the Institute, in his obituary notice, says: "Professor Delafosse died in 1926, only a few months after the acceptance of his new office; he had not only largely contributed to the formation of the Institute, but had started with great enthusiasm to take part in its work. His large experience, his erudition, and his familiarity with African problems—especially with those of West Africa—would have been a great asset for the Institute, and his death was a serious loss."—Cfr. *Journal of the International Institute of African Languages and Cultures,* London, Vol. I (1928), p. 7.

[61] Roncière, *Découverte de l'Afrique en Moyen Age,* Vol. I, p. 102 ff.

[62] Delafosse, l. c. Vol. I, p. 262; Vol. II, p. 12.

[63] St. Augustine, *Epistolae,* 196.—Paul Monceaux, *Païens Judaïsants,* Paris, 1902, p. 11: *Extrait de la Revue Archéologique.*

to the Chronicle of the Soudan, there succeeded one another up to the year 790.

**Ghana.**

"Their title of Ghana, from which their capital took its name, has nothing Arabic about it. 'Perhaps it belonged to the language of the first founders of the Empire of Ghana, that is to say to the language which without doubt was made up at the time of Aramean, Egyptian and Berber elements, that the Judaeo-Syrians spoke when they arrived in Aoukar.'

"Does not a Jew of the Tribe of Dan, who had been from Kairouan to the country of the Cannibals, tell us in the ninth century of a Jewish Empire in the Sahara which extended over a two hundred days' march? According to this Eldad the Danite [64] they had there in the interior of Africa a language seemingly Phoenician, a religion which was that of Joshua and a Jewish Emperor. This Emperor, elsewhere called Tloutan or Boulatan ben Tiklan, was converted in 837 to Islamism and began an era of sanguinary conflicts with the neighboring tribes, Jewish or otherwise." [65]

**Eldad the Danite.**

We might here digress for a moment from the account of De la Roncière, to say a few words about this Eldad the Danite. It was towards the end of the ninth century that the Jewish community at Kairwan in North Africa was aroused by a visitor from the heart of Negro Land with a strange story to relate. In the words of Max L. Margolis: " Eldad son of Mahli the Danite alleged that he was the descendant of the tribe of Dan. He related that his tribe had migrated from their Palestinian home so as not to take part in the civil war at the time of Jeroboam's seccession, and were residing in the land of Havilah beyond the rivers of Ethiopia. Three other tribes, Naphtali, Gad and Asher, were with them; these had joined them in the times of Sennacherib.[66] . . . They had the entire body of Scriptures barring Esther and Lamentations. They knew neither of the Mishna nor of Talmud; but

[64] Abraham Epstein, *Eldad ha Dani,* Wien, 1891; E. Carmoly, *Relation d'Eldad le Danite, Voyageur du ix Siècle,* Paris, 1838.

[65] Nahum Slouschz, *Étude sur l'Histoire des Juifs au Maroc,* Paris, 1905, p. 70; *Archives Marocaines: Raudh-el-Kartas,* ed. Thornberg, Upsala, 1843, Vol. I, p. 104.

[66] Margolis and Marx, *History of the Jewish People,* p. 278.

they had a Talmud of their own in which all the laws were cited in the name of Joshua son of Nun as he had received them at the hands of Moses. Eldad exhibited a Ritual dealing mostly with the rules pertaining to the killing of animals for food. It was written in a Hebrew containing many strange expressions with a slight Arabic coloring, though Eldad himself professed that he knew no other tongue but Hebrew, in which alone he conversed." [67] . . . Though criticised and questioned by Jewish authorities, "Eldad's ritual continued nevertheless to be cited by scholars of repute in subsequent ages. His account of the existence of other tribes of Israel sustained in many Jews the hope of a complete restoration." [68]

**Rodanites.**

We may now take up again the narrative of De la Roncière. He continues; "At the time when Eldad the Danite was writing his narrative, an Arabian geographer, Ibn Khordadbeh,[69] confirmed in 817 the power of the commercial expansion of the Jewish people: 'The Jewish merchants called Rodanites speak Hebrew, Persian, Rumi, Arabic and the languages of the French, Spaniards and Slavs. From west to east over the whole world, travelling sometimes by land, sometimes by sea, they carry away eunuchs, slaves, women, young boys, beaver-skins, brocades, martin-skins, furs and swords, and they bring from China musk, aloes, camphor and cinnamon. Arrived from the country of the French at El Farama (Peluse) they entrust their merchandise to the backs of camels, come by land, to cross the Isthmus of Suez, to Kolzum, over the Red Sea to come out at El Djar and by way of Djeddah and Arabia they pass to the Indies. Some of them ascend the basin of the Euphrates. Others travel through Central Asia to come out by way of the land of China. Others embark in Spain for Souss el-Akca." [70]

**Slave Merchants.**

It may be remarked in passing that the testimony of the Arab chronicler is confirmed by a recent writer, Lewis Browne, who tells us: "Under the tolerant rule of the Mohammedans, the Jews began to prosper.

[67] Idem, p. 279.

[68] Idem, p. 279 f.

[69] Ibn Khordadbeh, *Kitab el Macalek wa't mamalik,* ed. De Goeje, p. 117; Nahum Slouschz, *Hébræo-Phœniciens et Judéo-Berbères,* Paris, 1908, p. 393, XIV des Archives Marocaines.

[70] Roncière, *Découvertes de l'Afrique au Moyen Age,* Vol. I, p. 103 f.

They who had been poor and bedraggled pedlars for centuries, now became wealthy and powerful traders. They travelled everywhere, from England to India, from Bohemia to Egypt. Their commonest merchandise in those days, beginning with the eighth century, was slaves. On every highroad and on every great river and sea, these Jewish traders were to be found with their gangs of shackled prisoners in convoy. Slave-dealing seems irredeemably vile and hateful to us to-day, but we must remember here again the standards have changed." [71] And then, as if in defense of his race, the writer adds: "And in the light of the customs of those times, the slave-traffickers were actually doing almost a moral act. They alone were keeping the conquering armies from slaughtering every one of their defeated foes after each battle." [72]

**Legends of the Sahara.**

After this digression let us once more return to M. De la Roncière. He thus concludes his quotation from Delafosse: "The uninterrupted chain which at the time of Saint Jerome [73] the Jewish colonies formed from Mauritania to the Indies, has lost, we shall see, only a few of its links." [74]

De la Roncière having thus propounded the theory of Delafosse, adds on his own account: "The Sahara remains impregnated with biblical legends, from the Hoggar where the natives claim to have inherited from the prophet Daniel the secret of finding lost objects by means of magic characters,[75] to Koukiya on the Niger, which furnished the Pharao of Egypt with magicians to engage in dispute with Moses,[76] all the way to the Fortunate Islands of the Ocean where the body of Solomon reposes 'in a wonderful castle.' This immense extent was settled by Philistines, emigrants from Palestine after the death of Goliath: 'Djalout, son of Dharis, son of Djana,' so the legend has christened him, passed for the father of Berbers or 'Zenatas of

[71] Browne, *Stranger than Fiction,* p. 196.
[72] Idem, p. 196.
[73] St. Jerome, *Epistola ad Dardanum,* 122.
[74] Roncière, l. c. Vol. I, p. 104.
[75] Edrisi, *Description de l'Afrique et de l'Espagne,* trad. Dozy et de Goeje, Leyde, 1866, p. 42.
[76] Es-Sadi, *Tarikh es-Soudan,* trad. O. Houdas, Paris, 1900, p. 6; Edrisi, l. c., p. 53. Note:—The Koukiya in question was not on the Niger as will be shown later.

Maghreb.'[77] And everywhere his pseudo-sons clash with the sons of David, as if the biblical duel had not come to an end.[78]

"If the Jews actually do not form more than an islet in Abyssinia where they have been the royalty since the tenth century, if the Falashas are not more than a handful in the mountains where the Blue Nile takes its rise,[79] their race is still largely represented in the Saharan oases. In the Tripolitan Djebel there exists a Hebrew dialect mixed with Aramean.[80] At Tougart, in an isolated district, live the Meghearyeh, Jews who of old became perverts to escape death, but who do not mingle with the Mussulmans and marry among themselves: 'their women converse among themselves in Hebrew, when they desire not to be understood.'[81] Numerous also at Ouargla,[82] the

**In the Oases.**

[77] Ibn Khordadbeh, *Le Livre des Routes et des Provinces,* Paris, 1865, p. 212.

[78] Note:—Henri Basset would ascribe to Islamic sources many of the legends connected with biblical characters still current in Northern Africa. In many other instances, however, he would trace them to the Judaism as professed by certain Berber tribes before the Arab conquest. In either case, he regards them merely as legends "imported from abroad." He finds most popular of all "Josue, son of Nun," who would appear "to have been the principal hero of the Berber Jews; his remembrance is found in many places especially along the sea-coast. They show his sepulchre to the east of Nemours. . . . His father Nun is also well known; it is especially the Capes that are consecrated to him, not only along the shores of the Mediterranean—thus a little cape situated just in front of the tomb of Josue; so also Cape Noun, near Ceuta—but further along those of the Atlantic to extreme Southern Morocco, in distinctively Berber country. Without doubt, the connection between the cult of Josue and that of the fish appear really intimate; but it is not impossible that Nun, whose name signifies fish in Canaan as well as in Hebrew, has profited by this happy similarity of sound to have consecrated to him a certain number of Capes where the Phœnicians had established fisheries."—Henri Basset, *Essai sur la Littérature des Berbères,* Alger, 1920, p. 359 f. Of the legends concerning Solomon, the same author writes: "Solomon himself, Sidna Sliman, better known as master of the Jinns than as king of Israel, under which title he is universally celebrated, is far from enjoying in Berber countries the same popularity as in Arab lands."—l. c., p. 260. As regards the Goliath story, Abou-l-Hasan 'Ali el-Djaznai thus recounts it. "The causes of the establishment of the Berbers in Morocco, when they came from Palestine, are as follows: When the king of the Berbers, Djalout (Goliath) was killed by Dawoud (David) . . . the Berbers migrated towards Morocco."—Cfr. Abou-l-Hasan 'Ali el-Djaznai, *Zahrat el-As,* trad. Alfred Bel, Alger, 1923, p. 23. This passage according to Bel "is copied almost verbatim from Ibn 'Abd el Hakem."—l. c., p. 24, Note.

[79] C. Conti Rossini, *Notice sur les Manuscrits Éthiopiens de la collection d'Abbadie,* Paris, 1914, p. 28.

[80] Slouschz, *Un Voyage d'Études Juives en Afrique.*

[81] D'Avezac, *Études de Géographie Critique sur une Partie de l'Afrique Septentrionale,* Paris, 1836.

[82] Slouschz, *Hébræo-Phœniciens,* p. 437.

Jews multiply at Tagaost in the Souas,[83] at Auguelmin in Oued-Noun: [84] in Mauritanian Adrar they finance as of old the Berber caravans for Tombouctoo.[85]

"At Oualata, they were jewellers and goldsmiths. They are still in Tifilelt,[86] as they were from a remote period.[87] Swarming among the Mauritanian tribes they are blacksmiths, armourers, saddlers and jewellers, forming a special caste, the Mallemine: the legends of the Tagant make of them descendants of Jewish prisoners of war, especially distributed by the Prophet among his tribes, to there ply their trades.[88]

"The Jews, El-Bekri [89] tells us, at Sidjilmassa made a profession of masonry. Now by the side of the immense blocks which mark Medinet el-Hamra the site of the ancient capital of Tifilelt, a mass of flutings on the solid walls of brick, a well devised plan from floor to arch, testify to the ability of the masons,[90] pupils no doubt of the Romans. At Touat, they pay like honor to the irrigation works, the masonry of which still exists.

**On the Niger.**

"Lately, on the banks of the Niger, M. Bonnel de Mézières discovered the remains of a colony of Beni-Israel, who had sunk hundreds of wells for the irrigation of their gardens. These wells were preserved just as several centuries before the negro chronicler of Gao describes them, with their walls constructed of ferrigenous stones and coated over with the butter of aloes, which the action of a very hot fire had rendered as durable as cast iron.[91]

"If Ghana was a capital for the Jews, its ruins some day will yield up the secret. That is to say, the interest that the excavations of a city dead for seven centuries will present." [92]

[83] Marmol, *L'Afrique,* Paris, 1667, Vol. II, p. 41.
[84] Camille Douis, *Voyage dans le Sahara Occidental,* Rouen, 1888, p. 33.
[85] A. Colas, *Renseignements Géographiques sur l'Afrique Centrale et Occidentale,* Alger, 1880, p. 11.
[86] M. W. Harris, *Le Tafilelt,* pub. Le Comité de Maroc, 1909, p. 43; 62.
[87] *Leo Africanus,* ed. C. Schefer, Vol. III, p. 218.
[88] Vanelsche, *La Mauritanie—La Géographie,* March, 1923, p. 352.
[89] El-Bekri, *Description de l'Afrique Septentrionale,* trad. de Slane, Paris, 1859, p. 400.
[90] Harris, *La Tafilelt,* p. 43.
[91] Bonnel de Mézières, *Reconnaissance à Tendirma et dans le Région de Fati.—Bulletin de la Section de Géographie,* XXIX (1914), p. 128. Cfr. also reference in note 94 infra.
[92] Roncière, l. c., Vol. I, p. 105 f.

**Casserly's Comment.**

Thus far we have been quoting De la Roncière's written expression of his views. Lt. Col. Casserly's comment on the same, here seems timely. He says: "Before quitting the subject of the Sahara, I must record two interesting facts concerning it. The first is that a French Savant, M. de la Roncière, of the Bibliothéque Nationale, has recently made the remarkable discovery by means of reasearches in Genoa and elsewhere that Timbuctoo and the principal oases of the Sahara were known to and visited by Europeans in the Middle Ages. From the thirteenth to the sixteenth century commercial relations were established with the great centres of the Niger and of the Sudan. Spanish merchants and Italian artists were acquainted with the Sahara routes that were thought to have first been discovered by nineteenth century explorers. Andalusian architects built, and Genoese painters adorned, palaces on the banks of the Niger, palaces that have long disappeared, but of which the sites and foundations have been traced. M. de la Roncière has shown me maps made in those far-away centuries that plainly indicate the Hoggar, Adrar and other spots in the Sahara, the discovery of which in the nineteenth century was hailed as a great triumph of modern exploration." [93]

[93] Casserly, *Africa To-Day,* p. 255 f. Note:—In his latest volume, De la Roncière writes: "There are at the end of the Sahara, dead towns whose past was glorious. Through excavations, the foundations of one of them have been traced. May we not now look for a solution of the mystery of these ruins in stone, which are most likely the remains of Ghana, that beautiful town where they had, according to the Geographer Idrisi, sculptures and paintings? Was that town built by the Jews—the masons of the desert—as would seem to be indicated by the likeness of its ruins with those of Tindirma, near the Niger, attributed to-day also to the Children of Israel? Was this their capital? (There reigned there a certain number of 'white emperors' before the occupation of Sahara by Islam.) Was this a source of a Jewish migration of which certain elements have infiltrated into the negro population of the south? The problem offers as much breadth as complexity. . . . The solution of the problem will depend on the excavations which the governor of the French Soudan . . . has promised to undertake at Koumbi."—*La Découverte de l'Afrique au Moyen Age,* Vol. III (Cairo, 1927), p. ii f. Further, under date of May 25, 1926, M. de la Roncière wrote to me from Paris that he is preparing a volume to be entitled, "Has there been a Jewish Empire in the Sahara?" and he adds: "It will not see the light of day until the Governor of the French Sudan, M. Tarrason de Fougères, has caused excavations to be made at Koumbi Fhana, one hundred and twenty-five kilometers from Oualata, among the ruins of a mysterious city destroyed in 1240, where there were sculptures and paintings in the twelfth century." He also states: "I am now actually collecting all the documents which allow me to follow step by step the exodus of the Jews to the South and their constructions." While awaiting, then, the promised study

**Modern Researches.**

Writing in 1923, after devoting five or six months every year for ten years to scientific researches in this part of Africa, Bonnel de Mézières definitely "placed the Empire of Ghana in the region west of Néma, that is to say, to the north of Bakhounou and south of Aoukar," and determined that its capital was located at Koumbi or Settah.[94] The following year, 1924, Maurice Delafosse suggested that the word Ghana was not in reality the name of the ancient capital which he places at Koumbi, but rather " a title borne by the sovereign of the country," and adds: "I believe also that the founders of this state were of white origin and probably Semitic, but that by intercourse with women among their subjects of black race, they gave rise to descendants of greater and greater ethnic mixture, who ended by constituting the Sarakollé family, of which the actual representatives still bear the name, universally regarded as noble, of Sissé." [95]

**Arabic Records.**

Before leaving Ghana, however, reference should be made to one or two writers of the Middle Agas who were familiar with the history of the Sudanese Jews. Thus an Arabic manuscript of the twelfth century, the author of which is usually referred to as Edrisi, speaking of Lamlam, whence slaves were dragged into captivity by the inhabitants of Ghana, Tacour, etc. states that there were only two towns in this district which he places to the south of the kingdom of Ghana, and adds: "According to what the people of this country report, the inhabitants are Jews, but for the most part they are plunged in impiety and ignorance. When they have reached the age of puberty they brand the countenance or at least the temples with fire. This is with marks that serve to identify them. All the dwellings in their countries are built on the banks of a river which flows into the Nile." [96]

of M. de la Roncière, whose work always bears such a scholarly impress, we must be satisfied to let the matter rest here.

[94] Bonnel de Mézières, *Recherche de l'Emplacement de Ghana.—Mémoires présentés par Divers Savants à l'Académie des Inscriptions et Belles-Lettres de l'Institut de France,* Paris, Tome XIII (1923), p. 264.

[95] Maurice Delafosse, *Le Gana et, le Mali et l'Emplacement de leurs Capitales.—Bulletin du Comité d'Études Historiques et Scientifiques de l'Afrique Occidentale Français,* Tome IX (1924), No. 3.

[96] Edrisi, *Description de l'Afrique et de l'Espagne,* p. 4. Note:—As we shall see later, it was the common belief of the time that the Niger, which is clearly the River referred to in the present passage, actually formed an upper reach of the Nile.

Referring to Ghana as the most populous and the leading commercial city in Negro Land, the same author asserts that its king "possesses on the banks of the Nile (Niger) a solidly constructed castle, well fortified, and the interior of which is decorated with sculptures and paintings, and the windows glassed: this castle was built in the year 510 of the Hegira (1116 of the Christian era)." [97]

Hadji el-Eghwaati, writing in 1242, adds this testimony. "There is a race of people in Tuggurt called Medjehariah, who occupy one separate quarter of the town. They were Jews in former times, but to escape death, with which they were menaced by the natives, they made profession of Islam, and are now constant readers of the Koran, which they commit to memory. They are still distinguished by the complexion peculiar to the Jews; and their houses, like those of that nation, emit an offensive smell. They do not intermarry with the Arabs; and it rarely happens that an Arab takes a wife from among the Medjehariah. The governor of Tuggurt selects, from among these people, his scribes and book-keepers; but they are never admitted to the dignity of Cadhi, or Imam. They have mosques in their quarter of the town, and they pray at the stated hours, except on the day of djemat (Friday), which they do not observe as a sabbath. They possess great wealth. Their women appear in the market-places veiled, and converse in Hebrew among themselves, when they wish not to be understood." [98]

**Jews of the Sahara.**

According to Nahum Slouschz: "The tradition of the Jewish trader in the Sahara stretches back to biblical times." [99] And: "It is not at all surprising to encounter in every part of the desert traces—and even survivals—of a primitive Judaism which at one time played an important rôle in the whole region of the Sahara from Senegal to the very border of Somaliland." [100] He adds: "For many years

[97] Idem, p. 7.

[98] Hadji Ebn-ed-din el-Eghwaati, *Notes of a Journey into the Interior of Northern Africa,* trans. W. B. Hodgson, London, 1831, p. 21 f.

[99] Slouschz, *Travels in North Africa,* p. 104.

[100] Idem. p. 344. Note:—The following news item which appeared in the New York *Evening World* for November 15, 1928, p. 23, is suggestive of the general interest manifested in the whole question of the Jews of the Sahara. The article, which is signed by Pierre Van Paassen, Staff Correspondent of the *Evening World,* and is dated Paris, November 7, runs as follows. "A flourishing and tranquil Jewish community, numbering several thousand souls, in the

the author of this book has been gathering material for a history of the Jewish migrations into the Sahara and the Sudan. One part of the work is already done, the establishing of the authenticity of these migrations. The materials at his disposal will clear up many problems of the history of the Jews during the Middle Ages. To the writings of the Arabs and the oral traditions of the country he can now add the archaeological evidence furnished by

heart of the African desert, surrounded on all sides by savages and semi-civilized Moor and Berber tribes, is the discovery of M. René Leblond, French consul at Akka in Southern Morocco. M. Leblond descended on the outskirts of the Jewish settlement when his plane, forming part of a map-making expedition in the Sahara desert, strayed from its companions, developed engine trouble and was forced to come to earth. The Jews informed him that their settlement bore the name of Alouna and that he was at that point a ten-day journey by caravan from the proverbially inattainable Timbuctoo. . . . He goes on to say in his report, registered with the Geographical Society of France, that his surprise was more than agreeable when upon reaching terra firma, the folks surrounded his crippled airplane and by all manner of signs and tokens indicated that he was a welcome visitor and an honored guest. M. Leblond was taken to the home of the oldest inhabitant, a venerable patriarch, who bade him welcome with ancient ceremonial, proceeding even to wash his feet in the traditional Hebrew fashion, as mentioned frequently in the Scriptures. He was given the best room in the lowly dwelling and was invited to rest and eat before anyone was permitted to enter into conversation with him. The Jews spoke an Arabic dialect and some of the ancient ones had a smattering of French, archaic and mixed with Moroccan words. The first thing they told M. Leblond was that they considered themselves French subjects and proteges. They were hazy as to the name of the ruling monarch in France, reports the consul, but reports of a gigantic war had penetrated to them by way of the Berbers from South Morocco. The last white man they had seen, according to the testimony of the oldest inhabitants, had been a visitor, an explorer in 1866. Since that day no traveler from Europe had been in their midst. By dint of diligent questioning M. Leblond learned that the Jews hailed from North Morocco, but that their fathers, under pressure of persecution had left the Mediterranean shores many years ago. The intention of the fathers had been to travel 'by way of Egypt' to Palestine and settle there. Hostile tribes, disease, hunger, poverty, and other vicissitudes had interfered with the ancestral project of reaching the Promised Land, and they had remained in the desert. But the Jews assured him that they never had abandoned hope altogether of continuing their interrupted migration some day and of ultimately residing in the land 'that flows with milk and honey.' Although the Jews spoke Arabic, they used Hebrew lettering in their script. Their ritual service had undergone not the slightest modification, they assured the Consul, and their brethren in Israel would immediately recognize them by the ancient usages kept in honor amongst them. . . . M. Leblond's report states further that the Jews were courteous and highly civilized. Their features were bronzed to a degree that they might almost be taken for colored people. They wore white, flowing garments, lined with wool in the manner of mountain Berbers in the Atlas region. Most of the men were heavily bearded and spend their days between sheep herding, camel raising and the study of ancient Hebraic books that they had carried with them. There were several Talmudic commentators amongst them. M. Leblond reports that he was able to repair his plane after three days' sojourn in the Jewish settlement and that he proposes to go back to the Jews within a few weeks."

the ruins of ancient Jewish cities in the Sahara and the Sudan, and the documentary evidence of Hebrew inscriptions like those of Tuat which date from the thirteenth and the fourteenth centuries."[101] In particular, Slouschz states: "Two groups of the desert still retain their Jewish consciousness: the Mehajer, a settled population of Jewish origin, who are found at Tugurt and at Tuat, and the Daggatunes, a powerful tribe of Islamized Bedouins who camp on the route from Timbuctoo to the Sudan."[102] And further: "First of these groups of oases is the archipelago of Tafilelt, to which I have tried in vain to penetrate. . . . In this country there once flourished the great city of Sijilmasa, with a rabbinical college which was illustrious from the tenth century onwards."[103]

**In Salah.**

Comte René le More, passing through In Salah, towards the end of November, 1910, writes: "According to tradition, In Salah was founded by a Jewish colony that had migrated after the destruction of the Temple at Jerusalem. Its inhabitants dwelt quietly and under cover of the struggle not unlike persons shipwrecked in the desert, up to the time when the Moors were driven from Spain. At this period the Mussulmans, who heretofore had tolerated this Jewish population, now massacred them almost to a man. The town lost its importance, the more so as the massacre coincided with the subsidence of the springs; as happened in many other parts of the desert, where some entirely disappeared."[104]

**Mohammed and the Jews.**

The relations that had existed between the Mohammedans and the Jews had for the most part been friendly, after the initial hatred of the Prophet had worn itself out. In this connection, we are told by Samuel M. Zwemer, "In the seventh year of the Hegira (629 A. D.) Mohammed assembled a force of sixteen hundred warriors and marched against the Jewish strongholds at Khaibar; the Jews were subjugated or slain, and there was much booty, including a new wife for the prophet."[105] About two years previously he had conducted an expedition against the Jews of Bni Koraiza, when

[101] Slouschz, *Travels in North Africa,* p. 345.
[102] Idem, p. 346.
[103] Idem, p. 347.
[104] Comte René le More, *D'Alger à Tombouctou,* Paris, 1913, p. 34.
[105] Samuel M. Zwemer, *The Moslem World,* Philadelphia, 1908, p. 16.

seven hundred captives were slain.[106] In the sixth year of the Hegira also there had been "expeditions against the Jews and idolaters." [107] The Prophet's earliest hostilities then, would seem to have been against the Jews and idolaters.

**Personal Animosity.**

Lewis Browne thus explains this condition of affairs: "When Mohammed fled to Medina—it was the year 622—one of his dearest desires was to make followers of the Jews there. . . . The Jews showed some interest at first in the movement, for Mohammed claimed he had been sent by their God, and they thought he might be the Messiah. . . . But when they came to know Mohammed better and found out how ignorant he was, and how much fonder he seemed of pretty women than of what the Jews considered godly ways, they refused to have anything more to do with him. Their minstrels ridiculed him in sarcastic poems, and tried to make him the laughing-stock of Medina. The result was that as soon as enough Arabs had gathered under his banner Mohammed turned on the Jews and butchered them without mercy. He had made up his mind that the stubborn 'People of the Book' would not possibly be converted, and after decimating their ranks, he turned back to the more promising task of converting the rest of his brethren." [108]

**Forbearance of Islam.**

With the death of the prophet, however, his personal animosity against the Jews no longer influenced the hordes of Islamism, as Browne thus makes clear: "Early in the eighth century, however, the dawn of a new day began to break. As the Mohammedans drove the armies of Persia and the Christian nations before them, the Jews began slowly to lift themselves out of the dust. For the Mohammedans were now strangely tolerant of the Jews. Mohammed himself had long been dead, and with him had died his chagrin because the 'People of the Book' would not accept the Koran. His successors only knew the Jews as a people who by race and religion were somewhat like themselves. Perhaps they realized also that without the Jews to serve as scouts, they themselves would have been almost helpless. For they could trust the Jew alone to shew

[106] Idem, p. 15.
[107] Idem, p. 15.
[108] Browne, *Stranger than Fiction*, p. 190.

them the way about the vast world beyond the Desert. The Jews had travelled everywhere, and seemed to know every language. Without their aid the Arab invaders would have utterly lost their bearings as they swept on through the great countries to the right on the east, and to the left in the Mediterranean basin." [109]

Moreover, the vision of World Conquest never entered the Prophet's mind. His view was restricted by his immediate surroundings. For, as William Muir well remarks, "The command to fight angainst Jews, Christians and Idolaters . . . had reference to Arabia alone. . . . The Prophet's dying legacy was to the same effect:—'See,' said he, 'that there be but this one faith throughout Arabia.' " [110]

**Islamized North Africa.**

With the advent then, of Mohammedanism in North Africa, the progress and development of the Jews, for the time at least, was not impeded, and they extended their commercial enterprises to every part of the Sudan. E. F. Gautier, who has made exhaustive studies of this part of Africa, is most categorical in his statement: "The Jews of Figuig had certainly of old relations with the Soudan: they are hideous brutes, hairy, half-naked, fierce in countenance and as cunning as a Kabyle dog; they do not in the least resemble Israelitish merchants, and nevertheless that is what they are; they manufacture with what they call the 'gold of the Soudan' trinkets which very quickly become covered with verdigris." [111]

**"Time of the Jews."**

Again he says: "At Touat, when they recall the past, the expression 'the time of the Jews' recurs incessantly. It is the old order of things destroyed by El-Merili, of which the memory is kept alive after four hundred years; and this bears testimony to the violence of the upheaval.

"It is not easy to know in what precise measures this community was Jewish. It has left as monuments funeral inscriptions; one very beautiful inscription in Hebrew characters that are deep and clear, tells us that the lady Monispa is dead in bed, in the year of the creation of the world 5086 (1329 of our era).

"And it goes without saying that, to decipher it, it was necessary to address oneself to the Institute of France, and not to the

[109] Browne, *Stranger than Fiction*, p. 195.

[110] William Muir, *The Caliphate: Its Rise, Decline and Fall*, Edinburgh, 1924, p. 42.

[111] E. F. Gautier, *La Conquête du Sahara*, Paris, 1925, p. 46.

local lights. The time is distant when the Touat had erudite Rabbis and a school of Hebraists.

"Tamentit, an oasis actually in Touat, for a certainty was in the thirteenth and fourteenth centuries an industrial and commercial metropolis of the desert, a great legendary name, something like Timbuktu. The population was Jewish, at least as regards the dominant aristocracy.

"But it was not merely urban, mercantile and usurious. It must have been more or less rural, autonomous, deep-rooted in the soil. In any case at Gourara and in Northern Touat, the beautiful irrigation works, the pride of the oases, with their subterranean aqueducts and artesian wells, through their traditions pay honor to the Jews.

"It also seems to me, that the reversion of paganism and fetishism was maintained at Touat. Even to-day Tamentit has a black stone which has all the appearance of a fallen god, etc." [112]

**Desolation.**

Observing that: "Ancient Tamentit, with its synagogues, gave way in the storm; over its ruins, on certain feasts, even to-day the women go to weep," Gauntier makes the motive not piety, but a forlorn hope that the dead will disclose the secret of the hidden treasure.[113]

The massacre of the Jews at Tuat took place in 1492, the very year that the Moors were driven out of Granada.[114] And the previous influence of this Jewish people, especially in the North of Africa, may explain the reason why the Dominicans, when they undertook Mission work in Africa in the thirteenth century, required of their missionaries a knowledge of Hebrew as well as Arabic.[115] Another possible explanation of this might also be that while Ghana itself was finally destroyed in 1240,[116] the remnants of the Jewish empire was still scattered throughout the Sudan.

**Nda Family.**

Lieutenant Desplagnes asserts that when the Agni and Ashanti, whom he considers as branches

[112] Gautier, l. c., p. 135 f.
[113] Gautier, l. c., p. 138.
[114] Idem, p. 141.
[115] Reichert, *Monumenta Ordinis Fratrum Praedicatorum Historica,* Louvain, 1896, Vol. I, p. 263.
[116] Roncière, *Découverte de l'Afrique,* Vol. I, p. 86.

of the same tribe, sprung from the Nda family, reached approximately their present habitat in the twelfth century, they brought with them the germs of the Mediterranean civilization that they had imbibed during the long centuries of the tribal development through contact with the peoples of the recurrent migrations from the North.[117]

According to his theory, a race of pygmies constituted the initial population of West Africa. On these descended from the North and East tribes of good physique and stature. Among these early arrivals he numbers the Nda. Then began the constant intermingling of tribal families that has developed in West Africa such an involved ethnic complex as almost to defy analysis.

**Northern Influx.**

With the invasion of what Desplagnes calls the Red People from Carthage and its vicinity in the Roman period, and the arrival, as we shall see, of a White Race by way of Morocco early in the Christian era,[118] this intermixing was further accentuated.[119]

According to Desplagnes, too, it was the tributary tribes of the Carthaginians who introduced the religious ideas of the Sudan. During the Roman Conquest most of these tribes were driven into the desert, and found their way to the region of the Niger, where they mingled with the earlier tribes, including the Nda.[120]

Desplagnes also shows a constant influx of Egyptian and Asiatic influences, even preceding the Roman conquest of Carthage, that infiltrated throughout the Sudan,[121] and left a lasting impress.

**Jew or Christian?**

To our way of thinking then, with the arrival by way of Morocco of the Whites, who were presumably for the most part Jews, and who founded Ghana early in the Christian era, a great Jewish Empire was built up, as we have seen,[122] that dominated the country west of Lake Chad for many centuries. Desplagnes does not seem to recognize this Jewish element in the community. For, quoting from an

[117] Desplagnes, *Le Plateau Centrale Nigérien,* p. 135.
[118] Cfr. p. 251.
[119] Desplagnes, l. c., p. 105 ff.
[120] Idem, p. 113.
[121] Idem, p. 109 ff.
[122] Cfr. p. 228 ff.

Arabic Manuscript [123] in the National Library of Paris,[124] he says: "The inhabitants of the Soudan, of which Ghana was the capital, have professed the Christian religion in part up to the year 469 of the Hegira, 1076–1077, at which time they became converted to Islamism." [125] The original observer probably confused Judaism with Christianity.

However, here again we must be on our guard not to draw conclusions too quickly, as there are strong indications that after the destruction of the Church in North Africa, there was a considerable migration of Christians to the interior across the desert. Thus Francis Rennell Rodd reports of the Tuaregs: "The people are also given at times to using camel bells despite the injunction of the Prophet, who denounced it as an object associated with Christianity," [126] and, "Even so remote a part of Africa as Bornu was known to have been subjected to the influence of Coptic Christianity from the Nile." [127]

Furthermore, we are told by Mockler-Ferryman: "Borgu, the western boundary state of Nigeria, is a pagan kingdom situated almost entirely on the right bank of the Kwora Niger, and is known also by the name of Barida; in fact, Barida is the name by which the country and its people are always locally spoken of. Little is known of its early history, though native report says that at some period, many centuries ago, emigrants from the Barbary States settled in the country, and gave it its name by which it is still known. These Berber settlers, it is said, were driven out of Northern Africa by the Mohammedan conquerors, and brought with them their own religion, which appears to have contained some of the doctrines of Christianity. By their Mohammedan neighbours the Baridas, have, however, always been considered pagans, though they themselves assert that their belief is in one 'Kisra, a Jew, who gave his life for the sins of mankind.' Whatever they may affirm, there is little doubt that at the present day they are no better than pagans, the only trace that remains of their belief being an annual festival at which are

[123] Written by Abou-Abdallah-ez-Zohri. Cfr. *Tarikh es-Soudan,* Vol. II, p. 42. Note 1.

[124] *Manuscrit Arabe de la Bibliothèque Nationale,* n. 1873, f. 5, line 13.

[125] Desplagnes, l. c., p. 114.

[126] Rodd, *People of the Veil,* p. 293.

[127] Idem, p. 294.

commemorated certain events in the life of Kisra, intermingled with strange heathen rites." [128]

**Kisra.**

C. K. Meek, who declares: "There is nothing to connect Kisra with Christ," maintains: "The traditional date of the arrival of the 'Kisra kings in Borgu was apparently *circa* A. D. 1480." [129]

P. Amaury Talbot, on the contrary, is of the opinion that: "A wave of Christianity reached the Western Sudan about this time (seventh century A. D.) perhaps in connection with the expulsion of the Persians from Egypt, led by semi-white men from Nubia, who probably got their Christianity direct from Byzantium. According to some accounts, their principal leader was a Persian named Kisra, who first sought refuge at Bagada in Nubia (which one legend makes the starting point of the founder of the Hausa states) and later headed a migration to the west. The word Kisra is by some taken to be Christ, by others to be the mutilation of a Persian word such as Kosraf, a title given to kings." [130]

Ibn Khaldoun makes Kisra identical with the Persian Chosroes [131] while still others go so far as to derive the word from the Indian Krishna, making the migration from the East not of Christian but of Hindoo origin. In connection with Krishna, Sir J. G. Frazer relates: "A Hindoo sect, which has many representatives in Bombay and central India, holds that its spiritual chiefs or Maharajas, as they are called, are representatives or even incarnations on earth of the god Krishna. . . . And as Krishna looks down from heaven with most favour on such as minister to the wants of his successors or vicars on earth, a peculiar rite called Self-devotion has been instituted, whereby his faithful worshippers make over their bodies, their souls, and what is perhaps still more important, their worldy substance to his adorable incarnations." [132]

**Evidence of Christianity.**

But even previous to the Arab invasion of Egypt, Flinders Petrie finds evidence of a strong wave of influence that swept from Egypt to the Niger

[128] Mockler-Ferryman, *British Nigeria*, p. 144 f.
[129] Meek, *Northern Tribes of Nigeria*, Vol. I, p. 72.
[130] Talbot, *Peoples of Southern Nigeria*, Vol. I, p. 27.
[131] Ibn Khaldoun, *History of Yaman*, trans. Henry Cassels Kay, London, 1892, p. 138.
[132] James George Frazer, *The Golden Bough*, Vol. I, p. 406.

"due to the spread of Christianity, especially under the pious sway of Justinian." In his opinion, "This is seen perpetuated in the interwoven patterns found at Benin and other Nigerian centres."[133]

**Fulani.**

We come now to a question that is closely linked with that of the Jews of the Sahara, namely the origin of a race that has given ethnologists no end of trouble. De la Roncière writes: "For some time a problem has engaged the attention of ethnographers.

**Theories of Origin.**

"The Peuls, Pouls, Foulahs, Foulbe or Foutes, scattered to-day from Senegambia to Darfur, dark-complexioned, red, bronzed, copper-colored, recalling the warm tones of certain Egyptian types, the oval face, aquiline nose, the smooth hair, they stand out above the surrounding negroes. This contrast has given rise to the most extreme hypotheses.[134] Has it not been said that by their general character, by their traditions, by their language, by their method of counting, they may be considered as a branch of the Melasian races? Java is the point of the archipelago with which they present the closest affinity. Their first station in Eastern Africa seems to have been the Isle of Meroe, near Darfur, which took from them its name. They provided for themselves in the matter of currency with cowries or shell of Maldives, which originally came to them by the caravans of Egypt.[135]

"Others see in the Peuls the Leucoaethiopians or White Ethiopians whom Pliny placed to the south of the Getulians of Mauritania, the Pyrriaethiopians of Ptolemy. The latest data of anthropology and linguistics, in connecting them with the Semite

[133] *Ancient Egypt,* Part III of 1914, p. 169. Note:—It is just possible, too, that we may have a vestige of Christianity in what D. Amaury Talbot reports from Southern Nigeria. Eka Abassi (Mother of God), she says, is regarded as "the mother not alone of the Thunder God, Obumo, whom we had hitherto been assured was the head of the whole Ibibio pantheon, but also of all created things."—*Woman's Mysteries of a Primitive People,* p. 8 f.

[134] Note:—As an extreme view, Maurice Abadie in his turn cites a writer who would connect the Peuls of Africa with the Annamites, as well as with the Bretons of France, and who would further trace the settlement of Canada back to the Foulbe from the African kingdom of Ghana.—Cfr. Maurice Abadie, *La Colonie du Niger,* Paris, 1927, p. 57.

[135] Note:—According to Wilson D. Wallis, the cowries of West Africa which served so long as a medium of Exchange, were "introduced from the east coast, the shell fish from which they are made not being found on the west coast."—Wallis, *An Introduction to Anthropology,* p. 182.

Races, makes them Jewish immigrants who came from Palestine to the Soudan by way of Egypt." [136]

Louis Tauxier makes Foulbe the plural form of a singular that is variously spelt.[137] So that if we speak of Peuls, Fulani or Foulbe, we have reference to one and the same people.

Richard Jobson, who was trading along the Gambia River during 1620–1621, speaks of the wandering Fulbie as follows: "These are called Fulbies being a tawny people, and have a resemblance right unto those we call Egiptians: Their women amongst them are streight, upright, and excellently well bodied, having very good features, with a long blacke haire much more loose than the blacke women have, wherewith they attire themselves very neatly, but in their apparell they goe clothed and weare the same habite, the blacke women do; the men are not in their kinds, so generally handsome, as the women are, which may be imputed to their course of lives, whereof I proceede to tell you; Their profession in keeping of cattle, some goats they have, but the heards they tend are beefes, whereof they are abundantly stored; etc." [138]

Herbert C. Hall remarks of the Fulani men that as they pass middle age, "Their aspect becomes wonderfully Jewish and venerable, quite bearing out the idea that they were originally of that race." [139]

Doctor Lasnet, who classifies the Foulbe as Semites,[140] would connect them with the Fellahs of Egypt. He is one of those who regard them as the White Ethiopians, the Leucoaethiopians of Pliny, and would identify their migration with the rebellion of the soldiers in the time of Psammeticus, when the military garrisons started for the Upper Nile,[141] as will be noted in the following chapter. He furthed considers the Peul dialect as being related to the Semitic languages but greatly modified by the Arabic and the negro environment.[142]

Doctor Machat in turn would trace the Foulbe back to the

[136] Roncière, *Découverte de l'Afrique au Moyen Age,* Vol. I, p. 102.

[137] Louis Tauxier, *Le Noir du Soudan,* Paris, 1912, p. 609.

[138] Jobson, *The Golden Trade,* Chapter, "Wandering Fulbie."

[139] Herbert C. Hall, *Barrack and Bush in Northern Nigeria,* London, 1923, p. 9.

[140] Lasnet, *Une Mission au Sénégal,* Paris, 1900, p. 3.

[141] Idem, p. 37.

[142] Idem, p. 40.

Middle Nile, and he quotes the linguist Müller, as finding the inhabitants of Kordofan speaking a language very similar to the "foulfoulde" of the Foulbe.[143]

**Morel's Opinion.**

Edmond D. Morel, in his *Affairs of West Africa* devotes a most interesting chapter to the "Origin of the Fulani." He says: "Their own legend; their complexion and structure; their mental development and physical characteristics, all point emphatically to the East as the cradle of the Fulani race." [144] Morel entirely disagrees with M. Felix Dubois who would have them driven from Adrar, which is located north of the Senegal, by the Moors who had been expelled from Spain.[145]

In confirmation of his own view, Morel cites the results of Doctor Verneau's study of five skulls [146] of Fulani chiefs from Futa-Jallon, wherein he identifies them as being of the same type as the ancient Egyptians.[147] Doctor Blyden, too, is quoted as saying: "On entering a Fulah town the first thing which strikes a stranger is the Caucasian cast of features, especially among the older people; yet every now and then, in the children of the parents having all the physical traits of the Semitic family, there recurs the inextinguishable Negro physiognomy." The author explains this last observation by interrelations with the negresses.[148]

Morel is also of the opinion that "Fulfulde cannot as yet be definitely classed among the languages, but, as far as our knowledge extends, it has Semitic antecedents." [149]

After the overthrow of the Hyksos shepherds in Egypt, he conceives that many of them must have found their way into the interior of Africa by way of Cyrenaica,[150] and further remarks: "The Hebraic flavour—if one may put it so—which seems to permeate many of the Fulani customs, especially among the less contaminated elements of the race, has been recorded by careful observers. A friend, an officer in the employ of the Northern Nigerian administration, who was intimately acquainted with the

143 J. Machat, *Les Rivières de Sud et le Fouta-Diallon,* Paris, 1906, p. 267 ff.
144 Edmond D. Morel, *Affairs of West Africa,* London, 1902, p. 136.
145 Idem, p. 139 f.
146 *L'Anthropologie,* Tome X, No. 6.
147 Morel, l. c., p. 138 f.
148 Morel, l. c., p. 140.
149 Idem, p. 140.
150 Idem, p. 144.

Fulani, whose language he spoke, and who possessed considerable erudition, had prepared a number of notes for me on the subject, which, unfortunately, I never received, owing to his death while serving in Africa. One custom which had especially impressed him among the pure Fulani was the habit of setting aside the first-born. He found that the Fulani woman of unmixed blood in the Binue region never suckled her firstborn, but consigned it to the care of friends, and completely disinterested herself from its future career, while bestowing upon the second child, and subsequent children, the usual motherly solicitude. He connected this singular custom with a distorted rendering of the punishment visited upon the Egyptians in the time of the Captivity." [151]

Morel goes on to state: "The lecture delivered in 1886 by Captain de Guiraudon (who published a Fulfulde manual, and who resided for several years in the Fulani country in Senegambia) before the seventh Congress of Orientalists contains some interesting references to the subject under discussion. In the course of his relations with the Fulani, De Guiraudon was particularly struck by their peculiar knowledge of Jewish history. So familiarly did they speak of the chief Hebrew personalities of the Old Testament, and so well posted were they with the principal events related in it, that they could not, argued De Guiraudon, have acquired their knowledge merely through Arabic sources. They referred to those times as though dealing with their own national records. Moses and Abraham might have been individuals of the same race as themselves. 'In their oral legends Moses plays a very important part, and although certain passages of the Scriptures are transformed or rather assimilated, they have so intense a Biblical and Hebraic tone as to exclude all Arabic influence.' De Guiraudon noted, however, that their Israelitish chronicles ceased after Solomon. 'What they knew of the miracles of our Saviour was so distorted and erroneous as to prove that the New Testament had reached them from afar, in a vague and fragmentary condition.' De Guiraudon's conclusions are best given in his own words. 'It would seem as if the Puls (Fulani), if they themselves did not profess the Jewish faith, which I would rather be disposed to affirm than deny, were at least in permanent contact with the Jewish people in remote times, and that, influenced at one

[151] Idem, p. 148.

time or another by the Israelites, they received Old Testament legends directly from them.' "[152]

Morel concludes that the Fulani "are the lineal descendants of the Hyksos, having migrated westward with the overthrow of the Shepherd conquerors. Their customs bear record of their progenitors having been influenced both by the cult of ancient Egypt and by the Israelites, whose presence in the Nile Delta was contemporaneous with Hyksos rule. Their presence in West Africa dates back at least 2500 years."[153]

**Other Explanations.**

General Barrows, the President Emeritus of the University of California, in a little volume entitled *Berbers and Blacks,* recently published the record of his stay in the Sudan. Of the Peuls he remarks: "Some writers connect this people with the ancient Egyptians, but they are probably one of the mixtures of Berbers and Blacks."[154]

However, Maurice Abadie, another late writer on the subject, is quite positive in his views, when he asserts: "Without hesitation I side with those who ascribe a Semitic origin to the Peuls. . . . The Semitic origin of the Peuls of the Niger it seems to me cannot be questioned.

"As a result of what disturbances and by what route have these Jews come from Palestine to the Soudan?

"One knows in rough outline the history of the Israelitic migration into Egypt, at the time of Joseph, and the return to Sinai with Moses, movements which were undoubtedly connected with the invasion and exodus of the Hyksos. It is probable that many of the Jews who remained in Egypt were driven towards Ethiopia and especially towards Cyrenaica where they intermingled more or less with the Berbers. These Jews of Cyrenaica were rejoined about 330 B. C. by the Jews deported from Palestine after the seizure of Jerusalem by Ptolemy Soter. Thus they would form in Cyrenaica a Judaeo-Syrian population, mixed with Egyptian and a little Berber, and this would be the origin of the Peuls. (Did this population take the name of Foudh or Fouth in remembrance of its flight?)

[152] Morel, l. c., p. 148 f.
[153] Morel, l. c., p. 151.
[154] Barrows, *Berbers and Blacks,* p. 139.

"Persecuted by the Romans, in the course of the first century of our era, a part of these Jewish Foudh which St. Mark sought to evangelize, emigrated with their flocks towards the south-west, reached Aïr, then the Niger Bend, and finally the beautiful pastures of Macina (the Promised Land?) where the Soninké made them welcome. The Fouhd having succeeded in gaining the ascendancy over the Soninké, these latter rebelled and drove out the Fouhd, who proceeded to establish themselves in the vicinity of Nema. (Middle of the second century.) They were there joined shortly afterwards by another group of Jews from Cyrenaica, who had migrated by way of Tripoli, Tuat, and south of Morocco. It is this group of Jewish shepherds who came to enjoy a dominant role in the formation and development of the Empire of Ghana." [155]

Francis Rennell Rodd, too, after describing the Damergu Fulani as "Slender, fine-featured, but dark-skinned, with profiles of Assyrian statues," [156] and noting, "Their appearance is Semitic, though the nose is never heavy but straight, and this is the case even more among the women than the men," [157] adds: "The Fulani believe that one day they will return to the East, whence their tradition says that they came, but how or why or when they left this unknown home has not been explained. Obedient to tradition, numbers of them are settling year by year in the Nilotic Sudan." [158]

It is not surprising then, to find an official Guide to the Cameroons stating: "The Foulbes are established in central and northern Cameroon. They have come from Sokoto, and before that from Fouta, in Senegal. It is all but proven that the Foulbes are of a white race, come without doubt from Egypt. Appearing towards the fourth century in the region of Timbuktu, they have swarmed in Central Africa and above all in West Africa. In every country where they have dwelt, they have intermixed with the black race and the cross-breeding has become much more

[155] Maurice Abadie, *La Colonie du Niger,* p. 184 f. Note:—Abadie is of the opinion that Ghana was founded "towards the fourth century of our era."—l. c., p. 103.

[156] Rodd, *People of the Veil,* p. 57.

[157] Idem; p. 57. Note:—If of Judaic origin, the absence of the Hittite nose would connect the Fulani with an early period of the people.

[158] Rodd, *People of the Veil,* p. 58.

pronounced among those who have given up the nomadic life of shepherds." [159]

This view, however, is not favored by Delafosse who with equal assurance maintains: "To the west of Ghana, in the pasture district of the Termes, the mixture of Semitic nomads with the Sérères and above all the long cohabitation of these Semites in the midst of the Sérères effectively gave birth to the race of Peuls or Foulbe, who speak a language sufficiently near that of the Sérères." [160]

In a contribution to *L'Anthropologie,* the same author declares: "The true Peuls are incontestably of white origin and most probably Semitic. (I believe that here Anthropology is in accord with historical tradition.) I am almost absolutely certain that peul is not a hamitic language as Menihof and Westermann maintain, but a negro language by the same claim as the Bantou, to which it is nearly related." [161]

In a previous work, Delafosse had already said: "Driven from Ghana by the Soninkés of Ouagadou in the ninth century, the Judaeo-Syrians took possession of Fouta, Whites and Blacks mixed, with their flocks; a large number of blacksmiths were with them. Their Chief was named Ismael: and during two centuries, the authority remained in the hands of the Judaeo-Syrians, until their last Emperor was killed at Tekrourien. The people dispersed themselves among the tribes of the conquerors: the Judaeo-Syrians were become the Peul, 'the dispersed.' " [162] Now as these Judaeo-Syrians are in all probability to be identified with the Hyksos, the version of Delafosse differs little, after all, from the explanation by Morel.[163]

[159] *Commissariat de la République Française au Cameroun, Guide de la Colonisation au Cameroun,* Paris, 1923, p. 21.

[160] Maurice Delafosse, *Les Noirs de l'Afrique,* Paris, 1922, p. 44.

[161] Maurice Delafosse, *Les Langues de l'Afrique.*—L'Anthropologie, Paris, Tome XXX (1920), p. 546.

[162] Maurice Delafosse, *Haut-Sénégal-Niger,* Vol. II, p. 226; 353.

[163] Note:—Professor Dixon suggests the derivation of the Fulani from a "tall, light-skinned" people who, he assumes, entered Africa from the northeast "in early Neolithic times" and whom he classifies as of the Caspian type, that is Dolichocephalic or long-headed, Hypecephalic or high-skulled, and Leptorrhine or narrow-nosed. A branch of these Caspians, he surmises, passed by way of Nubia into the Sudan. "And so, perhaps as early even as late Neolithic times, some strain of this virile group reached as far as the Atlantic shores, and laid the foundations of the interesting people whose modern descendants are the Fula." He would thus make the Fulani and Berbers of common origin. For he remarks of the same migration: "In the north, along the Mediterranean

**Desplagnes' Theory.**

Louis Desplagnes, in his study of the ethnography of the Central Nigerian Plateau, finds that after the intermixture of the black tribes, first a so-called Red confederation formed from the North, which in turn was succeeded by a White confederation. True it is, that Desplagnes considers the color not as significant of the complexion of the people, but rather a sign of recognition which rendered a color "taboo.[164] Shepherd tribes allying themselves with the descendants of the tribes once tributary to Carthage eventually formed the Red wave with the consequent introduction of new religious ideas.[165] Among these shepherd tribes, he would include the Foulbe, which he declares ultimately of Egyptian origin.[166] The Whites, on the other hand, he would derive from the Roman period in North Africa, and would have them reach the Sudan from the northwest.[167] According to his view, they founded Ghana not very long after the beginning of the Christian era.[168]

By way of summing up, we may close our reference to the Fulani, by quoting from C. K. Meek, of whom Sir Hugh Clifford as Governor of Nigeria testifies: "Mr. Meek himself, whose interest in ethnological and anthropological studies marked him out for selection to superintend the taking of the Census in the Northern Provinces of Nigeria, supplemented the knowledge of which he already stood possessed by taking an anthropological course at Oxford." [169] This then, is Mr. Meek's conservative conclusion: "In marked contrast to the Negro is the Hamitic ele-

shores and in the eastern Atlas, the newcomers came to be supreme, forming the foundation of the Libyans and Berbers."—Dixon, *Racial History of Man,* p. 184 ff. Of the Fula, he writes again: "Indeed, it seems not impossible that in this case we are not dealing with a Negro people who have absorbed a certain element of the eastern immigrants of higher culture, but rather with a body of these ancient peoples from Asia who, early penetrating to the western margin of the continent, have, in the long period since, absorbed a large Negro element from the ancient population of this type, which is believed originally to have held not only the Sudan but most of the Sahara as well."—l. c., p. 237.

[164] Desplagnes, *Le Plateau Central Nigérien,* p. 105.

[165] Idem, p. 118.

[166] Idem, p. 121 ff.

[167] Idem, p. 125.

[168] Idem, p. 126. Note:—We prefer this date to the later one suggested by Buell: "Even before the arrival of the Arabs, the kingdom of Ghana was founded about 300 A. D. and reputed to have had 'white' rulers."—Cfr. Raymond Leslie Buell, *Native Problems in Africa,* New York, 1928, p. 679.

[169] Meek, *Northern Tribes of Nigeria,* Preface, p. v.

ment, whose purest representatives are the nomad Fulani. Their colour varies from a light to a reddish brown; their physique is slender and sinewy, and the head dolichocephalic, the forehead rather receding towards the temple, the nose straight or even aquiline, and often slightly rounded at the tip. There is little or no prognathism, the hair is ringletty and often straight, and never of the Negro peppercorn type. On his chin a man wears a scraggy tuft of beard.The eyes are almond-shaped and overhung by long black silken lashes. The beauty of countenance and graceful carriage of Fulani women are well known. In character the Fula is distrustful and shy, shrewd and artful. No African native can equal him for dissimulation and finesse. Such is the typical western Hamite. I avoid," he adds, "the word Libyan as being at this stage a question-begging term, and Semito-Hamite as being ultra-speculative." [170]

**Summary.** What conclusions may we draw from the foregoing? The Phoenicians, as we have seen, were named by the Greeks the "Red" people. In due course they founded Carthage and intermixed with the surrounding tribes, leaving on them the impress of their culture and their name. These tribes in turn mingling with the shepherd races south of them, founded the "Red" confederation [171] described by Lieutenant Desplagnes who would also identify with it the much-discussed Fulani. Might not all this indicate that the Fulani were in reality ultimately of Carthaginian origin at least in part, with a consequent intermixture of Hebrew and possibly Egyptian elements?

Recent excavations in Africa establish a close connection between Carthage and the interior of the Dark Continent. Thus, Byron de Prorok, speaking of a vast pyramidical mound located in the stretch of the range of hills to the south of Tamanrasset, which he regards as the tomb of an early Libyan ruler, states unequivocally: "Fragments of ancient pottery in the neighbourhood point to a similarity to the relics of the Carthaginian em-

[170] Idem, p. 25 f.

[171] Note:—Rodd declares: "The Tuareg of Aïr differentiate the coloring of people somewhat arbitrarily: they call the pure negro 'blue,' but the dark-brown Hausa, 'black'; the Arab is always 'white' whatever shade of bronze he happens to be; the Tuareg himself is 'red,' which is the most complimentary epithet he can apply to others."—*People of the Veil*, p. 162. Rodd also notes that Ihargarnen, literally the red ones, may possibly be the etymology of Ihaggaren, Tuareg form for the Hoggar group.

pire which we have already discovered in our five years' excavation at Carthage." [172]

This is in keeping with the general statement of Professor Rawlinson: "The extent of Carthaginian commerce is uncertain; but there can be little doubt that it reached, at any rate, to the following places; . . . towards the west, Maderia, the Canaries, and the Coast of Guinea; . . . Upper Egypt, Cyrene, the oases of the Sahara, Fezzan, perhaps Ethiopia and Bornou, carried on in this way a traffic with the great commercial emporium. By sea her commerce was especially with Tyre, . . . with the tribes of the African coast from the Pillars of Hercules to the Bight of Benin, etc." [173] And may we not safely assume, that, wherever that commerce was carried on, individuals at least of the Jewish race might well have found their way?

The White confederation of Lieutenant Desplagnes, in turn, can scarcely be any other than the Hebrew invasion from the North, that culminated in the Jewish kingdom of Ghana, of which we read in the old Arab chronicle: "It is certain that this kingdom existed before the Hegira. For twenty-two princes reigned here before this period, and there was an equal twenty-two who reigned afterwards. That makes in all forty-four kings. They were of a white race, but we are ignorant whence they took their origin." [174]

**Johnston's Assertion.**

Sir Harry Johnston has much to say, that serves well our present purpose. Thus: "The Jews who settled so abundantly in North Africa both before and after the fall of Jerusalem, brought thither the influence of Hebrew and Aramaic, and contributed to Semeticize North Africa in language and religion. So that Carthaginian rule paved the way for the Judaizing of certain tribes, before and after the Roman empire ousted Syria for a time as a colonizing agency." [175] He goes on to say: "The Jews, after the first century of the Christian era, settled numerously in North Africa from Cyrenaica to Western Morocco. They are believed to have preceded the Berbers in settling the oasis of Tuat in mid-Sahara, and other oases of the desert also; though they probably found

[172] Prorok, *Digging for Lost African Gods,* p. 346.
[173] Rawlinson, *Ancient History from the Earliest Times,* p. 70.
[174] Es-Sadi, *Tarikh es-Soudan,* p. 18.
[175] Johnston, *History of the Colonization of Africa by Alien Races,* p. 40.

these habitable regions still retaining a negroid population,"[176] Again the same author observes: "The Jews having settled numerously in North Africa, won over a number of Berber chieftains to the Jewish religion."[177] And further: "Before the arrival of the Arabs (about 650 A. D.) the Berbers in many districts had strong leaning towards Judaism."[178] He had previously stated: "It was, however, just as the Graeco-Roman rule in Northern Africa was coming to an end that its effects on Negro Africa became apparent. The great racial movements in the northern Sudan, which led to the creation of the Mandingo, Songhai, and Bornu kingdoms of the eighth century, were undoubtedly due to impulses coming across the desert from Greek and Roman Egypt, Tripoli, or Tunis. Christianized Berbers from North Africa even carried Jewish and Christian ideas of religion as far into the Dark Continent as Borgo, to the west of the Lower Niger."[179] Here perhaps is still another warning that some of our supposed Hebrewisms may be in reality a reflection of an early Christian influence!

**Conclusions.** As regards our present question then, while a great deal of excavation will be required before we can hope for any really satisfactory solution concerning the origin of the Tuaregs, the true history of Ghana, and the other mysteries of the desert, this much, however, we may take as certain. From an early date, there was a strong Hebraic influence in the North of Africa which through infiltration and commerce has left its impress on many parts of the Sahara, and even southward to the neighborhood of the River Niger. We may also regard it as proven, that up to comparatively recent times, Jewish groups, and probably also distinctively Jewish tribes, for a time enjoyed an independent existence south of the Sahara in close contact with the Negro tribes of the interior, and that intermarriage and assimilation must have led to a gradual absorption of the newcomers with a resultant ingraft of customs and manners that necessarily left an impress on the culture of the Negro tribes of their adoption.

Whether this Hebraic influence from the North was carried by

[176] Idem, p. 40.
[177] Idem, p. 50.
[178] Johnston, l. c., p. 58.
[179] Idem, p. 51.

Hebrews in the strict sense of the word, or to a great extent by Judaized Berber tribes, in the light of our present knowledge it is difficult to judge. Ghana would appear to have a closer claim to purity of stock than the subsequent waves that crept across the Sahara, and we are inclined to think that whatever cultural effect was produced, by these later infiltrations at least, must be ascribed to tribes that were actually Jews only by adoption.

In any case, we do not feel that we have the real explanation of the Hebrewism of the Ashanti as a whole, though some individual traits may possibly owe their origin to this source. The language traces, for example, such as appear in the name and attributes of the Supreme Being of the Ashanti, require a purer Hebrew than could be expected from the North, where the Hebraeo-Phoenician patois of the early Carthaginian Jews must soon have become impregnated with Greek loan words and constructions, especially in consequence of the commercial supremacy of Alexandria in its prime. It was principally through commerce that the early Jewish invasion of the interior of Africa was effected, and Greek was essentially the language of the commercial world after the founding of the Alexandrine city.

**Hebrew Patois.**

Nahum Slouschz actually found in the Tripolitan Sahara a Hebrew patois strongly marked by Aramaic and Greek words. He thus describes his discovery: "A chance excursion brought to my attention the existence of a Hebrew dialect in use in the Djebel Iffren which should show analogies with the ancient Jewish way of speaking under the Byzantine regime and even earlier. This patois is almost universally known by the Jews of the Tripolitan Sahara, even by the children and illiterate. They call it in the oases of the district: 'Lashon Haqodesh' (the sacred language) of the Djebel. . . . Most of the words which form the vocabulary of the Hebrew patois of the Djebel are Hebrew pure and simple, having undergone slight changes due to the influence of the Arab pronunciation." [180] However, he takes care to note: "The Aramaic words which endure are sufficiently numerous; they indicate a Palestinian origin. The Babylonian Talmud does not

[180] Nahum Slouschz, *Un Voyage d'Études Juives en Afrique—Mémoires présentées par Divers Savants à l'Académie des Inscriptions et Belles-Lettres de l'Institut de France,* Paris, Tome XII (1913) deuxième partie, p. 539.

seem to have contributed to the formation of this category of words." [181] And again: "The presence of Greek words in the dialect of the Djebel indicates a Greek origin at least in the case of some of the Jews of the interior of Africa." [182] Finally Slouschz concludes: "In any case, the Hebrew patois of the Djebel is in every way most instructive. At all events I should add that the Jews of Djerba, of the Tell, and of the Nomads of Southern Tunis have preserved some notions of it. However, the Aramaic and Greek elements which form, in point of view of antiquity, the principal interest of this dialect, are found neither in Tunis nor in Algiers. Further proof that the Jews of these countries are of an origin less autochthonous and more mixed than are the groups of the Sahara." [183]

We feel constrained then, to search further for the real Hebraic influence that has left its impress so lastingly upon the Ashanti, and it is now to Egypt that we are going to turn our attention.

[181] Idem, p. 541.

[182] Idem, p. 543.

[183] Slouschz, l. c., p. 544. Note:—Returning to the subject nearly fourteen years later, Slouschz writes of what he calls "Lashon ha-Kodesh de-Jebel" (Hebrew of the Mountain)—Cfr. *Travels in North Africa,* p. 173, as follows: "The Jews of the Jebel have a Hebrew dialect of their own which is slowly disappearing. This is the 'Lashon Hakodesh' of the Jebel. I have spoken of this elsewhere, but here I will indicate some of the peculiarities of this curious language: 1) Most of the words in the vocabulary are Hebrew, with only a change in the pronunciation. The Hebrew word persists even when it is common to Hebrew and Arabic, but it has been influenced by Arab vocalization. . . . 2) Words of Berber and Arab origin are numerous. . . 3) . . . words which are Hebrew in origin but which are used in a figurative or indirect sense. . . . Aramaic words are often used. . . . Several words are of Greek origin. . . . The elements of this language may be met with in Algeria and Morocco."—*Travels in North Africa,* p. 194 f.

## *Chapter X*

# THE FLESH POTS OF EGYPT

**Hyksos.** Professor Clay of Yale University writes: "In the first half of the second Millennium B. C. an Asiatic people called the Hyksos completely dominated Egypt for a century, or as some hold, a much longer time. Contemporaries call them 'Asiatic' or 'barbarians.' The late traditions of Manetho call them Arabians and Phoenicians, while Joshepus in his diatribe against Apion, calls them Hebrews." [1] Elsewhere Clay states positively: "It is now generally conceded that the Hyksos, who invaded and held Egypt in the middle part of the second Millennium B. C. were Semites from Syria." [2]

This is in keeping with the opinion expressed by Professor Mercer some years earlier: "About 1650 B. C. Jacob and his family went into Egypt and sojourned there, according to Biblical tradition, about four hundred and thirty years. This was a time of great migrations, and we find that the Hyksos, a Semite people,

[1] Clay, *Empire of the Amorites,* p. 138.

[2] Clay, *Origin of Biblical Traditions,* p. 39. Note:—Christopher Dawson says: "About the beginning of the seventeenth century, Egypt fell into the hands of the Asiatic conquerors—the so-called Hyksos or Shepherd Kings. These were probably Semites from Northern Syria, but their invasion of Egypt was not an isolated fact. It forms part of the great movement of peoples which was convulsing the whole of the Near East in the first centuries of the second millenium. The power of Babylon had fallen before a Hittite raid, perhaps as early as 1870 B. C. and a whole series of new peoples was making its appearance in the highland regions of the north."—Dawson, *The Age of the Gods,* p. 352. Of the Pre-Dynastic culture in Egypt itself, Dawson writes: "This fusion of cultures no doubt represents the mingling of two peoples and may well explain the union of Hamitic and Semitic elements which went to make up the historical Egyptian people. Linguistic evidence clearly shows the existence of these two elements, for while the ground-stock of the language is undoubtedly Hamitic, it differs from the other Hamitic tongues by the possession of a striking affinity to Semitic which suggests that Egypt had come under strong Semitic influence during the formative period of the language. From the anthropological point of view, however, a fusion of this kind would be hardly perceptible, for the Semites, the Hamites, and the Mediterraneans are all so similar in type that Professor Elliot Smith and other anthropologists have regarded them as three variants of a single racial stock."—l. c., p. 145.

a branch of whom Jacob and his family may well have been, entered Egypt and became rulers of the land. This rôle they played for fully a hundred years." [3] In a foot-note Mercer remarks: "It is interesting to note that scarabs of a Hyksos Pharao give his name as Jacob-her or Jacob-el." [4]

Now as the Hyksos were expelled from Egypt about 1580 B. C. the Pharaoh who showed friendship to Joseph and his brethern must really have belonged to the shepherd race of conquerors. This fact might easily explain the enmity and persecution to which the Hebrews were subjected after the expulsion of their kinsfolk, the Hyksos, and the establishment of what is known to-day as the Eighteenth Dynasty of Egypt.

**Hebrews in Egypt.**

Professor Pedersen observes: "We do not know how great a part of pre-historic Israel remained in Egypt," [5] and Mendelssohn points out that "Egypt may be regarded as the cradle of the Jewish race, and in all probability it has never been without a Hebrew or Jewish population since the days when Joseph and his brethren laid the foundation of the nation. In all the other countries of Northern Africa, the Jewish population has resulted from a later immigration, and in some cases, from successive waves of immigration." [6] Later the same author shows: "The Egyptian Kingdom was already nearly two thousand years old when the Children of Israel crossed the Red Sea. In all probability, the exodus was by no means universal, and a few laggards and shirkers stayed behind amid the alluring 'flesh-pots of Egypt,' or slipped back to their old haunts during the forty years wanderings in the desert.[7] Possibly others returned during the days of the Judges, or in the more exciting times of the Kingdoms of Judah and Israel, when perhaps a maritime traffic had developed between

[3] Mercer, *Extra-Biblical Sources,* p. 9.

[4] Idem, p. 9, Note.

[5] Johs Pedersen, *Israel: Its Life and Culture,* p. 17. Note:—He adds: "We must constantly bear in mind that it was pre-historic Israel which lived in Egypt; historic Israel and its tribes were created in Canaan." l. c.

[6] Mendelssohn, *Jews in Africa,* p. 2.

[7] Note:—There is a Rabbinic tradition that at the time of the Exodus "many Israelites whose heart was with Egypt remained with the Egyptians; but many Egyptians whose heart was with Israel followed the Israelites."—Cfr. Edmond Fleg, *The Life of Moses,* trans. Stephen Haden Guest, New York, 1928, p. 56 f.

Palestine and Egypt, and there were probably fair-sized colonies of Jewish inhabitants at Cairo and other Egyptian towns when the destruction of Palestine as a state dispersed the Jews in so many directions, especially Asia and Africa. Those who went to Egypt from time to time had no doubt to undergo many fluctuations of fate, but they appear to have been allowed to remain permanently in the country and shared in its vicissitudes of fortune throughout its many changes of government and domination."[8]

**Refugees.** As a matter of history, the fugitives from the wrath of the Chaldeans found many Jewish colonies already established throughout Egypt. Flinders Petrie thus explains their origin and development: "During the age of the Judges there was a continuous decadence in Egypt, so that on both sides it is improbable that trade led to any Jewish settlements. The rise of the Jewish kingdom, and the regular horse trade established by Solomon, together with his marriage to the royal family of Tanis, Zoan, and consequent connection with the royal family Bubastis,[9] must have led to some mercantile establishments. Still greater familiarity with Egypt came during the increasing troubles of the close of the Jewish kingdom. About seventy years before the fall of Jerusalem the new Saite King, Psamtek, had established a great frontier fort on the road to Palestine, at Tahpahnes; this was a settlement of Greek troops, and hence open to foreign residents.[10] Wherever there was trouble in Judea, especially from Assyria, this fortress would be the natural asylum of any refugees, and Greek and Jew first mixed here and learned each other's ways. The result of this mixture was evident in the reference to the five cities speaking the language of Canaan, and swearing by the Lord of Hosts, and in the address of Jeremiah to the Jews which dwelt in the land of Egypt, which dwell at Migdol, the desert frontier, and at Tahpahnes, the Delta frontier, and at Noph, Memphis, and in the country of Pathros, Upper Egypt, calling their attention to the desolation of Jerusalem and exhorting them therefore to give up burning

[8] Mendelssohn, *Jews in Africa,* p. 33.
[9] Petrie, *Egypt and Israel,* p. 68.
[10] Petrie, *Tanis,* p. 11; *Depennah,* p. 48 ff.

incense to other gods in the land of Egypt, where they had gone to dwell already, more than ten years before the fall of Jerusalem." [11]

**Mercenaries.** Heinrich Ewald further calls attention to the alliance that had been formed between Egypt and the Jews in the time of Manasses, in the following words: "The army of Psammeticus, who, in former years during the great disturbances in Egypt, had himself found shelter as a refugee in Syria, was for the most part made up of foreign mercenaries. He accordingly received regiments of Jewish infantry, which he conveyed to Egypt by sea from Joppa supplying Manasseh with war-horses in return. The two states thus mutually exchanged the kind of forces in which each was strongest, and active intercourse certainly sprang up between them which was not confined to military purposes." [12]

While, then, King Manasses was employing Arabian tribesmen in the defence of Jerusalem against Sennacherib,[13] and Carian mercenaries were also in the employ of the Judean Court,[14] it would appear that Jewish infantry was being spared to Egypt in exchange for much-needed war-horses, and that these exiled bands of soldiery, in turn, were forming, or possibly strengthening, the nuclei of future centers of Jewish influence in the midst of the flesh pots of Egypt.

**Steady Growth.** Again Ewald states: "It is true that from the eighth century, and even earlier, great numbers of individuals were driven from Israel to Egypt by a great variety of causes. Some went as fugitives, some as prisoners, some as settlers, either separately or in large masses, so that in some towns there certainly arose a permanent and more compact population of Israelites. Now since Nebuchadnezzar never concluded peace with Egypt, but, on the contrary, according to traditions, which of course we can no longer investigate at first hand, concluded an expedition against it which penetrated far into Africa, it might have been expected that the Egyptian

[11] W. M. Flinders Petrie, *The Status of the Jews in Egypt*, London, 1922, p. 20 f.

[12] Ewald, *History of Israel*, Vol. IV, p. 190. Note:—In a footnote Ewald quotes as additional authority the testimony in the book of Aristeas (p. 104, ad fin. Haverkamps's *Josephus*).

[13] Stanley A. Cook, Cambridge Ancient History, Vol. III, p. 390.

[14] Idem, p. 391.

sovereigns would have assisted a people whose territory had been wrested from them by these same Chaldeans, and of whom so many representatives, some of them distinguished men, had in recent times sought refuge and hospitality at their hands."[15] And in a note Ewald adds: "They were especially numerous at Migdol and Taphne (Tahpahnes) to the north-east, not far from Pelusius, in Memphis, and in Upper Egypt, in the last case perhaps having been compelled by the Egyptian sovereigns to migrate further to the south."[16]

**Exiles with Jeremias.**

As noted in a previous chapter, after Jehoiachin had been led captive into Babylon in 597 B. C. an interval of a decade elapsed before the Pharaoh Hophra or Apries induced the remnant of Juda and some neighboring states to make common cause with Egypt by revolting against Babylon. Nabuchodonosor forthwith laid siege to Jerusalem in 587, and while obliged to withdraw for a time to defeat Hophra, he returned and completely destroyed the city in 586 B. C. The scattered remnants of the people that were not led into exile, were placed under the care of Godolias who was appointed governor.[17] When, then, this Godolias was treacherously murdered at Masphath, the terrified Jews, fearful of the wrath of Babylon, naturally made haste to seek shelter in Egypt, since it was at Egypt's instigation that the last disastrous uprising against Babylon had taken place. The Prophet Jeremias strongly opposed their action, but despite the fact, was carried along by the remnant of the people in their flight to the land of the Pharaohs.[18]

**Idolatry.**

As Ewald remarks: "Here the number of Judahite settlers continued to increase; they were favoured by the government, and they spread all over the country. Jeremiah had consequently to renew his discourse, partly against idolatry, which was revived in this luxurious soil especially among women [19] partly against the vain hopes of an Egyptian victory over

[15] Ewald, l. c., Vol. V, p. 2 f.
[16] Idem, p. 3, Note.
[17] Mercer, *Extra-Biblical Sources*, p. 57.
[18] Jeremias xlii; xliii.
[19] Note:—According to Doctor Contenau, with the introduction of the vowel points into the Old Testament text, the Masoretes in writing the names of pagan divinities, employed the vowels o and e of the Hebrew בשת (boshet), meaning something shameful, an abomination. Thus Astarte became Ashtoreth to the eye, but it was not read in this way; "the presence of the vowels o, e,

the Chaldeans.[20] Yet while the majority would not let the aged prophet go out of their midst—he was a sort of relic of better times—they would not listen to his voice." [21] This divided service is easily explained.

Of the fugitives themselves, Margolis writes: "It was the poorest sort of Jews that took up their abode in the Delta. The Jewish settlement in Egypt was destined to become a center rivaling Babylonia, but the Jews had commenced to drift into the land of the Pharaohs at a much earlier period. The constant relations with Egypt since the rise of the Libyan dynasty in the times of Solomon, especially the trade in horses, led to many a Jew settling in that country. Others were carried away as slaves, and still others, among Asiatics in general, found employment as mercenaries in the Pharaonic army. After the expulsion of the Ethiopians, soldier colonies of Jewish descent guarded the southern frontier of Upper Egypt. Thus Jeremiah found Jewish communities both in Upper and in Lower Egypt. These Jews clung to their nationality and practised the religion they had known in the rural districts of Judea from which they were come. Jeremiah met with stubborn opposition when he upbraided the Egyptian Jews for their unwillingness to abandon the worship of the 'queen of heaven,' [22] and her cult persisted down to Persian times." [23]

warned to replace this name of Ashtar by boshet, when one had to pronounce it."—Cfr. Contenau, *La Civilisation Phénicienne,* p. 113.

[20] Note:—Henry Thatcher Fowler thus closes his chapter on "Jeremiah and the Fall of Jerusalem."—"In the land of the Nile, the prophet warned his countrymen that they were not yet safe, for Egypt would be conquered. There they practiced idolatry and were deaf to his warnings Our last glimpse of Jeremiah shows him pronouncing doom upon the idolaters, yet not without a glimpse of hope. A few, very few, he is sure will escape from Egypt to their own land. Thus the curtain falls on one of the most tragic stories in history. The night of exile has come. A remnant of the Jews are in Egypt, faithless to their God. In Judea, desolate and devastated, anarchy rules among the poor and ignorant elements left in the land. The hope of the future rests largely with the fifty thousand who are exiles in far Babylonia, yet few of them can see the hope. It needs a prophet's vision and faith to look through the long, dark night to the dawn. Jeremiah had this vision and faith and so his tragic story is a story of hope."—Fowler, *Great Leaders of Hebrew History,* New York, 1920, p. 59.

[21] Ewald, l.c. Vol. IV p. 270.

[22] Note:—Kortleitner thus explains the term: "Just as Baal was called king and his image was discerned in the brightest Sun, so Astarte was regarded as the Moon, which on a clear night stood out as queen among the stars. Therefore was she called the queen of heaven."—Kortleitner, *De Polytheismo Universo,* p. 249.

[23] Margolis and Marx, *History of the Jewish People,* p. 113.

**Flesh Pots.** The flesh pots of Egypt and all they signified had always been sweet to the Children of Israel. For even when Moses led them forth from bondage of oppression, scarcely had they entered the desert of sin, "which is between Elim and Sinai: the fifteenth day of the second month after they came out of the land of Egypt," [24] than they began to murmur and complain: "Would to God we had died by the hand of the Lord in the land of Egypt, when we sat over the flesh pots, and ate bread to the full." [25] The spiritual in them had not yet asserted the mastery over the sensual.

So, too, with the refugees from Jerusalem, nine long centuries later, when the true service of Yahweh had become in a sense obscured in the gross satisfaction of their carnal yearnings. Sensuality in its most debasing form of idolatry had brought God's curse upon the Nation, and returning to the flesh pots of Egypt, against the warning threat of their Prophet, these fugitives from the wrath of the Chaldeans sought to assuage their grief and forget their losses in the sensuous gratification of the unbridled lusts of Astarte.[26]

**Jeremias' Prophecy.** A Lapide surmises that Jeremias was stoned to death by the Jews four years after the exodus to Egypt, the year before the fulfilment of his prophecy that Nabuchodonosor would invade Egypt, and it was in all probability at Taphnis that he was martyred in consequence of his reproaches against the idolatry of his countrymen.[27]

[24] Exod. xvi, 1.

[25] Exod. xvi, 3.

[26] Note:—Kortleitner declares: "Shortly after the death of Joshue, the Hebrews began to worship Astarte (Judges ii, 13; x, 6. I Sam. vii, 3 f; xii, 10). Solomon erected a sanctuary in her honor on the Mount of Olives (II Kings xxiii, 13. Cfr. I Kings xi, 5, 33). This worship also appears among the causes of the breaking up of the Kingdom of the Twelve Tribes (I Kings xi, 33). At the time of Jeremias (vii, 18; xliv, 17–19, 25) Hebrew women, who persuaded themselves that they owed the abundance of all things to the idols whom they worshipped, gave and sacrificed to Astarte crescent-shaped cakes and libations. Wherefore they were severely upbraided by the Prophet (xliv, 20 ff)."—Kortleitner, *De Polytheismo Universo,* p. 255.

[27] Corneli a Lapide *Commentaria in Quatuor Prophetas Majores,* Antwerp, 1634, p. 563. Note:—Ewald says: "The tradition that he was stoned to death by his own countrymen at Taphne in Egypt is therefore not improbable; only we do not know it from its older source, as it is only found for the first time in the work of Epiphanius. *De Proph.* viii, and in still later books. It is probably derived from some Apocryphon from which another piece has been preserved through Alexander Polyhistor in Euseb. *Praep. Ev.* ix, 39."—Ewald. *History of Israel,* Vol. IV, p. 276, Note.

**Fulfilment.** According to John Skinner: "The predictions seem to have been partially fulfilled within the lifetime of some of Jeremiah's hearers, though not till after the prophet himself had passed from the scene. Obscure references in both Babylonian and Egyptian inscriptions combine to make it probable that a Babylonian invasion of Egypt took place in the year 568, in which the land was ravaged as far as the southern frontier of Syene." [28]

This is in conformity with what we read in Josephus: "God signified to the prophet that the king of Babylon was about making an expedition against the Egyptians, and commanded him to foretell to the people that Egypt should be taken, and the king of Babylon should slay some of them, and should take others captive, and bring them to Babylon. which things came to pass accordingly; for in the fifth year after the destruction of Jerusalem, which was the twenty-third of the reign of Nebuchadnezzar, he made an expedition against Cele-Syria; and when he had possessed himself of it, he made war against the Ammonites and Moabites; and when he had brought all these nations under subjection, he fell upon Egypt, in order to overthrow it; and he slew the king that then reigned, and set up another; and he took those Jews that were there captives, and led them away to Babylon; and such was the end of the nation of the Hebrews." [29]

**Survivors.** However, it was not, as we shall see, the extinction of the Jews in Egypt by any means. For, as Harold Hunting says: "There were probably almost as many Jews in Egypt at this time as in Babylonia. Indeed even before the destruction of Jerusalem the constant wars in Canaan had compelled great numbers to seek for peace and comfort for themselves and their wives and children in Egypt, in Damascus, and even in far-away Carthage and Greece." [30]

**Memphis.** While some of the refuges of 586 B. C. had passed up the Nile as far as Thebes, and in all probability even further, many of them settled at Memphis, which was located near the head of the Delta. Now Herodotus relates:

[28] John Skinner, *Prophecy and Religion,* Cambridge, 1922, p. 341.—References quoted by Skinner:—"Meyer, *Geschichte des Alterthums,* 1884, p. 497; Winkler, *Geschichte Babyloniens und Assyriens,* 1892, p. 312 sqq."

[29] Josephus, *Antiquities,* Bk. X, Chap. ix, # 6 f.

[30] Hunting, *Hebrew Life and Times,* p. 123.

"There is a sacred precinct of this king in Memphis, which is very beautiful and richly adorned, situated south of the great temple of Vulcan. Phoenicians from the city of Tyre dwell around this precinct, and the whole place is known by the name of 'the camp of the Tyrians.' [31] Within the enclosure stands a temple, which is called that of Venus the Stranger. . . . Among all the many temples of Venus there is no other where the goddess bears this title." [32]

Commenting on this passage, Professor Rawlinson notes: "This was evidently Astarte, the Venus of the Phoenicians and Syrians. Herodotus is correct in saying that nowhere else has she a temple dedicated to her under that name, and an intercourse with the Phoenicians may have led to her worship at Memphis." [33]

But may not this temple with equal probability have owed something in its origin, or at least support, to the refugee Jews who assembled at Memphis? Herodotus would scarcely have made much of a distinction, if any, between the Tyrians and the Jews, who, as we have seen, are viewed by him merely as Syrians of Palestine.

**Astarte.** Benjamin Martin in his system of Philology asserts: "Astarte having become the symbol of the Moon, and Adonis of the Sun, the Scriptures always join the worship of Baal, who represented that luminary, with that of Astaroth. We may also note, that the Groves consecrated to this Divinity, were always near the Temple of Baal, and while bloody sacrifices were presented to him, delicious cakes, liquors, and perfumes, were presented to her; and on the first day of every Moon, costly suppers were prepared for this goddess, and the same for Adonis. To show to what excess their superstitions towards these idols were carried, it suffices to mention, that Ahab had 459 prophets of Baal, and that Jezebel, his spouse, who introduced into Israel the worship of Astarte, had 400 belonging to that goddess." [34]

[31] Note:—The "Camp of the Tyrians" was in reality a group of Phoenician merchants who purchased the right to trade freely. They there worshipped Astarte in a temple which they had built according to Herodotus, shortly after the epoch of the Trojan war, 1180 B.C.—Cfr. Contenau, *La Civilisation Phénicienne,* p. 91.

[32] *Herodotus,* Bk. II, # 112.

[33] Rawlinson, *Herodotus,* Vol. II, p. 183, Note 6.

[34] Benjamin Martin, *System of Philology,* London, 1759, Vol. I, p. 170. Note:—The following citation from the *Jewish Encyclopedia* would indicate that the cult of Astarte among the Israelites antedated the days of Jezebel.

According to the *Jewish Encyclopedia,* "Astarte is the Phoenician name of the primitive Semitic mother-goddess, out of which the most important of the Semitic deities were developed. . . . Solomon is said to have built a high place to her near Jerusalem, which was removed during Josiah's reform. . . . Astarte, wherever worshipped, was a goddess of fertility and sexual love." [35] Aptly, then, was she called at Memphis, "Venus the Stranger."

It was particularly against this cult of Astarte, or Astaroth, as she is called in the Scriptures, that Jeremias inveighed, when he took the Refugees to task for their worship of the "queen of heaven." [36] If this temple at Memphis could be connected with the Exiles of 585 B. C. it would have a striking bearing on the question in hand!

**Terra-cotta Heads.**

Leo Frobenius organized the German Anthropological Expedition of 1910–1912 in Nigeria, and later published a general summary of the undertaking in a work entitled *The Voice of Africa.*[37] Among the finds of the expedition was a number of terra-cotta heads, picked up in the Yoruba country, and chiefly in Ilifé.[38] Flinders Petrie has classified these terra-cotta heads with similar objects found at Memphis, and already assigned to the fifth century B. C.[39]

[35] *Jewish Encyclopedia,* Vol. II, p. 239.

[36] Jeremias xliv, 17.

[37] Leo Frobenius, *The Voice of Africa,* London, 1913.

[38] Cfr. Talbot, *Peoples of Southern Nigeria,* Vol. I, p. 277. Note:—Frobenius tells us that the terra-cottas were "obtained from Ebolokun in part, and in part from the depths of Ilifé."—*The Voice of Africa,* Vol. I, p. 312. They were found "at a depth of from about eighteen to twenty-four feet in Ebolokum, and in the city under old walls, trees and in the sacred enclosures."—l. c., p. 313. We cannot entirely agree with Frobenius when he assumes as a "working hypothesis"—"The Yoruban philosophy must have been born and nourished on a pre-Christian, primeval foundation, which, considering the discoveries and statements made in Ilifé, must also, chronistically and essentially, have been coeval with the condition of ancient Etruscan civilization."—l. c., p. 322 f. Neither can we accept his theory that the Yoruba culture is closely allied to the Etruscan,—l. c., p. 241 ff., any more than we can admit his identification of Yorubaland with the mythical Atlantis of the ancients.—l. c., p. 345. Briefly Frobenius sums up his own viewpoint as follows: "The culture of Yoruba is the crystallization of that mighty stream of Western civilization which, in its Eur-African form, flowed from Europe into Africa, and, when it sank in volume, left behind it the Etruscans as its cognate and equally symphonic exponents."—l. c., p. 348. While, therefore, we unreservedly reject the conclusions of Frobenius, the authenticity of his archaeological finds are not to be impugned.

[39] Cfr. W. M. Flinders Petrie, *Memphis I,* London, 1909, p. 15 f.

Reviewing the work of Frobenius, Petrie passes the following judgment: "In every respect they are extremely close to the pottery heads from the foreign quarter of Memphis. if any of them had been found there they would—though larger—have been accepted as all of the same class. The Memphite work cannot have come from the Niger, it is too closely in touch with Persia and India, but the idea and even the workmen, may have come from Egypt to West Africa. The work of the fifth century B. C. may be the source, but nothing so late as the Roman age." [40]

**Memphis and Niger.**

The theory then, of a gradual migration of the Jews is perhaps the simplest, if not the only plausible, explanation of this connection between Memphis and the distant Niger, as we hope to make clear in the following chapter.

**Retreat up the Nile.**

Professor Rawlinson thinks that Nabuchodonosor invaded Egypt twice. First in 582 B. C. and again about 570 B. C. when he deposed Apries and set up Amasis, who was perhaps thereafter his tributary.[41]

In any case, at the approach of their old enemy, the refugees would naturally withdraw inland along the Nile River, and take up their abode with the more distant Jewish colonies, or even in the interior of Ethiopia.[42]

This appears the more probable when we recall the warning words of Jeremias: "There shall be none that shall escape and remain of the remnant of the Jews that are gone to sojourn in the land of Egypt: and that shall return into the land of Juda, to which they have a desire to return to dwell there: there shall none return but they that shall flee." [43] And again: "A few men that shall flee from the sword, shall return out of the land of

[40] *Ancient Egypt,* Part II of 1914, p. 84.

[41] Rawlinson, *Herodotus,* Vol. I, p. 532, Essay VIII.

[42] Note:—If we are to give credence to Ossendowski, there must have been a considerable intercourse between Egypt and the Negroes of the interior from a very early date. He says: "The divine trinity of Egypt remains unchanged in the mythology of some tribes in the Sudan. The word 'Hor' or 'Har' presumably derived from the Egyptian 'Horus,' is still kept by aristocratic families as having sanctity and importance. One tide of migration from the land of the Nile brought with it the Egyptian sun god, Ra, and we find the fetich Ragun to-day in the Fouta-Djallon Mountains. But sun worship is rare to-day in Africa, for the sun on either side of the Equator is regarded as a demon, the enemy of the people."—Ossendowski, *Cruel Gods Fill the African Olympus,* p. 13.

[43] Jeremias xliv, 14.

Egypt into the land of Juda." [44] What would be more natural then, than that some Jews should take these words to heart, and as the order was literally to flee from Egypt, with the approach of their sworn enemy, the only available outlet for their flight was to the interior of Africa by way of the Nile.

**Ethiopia.**

Quoting from Rawlinson again: "The Ethiopians held the valley of the Nile above Egypt, and the whole of the plateau from which descend the great Nile affluents, the modern country of Abyssinia. Their chief town was Meroe." [45]

**Mosaic Myth.**

It may be interesting to note in passing that it was this Meroe that Josephus says Moses proceeded against as general of the Egyptian Pharaoh, before God called him to lead the Children of Israel out of the Land of Bondage.[46] Commenting on the passage in question, William Whiston observes: [47] "This history of Moses, as a general of the Egyptians against the Ethiopians, is wholly omitted in our Bibles; but is thus cited by Irenaeus, from Josephus, and that soon after his own age: 'Josephus says that when Moses was nourished in the king's palace, he was appointed general of the army against the Ethiopians, and conquered them, when he married the king's daughter; because, out of affection for him, she delivered the city up to him.' [48] Nor perhaps did St. Stephen refer to anything else, when he said of Moses, before he was sent by God to the Israelites, that he was not only learned in all the wisdom of the Egyptians, but was also mighty in words and deeds." [49]

In reference to this same passage from Josephus, H. Lincoln Tangye asserts: "The expedition is confirmed by traditions quoted by the Arab historians Abu Salih and Selim-el-Aswam, who speak of his successes against Tafa, forty miles above Assuan." [50]

**Soldiers' Rebellion.**

Into this country, during the reign of Psammeticus I who died probably about 610 B. C.[51] retreated the 240,000 Egyptian soldiers who re-

[44] Idem, xliv, 28.
[45] Rawlinson, *Ancient History from the Earliest Times,* p. 52.
[46] Josephus, *Antiquities,* Bk. II, Chap. X, # 1.
[47] Flavius Josephus, trans. William Whiston, New York, p. 158.
[48] Cfr. *Fragments of Irenaeus,* ap. edit. Grab. p. 472.
[49] Acts of the Apostles, vii, 22.
[50] H. Lincoln Tangye, *In the Torrid Sudan,* Boston, 1910, p. 22.
[51] Rawlinson, *Herodotus,* Vol. II, p. 380.

belled, as Herodotus tells us, and took up their abode on an island in the Nile, as far above Meroe, as this capital of Ethiopia is above the First Cataract. [52] While the exodus was made up chiefly of native Egyptians, it appears quite probable that some at least of the mercenaries must have thrown in their lot with their brothers-in-arms, and if so, bands of the Jewish Infantry brought by Psammeticus from Joppa in accordance with his alliance with Manasses, may well have advanced far into the interior of the continent.

Mr. Talbot states: "There was no doubt a great upheaval and wide dispersion among the Sudanic peoples in connection with the invasion of Egypt by the Assyrians B. C. 670 and the flight of various tribes from the Pharaohs." [53] Then, having repeated the story of the rebellion of the mercenaries under Psammeticus, whom he would identify with the second of the name, fixing the date of the rebellion as about 590 B. C. he adds: "A similar exodus of discontented soldiers took place in the succeeding reign of Apries, or Haa-ab-Ra." [54]

**Elephantine Colony.**

James Henry Breasted, speaking of an Aramaic letter which was written by a Hebrew colony in Egypt to the Persian Governor in Palestine in the fifth century B. C. thus describes it: "This remarkable letter was discovered in 1907, with some other similar papers, lying in the ruins of Elephantine in Upper Egypt. Here lived a community of some six or seven hundred Hebrews; some of them had probably migrated to Egypt before Nebuchadnezzar destroyed Jerusalem. They had built a temple to Jahveh on the banks of the Nile. This letter tells how the jealous Egyptian priests formed a mob, burned the Hebrew temple, and plundered it of its gold and silver vessels. Thereupon the whole Hebrew community sat down in mourning, and for three years they tried in vain to secure permission to rebuild. Then in 407 B. C. their leaders wrote this letter to Bagaos, the Persian governor of Egypt, to permit them to rebuild their ruined temple. They refer by name to persons in Palestine who are also mentioned in the Old Testament. The letter is written with pen and ink on papyrus, in the Aramaic

[52] Herodotus, Bk. II, # 30.
[53] Talbot, *Peoples of Southern Nigeria,* Vol. I, p. 24.
[54] Idem, p. 25.

language, which was now rapidly displacing Hebrew. This writing used the Phoenician letters long before adopted throughout Western Asia." [55]

**Soldiers and Tradesmen.**

Of this same Hebrew colony, George Barton writes: "Numerous papyri found since 1895 at Elephantine, an island at the First Cataract of the Nile, reveal the existence of a Jewish community there. The documents are dated from the year 494 B. C. to the year 400 B. C. They show that this Jewish community had at Elephantine a temple to Jehovah, that they were soldiers, and that some of them were engaged in trade. One document declares that when Cambyses conquered Egypt (525 B. C.) he then found the temple of Jehovah in existence there, and that it had been built under native Egyptian kings." [56]

Elsewhere Barton surmises: "It has been conjectured that this colony, connected as it was with a fortress, was placed at this point by Psammeticus II.[57] While this theory cannot be confirmed it seems quite probable. . . . As the Deuteronomic law provides that there should be but one sanctuary, it has been plausibly conjectured that the temple at Elephantine was constructed after the destruction of the temple at Jerusalem in 586 B. C.[58] In this temple in the land of Egypt Yahveh was worshipped under the name Yahu or Yaho." [59]

Again Barton suggests: "If the founders of the temple at Elephantine had no thought of violating the law of Deuteronomy, having erected their temple when that at Jerusalem was in ruins, their descendants clung passionately to the possession of their place of worship after the one in Jerusalem had been rebuilt. This was most natural. Long association aided them in regarding the spot as sacred to Yahveh, and such associations are not easily set aside. Then, too, they might naturally reason that, if the erection of their temple was ever right, changes in conditions at Jerusalem could not make it wrong. At all events, they persisted in maintaining it." [60]

[55] Breasted, *Ancient Times,* p. 215.
[56] Barton, *Archæology and the Bible,* p. 447.
[57] Cfr. *Herodotus,* Bk. II, # 161.
[58] H. Anneler, *Zur Geschichte der Juden von Elephantine,* Bern, 1912, p. 194 ff.
[59] Barton, *Religion of Israel,* p. 266 f.
[60] Idem, p. 268.

**Jewish Strength.**

Flinders Petrie, in turn, observes: "Though this temple was destroyed in 411 B. C. by the enmity of the Egyptian priests of Khnum, and the cupidity of the Persian governor Widarnag, yet the parties were so nearly equal that before 408 the governor and all his accomplices had perished by violence, and in revenge by 405 Yedoniyeh bar Gamariyeh, a principal Jew of Elephantine, had fled to Thebes, where he was killed." [61] And again: "It is evident that there was no hestitation in establishing temple worship at the Cataract, and probably also in the other cities that 'called on the name of Yahveh,' as a substitute for the destroyed temple of Jerusalem. This is in accord with the establishing of the temple of Onias some three centuries later. . . . A rival temple would probably have been illegitimate at any time; but if the temple at Jerusalem was destroyed, or in the heretical hands of the Hellenic party, then it was looked on as more important to maintain the worship, rather than to abandon it because its true centre was unattainable. This was in accord with Western Judaism, which would subordinate the letter of the law to the keeping the spirit of it; in contrast to Babylonian Judaism, which by concentrating on the letter of the law forgot the more important value of it, and thus 'tithed mint, anise and cummin, and omitted the weightier matters of the law.' " [62]

**Proselytes Present.**

Here again we should notice what Flinders Petrie expressly calls to our attention, and which confirms what we have already remarked in the Jews elsewhere, that "regarding the relations of Egyptians to Jews, it is notable that proselytes were not uncommon. Ashor, an Egyption, married a Jewess, and took the name of Nathan. Hoshea, was a son of an Egyptian, Pedu-khnum; Hadadnuri the Babylonian had a son named Yathom, and grandson Melkiel." [63] Petrie too, is of opinion that the colony "probably dates from the time of Hophra's foreign policy before 570." [64]

Professor Cowley, who has made a special study of the whole question and has reproduced "all the legible pre-Christian Aramaic

[61] Petrie, *Status of the Jews in Egypt,* p. 22.
[62] Idem, p. 26 f.
[63] Idem, p. 24.
[64] Idem, p. 23.

papyri known" to him,[65] calls attention to many interesting points in connection with this colony at Elephantine.

**Judeans.**

While he sees in this military group "mercenaries in the employment of the Persian king," [66] Cowley positively maintains that "they lived on equal terms with the Egyptians, transacted business with people of various races, intermarried, and sometimes bore alien names." [67] He further shows that the people were Judeans, and not Samaritans " as argued by Hoonacher," [68] nor yet Israelites from the destroyed Nation of the North.[69] And again: "When these papyri begin, early in the fifth century, the colony, while retaining its military organization, had become a settled community. Its members could buy and sell land and houses, they engage in trade, they could go to law before the civil courts and they held civil posts under government. Moreover they had their wives and families, and the women could hold property and take legal action in their own right, etc." [70]

**Temple of Ya'u.**

Cowley goes on to show that the service of the temple at Elephantine varied little from the norm set in the time of Manasses, a possible indication that the founders of the colony may have been some of the infantry sent to Egypt by Manasses, and that the worship of Yahweh was still defiled by being associated with idolatry. "The colonists," he observes, "were not better than their fathers—perhaps much worse. To begin with, they regarded themselves as especially devoted to the worship of the national God whom they called Ya'u.[71] This name, as I have argued elsewhere, is not an abbreviation of Jahve,[72] but an earlier form, and only another way of writing the earliest form Yau.[73] As the 'He' [74] seems to be a mere vowel-sign, or perhaps hamza, I have adopted here the

[65] A. Cowley, *Aramaic Papyri of the Fifth Century B.C.*, Oxford, 1923, Introduction, p. xiii.
[66] Idem, p. xvi.
[67] Idem, p. xvii.
[68] Hoonacher, *Schweich Lectures for 1914, Une Communauté Judaeo-Araméene,* London, 1915.
[69] Cowley, l. c., p. xv.
[70] Idem, p. xvi.
[71] יהו
[72] יהוה
[73] יו
[74] ה

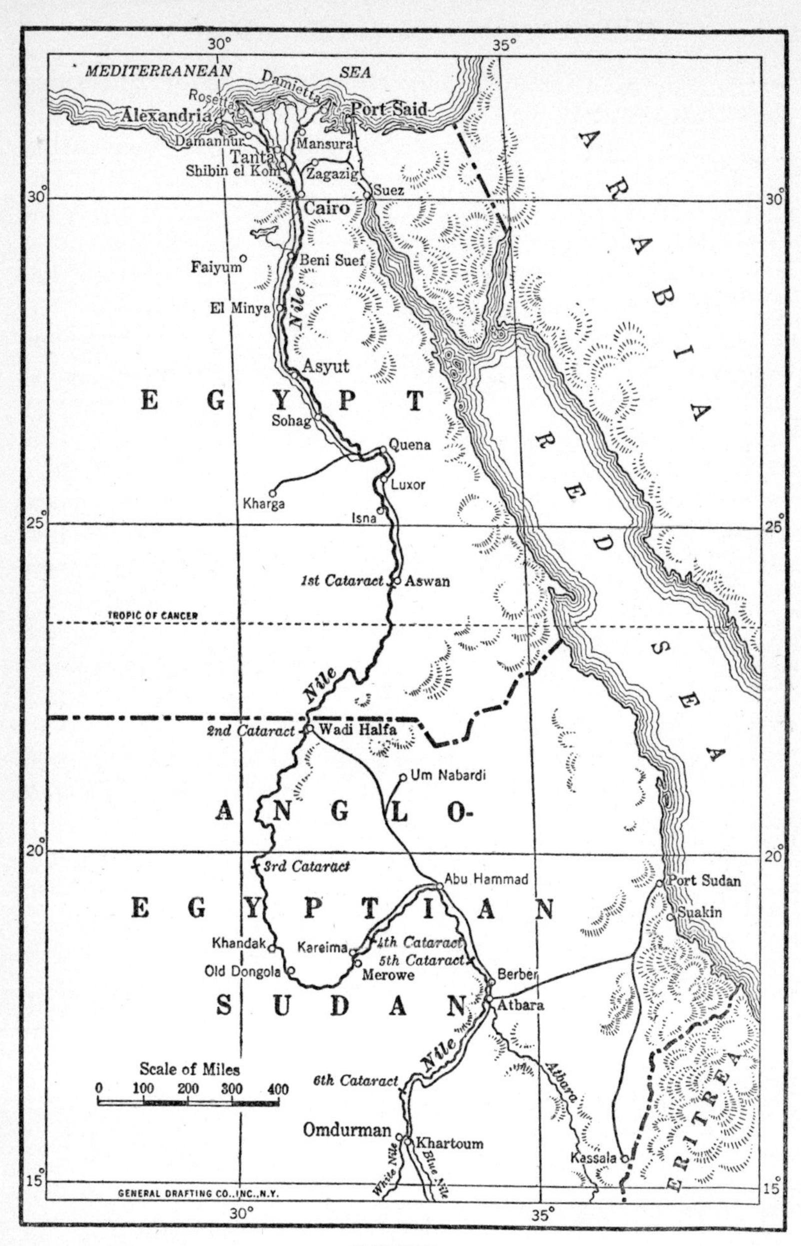
MEDITERRANEAN SEA
Rosetta
Damietta
Alexandria
Port Said
Damanhur
Mansura
Tanta
Shibin el Kom
Zagazig
Suez
Cairo
Faiyum
Beni Suef
El Minya
Nile
Asyut
E G Y P T
Sohag
Quena
Luxor
Kharga
Isna
1st Cataract
Aswan
TROPIC OF CANCER
Nile
2nd Cataract
Wadi Halfa
Um Nabardi
A N G L O-
E G Y P T I A N
S U D A N
3rd Cataract
Abu Hammad
Khandak
Kareima
4th Cataract
5th Cataract
Merowe
Old Dongola
Berber
Atbara
Nile
6th Cataract
Atbara
Omdurman
Khartoum
White Nile
Blue Nile
Kassala
Port Sudan
Suakin
ARABIA
RED SEA
ERITREA
Scale of Miles
0 100 200 300 400
GENERAL DRAFTING CO., INC., N.Y.
30°
35°
25°
20°
15°

EGYPT

transliteration Ya'u, as an approximate pronunciation, rather than the customary Yahu or Yehu, which are no forms. . . . Yet we also find other gods mentioned besides Ya'u. The most explicit case of this is where the temple-fund is to be divided between Ya'u and 'Anathbethel in nearly equal shares, and Ishnumbethel who receives much less. In the law-courts they swear usually by Ya'u, but an oath is recorded 'by the temple' and 'by 'Anathya'u' and a man is challenged to swear 'by Ḥerembethel the god.' . . . It would seem that besides Ya'u they recognized 'Anath, Bethel, Ishum and Ḥerem. There may have been others, but it is at least a coincidence that we have the names of five gods and that there were five gates to the temple.

"Of these names 'Anath is known as that of a goddess in Syria and elsewhere, so that it has been suggested that 'Anathya'u was intended as a consort of Ya'u—the queen of heaven." [75]

Cowley further adds: "Yet the national God was Ya'u. Whatever may have been their doctrine as to his relation to the other gods, there is no sort of doubt that he was pre-eminent. It was to him that the temple belonged, although it seems that other gods were also worshipped there. The temple of Elephantine was not a mere synagogue, but a considerable building, with an altar and all the appurtenances of sacrifice." [76]

These Jews, whatever their origin, had eaten their fill of the flesh pots of Egypt, and yet they clung to the external forms of their national sacrifice to Yahweh, entirely unmindful, however, of His warning: "Adore not any strange gods. The Lord his name is Jealous, he is a jealous God." [77] The flesh pots of Egypt had certainly done their work!

**Onias-Temple Compared.**

Comparing this temple at Elephantine with the later temple in the Delta, Cowley maintains: "The case of the Onias-temple, built at Leontopolis about 154 B. C. was on an entirely different footing. That was definitely schismatic, and whatever way the supporters of it might defend their action, they knew at least that it required defence. The colonists of Elephantine had no such misgivings. After their temple was destroyed in a riot of the Egyptians (in 411), they sent a

[75] Jeremias xliv, 17.
[76] Cowley, l. c., p. xx.
[77] Exod. xxxiv, 14.

petition to the High Priest at Jerusalem, asking for help to rebuild it. When this was disregarded, they appealed to the Persian governor at Jerusalem. There is no hint of any suspicion that the temple could be considered heretical, and they would surely not have appealed to the High Priest at Jerusalem if they had felt any doubt about it. On the contrary they give the impression of being proud of having a temple of their own, and as pious devotees of Ya'u (no other god is mentioned in the petition) seriously distressed at the loss of religious opportunities caused by its destruction. . . . But it is quite intelligible that the High Priest took no notice of their appeal. We can also understand why they afterwards wrote to the Persian governor, who had no interest in Deuteronomy, and to the Samaritans, who interpreted it in their own way, and that they received a reply." [78]

After showing that in the case of the Elephantine temple the term sacrifice must be understood in the strict sense of the word, Cowley concludes: "Thus there are several indications that the colonists of the fifth century B. C. remained at the same stage of religious development (if that is what we ought to call it) as their fathers in Judaea in the seventh century." [79]

**Language Indications.**

Finally, in commenting on one document, Cowley takes care to note: "The many mistakes, solecisms and corrections in this text, and the frequent Hebrewisms here and elsewhere, give the impression that the writer was not really at home with Aramaic as a means of expressing himself. Although no Hebrew document is found in the collection, it is not impossible that these Jews commonly spoke Hebrew among themselves. They would be compelled to use Aramaic in business transactions, as the language of the Government, and as long as composition was confined to legal documents, with their familiar phrases, they could manage it well enough. But they came to regard it as the natural vehicle for literary expression, letters, etc., and when they went outside the legal formulae the task was beyond their powers." [80]

**Possible Origin.**

From all this it is clear that the temple at Elephantine differed little in its service from what we would expect to find among the descendants of the

[78] Cowley, l. c., p. xx f.
[79] Idem, p. xxii.
[80] Cowley, l. c., p. 119.

Judean refugees of the days of Jeremias, some of whom in all probability may have found their way to the First Cataract of the Nile in their flight at the approach of Nabuchodonosor. This is precisely the view of Arendzen, who would connect the Elephantine colony directly with the fugitives who carried Jeremias into Egypt. Thus he declares: "In the days of Jeremias the Prophet, great numbers of Jews went into voluntary exile in Egypt, and formed self-contained communities on the Nile. They even built a temple to Jahveh at Elephantine; and could boast that Cambyses the Conqueror, though he destroyed so many Egyptian temples in 525 B. C., left the temple of Jahveh, on the Nile, untouched." [81] Doctor Hyvernat inclines to the same opinion when he writes: "When, however, the remnant of the Jews fled to Egypt, taking Jeremiah with them, Apries received them and allowed them to settle in different cities of the Delta, at Memphis, and in Upper Egypt. Such, very likely, was the origin of the Jewish colony established in the island of Elephantine 'before Cambyses,' as related in the Judaeo-Aramaic papyri recently discovered there." [82]

**Divided Worship.**

As regards the cult practiced in the Elephantine temple, it is instructive to read what Max L. Margolis has to say of the habitual divided service of Yahweh which characterized so many of the Pre-Babylonian Jews. He is writing from the Jewish viewpoint and can scarcely be accused of prejudice. He thus describes the early days under the rule of the Judges: "The Canaanite inheritance made itself felt also in the religious sphere. Of an out and out adoption of Canaanite polytheism there could be no question. But the worship of the Lord assumed more and more the features of the indigenous Baal cult. . . . The popular religion gave itself over to all sorts of magic and witchcraft: the Canaanite worship of demons and departed souls was wide-spread. The grossest aberration consisted in the adoption of human sacrifices strictly forbidden by the Mosaic Torah." [83]

Speaking of the Monarchy in both Kingdoms, he writes: "There was piety in the land; but in the popular religion it took on forms bordering upon heathenism and retained outworn super-

[81] Arendzen, *Men and Manners in the Days of Christ,* London, 1928, p. 94.
[82] Henry Hyvernat—*Catholic Encyclopedia,* Vol. V, Article "Egypt," p. 342.
[83] Margolis and Marx, *History of the Jewish People,* p. 32.

stitions." [84] And of the days of King Manasses in particular he specifies: "The ancient forms of augury and divination, repeatedly suppressed, were revived. The Assyrian cult of the heavenly constellations was particularly favored. In the Temple itself an image of the Assyrian Ishtar, 'the queen of heaven,' was erected." [85]

According to the same author, immediately before the destruction of Jerusalem, during the reign of Sedecias, "The political division involved religious consequences: on the one side men, and especially women, gave themselves up to the worship of the Babylonian goddess of love (Ishtar) and her son Tammuz, as well as of the sun-god; and on the other side the cult of the sacred animals of Egypt was carried on in an underground chamber." [86]

It is not surprising then, to find Margolis concluding in regards to the Elephantine Colony: "The worship of these Jews was not free from an admixture of heathenish conceptions such as their fathers had carried away from their rural Judaean homes." [87]

**Destruction of Colony.**

Cowley with good reason suggests that the Jewish colony at Elephantine did not long survive the last document which was probably written about 407 B. C. and adds. "Egypt was getting into a very unsettled state, and apparently threw off the Persian yoke in or about 404 B. C. It may well be that the Egyptians took the opportunity of the prevailing unrest to get rid of the Jewish Garrison, and began by making away with (or killing) the chief men of the colony." [88]

**In the Interior.**

Another explanation might suggest itself. The Jews, at least in part, may again have sought safety in flight and escape from the Egyptians by retreating further up the Nile into the territory of the Ethiopians, where there were already many centers of Jewish influence. Nor is this any mere idle conjecture. Not only have we seen in a previous chapter [89] the tradition of the presence of Jewish colonies in what is now Abyssinia from a very early date, but there is con-

[84] Idem, p. 88.
[85] Idem, p. 108.
[86] Idem, p. 110.
[87] Idem, p. 127.
[88] Cowley, l. c., p. 127.
[89] Cfr. Chapter VII.

siderable probability that the Soldiers' Rebellion in the time of Psammeticus had its quota of Jews in the movement, since it was apparently resentment against the preference shown to the Ionians and Carians that had led to the mutiny,[90] and the Hebrew mercenaries, under the circumstances, would naturally unite with the native Egyptian element against the Greeks.

Furthermore, if we make due allowance for the allurement of commerce and the innate restlessness of the Jew in exile, it is safe to conclude that there must have been many Jewish centers throughout the great border country of Ethiopia at the time of the troubles at Elephantine. It is only reasonable, then, to suppose that many, if not all of the Jewish garrison, must have sought safety, for the non-combatants at least, among their brethren of the hinterland.

**El Yahud.** H. A. MacMichael of the Sudan Political Service published a few years ago, *A History of the Arabs in the Sudan and some account of the people who preceded them and of the tribes inhabiting Darfur*. He incorporated in his work "translations of thirty-two native manuscripts, with explanatory notes, etc." [91] One of these manuscripts is a copy of a work by Seyyid Ghumalla ibn 'Aid who migrated from el Yemen probably in the fifteenth century, and which bears annotations of succeeding generations of his descendants.[92] This manuscript refers to a Jewish tribe in what is now the English Sudan as el Yahud, and while the writer seeks to derive the name from the Arabic word hada, to repent,[93] it is more likely the generic term used by the Arabs for the Jews. There is a remote possibility, of course, that the word may be distantly connected with Ya'u, the name of the Supreme Being as used in connection with the Elephantine Temple. These Jews then, might be the descendants of the old colonists of the Nile, to whom the title Yahudites would be perfectly applicable.

**Heart of Africa.** Sir Harry Johnston assures us: "The Dynastic Egyptians ruled and populated the narrow valley of the Desert Nile as far south as the First Cata-

[90] Desplagnes, *Le Plateau Central Nigérien*, p. 131.
[91] H. A. MacMichael, *A History of the Arabs in the Sudan*, Cambridge, 1922, Vol. I, Introduction, p. vii.
[92] Idem, Vol. II, p. 181.
[93] Idem, Vol. II, p. 199.

ract, and also its broad delta to the shores of the Mediterranean. South of the First Cataract there was a mixed population of Egypitans, Hamites and the negroes of the Nubian race.[94] Above the Second Cataract the country of the Nile was, while dynastic Egyptian rule lasted, entirely negro in population." [95] And again, after tracing Egyptian trade from time immemorial "through Nubia to Kardofan and Darfur, Bornu, Tibesti, Agades and the Niger," he continues: "Hamitic peoples and Semitic colonists in Abyssinia and Northern Galaland were in touch with Egypt of the last dynasties and the Egypt of the Ptolemies, and pushed a trade in Egyptian goods inland as far as Mt. Elgon and the shores of the Victoria Nyanza. Their ancient, blue, Egyptian beads are dug up occasionally in the sub-soil of Kavirondo. Egyptian or Gala adventurers appeared (outcasts, criminals, or mutinous soldiers in origin, it may be) in the lands of the savage negroes about the sources of the Nile. They were looked upon as demi-gods; and their descendants to this day (with a striking Pharaonic physiognomy) are often called by a name which means 'spirits,' 'white men,' or 'gods.' They or traders whom they attracted, brought with them the domestic animals of Egypt and the cultivated plants, besides a knowledge of metal working. Is it generally realized that the whole of negro Africa, south of the Northern Sahara, received its first and principal domestic animals and cultivated plants from Egypt and Egypt alone?" [96]

Here then, we have an explanation of the terra-cotta heads which were found on the Niger and which have been identified as being of common origin, at least as regards workmanship, with similar objects found in the foreign quarter of Memphis. This also would explain the coins of the Machabees picked up in East Africa, and would fully be in conformity with Morel's theory of the origin of the Fulani or Foulbe as outlined in the preceding chapter. A further confirmation may also be found in the observation of W. G. Browne, when, towards the end of the eighteenth

[94] Note:—Christopher Dawson speaking of the decline of the Old Kingdom in Egypt, that is, probably about the 27th century B.C. maintains: "At the same time Negro peoples from Central Africa had penetrated up the White Nile as far as Nubia and already made their first appearance on the scene of history in the latter part of the Sixth Dynasty."—*The Age of the Gods,* p. 161.

[95] Johnston, *History of the Colonization of Africa by Alien Races,* p. 18.

[96] Idem, p. 19.

century, he is describing the district between the Nile and Lake Chad. He says: "On the east of Fur there is a particular tribe of Arabs, who curl their hair, as it were, in a bushy wig, resembling that of the ancient figures in the ruins of Persepolis. It is probable that many fragments of ancient nations may be found in the interior of Africa." [97]

**Land of Hebrews.**

At a much earlier date, John Pory in publishing an English translation of Leo Africanus, subjoins a discourse which he entitles: "A Summarie discourse of the Manifold Religions professed in Africa." Herein, after repeating the Abyssinian story of the origin of the House of Menilek, he adds: "At this day also the Abassins affirm that upon the Nilus towards the West, there inhabiteth a most populous nation of the Jewish stock, under a mightie King. And some of our modern cosmographers set down a province in those quarters, which they call the land of the Hebrews, placed as it were under the equinoctial, in certain unknown mountains, between the confines of Abassin and Congo." [98]

**Growth of Judaism.**

But whatever may have been the fate of the garrison at Elephantine, the Jewish influence and power in Egypt soon began to rapidly develop. For, in the words of Flinders Petrie, "The close of the Persian age brought in new conditions under Alexander. Wide as had been the liberty of Judaism under the international empire of Persia, it obtained still more liberal treatment from the Macedonian conqueror. In consequence of the assistance that the Jews had given against the Egyptians, Alexander granted to them equal rights with the

[97] W. G. Browne, *Travels in Africa, Egypt and Syria; from the Year 1792 to 1798*, Second Edition Enlarged, London, 1806, p. 274 N. Note:—We are told by Newbold: "South of Lat. 15° 45′ . . . northern Kordofan and northern Darfur are full of archæological remains. . . . It is probably in these latitudes that the Tamahu or Southern Libyans first encountered the black aborigines in the third millenium B. C. The resulting fusion produced the Leucoæthiopes or Nuba. There were moreover cross-currents of migration from east to west. An ethnic tangle was created which makes it impossible to draw any definite archæological conclusions from finds in this area."—D. Newbold, Rock-pictures and Archæology in the Libyan Desert—*Antiquity*, Gloucester, Vol. II (1928), p. 284. He has already spoken of "the Garamantes, who inhabited Fezzan,"—l. c., p. 263; and "the Leucoæthiopes, the 'white Sudanese' probably inhabiting the Halfa-Gondola reach of the Nile and Selima, and possibly north-east Kordofan."—l. c., p. 263.

[98] John Pory, *A Geographical Historie of Africa, Written in Arabicke and Italian by John Leo a More, borne in Granada, and brought up in Barbarie.* Translation. London, 1600, p. 379.

Greeks in the new foundation at Alexandria.[99] They had there a separate quarter called the Delta,[100] and they were allowed to be called Macedonians,[101] to mark them as being under the royal protection. This status in Alexandria, though suspended by Caligula, was renewed by Claudius. The Jews had also other places assigned to them in Egypt, and were ruled by an ethnarch, who was chief judge and registrar of the whole of the settlers." [102]

According to Wallis Budge: "On the death of Alexander II of Egypt, Ptolemy ruled the country in his own name, and he inaugurated the policy under which Egypt became the richest country in the world. This result was brought about, not by Nubian and Asiatic wars, but by a steady development of the trade of the country. Under the influence of the shrewd and business-like abilities of the Ptolemies Egypt became a kind of central market and clearing-house for all the commerce of East Africa, Southern Arabia, the Red Sea, the Egyptian Sudan, Palestine and Syria, Cyprus and the Islands and coasts of the eastern half of the Mediterranean. The Jews were encouraged to settle in Alexandria, and the merchants contributed to making that port the most important in the world at the time. A Jewish colony existed at Elephantine long before the rule of the Ptolemies, and when the Macedonians established a strong and settled government in Egypt, Jewish merchants were to be found in the markets of all the large towns in the country." [103] They had prospered among the flesh pots of Egypt.

**Alexandrine Jews.**

Norman Bentwich well summarizes the story of the Alexandrine Jews as follows: "From the time of the post-exilic prophets Judaism developed in three main streams, one flowing from Jerusalem, another from Babylon, the third from Egypt. Alexandria soon took precedence of existing settlements of Jews, and became a great centre of Jewish life. The first Ptolemy, to whom at the dismemberment of

[99] Josephus, *Wars,* Bk. II, Chap. xviii, # 7. Note:—Professor Dixon tells us: "There have been Jews in Egypt since very early times, but with the foundation of Alexandria they flocked thither in large numbers, and are said to have formed a fifth of the population of this great city at the beginning of the Christian era."—*Racial History of Man,* p. 169.

[100] Josephus, *Wars,* Bk. II, Chap. xvii, # 8.

[101] Idem, Bk. II, Chap. xviii, # 7.

[102] Josephus from Strabo, *Antiquities,* Bk. XIV, Chap. vii, # 2.—Petrie, *Status of the Jews in Egypt,* p. 27.

[103] Budge, *Short History of the Egyptian People,* p. 152.

Alexander's empire Egypt had fallen,[104] continued to the Jewish settlers the privileges of full citizenship which Alexander had granted them. He increased also the number of Jewish inhabitants, for following his conquest of Palestine (or Cœle-Syria, as it was then called), he brought back to his capital a large number of Jewish families, and settled thirty thousand Jewish soldiers in garrisons. For the next hundred years the Palestinian and Egyptian Jews were under the same rule, and for the most part the Ptolemies treated them well. They were easy-going and tolerant, and while they encouraged the higher forms of Greek culture, art, letters, and philosophy, both at their own court and throughout their dominions, they made no attempt to impose on their subjects the Greek religion and ceremonial. Under their tolerant sway the Jewish community thrived, and became distinguished in the handicrafts as well as in commerce. Two of the five sections into which Alexandria was divided were almost exclusively occupied by them; these lay in the north-east along the shore and near the royal palace—a favorable situation for the large commercial enterprises in which they were engaged. The Jews had full permission to carry on their religious observances, and besides many smaller places of worship, each marked by its surrounding plantation of trees, they built a great synagogue, of which it is said in the Talmud, 'He who has not seen it has not seen the glory of Israel.' [105] It was in the form of a basilica, with a double row of columns, and so vast that an official standing upon a platform had to wave his head-cloth or veil to inform the people at the back of the edifice when to say 'Amen' in response to the Reader. The congregation was seated according to trade-guilds, as was also customary during the Middle Ages; the goldsmiths, silversmiths, coppersmiths, and weavers had their own places, for the Alexandrine Jews seem to have partially adopted the Egyptian caste-system. The Jews enjoyed a large amount of self-government, having their own governor, the ethnarch, and in Roman times their own council (Sanhedrin), which administered their own code of laws. Of the ethnarch Strabo says that he was like an independent ruler, and it was his function to secure

**Religious Freedom.**

**Civic Autonomy.**

[104] Cfr. Josephus, *Antiquities,* Bk. IX, #1.
[105] Sukkah 51b.

the proper fulfilment of duties by the community and compliance with their peculiar laws.[106] Thus the people formed a sort of state within a state, preserving their national life in the foreign environment. They possessed as much political independence as the Palestinian community when under Roman rule; and enjoyed all the advantages without any of the narrowing influences, physical or intellectual, of a ghetto. They were able to remain an independent body, and foster a Jewish spirit, a Jewish view of life, a Jewish culture, while at the same time they assimilated the different culture of the Greeks around them, and took their part in the general social and political life.

**Rejuvenation.**

"At the end of the third and the beginning of the second century Palestine was a shuttlecock tossed between the Ptolemies and the Seleucids; but in the reign of Antiochus Epiphanes (c. 150 B. C.) it finally passed out of the power of the Ptolemaic house, and from this time the Palestinian Jew had a different political history from the Egyptian. The compulsory Hellenization of Antiochus aroused the best elements of the Jewish nation, which had seemed likely to lose by a gradual assimilation its adherence to pure monotheism and the Mosaic law. The struggle of Judas Maccabaeus was not so much against an external foe as against the Hellenizing party of his own people, which led by the high priests Jason, Menelaus, and Alcimus, tried to crush both the national culture, and also a revival of the national religion. Before, however, the deliverance of the Jews had been accomplished by the noble band of brothers, many of the faithful Palestinian families had fled for protection from the tyranny of Antiochus to the refuge of his enemy Ptolemy Philometer. Among the fugitives were Onias and Dositheus, who, according to Josephus [107] became the trusted leaders of the armies of the Egyptian Monarch. Onias, moreover, was the rightful successor to the high-priesthood, and despairing of obtaining his dignity in Jerusalem, where the office had been given to the worthless Hellenist Alcimus, he conceived the idea of setting up a local centre of the Jewish religion in the country of exile. He persuaded Ptolemy to grant him a piece of territory upon which he might build a temple for

**Onias and Dositheus.**

[106] Quoted by Josephus, *Antiquities,* Bk. IV, # 7.
[107] Josephus, *Antiquities,* Bk. XII, # 5, 9; Bk. XX, # 10.

Jewish worship, assuring him that his notion would have the effect of securing forever the loyalty of his Jewish subjects. Ptolemy 'gave him a place one hundred and eighty furlongs distant from Memphis, in the nomos of Heliopolis, where he built a fortress and a temple, not like that at Jerusalem, but such as resembled a tower.' [108] Professor Flinders Petrie has recently discovered remains at Tell-el-Yehoudiyeh, the 'mound of the Jews,' near the ancient Leontopolis, which tally with the descriptions of Josephus, and may be presumed to be the ruins of the temple." [109]

**Temple of Onias.**

Professor Petrie's version of the founding of the Temple of Onias is as follows: "When Jonathan the Maccabee was made high priest in 153 B. C. Onias, the son of Onias III, the deposed high priest, having fled to Egypt, obtained a grant of land at Leontopolis, as the ancient city of Bubastis was then called, and erected a temple to Yahweh there, which was modelled on the temple at Jerusalem. Ptolemy VII, anxious to cement the loyalty of the Jews resident in Egypt, gave Onias the revenues of a considerable territory to support the temple. Excavation has within a few years brought this temple to light, confirming the statement of Josephus at many points.[110] This temple of Leontopolis continued to exist until after the destruction by Titus of the temple at Jerusalem in the year 70 A. D. The movement headed by Onias was a schism due to personal ambition. Both he and the Jews who worshipped with him in Egypt reverenced the whole Pentateuch as coming from Moses, but, as the Maccabees were not of the direct line of Zadoc, Onias and his supporters apparently felt justified in regarding the Jewish temple as administered by them as a schismatic organization. This temple and the one at Elephantine show what vagaries were possible even among orthodox Jews of the dispersion." [111]

Elsewhere the same author observes: "The importance of the Jewish sub-kingdom in the east of Egypt is shown by a sidelight. We read that the land called after the High Priest Oniah, stretched from near Cairo down to the coast, and that the Jews

[108] Josephus, *Jewish Wars,* Bk. VII, # 10.

[109] Norman Bentwich, *Philo-Judaeus of Alexandria,* Philadelphia, 1910, p. 15 ff. Note:—The next citation from Flinders Petrie does not place Onias in so favorable a light.

[110] Barton, *Archæology and the Bible,* p. 33 ff.

[111] Petrie, *Religion of Israel,* p. 269.

who occupied it could bar the way of the auxilaries of Caesar when passing from Syria to Alexandria." [112] Petrie further offers the following explanation of the closing of Onias' temple. "The wreck of the whole," he says, "came after Titus had taken Jerusalem, and when the Zealots tried in utter folly to start a revolt in the Jewish region of the Eastern Delta. This mad attempt could not be tolerated in the valuable province of Egypt: so the temple was closed, after its treasures had been removed. Thus the place fell into decay and perished." [113]

**Septuagint.**

Again Bentwick remarks; in connection with these Alexandrine Jews: "Within a hundred years of their settlement Hebrew and Aramaic had become to the Jews a strange language, and they spoke and thought in Greek. Hence it was necessary to have an authoritative Greek translation of the Holy Scriptures, and the first great step in the Jewish-Hellenistic development is marked by the Septuagint version of the Bible." [114] Bentwich's further observation is worth recording here. "At this epoch," he says, "and at Alexandria especially, Judaism was no self-centred, exclusive faith afraid of expansion. The mission of Israel was a very real thing, and conversion was widespread in Rome, in Egypt, and all along the Mediterranean countries. The Jews, says the letter of Aristeas, 'eagerly seek intercourse with other nations, and they pay special care to this, and emulate each

[112] W. M. Flinders Petrie, *Egypt and Israel,* London, 1911, p. 97.

[113] Idem, p. 110. Note:—An interesting description of the Temple may be found in W. M. Flinders Petrie, *Hyksos and Israelite Cities,* London, 1906, p. 19 ff.

[114] Bentwich, *Philo-Judaeus of Alexandria,* p. 25. Note:—According to H. St. John Thackery: "There can be little doubt that it was the religious needs of this thriving community (Alexandria) which stimulated the ambitious project of translating the Scriptures. Hebrew, even in the homeland, had long since become a learned language; but in Egypt even the Aramaic paraphrase which served the need of the Palestinian synagogues, had, at least to the second and third generation of immigrants, ceased to be intelligible. Clinging tenaciously to their faith, but driven by circumstances to abandon the use of Aramaic, this enterprising colony determined that their Law should be read in a language 'understanded of the people.' The Greek Bible, it seems, owed its origin to a popular demand for a version in the vulgar tongue. It must be admitted that this is not the motive assigned by ancient tradition." He then proceeds to reject the common tradition of its composition by the 72 Scribes at the Royal command, and says: "It is the work of a company, probably a small company. The traditional number (seventy or seventy-two) is legendary; the alternative number five, found in a Rabbinic version of the story (Masseketh Sopherim, i. 8. ed. J. Muller, 1878) is more likely to be true."—H. St. John Thackery, *The Septuagint and Jewish Worship,* London, 1921, p. 11 f.

other therein.' And one of the most reliable pagan writers says of them, 'They have penetrated into every state, and it is hard to find a place where they have not become powerful.' "[115]

**Monasticism.**

There is still another phase of the Jewish religious life in the Alexandrine period that should not be passed over in silence. It is thus referred to by S. H. Leeder. "Seeing the epoch-making developments which had their birth in Egypt, through the early passion of the Christians for monasticism, a brief note may be permitted on an extraordinary development of Alexandrine Judaism, by which a community of Jews, settled near Lake Mareotis, formed themselves into an ascetic brotherhood. Philo (in *De Vita Contemplativa*) describes how each member of the brotherhood lived in a separate cell, called monasterium, in which he spent his time in mystic devotion and ascetic practices, and especially in the study of the Torah, and in reciting the psalms; practicing the while great self-denial. Women, he says, were admitted into the Order; they spent their time in caring for orphan children, and they listened 'behind a separating wall' to the law as read by the men at their devotions. Which incidentally may be thought to dispose of the oft-repeated charge that the dividing screen was the later invention of the terrible Moslem."[116]

**Jewish Element in Copts.**

Leeder, too, is a stout defender of the theory that the Copts of the present day are descended from the ancient Egyptians with a strong inmixing of Jewish blood. "I think," he writes, "sufficient attention has never been given to the Jewish element in the Coptic people. It is not a popular suggestion, I know, but the prejudice which has gathered through the long Christian era against the Jews, and which the Copts share to the full, ought not to make us stupidly blind to historic fact. From the days of Jeremiah, when

[115] Cfr. Strabo, Frag. 6, Didot.—Bentwich, l. c., p. 32.

[116] S. H. Leeder, *Modern Sons of the Pharaohs,* London, 1918, p. 319. Note: —In passing attention should also be called to the statement of Arendzen: "The Sibyllines illustrate the Jewish mind outside Palestine and especially the mind of Jewry living in Egypt, for a great number of indications make it quite sure that much if not the bulk of the Jewish Sibyllines is due to Egyptian Jews. The book illustrates so-called liberal Judaism. Neither circumcision, nor Sabbath, nor the avoidance of unclean meats, nor any ceremonial laws are so much as hinted at, only monotheism, the Messianic hope, and chaste, charitable behaviour are emphasized. This accounts for the fact that the Sibyl is completely unknown to Talmudic literature, except in one passage."—Arendzen, *Men and Manners in the Days of Christ,* p. 170.

Johanan the son of Karesh led a band of Jews into Egypt, there has been a steady stream of immigration of Jews from Palestine. In this connection the very ancient tomb, preserved in a synagogue at Old Cairo, which the Jews have always persisted contains the body of the prophet Jeremiah, is of great interest. By the first century, we have the authority of Philo for saying the Jews resident in Alexandria, did not fall short of a million." [117]

**"Jeremias' Tomb."**

Of the supposed tomb of Jeremias, Leeder notes: "Until a few years since, a roll, which all agreed was written by the prophet Ezra, was preserved here, with a curse on any who should remove it. It was only through the treachery of a Jew that its existence became known to outsiders. Two zealous antiquarians forced their way into the synagogue, discovered the roll, and tried to unloose it. Evidently it had never been opened for centuries, for the remains of a serpent were found in its hiding-place, where it must have taken refuge. The edges of the roll were so glued by the discharge of the serpent, that it was found impossible to separate them without great damage. The antiquarians, after seeing enough to satisfy them that it was of marvellous age, departed, hoping to make a further examination under favourable conditions. But the guardians took alarm, and a fresh hiding-place, unknown to Gentile prying, has been found for the roll." [118]

**Conclusions.**

From all that has been said in the present chapter, it is safe to conclude, that, from the time of the Babylonian Exile, the Jews in Egypt, in ever increasing numbers, built up their power and influence, until they became an important factor in the State, with their own leaders at the head of the Pharaoh's armies. They had habitually made themselves the friends of the power in control. While in the service of Persia, it is true, they had drawn down upon themselves a brief persecution at the hands of the Egyptian rabble. But this very period of oppression only tended to make them the more devoted to the cause of Alexander, who requited the service by bestowing on them the most flattering privilege within his power, the right to call themselves Macedonians.

It would be against reason to suppose that the commercial spirit,

[117] Leeder, *Modern Sons of the Pharaohs,* p. 315.
[118] Idem, p. 316 Note.

that was steadily making for the Jews a unique place in history, would permit their confining their energies to Egypt alone. If persecution started them on a trek towards the upper reaches of the Nile, the claims of commerce drew the Jews not only along the entire littoral of the Mediterranean, but also to the utmost recesses of Africa, West, East and South, wherever in fact there was hope of trade and profitable returns.

And yet, the flesh pots of Egypt had a devitalizing effect, that sapped away their spiritual energy and worked havoc with the most sacred traditions of their Faith. The schismatical temple at Leotonpolis bespeaks a weakening of the bonds of the Law of Moses, and the admission of idols to the temple at Elephantine, where Yahweh was worshipped under the title of Ya'u, indicates a continuation of the very type of religion, which in the days of King Manasses had drawn down God's vengence on the Nation. The warm breath of Africa fanned human passions into flame, and the Hellenistic spirit of the Alexandrine Jews begot a gross materialistic tendency and developed a condition of general laxity and compromise that was entirely unknown to the Talmudists of Babylon.

Truly, the flesh pots of Egypt had done their work effectively, and it was a people enervated by luxury and weakened in faith, that followed the paths of commerce to the very heart of Africa, only to lose eventually their identity and become absorbed by the Negro tribes of the Niger, and elsewhere, almost as completely as their brethren of the Northern Kingdom had become assimilated by the Assyrians and Medes along the banks of the Euphrates so many centuries before.

We are ready now to try and follow the Jews into the heart of the Black Man's Country, and to show how one Negro tribe at least gives evidence of its early origin in Upper Egypt, where it might easily have become impregnated with an Hebraic element. We are going to try and follow that tribe in its wanderings across the entire continent, to establish perhaps the greatest negro empire of all time, which even after its fall left its impress on the whole of western Africa. We are going to try to establish the plausibility of identifying a Jewish element with the white aristocracy which gave this Negro tribe its first two ruling dynasties.

## *Chapter XI*

## THE LONG TREK

**Songhois.**

Sir Harry Johnston says of the Songhois,[1] or as he calls them the Songhai—the word is variously spelt—"Though black-skinned and woolly-haired, their features are often of Caucasian cast, and their characteristics generally those of negroids rather than negroes. Their language (the common speech of Timbuktu) is at present an unsolved mystery, its affinities are unguessed at. The Songhai seem to have dwelt first (where they still live under Tuareg influence) in the Oasis of Agades, a country on the southern verge of the Sahara, due east of the great Niger bend. Here they appear to have received immigrants from Ptolemaic or Roman Egypt, who brought with them Egyptian domestic animals and the Egyptian style of architecture. This last they applied to buildings in mud instead of stone. But although much modified since by Berber and Arab (Saracenic) influence from the north, this massive Egyptian style of mud-built walls, palaces and mosques still prevails throughout northern Nigeria from the Upper Niger to the vicinity of the Shari River." [2]

**White Infiltration.**

Verneau, on the other hand, while showing conclusively the presence of a white element in the Songhois, is inclined to attribute it to a Moroccan origin.[3] In this, however, as we shall see, the consensus of proof seems to be against him.

Of the Songhois, too, it is recorded by Henry Barth: "It would seem as if they had received in more ancient times several insti-

[1] Note:—We have accepted the spelling of Felix Dubois for reasons that will be quoted from him later. The transliteration for the English pronunciation of the word would approximate Sohgwa.

[2] Johnston, *History of the Colonization of Africa by Alien Races,* p. 13.

[3] R. Verneau, *Résultats Anthropologiques de la Mission de M. de Gironcourt en Afrique Occidentale.—L'Anthropologie,* Tome XXVII (1916) p. 567.

tutions from the Egyptians, with whom, I have no doubt, they maintained an intercourse, by means of the energetic inhabitants of Aujila, from a relatively ancient period; and among these institutions I feel justified in reckoning the great care which the Songhay bestow on their dead." [4]

In this connection it may be interesting to quote from C. K. Meek: "It is well worth noting that the Songhai appear to have embalmed the bodies of their chiefs. The author of the *Tarikh-es-Sudan* records how on the death, in 1492, of Sunni Ali, the Kharijite king of Songhai, 'His sons opened his stomach, removed the entrails, and filled the cavity with honey, to prevent putrefaction.' " [5] This practice certainly savors of Egyptian origin, particularly as regards the use of honey for the purpose.

Even to-day travellers remark among the Songhois element at Timbuktu "a notable elegance of manner," [6] and comment on the "Egyptian look" of the porticoes of their houses.[7] And P. Amaury Talbot has also quite recently added his testimony: "The mass of the Songhai," he says, "are certainly negroes, though there is little doubt that their ruling families had a strain of Hamitic or even Semitic blood." [8]

**Conjectural Source.**

If then, we might be allowed a conjecture as to the ultimate fate of the Judaeans who took refuge in Egypt in 586 B. C. we would suggest that possibly, after a series of migrations of their own, they eventually lost their identity in the Jewish settlements of Egypt, and that these in turn, at least in part, migrated further and further inland, ever carrying with them their perverted and divided worship of Yahweh, and gradually through intermarriage with the natives came to exercise a widespread influence in many parts of Africa, as for example possibly among the Songhois, and while they are long since extinct as a people, they have left, as we believe, manifold evidences of their infiltration among the Blacks, so that we find even to-day many vestiges of their belief and customs. This assumption would explain much that has mystified African travel-

[4] Henry Barth, *Travels and Discoveries in North and Central Africa,* New York, 1857, Vol. III, p. 285.
[5] Meek, *Northern Tribes of Nigeria,* Vol. II, p. 114.
[6] Leland Hall, *Timbuctoo,* New York, 1927, p. 68 f.
[7] Idem, p. 37.
[8] Talbot, *Peoples of Southern Nigeria,* Vol. I, p. 27.

lers and would serve as a basis for the solution of more than one ethnological problem which is at present shrouded in mystery. That the hypothesis is no mere figment of the imagination, we hope now to show in due course.

**Statement of Leo Africanus.**

Hassan-ibn-Mohammed-el-Ouzzan of Granada, better known as John Leo the African, writing some three centuries ago, declared: "The ancient Africans were addicted to idolatry, even as the Persians to this day, some of them worshipping the sun as God and others fire. The Africans, as already noted, had a magnificent and extensive temple erected in honor of the sun and fire conjointly. In this a fire was kindled day and night, and care was taken lest anything should extinguish it, even as we read the Roman Vestals were accustomed to do; all of which may be perused in detail in the historians of the Persians and Africans. The Africans who dwell in Numidia and Libya, each one adored some planet, to which they offered sacrifices and vows. Some of them, whom we have before indicated by the word Negroes, worshipped Guighimo, i. e. the Lord of Heaven, and this saner condition of mind was induced not by a prophet or teacher, but by a kind of divine intuition. Later they adopted the Judaic Law, in which they are said to have spent many years. Afterwards they were professors of the Christian faith, and remained as such until the superstitions of the Mahometans were taken up, which happened in the 208th year of the Hegira." [9] The reference apparently is not to the Abyssinians and the supposititious introduction of the Mosaic Law by the Queen of Sheba, as these never became Mohammedans. Moreover, Leo Africanus is speaking of Negroes, such as are west of the Nile.

**Ogilby's Version.**

John Ogilby, "Master of His Majesties Revels in the Kingdom of Ireland," published in 1679 a volume on Africa, wherein he speaks of the Coast of Guinea as follows: "Many Jews also are scattered over this region; some Natives, boasting themselves of Abraham's seed, inhabiting both sides of the River Niger: Others are Asian

[9] John Leo Africanus, *Africae Descriptio,* Amsterdam, 1632, p. 59 f. Note:—Hassan ibn Muhammed el Ouzzan was born about 1495 at Granada. Converted to Christianity he abandoned his original name, assuming the title John Leo to which the appellation "the African" came to be added. His life was spent for the most part at Rome or in Northern Africa, where after travelling extensively, he died at Tunis in 1552.

Strangers, who fled thither either from the desolation of Jerusalem by Vespasian; or from Judea wasted and depopulated by the Romans, Persians, Saracens, and Christians: Or else such as came out of Europe, whence they were banished, etc." [10]

According to the Map of Africa included by Ogilby in his volume, Lake Chad is marked as Borno Lake, and the Niger is supposed to flow through it. On this map the Niger rises in a lake called Lake Niger situated a few degrees north of the Equator, and some ten degrees east of the longitude of Lake Chad. It flows almost due north until approaching Lake Borno (Chad) when it turns to the north-west to enter the Lake. Passing thence, it flows almost due west until it reaches Lake Guardo, which by its location must be in reality Lake Fagibine. Thence it continues westward only to break up into a number of outlets to the Sea, as the Gambya, Rio Grande, etc. This last stretch is evidently confused with the Senegal, the middle reach is most likely the Niger proper, and the early stage is the watershed of the Congo, or possibly the Shari and Logone Rivers. All this should be kept in mind in identifying the location of the Jews "inhabiting both sides of the Niger River."

Later Ogilby paraphrases the citation we have already taken from Leo Africanus, in which he adds nothing material, except to place the Africans in question inland from the Guinea Coast, and distinct from those near the Sea.[11]

**Origin of Songhois.**

Now to return to the Songhai, or Songhois as we shall hereafter call them. Felix Dubois, towards the close of the last century, made a special study of this people, and came to some rather startling conclusions that are much to our purpose. We may be pardoned then, if we quote him at some length. He states: "Arriving at Jenne the traveller finds himself face to face with an entirely new ethnological entity, namely the Songhois. Most Europeans miscall them the Sonrhais, but the natives refuse to recognise the word disfigured in this fashion. During the whole forty years in which the interior of Africa has occupied the attention of the world, the name has only appeared before us once. Among ancient geographers Leon the African alone has mentioned them, and that in

[10] John Ogilby, *Africa,* London, 1679, p. 34.
[11] Idem, p. 318.

a paragraph of—two lines! Among moderns, the famous German traveller Barth mentions them at greater length, but all his remarks are wrongly based, for he reckons the Songhois among the aboriginals of the Sudan, and places their cradle between Tindirma and the Dira, to the south-west of Timbuktu. Quite other is the tradition of the Songhois themselves. They invariably told me that they did not originate in the countries of the Niger, and when questioned concerning the home of their fathers they all gave the same reply. The right arm of the human document was raised, flinging back the numerous white draperies that serve as clothing, and a black hand pointed unhesitatingly to the direction of the purple dawn. It was their unvarying response in Jenne and elsewhere, and it was never the west, where Tindirma and Dira lie, that they indicated. . . . After the human documents I consulted the written, and among all the historical manuscripts collected in my travels the only one to refer to the origin of the Songhois is the Tarik.[12]

**Dialliaman.**

"It must be attentively read, too, for its most precious indications are very concisely enclosed. 'The first king of the Songhois,' it says, 'was called Dialliaman. His name comes from the Arabian Dia min al Jemen, signifying, He is come from Yemen. Dialliaman,' the narrative continues, 'quitted Yemen in company with his brother. They travelled through the country of God until destiny brought them to the land of Kokia. Now Kokia was a town of the Songhois people situated on the banks of a river, and was very ancient. It existed in the time of the Pharaohs, and it is said that one of them, during his

[12] Note:—The Reference is to *Tarikh es Soudan* by Abderrahman ben Abdallah ben $^{c}$Imram ben $^{c}$Amir es-Sadi, trad. O. Houdas, Paris, 1900. Es-Sadi or Es-Sa$^{c}$id or Es-Sa$^{c}$idi (Introd. p. xii) was born at Timbuktu May 28, 1596 (Intro. p. xiii) and published the *Tarikh es-Soudan* in 1652. He added another chapter and completed the work in 1655 (Intro. p. xiv). The first part is little more than a résumé that the author collected from oral and written traditions; the second part is rather a personal memoir (Intro. p. ii). Es-Sadi tells us that there were fourteen pagan kings before Za-Kosoë who was converted to Islamism in the year 400 of the Hegira (A.D. 1009–1010); that Za-al-Ayaman was derived from dja min el-Yemen, he is come from Yemen, (p. 6) to which Houdas in a footnote remarks that the word dja, orthographically Za, is pronounced Dia. Es-Sadi further states: "We are ignorant as to what epoch Za-al-Ayaman left Yemen, at what time he arrived at Koukiya and what was his real name." (p. 8.) And that the descendants of Za-al-Ayaman "were all energetic men, bold and brave. They were moreover of good physique and of tall stature." (p. 9.)

disputes with Moses, sent thither for the Magician whom he opposed to the prophet.' "[13]

In passing, it should be remarked, that the "country of God" might well be the "Promised Land," and the city Kokia, "situated on the banks of a river" whence the Pharaoh had summoned the Magician to oppose Moses, throws its own light on the subject.[14] For S. H. Leeder, during his journeys through Egypt secured a photograph which he has published with this caption: "The distant village in Upper Egypt from which it is said the Magicians came who pitted their arts against those of Moses and Aaron. The author happened to be passing this village when on a country journey, and native friends with him spoke of the tradition as though it belonged to almost recent times."[15] Is this parallel tradition of the Songhois and the Modern Egyptians nothing more than another coincidence?

As regards Dialliaman, Meek suggests: "He was possibly a member of one of the Jewish colonies (Falasha) said to have been transported from Yemen by the Abyssinians in the sixth century A. D." and immediately adds: "Whether this story is a philological after-thought or really represents a tribal influx from southern Arabia need not be discussed here."[16]

**Yemen.**

As we shall see later, other tribes, such as the Jukun of Northern Nigeria, claim to derive their origin from Yemen, and in this connection it is interesting to find Omarah al-Hakami in his history of Yemen referring to the use of "the royal umbrella" as early as the year 866 of the Christian era,[17] and Makrizi in his Khitat giving a detailed description "of the Imperial umbrella which was borne on state occasions over the head of the Khalif,"[18] in a way that bears a striking resemblance to the state umbrellas used by the Ashanti and other West Afri-

[13] Felix Dubois, *Timbuctoo the Mysterious,* trans. Diana White, London, 1897, p. 89 f.

[14] Note:—The *Tarikh es-Soudan* spells the word Koukiya, and states: "This town existed already at the time of Pharaoh, and it is thence, they say, that he brought the group of magicians which he engaged in the controversy that he had with Moses."—Es-Sadi, *Tarikh es-Soudan,* Vol. II, p. 6.

[15] Leeder, *Modern Sons of the Pharaohs,* opp. p. 112.

[16] Meek, *Northern Tribes of Nigeria,* Vol. I, p. 66.

[17] Najm ad-din Omarah al-Hakami, *Yaman: Its Early Mediaeval History,* trans. Henry Cassels Kay, London, 1892, p. 15.

[18] Idem, p. 241, Note 18.

can tribes that have never fallen under the influence of the Moslem.[19]

It should also be remembered that at the beginning of the seventh century, the country of Hidjaz in Arabia which was to become later Mohammed's center of activity, was thickly inhabited by the Jews. The oases with the exception of Tabouk were in their possession, while at Medina though slightly outnumbered [20] they exercised the dominant commercial influence, and held the Arabs in the position of clients.[21] At Mecca, it is true, the Jews were represented only by transient merchants, but at Yemen they had actually established a Jewish State.[22] What are we to think then, of the following assertion of Nahum Slouschz? "We are told," he writes, "of the Yehud Chaibar (the Rechab), a tribe of shepherds and agriculturists, intrepid horsemen who at one time camped on the shores of the Red Sea, and who finally crossed the Sudan and penetrated to the farthest points of the Sahara. To them the Moorish natives, as well as the Arabs and negroes, attributed the founding of the first empires, the erection of the first public buildings in the country, the construction of the first canals and irrigation systems, and the institution of a social and economic regime which still survives in all Saharan communities." [23] If such a migration actually did take place, is it reasonable to suppose that this "tribe of shepherds and agriculturists" would to a man, spurning the fertile lands south of the desert, bury themselves amid the oases of the Sahara? Might not the same or even earlier migrations have found their way into the heart of Negro Land, only to be gradually assimilated? The legend of Dialliaman then, may possibly be traced to some such migration from distant Yemen.

**Kokia.** But now let us return to Felix Dubois and his description. He says: "With the Tarik in my hand, I questioned the Songhois concerning the whereabouts of this city Kokia. 'The city of Kokia was far, very far away in the east, beyond Gao,' was their unanimous reply; and upon two occasions the marabuts added, 'It was a town in the country of Misr.' Now

[19] Cfr. Rattray, *Religion and Art in Ashanti,* p. 130.
[20] Henri Lammens, *L'Islam, Croyances et Institutions,* Beyrouth, 1926, p. 9.
[21] Idem, p. 26.
[22] Idem, p. 27.
[23] Slouschz, *Travels in North Africa,* p. 344.

in the Sudan the country of Misr means Egypt, the valley of the Nile, and the name comes from Misra, signifying Cairo." [24] Here we might take exception to the derivation of the word Misr, and rather suggest its Hebrew origin, where the word for Egypt is Misraim [25] and dropping the plural, or perhaps more properly the dual, termination, it becomes Misr, which is practically identical with the Songhois word in question. Can this again be only another mere coincidence?

Dubois continues: "What river do we find in the map east of Gao? None, large or small, but the Nile, and it is in Egypt alone that Kokia, 'situated near a great river,' could have existed. Moreover, this will explain why the author said, to indicate the great antiquity of the town, 'it already existed in the time of the Pharaohs,' and that 'one of them sent thither for magicians to defeat Moses.' It would probably be a neighbouring and vassal country to which they would apply." [26]

**Malfant's Testimony.**

Charles de la Roncière reproduces the Latin document of Anthony Malfant supposedly written at Tamentit, the capital of Tuat, in the year 1447, to which reference was made in a preceding chapter. Relying on his own interpretation of this document, Roncière places this Kokia or Koukiya, called by Malfant Chouchia or Chuchia, and which he styles the ancient capital of the Songhois Empire, on the River Niger, mid-way between Gao and Niamey, That there was a town named Koukiya situated in that locality on the Niger about 150 kilometers to the south of Gao, and, that it was for a time the capital of the Songhois, is beyond all question an established fact. Its ruins have been fully identified by Louis Desplagnes.[27]

Nevertheless, the document of Malfant would seem to refer, not to this Koukiya, but to a more remote town of the same name. For it estimates that Koukiya is fifty days' journey from Tamentit, and De la Roncière declares that this is in accord with the figure given by Ibn Batoutah. Now the document of Malfant clearly states that the same Tamentit is only twenty days' journey from Tripoli, a distance as a matter of fact of approximately a thou-

[24] Dubois, *Timbuctoo the Mysterious,* p. 91.
[25] מִצְרַיִם
[26] Dubois, l. c., p. 91.
[27] Desplagnes, *Le Plateau Centrale Nigérien,* p. 73 f.

sand miles. This would bring Koukiya 2,500 miles from Tamentit, or well into Upper Egypt. Again, as Malfant makes the Niger, which he confuses with the Nile,[28] only twenty days' journey from Tamentit, it is clear that Koukiya must be thirty days further on, which certainly carries it far to the east of Lake Chad.[29] It should be noticed, too, that Malfant is drawing his information from his host at Tamentit, who in all probability had never visited Koukiya,[30] even if existent in his day, and who is relying on such authorities as the *Tarikh-es-Soudan.*

**Several Kokias.**

The probable explanation would seem to be that, as so often happens with the transfer of a people, the old name was carried from the abandoned town to the new one. In fact, Dubois actually suggests: "The name was probably given to it by the Songhois in memory of their first home." [31] Thus there may have been two or even more Kokias, marking successive steps along the way of migration.

In support of this theory we find to-day to the west of Lake Chad the town of Kouka,[32] which is called Kikoua by the natives who belong to the group of the Kanori, a people "as a rule with-

[28] Note:—Even Arabic geographers commonly confused the Nile and the Niger, and regarded them as one and the same river. Thus, reaching the Niger for the first time, Ibn Batoutah calls it "the Nile or Niger." He then proceeds to trace it, under the name of Nile, to Tombuctu, Caoucaou (Gao) and so on to the country of the Nubians and Egypt. Throughout he regards the Niger as an upper reach of the Nile.—Cfr. *Voyages d'Ibn Batoutah,* trad. Defremery et Sanguinetti, Paris, 1922, Vol. IV, p. 395 f.

[29] Note:—Even to-day in the Anglo-Egyptian Sudan there is a Kuke on the west bank of the Nile below the Third Cataract (N. 20; E. 30½) and a Kaka on the west bank of the Upper Nile (White Nile) on the border of the Shilluk country (N. 10¾; E. 32¼).

[30] Note:—De la Roncière positively asserts the contrary, but he is evidently led astray by the erroneous translation of the following words of Malfant: "Dixit mihi dominus meus non esse multum tempus quod in Cuchia, etc." i.e. "My host told me that not long since in Cuchia, etc." In the French version, which De la Roncière quotes, it runs as follows: "Il n'y a pas longtemps que j'ai été à Koukiya, etc." which would be, "It was not long since that I was in Koukiya, etc." And this last is certainly far from the true meaning of the Latin original.

[31] Dubois, l. c., p. 92 Note.

[32] Note:—Francis Rennell Rodd, after stating: "With the opening of the Mohammedan era we find a kingdom at Ghana in Western Negroland with a ruling family of 'white people,' and the Libyan dynasty of Za Alayamin (Za el Yemani) installed at Kukia," takes care to note that the Kukia in question was situated "Fifteen days east of Ghana in the Upper Niger country. Not to be confused with Kuka on Lake Chad, or with Gao (Gago) on the middle Niger, Kukia is called Kugha in el Bekri, Cochia by Ca' da Mosto."—*People of the Veil,* p. 404.

out the negro character much accentuated." [33] This Kouka, also written Koukaoua, was founded at the beginning of the 19th century. It was named after the large number of kouka, calabash-trees or gourds, found in the vicinity. Koukaoua, which means city of calabash-trees, was contracted simply into Kouka.[34] Now the surprising point is this. The Songhois influence extended over all this country to the west of Lake Chad,[35] where its impress has endured to the present day.[36] Moreover the Hebrew word for gourd is Qiqayon,[37] which might suggest that the Songhois Kokia, and also the Kanori Kouka, may owe their derivations to the same Hebraic root. Again Lake Chad is called by the Kanori "Tsade" or "Tsadi" [38]; while Tsade in turn is the name of the eighteenth letter of the Hebrew Alphabet, and the usual meaning suggested for the word is "fish-hook," though this meaning is by no means certain.[39] Furthermore, there is an Hebraic suggestiveness about the word Kanori itself,[40] Kinor [41] being the Hebrew word for the string instrument known as a Lyre.

That there actually was another Kouka situated well to the east of Lake Chad is shown by a map published by M. Perron in connection with his translation of the *Voyage au Ouaday* by Mohammed ibn-Omar el-Tounsy. It is dated Cario 1845, and is entitled

[33] Cfr. F. Fourneau, *Documents Scientifiques de la Mission Saharienne—Mission Foureau-Lamy, D'Alger au Congo par le Chad,* Paris, 1905, p. 951.

[34] P. L. Monteil, *De Saint Louis à Tripoli par le Lac Tchad,* Paris, 1895, p. 341.

[35] Note:—Rodd tells us: "What seems to have struck Barth most about Agades was that the people spoke Songhai and not Tamajegh; it was in fact, one of the few places left where the language of the greatest Empire of the Niger still survived."—*People of the Veil,* p. 117.

[36] Léon Peyrissac, *Aux Ruines des Grandes Cités Soudanaises,* Paris, 1910, p. 134.

[37] קִיקָיוֹן.—Cfr. Jonas, iv, 6. Note:—The LXX and the Itala have κολοκύνθη. The exact translation is still matter of controversy. Besides gourd we also find suggested ivy and castor oil plant. Of the ancient authors, Pliny alone renders it "ricinus" or gourd.

[38] Monteil, *De Saint Louis à Tripoli par le Lac Tchad,* p. 339.

[39] Cfr. Wood and Lancaster, *Hebrew Grammar,* London, 1920, p. 7.

[40] Note:—The Kanori with other tribes located to the east of Lake Chad, according to Maurice Abadie, are derived from a mixture of the autochthonous Blacks and conquering Whites who advanced from the North and the East.—Cfr. *Abadie, La Colonie du Niger,* p. 191. According to their own traditions, the Kanori came from Yemen, and found their way into Africa by way of Darfur and the Bahr-el-Ghazal.—Abadie, l. c., p. 387.

[41] כִּנּוֹר

*Ouaday ou Dar Saleih*. This district which we are told was also called Dar Wadai,[42] or Land of Wadai, is located just to the west of Darfur, and is unquestionably to be identified with the present Wadai. Now in the south-east corner of this map we find the notation: "Dar Kouka [43]—Origin; The Koukas are of the Djenakhérah, they form in the Dar-el-Djenakhérah [44] a numerous people celebrated for the beauty of their women." [45] This last-named district is situated to the north of a stream marked Bahr-Jro, and Kouka is located on the northern bank of the stream. As far as one can judge then, Kouka was the present Kuga on the River Auk.[46] And it should further be noted, that the Kouka of El-Tounsy would also appear to owe the name to the abundance of gourds to be found in the district,[47] resembling in this the Kouka that is west of Lake Chad.[48]

**Songhois Migration.**

As regards the date of the Songhois migration, Dubois conjectures: "The reconstruction of the exodus is, unfortunately, not so simple as the demonstration of their origin, but the following version seems to be the most probable. The emigration must have begun towards the middle of the seventh century, for Jenne was founded one hundred and fifty years after the Hegira (about 750 of our era), and Jenne is the extreme western point of their invasion. From a

[42] Mohammed ibn-Omer el-Tounsy, *Voyage au Ouaday,* trad. Perron, Paris, 1851, Preface, p. xxiv.

[43] Kouka Country.

[44] Country of the Djenakhérah.

[45] El-Tounsy, l. c., Map at end of Volume.

[46] Kuga is located about N. 10; E. 21. Note:—Among other African towns of similar name, we might mention the Abyssinian Koka, in Gojjam, near the southern bank of the River Abbai or Blue Nile (N. 10¼; E. 36); Kouki in French Equatorial Africa, about one hundred and fifty miles south-west of Fort Archambeault on the Shari River (N. 7¼; E. 17¼); Kachia in Northern Nigeria, about fifty miles south-east of Kaduna (N. 9¾; E. 7¾); Kokoe in the Cameroons, sixteen miles south-east of the bend of the Sanaga River (N. 4¾; E. 13½); besides the Kuka in Northern Territories, to which reference will be made later in connection with the Ashanti. Then there is also the Kaka Tribe in the Cameroons along the Kadei River (N. 4½; E. 14).

[47] El-Tounsy, l. c., Preface, p. xxx.

[48] Still another conjecture might be made as regards the meaning of the word Kokia. In Hebrew Kokab (כּוֹכָב) means star. The Aramaic Kokeba (כּוֹכְבָא) is a feminine form specifically used of the planet Venus. Can the Kokia then, of the Songhois have any possible connection or reference to the city of Venus? If so, have we here perhaps another connecting link between the terra-cotta heads of Memphis, the city of the temple of Venus the Stranger, and the similar statuettes found in West Africa?

hundred to a hundred and twenty years would be sufficient length of time to include the years of wandering and those of settlement and occupation of the Songhois countries." [49] While this is an unnecessary restriction of the duration of the exodus, it effectively fixes its close.

In fact, Léon Peyrissac who specialized in the ruins of the ancient cities of the Sudan assigns as the date for the founding of the Niger Koukia, three hundred years before the Hegira, or about 300 A. D.[50] He further states that the capital was transferred to Gao in the 11th century when the recently arrived Tuaregs had driven the Songhois from Koukia.[51] While all other quotations cited place the founding of Koukia on the Niger at a much later date, it must be remembered that these authors for the most part based their calculations on rough estimates and without any definite data. Peyrissac, on the contrary, studied the question on the site of the ruins, and we feel justified in accepting his conclusions, at least as a working basis.

**Probable Route.**

Dubois has further reconstructed for us the probable line of march of the Songhois,[52] as follows: "The route taken by the emigrants, keeping south of the Libyan desert, passing by Agades and the north of Lake Chad, would meet the Niger somewhere near Gao. They would naturally follow the outskirts of the desert, as the line of less dense population would be the least likely to impede progress. In this manner they would reach the Niger, in spite of the enormous tract of land to be covered, in a comparatively short time. Several details favor this theory. A language similar to that of the Songhois is spoken at Agades, the people bordering the desert between Chad and the Niger are also Songhoi; and there is no doubt that many more analogous ethnological and linguistic traits will be found to exist when the countries lying between Lake Chad and the Nile are

[49] Dubois, l. c., p. 92.
[50] Peyrissac, *Aux Ruines des Grandes Cités Soundanaises,* p. 23.
[51] Idem, p. 23.
[52] Note:—Not only has Dubois good grounds for determining this route, but even to-day it is the main line of commerce from the Nile to the Niger. Thus, Dugald Campbell, describing the Trail of the Tuareg, records: "From east to west, between Khartoum on the Nile to Kano near the Niger, via El Obeid, El Fasher, and every other important south Sahara city—in almost a straight stretch of about three thousand miles—are to be found villages and encampments of the many families of Tuaregs."—Campbell, *On the Trail of the Veiled Tuareg,* p. 19.

better known. Finally, in the country of Bourrousu, near the city of Gao, local tradition preserves the arrival in those parts of an Egyptian Pharao, who is really none other than Dialliaman, or the leader of the Songhoi emigration." [53]

**Caucasian Blood.**

Sir Harry Johnston has this to say of the Songhois of Sokoto: "Their language at present shows no indication of affinity with other groups of Negro or non-Negro speech, but the people themselves have obviously absorbed in past ages a considerable proportion of Caucasian blood, no doubt by mixing with the people of the Libyan Desert, with Arabs, Fula, and even possibly with ancient Egyptians, whose commerce certainly extended into these regions." [54]

And more recently Meek expresses his opinion thus: "It is quite probable that the Songhai did find their way from Egypt to the western Sudan about the time of the first Arab invasions of North Africa." [55] And again: "On the death of Sunni Ali in 1492 the throne was seized by a negro native of Songhai, Muhammad Askia.[56] As we have seen, the rulers of Songhai were foreigners of Himyarite, Libyan, or Nilotic extraction, but they had no doubt lost the purity of their ancient stock." [57] Here, of course, Meek does not agree with our date for the founding of Koukia, but in all probability he was not familiar with the work of Peyrissac.

Writing from Gao on February 25, 1911, Count René le More notes in his diary: "One traces back the foundation of Gao to the year 640. It is thought that it was built by Songhois emigrants come from the banks of the Nile and fleeing from the Arab invasion which at this period had laid waste its borders. . . . I understand that they are finding many analagous traces in language and ethnography at Tchad, Gao and the Nile. Moreover it is thought

[53] Dubois, l. c., p. 94 f.

[54] Johnston, *British Empire in Africa,* p. 335.

[55] Meek, *Northern Tribes of Nigeria,* Vol. I, p. 66.

[56] Note:—Cfr. Buell, *Native Problems in Africa,* p. 679: "Probably the greatest figure in the history of the interior of Africa, at least in the sixteenth century, was Askia the Great, who made the Songhai kingdom renowned not only in the Sudan but along the Mediterranean. In 1500 this leader shattered the Melle Kingdom. But the Songhai Kingdom was itself finally overthrown by the Moroccans in 1591, following which the shattered bits have become subject to the Hausas, Tuaregs, and Fulani. When the Moors were driven out of Spain, they took their revenge in breaking up these Soudan Empires."

[57] Meek, l. c., Vol. I, p. 67.

that one may visualize their route to the south of the Libyan desert, Agades where one finds the same people, north of Tchad and Gao where they came upon a river having some resemblance to the Nile, broad as it and like it subject to periodic and fertilizing overflows."[58] At first glance, this might seem like a mere quotation from Dubois. But in fixing so early a date for the founding of Gao, which event occurred long after the settlement of Koukia, he not only supports Peyrissac's computation, but establishes his report as independent testimony.

**Language.** Again Dubois observes: "The Songhois themselves furnish further proof that they were originally strangers in the country. Their speech is totally different from the numerous Sudanese dialects, and its roots are those of the languages of the Nile. Moreover, their physical type owns nothing in common with that of the West African negro. In the most mixed group of negroes a Songhois may be identified at the first glance; his skin is as black as theirs, certainly, but nothing in his mask conforms to their well known characteristics. The nose of the Songhois is straight and long, pointed rather than flat; the lips are comparatively thin, and the mouth wide rather than prominent and broad; while the eyes are deeply set and straight in their orbit. A cursory glance shows that the profile resembles that of the European, and one is struck by the remarkable intelligence of their physiognomy and expression. In addition they are tall, well-made, and slender."[59]

**Location.** "They founded Jenne," according to Dubois, "their most western territory, in 765, and made it the market of the empire. We may conclude their dominion to have attained its normal and present boundaries towards the end of the eighth century. These limits comprise the countries from the east of Gao to Lake Chad, and that portion of the valley of the Niger below Jenne and Say. The Sahara bound them on the north, the empire of the Mali in the west, and the countries of the Bambara, the Mossi, and the Sokoti in the south; while the vague regions between Agades and Lake Chad limit them in the east."[60]

[58] René le More, *D'Alger à Tombouctoo,* p. 107 f.
[59] Dubois, *Timbuctoo the Mysterious,* p. 96 f.
[60] Dubois, l.c., p. 99.

**Songhois and Ashanti.**

It was from this very district that the Ashanti came at a period that would certainly synchronize with the Songhois Empire.[61] If not actually ethnically related, perhaps we may be able to ascribe to the Songhois some of the Hebrewisms of the Ashanti. At least this offers as plausible an explanation as any thus far advanced. Besides, we find some confirmation of this theory in the fact that the peculiar derivation of the Ashanti and kindred peoples from twelve tribes or families [62] is reported also by Doctor Barth in the Kingdom of Bornu to the south-west of Lake Chad, wherein the sphere of Songhois influence still endures. He describes them as "Twelve great officers or alan which constitute the chief machinery of the empire, and which are already indicated by Makrisi [63] in the words, 'and they have twelve princes.' " [64]

**Petrie's Theory.**

Professor Petrie, the noted Egyptologist, contributed to *Ancient Egypt,* of which he was the Editor, a couple of articles on "Egypt in Africa," wherein he speaks of parallels between West Africa and Egypt, which he explains either as descents, in Egypt and Africa, from a common source, or as a result of Africa borrowing from Egypt. He then enumerates instances in question.[65] In a succeeding number he states: "There appear to have been at least three periods when influence spread in Africa either from or through Egypt. The earliest is under the strong power of the XXVth dynasty at Napata; this kingdom borrowed its writing and much of its culture from Egypt, and spread it to the outlying regions of the rule. This, however, did not apparently spread as far as the Equator or Niger.

"The great activities of the sixth century B. C. spread as far as the Niger, as is shown by Terracotta Nigerian heads . . . the style of art and the solid modelling (not hollow moulding) stamp these as the same school as the best modelled heads found in Mem-

[61] Note:—Is it still another mere coincidence that the name of the old Songhois capital appears again in Kuka which is located in Northern Territories, across the line from Ashanti, and just south of the Volta River (N. 8¼; W. 1½), eleven miles north-east of Kintampo?—Cfr. Claridge, *History of the Gold Coast and Ashanti,* Vol. I, Map. opp. imprint.

[62] Dubois, l. c., p. 113.

[63] Hamaker, p. 12.

[64] Barth, *Travels in Northern and Central Africa,* Vol. II, p. 591.

[65] *Ancient Egypt,* Part III of 1914, p. 122.

phis, of the Persian age. They cannot have been derived from the much rougher hollow moulded figure of Ptolemaic or Roman work. The style is admirable, and could not be surpassed for a racial portrait, identical with the present type of the people." [66]

It is to be noted carefully that Professor Petrie is only interesting himself in the common origin of customs in West Africa and Egypt, and says nothing beyond the fact that the West must have derived them from Egypt, and that, probably, due to an impulse set on foot in the sixth century B. C. While he makes not the slightest reference to the Jews, there is nothing in his view that contravenes our theory in the least. Rather he tends to confirm it, by setting the sixth century B. C. as the beginning of the spread of Egyptian influence to the Niger, the exact period when the refugee Jews were moving along the very line indicated.

**Architecture.** In the last article mentioned, Professor Petrie [67] quotes from Sir Harry Johnston, as follows:

[66] Idem, Part IV of 1914, p. 169. Note:—These Nigerian heads are the ones already referred to in the preceding chapter (p. 266 f.), as having been picked up by Frobenius in the Yoruba Country and chiefly at Ilifé. Christopher Dawson speaks of Ifé as one of the Yoruba theocratic states, "which retain down to the present day their sacred character and their ancient theocratic polity."—Dawson, *The Age of the Gods,* p. 117. Eckert von Sydow, speaking of the history of African Art, recently remarked the "close connexion between Benin and Ife,"—Cfr. Eckert von Sydow, African Culture—*Journal of the International Institute of African Languages and Cultures,* Vol. I, (1928) p. 215, especially as regards the clay heads discovered and adds: "The similarity between the two types is so great that the specimens from Ife must be assigned to the same period as the other series of heads, and therefore they too will date from the end of the fifteenth century, and not from the first millenium B. C. as Frobenius thinks."—l. c., p. 216. However, Samuel Crowther, a native missionary, prefaced his *Grammar of the Yoruba Language* in 1852 with a short digest of the early traditions of the Yorubas, and after calling attention to the fact that the Kingdom of Yoruba formerly extended to Benin, informs us: "Ife is still regarded as the origin of the Yoruba nation, as well as the spot from which all other nations derived their existence. The priests who are very superstitious, and much celebrated for their superior arts of divination, impose upon the natives many fabulous stories connected with Ife the land of their ancestors. Ife is the pantheon of Yoruba: all kinds of idols are to be had there, and celebrated gods are frequently purchased there by the people of other tribes. So much has superstition taken hold of the minds of the people, especially the old, that, during our residence at Abbeokuta, several such gods have been purchased and brought in from Ife, one of which (Odudua) is now situated in the front of the council-house at Ake, and sacrifices of beasts and fowls are made to it every five days, in order to obtain children, wealth, and peace." —Crowther, *Grammar of the Yoruba Language,* London, 1852, p. ii f. May not this indicate that the statuettes of Benin also owe their origin to Ife? They may well have been brought to Benin in the 15th century as Von Sydow thinks. But this would not prove that they had not rested at Ife for many centuries previously in accordance with the view of Frobenius and Petrie.

[67] *Ancient Egypt,* Part IV of 1914, p. 170.

"The Songhai seem to have adopted an imitation of ancient Egyptian architecture in clay and wood instead of stone. They in their turn subdued the Madingoes . . . in the city of Jenne, at the confluence of the Niger and the Bani. From Jenne radiated over all the Western Sudan a diluted Egyptian influence in architectural forms, in boat building, and other arts." [68]

More than a century ago, as already mentioned,[69] T. Edward Bowditch wrote his book to show some connection between the Ashanti and the Abyssinians and Egyptians. His views were too radical to be accepted by his contemporaries. No Flinders Petrie had then come to practically the same conclusion, albeit by a very different process of reasoning.[70]

Maurice Delafosse, it is true, absolutely rejects the suggestion that the style of architecture surviving at Jenne and elsewhere is derived from Egyptian sources. He rather ascribes it to an Arabic-Berber influence from the North.[71] Professor Petrie, on the other hand, is equally positive in his statement: "That the Songhai have continued the Egyptian style of brick and woodwork, which has been best preserved to us by the architectural copies in stone. The general unity of style in building from Upper Egypt across North Africa is very marked." [72]

**Egypt and West Africa.**

Furthermore, when Ibn Batoutah visited the Sudan in the middle of the fourteenth century, he remarked at Ioulatan that "the garments of the inhabitants are neat and imported from Egypt." [73] The majority of the population at the time were evidently Tuaregs, as he describes them as veiling the lower half of the face.[74] He later speaks

[68] H. H. Johnston, *Racial and Tribal Migrations in Africa—Journal of the Royal Geographical Society,* 1913, p. 10.

[69] Cfr. Page 32 ff.

[70] Note:—Kroeber asserts: "Any specific culture trait common to ancient Egypt and the modern Negroes is suspected of a common origin, which ordinarily—though not universally—would mean an Egyptian or more remote origin. Yet the resolution of such a suspicion is not always easy. Much depends on the extent and continuity of the geographical distribution of the trait, and on the actuality and specificity of the resemblance. On these points the necessary information is often still incomplete."—Kroeber, *Anthropology,* p. 499.

[71] Delafosse, *Les Noirs de l'Afrique,* p. 31.

[72] *Ancient Egypt,* Part IV of 1914, p. 170. Note:—P. Amaury Talbot supports the same view. He writes: "The Fulani, Hausa and Bornuese style of architecture came in all likelihood from Egypt via the Songhai."—*Peoples of Southern Nigeria,* Vol. I, p. 30.

[73] Ibn Batoutah, *Voyages,* Vol. IV, p. 387.

[74] Idem, p. 430.

of the merchants of Tacadda who journey to Egypt once a year for all their supplies.[75] And once again, he refers to the "road to Ghat, which leads to Egypt." [76] All this would indicate that even in the fourteenth century the tribes of West Africa were in close contact with the commerce and culture of Egypt and not with the nearer centers of the North. From which we well might argue, that they would naturally keep in touch with the country whence their dominant influence and culture had been ultimately derived.[77]

It is with reason then, that Nahum Slouschz declares: "The history of the time tells us that, on the eve of the Roman invasion, there existed, between Elephantis and Ethiopia, autonomous Jewish colonies, which were military, agricultural and industrial in character, with a republican form of government, and which exercised a civilizing religious influence on the natives of the country. This view was held also by the geographer Elisée Reclus.[78] And without being certain of it, we may conclude that this colonization had penetrated the African continent to a considerable depth before the coming of the Romans." [79]

**Ivory Coast.**

Maurice Delafosse, after showing the influence of ancient Egypt on the civilization of the Agni of Baoulé on the Ivory Coast,[80] later returns to the subject and in great detail establishes the existence of a strong eastern influence which he unhesitatingly ascribes to Egypt, not only among the Agni and their kindred the Ashanti, but also throughout West Africa in general. However, he takes care to state: "I no longer claim that the Agni or their ancestors the Ashanti have come from Egypt, or from countries near Egypt: it

[75] Idem, p. 439.
[76] Idem, p. 445.
[77] Note:—According to Kroeber: "Ancient Egyptian influences have penetrated Africa more significantly than has generally been thought. It is only recently that a beginning has been made in tracing them out in detail in the Nile Sudan. For so intensive a civilization as that of Egypt to exist in juxtaposition to the southeastern Hamitic tribes and the Negroes for five or six thousand years without radiating innumerable elements of culture into their life would be unparalleled. In fact the dynastic Egyptians used materials like ostrich feathers that were imported from the south, and depicted Negroid physical types. The trade and association involved must have flowed both ways." —Kroeber, *Anthropology*, p. 497.
[78] Elisée Reclus, *L'Homme et la Terre*, Vol. II, p. 239.
[79] Slouschz, *Travels in North Africa*, p. 213 f.
[80] Maurice Delafosse, *Les Agni—L'Anthropologie*, Paris, Tome IV, (1903), p. 402 ff.

seems proven that their race originated from Gondja (part of Salaga, on the Upper Volta). I do not wish to say more than that there have been Egyptian migrations to Baoulé."[81]

Then, after enumerating many instances of Egyptian influence on the civilization of the Ivory Coast, Delafosse expresses the opinion: "But the Touaregs, and above all the Peuhls, cannot be regarded as the true propagators of the Egyptian civilization."[82] In his way of thinking, their nomadic life precludes any such possibility. His own conclusion is: "The true agents of propaganda of the Egyptian civilization in the black countries have been probably the Haussa, who, having themselves received the civilization from the Ethiopians and the peoples of the Upper Nile, have transmitted it progressively to all their neighbours of the West: The Songhai, the Yoruba, and the Nta of Gondja (ancestors of the Ashanti and of the Agni and in consequence of the Baoulé). The Songhai in their turn civilized the Mande, the Yorouba have civilized the Dahomans, etc."[83]

While agreeing with the French Savant, that the influence was in reality derived by emigration from Egypt, it is our belief that these emigrants were not themselves Egyptians, but exile Hebrews, in great part identified with, and absorbed eventually by, the Songhois, in their migration from the East. The Hausa, as we have seen,[84] are not a race at all, but rather a conglomeration of peoples of various origins. They, too, may have imbibed some of the same influence, but they cannot be the main carriers.

**Ichthyolatry.** In the case of the Songhois, however, we must admit the possibility of a flaw in our argument. For according to their tradition, at the time of the advent of Dialliaman in their midst, they had been worshippers of a fish which the new-comer destroyed.[85] This might indicate that they had

[81] Maurice Delafosse, *Sur les Traces probables de Civilisation Egyptienne et d'Hommes de Race Blanche à la Côte d'Ivoire—L'Anthropologie,* Tome XI (1900), p. 432.

[82] Idem, p. 688.

[83] Idem, p. 689.

[84] Cfr. Page 106 f.

[85] Dubois, *Timbuctoo the Mysterious,* p. 90. Note:—Speaking of the superstitions of the Jews of Tunis, Nahum Slouschz writes: "We will mention first a whole series of beliefs which have sprung up from the cult of the fish, a cult that traces of whose ancient predominance may be found scattered across the whole Mediterranean. Thus the Jewish fortune-tellers practice divination with fish. At Tunis, even at Tangiers, there are certain kinds of fish which it is forbidden to eat, on account of their use in divination. It is not in good taste to

actually been Christians, as the fish was the symbol in the early days of the Church, whereby the true worshippers of Christ might recognize one another without awakening the suspicions of the Pagans. In this case, Dialliaman might have crushed out Christianity in the tribe, and so given rise to the fable, a supposition that seems highly improbable.

**Ophiolatry.** But let us now return to Desplagnes and his theory which was already referred to in a previous chapter.[86] It is his opinion that to the south of Egypt, from earliest times, groups of black people, who were devoted to ophiolatry, and themselves of mixed lineage, were further adding to their racial complex by absorbing the wastage of Egypt. First came pastoral tribes, then conquered nations or nomads, who arrived as individuals or in groups, and finally the rebellious mercenaries who marched up the Nile and located, he maintains, at Bahr-el-Azrak, near Khartoum, and at Bahr-el-Ghazel.[87]

Desplagnes would locate this heterogeneous tribal conglomeration in the great plains that border the Upper Nile, and he suggests that under the name of Sousou they were started on a migration westward by the advance of Islamism in the eighth century, bringing with them their cult of ophiolatry.[88]

It was about this period that Dubois thinks that the Songhois left Egypt, when the tranquillity "was rudely disturbed in the seventh century by the Lieutenants of the first Khalifs; and the country received a shock that would fully justify such an exodus. . . . The Lower, Upper and Middle Egypts were all overrun towards the year 640." [89] But, as we have already seen, the Songhois must have been on the Niger long antecedent to this date.[90]

use the word 'hut' (Fish); its use is replaced by the phrase Mta el hara or el hahra (beings of the sea)."—*Travels in North Africa,* p. 282. It should be noticed, too, that the god of the Philistines was the fish-god Dagon.—Cfr. I Kings v, 2–7.

[86] Cfr. Page 240 f.

[87] Desplagnes, *Le Plateau Central Nigérien,* p. 130 f.

[88] Idem, p. 132 f. Note:—Ellis speaks of Whydah as Juida, though there is probably no significance in the name, and makes it the original center of the serpent worship in West Africa. It was only after the capture of the kingdom of Juida in 1726 that the Dahomans adopted ophiolatry. It was through the Dahomans, as we have seen, and prisoner Juidans, that the practice found its way to the West Indies.—Cfr. Ellis, *The Ewe-Speaking Peoples of the Slave Coast of West Africa,* p. 54.

[89] Dubois, *Timbuctoo the Mysterious,* p. 93.

[90] Cfr. Page 300 f.

Passing Lake Chad, and reaching the Niger Bend, the Sousou, according to Desplagnes, imposed their worship of the serpent on such of the Songhois and other tribes as submitted to them. Those who would not adopt the cult were driven before them or exterminated. Thus it happened that the Nda who occupied the Nigerian plains and doubtless other branches of the family who had become closely allied with the Songhois and had been driven in from the East, were forced to retreat to the South, "for we see them in the twelfth century penetrating into Dahomey and under the name of Ashanti-Agni [91] crossing the forests of the Ivory Coast and stopping only at the shores of the ocean." [92]

**Ashanti.**

Captain Figiac [93] is also of the opinion that "the people Nda is actually called Agni-Ashanti or Appolians. It is to be found scattered more or less intermingled in the Ivory Coast Colony, Togo, the Gold Coast and Dahomey." [94]

While not prepared either to affirm, or to deny, this suggestion as regards the derivation of the Ashanti from the Nda, in any case, we look to the East and not to the North as the origin of their tribal culture. And whether this same culture as we find it to-day among the Ashanti was also proper to the Nda themselves, or an ingraft from a later migration, we are convinced that what is really characteristic and distinctive of the Ashanti must be traced ultimately to the far East, and that too at a very early period.

**Human Sacrifice.**

The very sacrifice of human life that so long marked the royal funerals, notably in Ashanti and Dahomey, only strengthens the presumption of the Eastern origin of the antecedents of these tribes. For no less an authority than Professor Flinders Petrie asserts: "At Abydos we found that the burials which surrounded King Qa were made before the brick chambers were hard, so that the walls squeezed down upon them, and it seems that the servants were killed all together at the funeral. The human sacrifices appear to have been retained in the royal burials of the XVIIIth dynasty (1580–1350

[91] Note:—The Agni word for sand is Agné.—Cfr. L. Tauxier, *Le Noir de Boudoukou,* Paris, 1921, p. 623. It is just possible then, that the tribal name may have some reference to the desert and might imply that the Ashanti were of desert origin. This, however, does not seem likely.

[92] Desplagnes, l. c., p. 134.

[93] *Bulletin de Société de Géographie de Rochefort,* 1903–1905.

[94] Desplagnes, l. c., p. 110, Note 3.

B. C.) and the teknu appears to have been a mock human sacrifice in private tombs of the same age." [95]

So much horror is expressed with the comparatively recent human holocaust that was practiced among the Ashanti, that it may appear repellant to ascribe any connection, however remote, between this tribe and the Chosen People of God. But it is well to recall to mind, that human sacrifice was far from being uncommon in both the Northern and the Southern Kingdoms before the Babylonian Exile.

**Biblical Precedent.**

Thus in the Fourth Book of Kings, we read of Israel: "They served Baal. And consecrated their sons, and their daughters through fire: and they gave themselves to divinations, and soothsayings: and they delivered themselves up to do evil before the Lord, to provoke him. And the Lord was very angry with Israel, and removed them from his sight." [96] And later in the same chapter we are told of the new generation that sprang up in Samaria from the remnants of Israel intermarrying with the colonists planted there by the Assyrians: "And they that were of Sepharvaim burnt their children in fire, to Adrameleck and Anameleck the gods of Sepharvaim. And nevertheless they worshipped the Lord." [97]

Meanwhile a like condition of affairs prevailed also in Juda. For of Achaz it is written: "He walked in the way of the kings of Israel: moreover he consecrated also his son, making him pass through the fire according to the idols of the nations: which the Lord destroyed before the children of Israel." [98] Of Manasses, too, it is recorded: "He built altars in the house of the Lord, of which the Lord said: In Jerusalem I will put my name. And he built altars for all the host of heaven in the two courts of the temple of the Lord. And he made his son pass through fire: and he used divination, and observed omens, and appointed pythons, and multiplied soothsayers to do evil before the Lord, and to provoke him.' [99] And again: "He made his sons to pass through the fire in the valley of Benennom." [100] The Ashanti at their worst never fell any lower than that!

[95] *Ancient Egypt,* Part III of 1914, p. 124.
[96] IV Kings xvii, 16–18.
[97] IV Kings xvii, 31, 32.
[98] IV Kings xvi, 3.
[99] IV Kings xxi, 4–6.
[100] II Paral. xxxiii, 6.

Of Amon, too, we read: "He did evil in the sight of the Lord, as Manasses his father had done; and he sacrificed to all the idols which Manasses his father had made, and served them." [101]

Of the earlier lapses the Psalmist had cried out in horror: "They sacrificed their sons, and their daughters to devils, and they shed innocent blood: the blood of their sons and of their daughters which they sacrificed to the idols of Canaan." [102] And the prophets in their turn waxed eloquent against this ungodly sacrifice. Thus, for example, Jeremias: "The Lord hath rejected, and forsaken the generation of his wrath, because the children of Juda have done evil in my eyes, saith the Lord. They have set their abominations in the house in which my name is called upon, to pollute it; and they have built the high places of Topheth, which is in the valley of the son of Ennom to burn their sons, and their daughters in the fire." [103] And Ezechiel is no less outspoken, as in the name of the Lord he upbraids Juda: "Thou hast taken thy sons, and thy daughters, whom thou hast borne to me; and hast sacrificed the same to them, to be devoured. Is thy fornication small? Thou hast sacrificed and given my children to them, consecrating them by fire." [104]

**Legal Penalty.** In connection with human sacrifice among the Ashanti, Walton Claridge has said in extenuation of the practice: "A very large proportion of the so-called human sacrifices that are always adduced as evidence in support of this

[101] II Paral. xxxiii, 22.
[102] Ps. CV, 37, 38.
[103] Jeremias vii, 29–31.
[104] Ezechiel xvi, 20, 21. Note:—According to Kortleitner: "By almost every nation even men were immolated to the gods and that especially in the time of public calamities, because there existed no more precious gift, with which the wrath of the gods might be placated. Wherefore it was the custom to offer the most beloved sons, especially an only child, and those born of the most noble lineage. By these sacrifices is proven partly the memory of the fall from primal state and a desire of expiation, partly the depraving of the first concept of sacrifice."—Then follows a long list of references showing the existence of the practice among practically all the leading nations of Ancient Times, from the rudest to the most refined.—Cfr. Kortleitner, *De Polytheismo Universo,* p. 122. Wallis, too, observes: "It has been said that one of the most noteworthy features of savage and barbarian as opposed to civilized society is the relative unimportance in the former of the individual as compared with the community, as shown, for example, by the various forms of human sacrifice which apparently shock no one. But human sacrifice is seldom if ever found in the lower stages of savagery, characterizing rather the higher stages, the more advanced barbarisms, and semi-civilizations. It was a feature in most of the older Mediterranean cultures."—Wallis, *An Introduction to Anthropology,* p. 296 f.

charge (cruelty) were really nothing more than public executions of criminals who, after condemnation, had been reserved until victims were required for some religious ceremony in which the sacrifice of human life was considered essential." [105] In some of our States to-day death is the penalty for other crimes than murder, and the guillotine of France is no less grewsome than the executioner's sword of the Ashanti used to be.

Moreover, as regards the Ashanti themselves, Captain Rattray is insistent: "Ashanti tradition everywhere records a time when human sacrifices and capital punishment were not known, and disputes were settled between clans by single combat of leaders of the clan." [106] In some respects this practice was not unlike the struggle between David and Goliath.[107]

**Jukun.**

Among the smaller tribes of Northern Nigeria, and located for the most part on the south bank of the River Benue,[108] are the Jukun who show not only much in common with the Ashanti, but in their traditions may be connected with the Songhois and the latter's trek from the East. Here then, we have possibly a connecting link between the Ashanti and the Songhois.

**Akin to Ashanti.**

Unlike most of the surrounding tribes, these Jukun "are devoid of all tribal marks." [109] Also, while the condition of absolute nakedness is common among the pagan tribes of their vicinity [110] and "the great majority of Animistic tribes wear natural clothing" such as aprons of goatskin, etc.[111] the Jukun claim that they cannot "recall a time when they did not affect manufactured clothes," and they "have a characteristic method of wearing a cloth tucked in at the waist and extending to the feet." [112] In all this they are not unlike the Ashanti.

The idea of multiple souls and the belief in reincarnation is common to the Jukun [113] and to the Ashanti.[114] "Human sacri-

[105] Claridge, *History of the Gold Coast and Ashanti,* Vol. I, p. 188.
[106] Rattray, *Religion and Art in Ashanti,* p. 135 Note.
[107] I Kings xvii.
[108] About N. 8°; E. 10°.
[109] Meek, *Northern Tribes of Nigeria,* Vol. I, p. 29.
[110] Idem, p. 40.
[111] Idem, p. 41.
[112] Idem, p. 42.
[113] Idem, Vol. II, p. 35.
[114] Rattray, *Ashanti,* p. 80.

fice is another feature of Jukun-Yoruba culture," [115] even as it is distinctive of the Ashanti.[116] Moreover, if the Jukun king "even touch the ground with his hands or uncovered feet the crops would be ruined." [117] So also, "The feet of the King of Ashanti were likewise never to touch the ground 'lest a great famine should come upon the nation.' " [118]

Achidong, the Supreme Being of the Jukun, has much in common with Nyankopon of the Ashanti. The two words have a similarity of ring, at least as much as might be expected from two divergent and unwritten languages, and Achidong is as near to Nyankopon as is the Accompong of Jamaica. With the Jukun, Achidong is the God of Justice,[119] has charge of the souls of the dead, etc.[120]

**Linked with East.** Tracing the Jukun to the East, we find that according to their tribal traditions, they "left Yemen through fear of Muhammed." [121] Claiming a descent from Yemen, they are not unlike the Dialliaman of the Songhois,[122] and the motive fear of Mohammed, might easily be a later ingraft on the tribal legend, as all the pagan tribes after centuries of experience had reason to fear the devotees of Mohammedanism.

The West African harp, used only by the Jukun and a few other tribes, "appears to be identical with that depicted in ancient

[115] Meek, l. c., Vol. II, p. 39.
[116] Rattray, *Ashanti,* p. 100.
[117] Meek, l. c., Vol. I, p. 254.
[118] Rattray, l. c., p. 216. Note:—A similar custom existed among the Bakuba, another tribe that shows an early Hebraic influence, as will be noted in the next chapter. Conway T. Wharton says: "The traditions of the Bakuba show that their former kings were never permitted to touch the ground. The king was carried by his subjects wherever he willed to go; when a halt was called they first spread out mats that the royal feet might not come in contact with the polluted soil which ordinary mortals trod."—*The Leopard Hunts Alone,* New York, 1927, p. 44.
[119] Meek, l. c., Vol. II, p. 31
[120] Idem, Vol. II, p. 28.
[121] Idem, Vol. I, p. 67.
[122] Note:—In reference to the Nomadic Jews of Africa, Nahum Slouschz writes: "There are Jewish traditions also in the south, where a group of oases forms the Ksur of the Sahara. Entire tribes, like the Hanancha and the Smul, and various ethnic groups, claim to be descended from the Jews of Arabia, the famous Yehud Chaibar (the Beni Rechab of Jewish tradition), with whom Mohammed carried on such a bitter struggle."—Cfr. *Travels in North Africa,* p. 296. However, we are not inclined to connect the Jukun with these Nomads of the North, but rather with the Songhois and kindred influences from the East.

Egyptian paintings. It is found in Upper Egypt at the present day." [123] So too, "the trumpet known as the kakaki" which is a "royal instrument," and "usually about eight feet long and made out of white metal" was supposedly introduced by the "founders of the Jukun state." [124] It is certainly not an African instrument, and distinctively savors of the East.

Meek further remarks: "The number seven has among the Jukun as among the Semites, a sacred significance." [125] And in his chapter on "Ethnological Conclusions," he observes: "The Jukun-Yoruba culture complex presents many striking similarities with that of the Shilluk—a tribe belonging to the Egyptian Sudan." [126] Meek had previously noticed: "The Jukun, who claim to be the earliest inhabitants of Bornu, say that when they first entered Bornu they found no other inhabitants there." [127] This tribal tradition would seem to imply that they had migrated west at a very early period.

**Shilluks.** Among the Shilluks, too, it should be observed that the more or less mythical leader who brought them to their present location, and established the reigning dynasty, has traditionally been known as Nyakang. Can this Nyakang of the Shilluk possibly share a common origin with the Nyankopon of the Ashanti and the Achidong of the Jukun? Sir James G. Frazer asserts that Nyakang is "now universally revered by the people as a demi-god," [128] and he quotes as his authority the statement of C. G. Seligman: "The whole working religion of the Shilluk is a cult of Nyakang, the semi-divine ancestor of the kings, in each of whom his spirit is immanent." [129] But is it not possible that the legend has reference to the Divinity who guided the Chosen People throughout their wanderings in the Desert and established them in the Promised Land, and who subsequently invested, as it were, the anointed of Samuel with His spirit, when he entrusted to Saul and his successors the right of authority? For, ultimately all authority comes from God alone,

[123] Meek, l. c., Vol. II, p. 157.
[124] Idem, Vol. II, p. 159.
[125] Idem, Vol. I, p. 183.
[126] Idem, Vol. II, p. 163.
[127] Idem, Vol. I, p. 58.
[128] Frazer, *The Golden Bough,* Vol. VI, p. 164.
[129] C. G. Seligman, *The Cult of Nyakang and the Divine Kings of the Shilluk,* Khartoum, 1911, p. 220.

no matter how the individual, in whom it is to be vested, may be designated.

**Summary.** Briefly then, to sum up the present chapter, we may accept the Songhois as an ethnic complex that evolved at an early date not far from the banks of the Nile. In this, tribal tradition is strongly supported by the fact that in all probability it was the Songhois who introduced, clear across Africa, a type of architecture that is distinctly Egyptian in its characteristics. We feel secure, too, in concluding that the Songhois originated in a conglomeration of peoples and tribes,[130] black, white and every intervening shade, with the negro element numerically in the ascendancy, but a distinctively light-complexioned aristocracy which must have included Egyptians, Abyssinians and probably a strong influx of refugee Jews who gradually asserted a cultural dominance over the entire mass. Certain it is that the two first recorded dynasties which ruled the Songhois when once they had developed into a powerful African State were distinctively white, and there is every indication that they did not belong to any late accretion to the nation, but rather that they had been the dominant aristocracy from the earliest days.

The migration to the west must have commenced well before the Christian era. The discoveries of Peyrissac on the site of the Nigerian Koukiya places the founding of the first Songhois capital on the Niger at about 300 A. D. And René le More, in independently assigning the foundation of Gao to 640 A. D., confirms this estimate. For fully three centuries had passed before Koukiya was abandoned and the new capital was established higher up the Niger.

The departure from Upper Egypt was presumably caused by tribal unrest and the pressing need of new pastures and sources of food for the expanding population. The progress then, would naturally be slow, as it would only be the exhaustion of a present site and the necessity of pressing deeper and deeper into the interior, that would urge a pastoral people to a further migration into the heart of the Continent.

The line of trek, almost of necessity, would be determined by

[130] Note:—Professor Hankins whole-heartedly defends the thesis: "That all important historical groups have been heterogeneous in racial composition; and that all areas of high culture have been areas of extensive population movement and race mixture."—*Racial Basis of Civilization,* Preface, p. viii.

the main route of commerce that flowed from the Nile to the Niger, and which of course followed the well-watered section with plentiful pasturage and ample supply of animal food, that extended between the dense tropical forests on the south and the desert wastes on the north. This highway, if we may so term it, passed by way of Khartum, Kordofan, Darfur, Wadai and Chad, around to the north of the Lake of that name, and then along the Yobe and Hadeija Rivers to Kano, and so on to the Niger itself, which in many ways was the counterpart of the distant Nile.

Long centuries must have been spent in covering the thousands of miles that separate the two great rivers, and during this entire period the Songhois were steadily evolving into a powerful and conquering State. On reaching the Niger they gradually spread out, overran the surrounding country, absorbed various other elements, including no doubt other waves of immigration that had followed from the East, until finally they built up the famous Songhois Empire which for a time dominated West Africa and was finally annihilated only when the refugee Moors of Spain, armed with the deadly firearm, hitherto entirely unknown in Central Africa, retreated through Morocco and wreaked their vengence on the thriving Negro Kingdoms of the interior.

A natural consequence of the advance of Mohammedanism has always been the blotting out of all local tribal culture and the complete Islamization of conquered peoples. The Songhois, perhaps, have resisted this influence to an unwonted degree. Still, it is not surprising to find that it is only a struggling vestige of ancient culture that yet lingers among the remnants of the Songhois proper. True tribal traditions and indications of cultural traits are better preserved among the early offshoots from the parent-stock that have successfully resisted the inroads of Islam.

That the Ashanti themselves at one time fell under the influence of the Songhois before the advent of Mohammedanism is almost undeniable. Every indication traces them back to the very field of the Songhois' greatest activity along the Niger; and to our mind, the characteristic traits of the Ashanti would indicate that it was active resistance to the advance of Islam that forced them to take refuge in the great tropical forests where the tsetse-fly rendered it impossible for the mounted invaders to follow them.

That diffusion may prove acceptable to the exactions of modern research, it is necessary to show between dissociated areas traces of the gradual expansion of a culture. And this requirement we feel has been satisfied in parallelisms with the Ashanti established notably among the Yoruba and the Jukun, and through these tribes with the Shilluk of the Egyptian Sudan.

We are now ready to draw our final conclusions and to try and evaluate in some small way the mass of facts already placed before the reader.

## *Chapter XII*

## CONCLUSIONS

**Pittard's Warning.**

Professor Pittard warns us: "Travellers in a hurry to write their accounts of their travels and anxious at any cost to provide 'something new' have also disturbed the even course of our knowledge of human races. Insufficiently qualified with scientific knowledge and devoid of judgment, they have sometimes arrived at the most unexpected approximations."[1] And again: "Degrees of ethnic purity are perceptible to Anthropology alone—that is to say, they are appreciable only by detailed analysis based on exact methods. No traveller's description—unless the traveller be a specialist—can be taken into serious consideration." [2] Professor Pittard goes on to explain his attitude. "Most travellers," he says, "pay far more attention to the expression of the face, to gestures and costume, or, often enough, to the desire to make the type conform to the requirements of some intellectual theory, than they do to objective morphological observations which entail the taking of a great deal of trouble." [3]

Keeping all this in mind, we have to make due allowance in evaluating the testimony of the travellers cited in the course of our present study. However, in many instances the quotations were in reality admissions directly contrary to the observer's preconceived notions, and not infrequently our witnesses have been scientists of no mean standing who were unquestionably competent to give evidence in their own peculiar fields of research.

**Hebrew Influences in Negro Land.**

We feel safe then, in formulating our first conclusion:—Somewhere in the dim past, a wave, or more probably a series of waves, of Hebraic influence swept over Negro Africa, leaving unmis-

[1] Pittard, *Race and History,* p. 10.
[2] Idem, p. 18.
[3] Idem, p. 19.

takable traces among the various tribes, where they have endured even to the present day.

**Among Ashanti.**

This is demonstrated, as we have seen, by such culture elements among the Ashanti as the Ob cult; religious dances; use of "Amen"; vowel value; patriarchal system; parallel symbolism of authority in "stool" and "chair"; endogamy; cross-cousin marriages; familial names; exogamy; simplicity of marriage rite; uncleanness after childbirth; purification ceremonies; menstrual seclusion; ceremonial ablutions; and Ashanti loan words of apparent Hebrew origin. Then in matters of religion, we have the truly remarkable similarity of the Ashanti Yame and the Hebrew Yahweh, first as regards the etymological derivation of the words themselves; and then in the tribal concept of Divine Attributes and the created channels of Divine Influence; and finally in the divided service accorded; the adoption of fetishism or its equivalent without any apostasy from monotheism; the subtle reference to a Redeemer; Ta Kora, the "son of the supreme God"; the "altar of Nyame" preserved in the stamp pattern of Ashanti cloth; the survival of what appears to be the breastplate and the misnefet of the Jewish High Priest; sterility a curse; the traditional twelve-tribe theory; the raven story of Elias and its counterpart; New Year festivals; legitimate violation of a sacred taboo; and reference to the Natural Law.

**Elsewhere.**

That the Hebrew cultural elements are not isolated instances among the Ashanti, but are to be found in less degree broadcast through Negro Land, is shown from similar traits in other tribes. Thus, for example, in floggings, the traditional number of strokes, "forty less one"; the common practice of New-Moon festivals; the oath-drink akin to the scriptural "bitter waters"; expectation of a Messias; Jewish distinction between diaboli and daemonia; the duodecimal division of tribes into families; exogamy; bloody sacrifices with the sprinkling of blood upon altar and door-posts; mourning customs; obsessions; legal defilement; Jewish octave; law on adultery; Sabbath rest; Levirate marriages; circumcision; priestly garb; etc. While the glass manufactured at Nupe and the carvings on window shutters indicate a Palestinian influence, the terra-cotta heads found in Yoruba postulate ultimately a Memphitic influx of culture.

**Possible Explanations.**

How are we to account for this mass of evidence? The environmental theory might possibly explain most of the facts individually.[4] However, the startling similarity between the Ashanti Yame and the Hebrew Yahweh, with all its ramifications, certainly requires a more plausible reason.

Convergent evolution, in turn, might satisfy in the case of small groups of these cultural traits. But scarcely so when we consider them as a whole, especially since we find these traits not isolated, but stretching out in the very direction from which tribal contact might be expected.[5]

The parallels established, too, are so numerous and so detailed that diffusion would appear to be the only plausible explanation for these trait-complexes. This is particularly true, as we have been able to build up a strong presumption, to say the least, for historic contact in pre-Christian days between the Hebrew People and the Negro tribes of West Africa.

In our present study, we may neglect any cultural waves that may have been derived from the Jewish hybrids of Abyssinia who are probably of more recent origin, and confine our consideration to the influx from pre-Christian Jews who from the north and the east exerted a cultural influence on Negro Land.

**Northern Influx.**

The initial Hebraic influence on West African Negro tribes may quite possibly have begun with Hebrew merchants who were identified with the

[4] Note:—Professor Dixon has well said: "On the whole, the physical effects definitely attributable to environment are disappointingly few. The belief long held, for example, that the skin color of the Negro and other dark-skinned peoples was the direct result of tropical climate can, in the light of our present knowledge, no longer be maintained. The almost black-skinned Tasmanian lived, and had lived apparently for countless ages, in a temperate environment comparable to that of southern England, whereas some peoples of Indonesia and tropical America are little if any darker than many Europeans. The real explanation for the development of excessive pigmentation is still in a measure uncertain, and although a climatic factor is probably involved, there are clearly others which are equally if not more important."—Dixon, *Building of Cultures,* p. 8.

[5] Note:—Professor Wallis enunciates the principle: "When similar traits are found in distant tribes with no such traits bridging the geographical interval there is reason to attribute the similarity to independent origins, unless historical contacts can be shown or inferred."—*An Introduction of Anthropology,* p. 467.

Egyptian commerce that pushed its way from the Nile to the very banks of the Niger. But before taking up this particular phase of the question, it seems well to review in some detail the more pronounced Hebraic influx that reached Negro Land from the north across the Sahara.[6]

**Hebrews and Phoenicians.**

The close association of the Hebrews and the Phoenicians, especially during the days of Solomon, would naturally lead one to suspect that Hebrew merchants and sailors, individually or in small groups, must have early been identified with the Phoenician projects along the coast of North Africa. More or less mythological legends as well as the living tradition from earliest times support this supposition. And recent archaeological discoveries are strengthening its plausibility.[7]

The later commercial activities of Phoenicia, but more particularly of Carthage, along the Atlantic Coast, no doubt in turn also included individual Hebrews in the personnel. But, even if colonies were actually established along the Guinea Coast, all this could little more than pave the way for later and more lasting influences. For, such early efforts as were made must have been sporadic, and a generation or two would obliterate all traces of the scattered individuals, and no enduring impress could be left on the manners and customs of the tribe that absorbed these little groups or colonies, if they did really ever exist. We must look, then, to a

[6] Note:—Shortly before the close of the past century, the Sheik El-Hachaichi of Tunis, a devout Mussulman, writing of a journey through the Tuareg country, states: "I have not, either in the Sahara or among the tribes, encountered a single Jew. They assure me that they do not exist in the Soudan, except in the southern part, where some autochthonous people profess the Jewish religion."—Cfr. Mohammed ben Otsmane el-Haichaichi *Voyage au Pays des Senoussia,* trad. Serras et Lesram, Paris, 1912, p. 243. Naturally as a Mussulman he minimizes the presence of the Jews as much as possible, and his admission that "autochthonous peoples profess the Jewish religion," even if the word autochthonous is not taken in its strict technical sense, should carry great weight.

[7] Note:—According to Slouschz: "We can no longer ignore the traditions attaching to the Judaism of pre-Islamic times—traditions which cover the whole of Northern Africa. And these traditions speak now of David and Joab, now of Joshua and Solomon, and even Esdras, the last in connection with clans of Aaronides and with Cohens."—*Travels in North Africa,* p. 214. While too much credence should not be given to the personal conclusions of Slouschz who as an enthusiast is apt at times to make the wish father to the thought, still we cannot brush lightly aside the accumulation of facts which he has so painstakingly amassed during his years of tireless research and personal investigation.

later date for a much more extensive and continuous infiltration of Hebrews into the stronghold of Negro Africa.

**North African Judaism.**

In the foundation of Carthage and the Semiticizing of the neighboring tribes, the Hebrews quite probably played no inconsiderable part. And, as the early adventurers, almost without exception, were undoubtedly men, the absence of women of their own kind must of necessity have led to some intermarriage on the part of individual Hebrews with other elements, thus early introducing an ethnic mixture, which was naturally increased by subsequent proselyting.

These early pioneers were followed by other Hebrew groups including entire families with their women and children, thus building up well-defined colonies especially at Carthage and later at Cyrenaica. With the advent of the Ptolemies in Egypt, these Jewish centers, many of which began to take on a military character, made rapid strides until in certain parts the Hebrews became a very considerable faction, especially in the cities.[8]

**Jewish Colonial Africa.**

Meanwhile proselyting had won over many Berber Tribes, not only of the coast but also of the hinterland. And it would be difficult at this distant date to distinguish these Judaized Berbers from the colonized Hebrews with the infusion of Berber blood that was entailed by their early associations and subsequent intermarriages. For all practical purposes, in religious matters they acted as a unit, especially in opposition to Grecian and Roman paganism, and the prosperity of what we might call Jewish Colonial Africa was at its height.[9]

While the destruction of Jerusalem by the Romans undermined the national prestige of the Jews, the arrival of large contingents of exiles tended to increase their numerical strength in North Africa, until Colonial Juda felt called upon to challenge the destroyers of the Mother Country.

[8] Note:—Slouschz maintains: "It is certain that shortly before the destruction of Jerusalem, Jews and Jewish proselytes formed a large part, if not the majority of the population of Libya."—*Travels in North Africa,* p. 215.

[9] Note:—Slouschz writes: "In the Roman epoch, at the beginning of the Christian era, there was a prosperous Jewish diaspora spread over the whole of Northern Africa as far as the shores of the Atlantic."—*Travels in North Africa,* p. 274.

The rebellion of 115 A. D. was a disastrous one for the African Jews. And while it required all the power Rome could muster three long years to crush the uprising, eventually the infuriated legions wrought the same havoc throughout Cyrenaica that they had accomplished in stricken Palestine. On the coast at least, Judaism was annihilated, but back in the Jebels, refugee Jews and Judaized Berbers began a new order of things.

**Jewish Sanctuaries.**

Up to this period, it would appear, the African Jewry had prospered, probably under the aegis of local sanctuaries entirely controlled by clans of Cohanim according to the method in vogue at Jerusalem, until the destruction of the Temple. Only the late-comers had become accustomed to a state of affairs whereby the Rabbi disputed the religious supremacy of the Cohen.[10]

**Survival of the Cohanim.**

After finding refuge in the Jebels, wherever possible the survivors of the old régime would naturally cling to their time-honored system of having Cohanim at the head of religious affairs. The newcomers, on the other hand, either through choice or from necessity, would readily dispense with their services. In many cases, too, the Cohanim must have been exterminated in the general massacre,[11] and replacements were not to be had, while nomadic

[10] Note:—Among the early Jews in North Africa, Slouschz would include: "Clans of Aaronides, who like Onias in Egypt, founded Bamot, or sanctuaries, in various places throughout the country."—*Travels in North Africa,* p. 273. He tells us: "One of the peculiarities of native African Judaism is the tendency of Cohanim to group themselves as a sort of clan apart from the laity. The few Levites that are there come of Spanish or Italian stock, and are often not favorably regarded by the Cohanim. . . . What is the origin of this curious separation which is peculiar to the Jews of Africa? As long as the Temple was standing the sons of Aaron formed a caste which had the monopoly of holy service. At the time of the exile they had their bamot in Palestine as well as throughout the diaspora. The rabbis who disputed the religious supremacy with them were not successful until after the destruction of the second Temple. But in Africa and Arabia where the settlement of Jews preceded the destruction of Jerusalem, the Aaronides continued at the head of religious affairs for many centuries."—l. c., p. 287. "The religion of Gabes, or the Jerid in particular lays claim to having the birthplace of a priestly clan of Zadokite origin, that is, of the same origin as Onias, the founder of the Temple of Leontopolis. A vague talmudic allusion would make it appear that the house of Onias ministered up to the fourth century. (Bab. Talmud, Magillah, 10a)."—l. c., p. 288 f. "The struggle between the Cohanim and the vulgus, which has nearly everywhere disappeared, is still going on in more than one corner of Africa, though its bitterness has been mitigated. In the end the tribes of Cohanim came to model themselves very closely on the Mussulman tribes of the Shurefas, the descendants of Mohammed."—l. c., p. 290.

[11] According to Slouschz: "A curious fact which is characteristic of the Jews

tribes devoid of sanctuaries would have no need for Cohanim and would quickly adjust themselves to new conditions. Hence, there sprang up two classes of Jewish tribes differentiated by the presence or absence of Cohanim. And it is a strange fact, that while to-day Aaronides are to be found along the entire littoral of North Africa, they are apparently unknown among the Berbers no less than among the Jewish tribes of the Desert.[12]

**Lack of Records.**

The coastal towns of Algeria and Morroco had not suffered the destruction that overwhelmed those of Tripoli, and their Jewish colonies, for the time being at least, were allowed to continue along their own lines. However, the pioneer Jews of North Africa, merchants and sailors, followed by agriculturists and soldiers, were men of toil, and not of education.[13] Consequently they committed little, if anything, to writing until after the destruction of the Temple in Jerusalem, when the newly-arrived exiles must have included scribes and other men of letters. This will explain the absence of written records prior to the Christian era.[14]

**Across the Sahara.**

In consequence of conditions along the Coast of the Mediterranean, we may safely conclude, that as the Carthaginian control of North Africa gave way to the Roman, and this in turn gradually yielded in part at

of Tripoli is the complete absence of Cohanim and Leviim in the interior and even in Tripoli. The few families of Cohanim to be found in Tripoli are of foreign birth." *Travels in North Africa,* p. 206. "It is an established fact that in Tripoli, amongst the Jews of the interior, there are no Cohanim indigenous to the country."—l. c., p. 158.

[12] Slouschz testifies: "Among the Berbers there are neither Cohanim nor Levites. We have noted the same phenomenon among the desert Jews of Tripoli and Algiers."—*Travels in North Africa,* p. 433.

[13] Note:—Blunt remarks: "No schools had existed in Israel before the Exile. But, though it may have been an uncommon accomplishment to read and write, the line of illiteracy cannot have been drawn very high, for Amos and Micah among the prophets belonged to the masses, and the workmen on Hezekiah's Siloah conduit were able to carve the manner of their work on the rock."—*Israel before Christ,* p. 130.

[14] Note:—Slouschz says:—"Agriculturists or nomads, military colonists or civil immigrants, these Hebrews wrote but little—and that in the 'Ibrit or Phoenician characters—so that they have survived only in local folk-lore and in the ethnic characteristics which they have transmitted to their posterity. Very different were the conditions obtaining among the Jews who came to the country after the destruction of the Temple. In the first place, most of them were thoroughly imbued with the Law of the Pharisees; in the second place, they had already become Romanized; these are the Jews referred to in the very earliest documents which we have concerning Judaism in this part of the world —the inscriptions unearthed concerning their rituals, and the testimony of the Fathers of the Church."—*Travels in North Africa,* p. 273 f.

least to the Grecian influence in Egypt, the migration from the north across the Desert of large bodies of Hebrews and of more or less Hebraized tribes, must have steadily increased. Then, with the rise of the commercial power of the Jews themselves in Alexandria and Cyrene, their coreligionists would inevitably have established themselves in regular organized colonies or commercial centers not only around the oases which marked the line of trade across the Sahara, but even to some degree among the Negro tribes of the Sudan.

The advance of Christianity must have driven many Jewish tribes further and further into the interior. As elsewhere, Christianity in North Africa claimed its first followers, for the most part, from among the devotees of the Synagogue. And as entire districts became Christian many defenders of the old faith sought the companionship of their brethren among the nomads of the desert.

The reign of the Vandals in North Africa gave the Jews a respite and incidentally afforded them an opportunity of further Judaizing the Berbers over whom they gradually gained a dominant influence.[15] This Judeo-Berber régime reached its climax in the heroic resistence of Cahena, the Jewish Berber Queen, to the encroachment of the hosts of Islam.

While many Jewish tribes in course of time embraced Mohammedanism, at least externally, others preserved their faith by retreating deep into the desert or possibly into Negro Land itself. This may explain in part how the Jews early became the chief merchants of the Sahara and the connecting link between the Negro Nations of the South and all the great commercial centers of the Mediterranean Coast.[16]

[15] Note:—According to Slouschz:—"The consolidation of Christianity, in the fourth century, was to deal the first blow to the Jewish prosperity. Recovering again under the rule of the Vandals (fifth century), the Jewish population again expanded. The Jews established themselves among the Berbers and there became the predominating element."—*Travels in North Africa,* p. 274.

[16] Note:—We have it on the authority of Slouschz: "The traditions of the Jewish trader in the Sahara stretch back to biblical times. The Talmud and the Midrash mention various articles which were imported into Palestine from Libya, such as donkeys, silk-worms, etc. At the beginning of the ninth century the caravans of the Rodanite Jews traversed the desert in every direction. During the Middle Ages the Jews were able, in the face of constant persecution at the hands of the Mussulmans, to maintain commercial relations with every part of the desert as far as the Sudan. These relations continued unbroken down to the middle of the last century."—*Travels in North Africa,* p. 104.

**Decline of Judaism.**

It was in the twelfth century, however, that the Judaism of North Africa suffered its most serious check. The fanatical Almohades swept down from the mountains with the avowed purpose of exterminating all non-Mussulmans.[17] The Jews of the cities found the only alternative for death was either apostasy or flight. While the majority embraced Mohammedanism, many there were who chose death and still others found a refuge with their coreligionists among the inland Berbers.[18]

**A new Kingdom.**

Long before all this had happened, however, south of the Sahara, a Jewish Kingdom had arisen, flourished for several centuries, and then been so entirely obliterated that its very existence was long questioned and the site of its capital has only quite recently been located. This Jewish Kingdom of Ghana, asserting as it did the mastery over the greater part of Negro Land, must have had a widespread influence on Negro customs and manners almost to the Coast of Guinea.

And yet, even this great influx of Jewish influence fails to explain many of the Hebrewisms of West Africa, especially among the Ashanti. For the language of the colonists from the North was not the Hebrew that has in so many ways left its impress. The early advance-guard from Carthage had perhaps spoken Hebrew or a patois of Hebrew and Phoenician blended, but the Hellenistic spirit of Alexandria must inevitably have made Greek the language of commercial North Africa long before the infiltration of the Jews could have reached a stage when it might exercise any real influence on the distinctively Negro tribes of the interior.[19]

[17] Note:—This is Slouschz's view: "This period of Jewish development came to an end with the rise of the mountain fanatics known as Almohades ('Unitarians') who began a war of extermination against all non-Mussulmans."—*Travels in North Africa,* p. 366.

[18] Note:—Slouschz says:—"As a matter of fact, while most of the Jews of the cities were converted, the Jews of the Berber country were not pressed, and their numbers were even swelled by refugees from the cities. . . . This persecution which lasted until the year 1288—that is, for one hundred and forty years —was the cause of the decline of a whole people, of the Jews who had been established in Mauritania since the Roman occupation and had written one of the most important chapters in the history of Israel."—*Travels in North Africa,* p. 368 f.

[19] Note:—The vestiges among the Ashanti of the Feasts of Rosh Ha-Shanah and Yom Kippur also demand contact with an early Hebraic influence, if we

**Ghana and Mohammedanism**

A strong Hebrew impress, no doubt, was actually left on the Negro tribes that were once subject to Ghana. But Mohammedanism has for the most part completely absorbed these tribes, and so fixed on them its own peculiar culture which in many respects is only a depreciated form of Judaism, that it is simply impossible in their regard to differentiate what is really Judaic from what is Mohammedan.

**Pagan Tribes.**

However, in our present study we are dealing especially with such West African tribes as have never yielded to the advance of Mohammedanism, and which are still classified as pagan or idolatrous. And here we feel constrained by the weight of evidence to look to the East and not to the North for the dominant influence that to-day manifests itself throughout West Africa. For, while no doubt the Northern infiltration left some impress on these tribes also, the status of the Jews who found their way along the valley of the Nile, and thence across the plains of Central Africa by Lake Chad, is more in accord with the traditions and culture of the Negro tribes as we actually find them at the present time.

**Talmudists.**

Lewis Browne has said of the Jews: "When the Temple was destroyed and the old priestly cult ended the whole technique of the religion had to be radically altered. The priestly organization was no more, and a new organization had to be erected. So the rabbinical cult resulted. A gigantic legal literature called the Talmud was developed in the first five centuries after the Destruction, and later an even more gigantic literature of Talmudic commentators and super-commentators." [20]

Nor is this hard to understand from the viewpoint of the Babylonian Jews who had spent the centuries since their establishment as a separate political entity, in the evolving of this new religious ceremonial which practically substituted Judaism for the Hebrewism of the Prophets. As a matter of fact, the community on the

may credit the words of Solomon Zeitlin: "The Jews after the destruction of the Temple (Second), paid no attention to the holidays except Purim and Hanukkah, as the raison d'être for celebrating them had ceased. It is true, we do find some discussion by the Tanaim and Amoraim concerning them, but they were purely of a theoretical nature, while the people in actual life knew nothing of them."—*Megillat Tanit as a Source for Jewish Chronology and History in the Hellenistic and Roman Periods,* Philadelphia, 1922, Preface, p. ix.

[20] Lewis Browne, *The Believing World,* New York, 1926, p. 249.

banks of the Euphrates had eventually come to prefer themselves as racially purer than the possessors of the Temple in Jerusalem, and in due course they stressed more and more the principle of exclusiveness and adopted an almost fetish adherence to the letter of the Law to the sacrifice of its true spirit and observance. And long before the loss of the Temple in Jerusalem, such was the influence of the Babylonian Jews, that they had in many respects effectively imposed upon their brethren in Palestine the spirit and practice of Judaism.

We see nothing of all this in the Hebrewisms of West Africa, and must consequently look to an earlier period of the history of Israel with which to connect our migrations to the heart of the Black Man's Country.

**God of Israel.**

Professor Macalister, speaking of pre-exilic times, says: "From time to time prophets arose, to lead the people to a purer conception of their national God. . . . But the Exile opened to the champions of monotheism their opportunity. They taught the returned remnant to look upon that national calamity as a judgment, executed by an offended God in expiation of their continued breach of the first commandment of the Decalogue. To this God they were henceforth to consecrate themselves as a peculiar people, governed by a strict religious law. But while this law nurtured their faith, its insistence upon forms and ceremonies had an increasingly deadening despiritualising effect. The persecutions which the Jewish people suffered, especially at the hands of Antiochus Epiphanes, strengthened their devotion to the law. Not long afterwards Jesus of Nazareth made his appearance. His contempt for empty ceremonial angered those to whom ceremonial was the whole substance of religion." [21]

**Pre-Exilic Hebrews.**

Later, the same author writes: "The pre-exilic Hebrews, as a body, were hardly more than pagan. Their 'lapses' into idolatry were not really lapses; they were the normal condition of their religious life. Reforming kings arose from time to time, in every case under the influence of a prophet. . . . These reforms were never more than temporary. . . . The papyri of Elephantine have cast a lurid light on the religion of the rank and file of the Hebrew people. These docu-

[21] R. A. S. Macalister, *A Century of Excavation in Palestine,* London, 1926, p. 268 f.

ments, which must rank among the greatest discoveries made in recent years, in the countries of the ancient East, relate to affairs of a Jewish colony, which must have entered the service of the king of Persia shortly before the Exile, and which, at first established as an outpost on the island called Yeb, at the frontier of Egypt, had there setttled down and had entered civil life. The period over which the papyri permit us to watch their proceedings covers most of the fifth century B. C." [22]

**Relative Idolatry.**

While accepting in a general way Professor Macalister's statement as regards the condition of affairs in pre-exilic Israel, exception must be taken to the inference which might be drawn, that the idolatry of the Chosen People was that of an intermediate stage between polytheism and monotheism. In other words, that the monotheism of Esdras was an evolution from previous polytheism, and not rather a rejuvenation of pristine belief.

That idolatry was recurrent, and often widespread, from the days of the Judges down to the Babylonian Exile, cannot be denied.[23] But we must take care to distinguish between the absolute cult of a false god and the veneration of images kept subordinate to the adoration of the one Supreme God. This latter condition, which we may refer to as a relative cult, was also actually forbidden by the Mosaic Law and consequently was likewise termed idolatry—a juridical, legal idolatry. The prophets in inveighing against the abuses of their times as a rule made no distinction between the two forms of idolatry. It is an easy matter then, to overstress the testimony of the Old Testament and to paint an exaggerated picture of conditions in pre-exilic Israel.

No conclusions of general idolatry among the Hebrews can be drawn legitimately. There are spasmodic outbursts of legal idolatry, that do not constitute an apostasy from Yahweh, but rather an adoption of extraneous ceremonies and practices. Moreover the idolatry of Israel, such as it was, in no one instance was indigenous or endemic. The deity whose image is worshipped is invariably a foreign god. If Israel fell into the natural polytheism of the surrounding peoples then, this was no abjuration of its own

[22] Idem, p. 295 f.
[23] Cfr. Kortleitner, *De Polytheismo Universo,* especially Sectio Tertia.

God, and Monotheistic Faith at least was widespread in Israel, even when the relative cult, which was juridically idolatry for the Jew, was most rampant.

**Modern Parallel.**

And even in the case of those who actually lapsed into idolatry in this broad sense, the condition was not unlike that recently outlined by Diederich Westerman, Professor at the University of Berlin, who thus describes the conceptions of God found in West Africa: "Local deities form the chief objects of worship. Most of them are the incorporation of natural objects or of natural phenomena. . . . The gods, however, are never identified with these objects; they are invisible and the objects in question are inhabited by them temporarily, they serve as places to which offerings can be brought and where gifts can be asked for. . . . The deity receives its power from the God of Heaven who delegates to the deity the administration of a definite sphere of living beings." [24]

**Compatibility with real Monotheism.**

The system at heart is Monotheistic. Only in the widest sense of the word is there the semblance of real idolatry. Some such condition of affairs existed in the lapses of pre-exilic Israel. There was no actual apostasy from the God of Abraham, of Isaac and of Jacob. The minor deities who engrossed the attention of the worshippers were at best beholden to Yahweh for their influence and power. True it is, that this divided service was destructive of the true concept of the One, Omnipotent God, and was at variance with all the precepts of the Law. Still it was absolutely compatible with the spirit of the times and a natural consequence of the neglect of the legal restrictions as regards intercourse with the tribes that surrounded and intermingled with the Chosen People. For, as the late Doctor J. M. Casanowicz of the United States National Museum once wrote to me: "As regards the worshipping or acknowledging the existence of one supreme being alongside of 'gods many and lords many,' this is found among all or many primitive and even civilized peoples who conceived of a unique transcendental creator with a host of *dei minores* who act as his delegates or manifestations." [25]

[24] Diederich Westerman, *Gottesvorstellungen in Oberguinea—Africa,* Oxford, Vol. I (1928), p. 282.
[25] Letter dated Washington, D. C., July 13, 1926.

**Effect of Exile.**

The monotheism of Esdras then, was no evolution from polytheistic practice, but a recalling of the People to their original purity of religion. What the Exile did effect was a whole-souled horror of sin, especially of the sin of the divided service of Yahweh. For it was sin that had led up to the Exile. The Exile was literally the price of sin. And yet the very horror of the external act became almost a fanaticism to the exclusion of the true internal motive. The Pharisaic School stressed more and more the material observances of every letter of the Law, and by Law (Torah) they understood not merely the precepts of the Pentateuch, but also the countless explanatory traditions that had been handed down with their meticulous details of potential violations which each learned Rabbi in turn sought to amplify and multiply, until a new danger threatened the Chosen People. External formalism began to undermine the most fundamental concepts of the service of Yahweh as prescribed in the Mosaic Code, and gradually the spiritual became subordinate in a way to the material. As a consequence, in due course the Promised-One, the Messias, lost His real spiritual character in the popular esteem, and became in common expectation a temporal leader and an irresistible conqueror. As A. W. F. Blunt, writing of post-exilic times, expresses it: "So tremendous was the insistence of later Judaism on sin, so vast the distance that it placed between God and man, that it tended to drive between them an immeasurable chasm and to declare that nothing could really bridge it. The idea of a God who should himself bridge it by becoming man, and so affect the at-one-ment of divine and human, was something which Judaism became sheerly incapable of conceiving or receiving." [26]

**Canaanitish Influence.**

It is only with restrictions then, that we may accept the view of Professor Hopkins. After stating: "The Israelites who invaded Canaan mingled with the earlier population and gradually overcame them, though in the process they became assimilated to the Canaanites," [27] goes on to say: "Israel could not live in such an environment without modifying its own religion." [28] This he illustrates by many ex-

[26] Blunt, *Israel before Christ,* p. 114.
[27] E. Washburn Hopkins, *History of Religions,* New York, 1926, p. 420.
[28] Idem, p. 423.

amples of false worship, and then continues: "This polytheism was not easily stamped out. It was really the popular religion of Israel until after the Exile. One cannot read the accounts of 'Israel's adultery' throughout the Old Testament without being impressed with the fact that Yahweh's strict worshippers were only a small group in a great host of idolatrous Israelites, who even admitted foreign gods into Yahweh's very tabernacle and were always ready to worship Baal. So say even the Jews;[29] 'Excepting David, Hezekiah, and Josiah, all the kings of Judah forsook the Law of the Most High.'"[30]

**Elephantine Worship.**

As we have seen, the relative idolatry, or as we may term it, the divided service, of the reign of King Manasses was duplicated in the Temple at Elephantine. In each case, Yahweh or Ya'u found idols actually sharing with Him His Temple. And it does seem only reasonable to connect our similar West African cult with this particular period of Hebrew History.

According to Doctor H. R. Hall: "Semites were always making their way into Egypt, in single spies when the native power was strong, in battalions when the native power was weak; the fleshpots of Egypt were always an attraction, whether to the desert Arab or to the fellah of Palestine."[31]

These flesh pots in a way symbolize the sensuous tendency of Egypt, in placing the carnal claims above the spiritual, and we have seen that the fugitives from Assyrian wrath in the times of the Prophet Jeremias, fell under the spell of their surroundings, and that the worship of Yahweh in consequence became vitiated by the ingrafting of the impure cult of Astarte. The general condition at Elephantine in the succeeding century fully corroborates this assumption.

**Jews of the Nile.**

According to our way of thinking, then, there was a constant movement up the Nile of such Jews as had for one reason or another taken up their abode in the land of the Pharaohs and then turned inland from the shores of the Mediterranean. Their stay among the flesh pots of Egypt, whether for a longer or a shorter period, had a correspond-

[29] Ecclus. xlix, 5.
[30] Hopkins, *History of Religions*, p. 424.
[31] Cfr. Arthur S. Peake, *The People and the Book*, Oxford, 1925, p. 4.

ingly enervating effect on their spiritual principles, and while they preserved Yahweh as their supreme God, to a certain extent they adapted themselves to their surroundings and continued that divided service which had characterized the days of King Manasses. And yet, they still remained in their own esteem the Chosen People of God, and the Children of Yahweh.

Whether as Egyptian merchants, or associated in Phoenician commerce, no doubt they established themselves in centers of trade throughout the hinterland. But anything like colonization, if it existed at all, must at the start have been restricted to Upper Egypt and adjacent Ethiopia.[32]

**Soldiers' Rebellion.** The soldiers' rebellion in the reign of Psammeticus may conceivably have carried bands of Jews well into the interior, to swell the scattered groups of their coreligionists. But it would seem that, thus far at least, there could have been but few, if any, women included among them—it was almost exclusively a movement of the male element of the people. As a consequence, intermarriage with the native tribes was practically a necessity, especially as the restrictive law of the Talmudists had not yet been enunciated, and its spirit exercised no restraining influence over the pre-exilic Jews and the refugees in Egypt.

**Refugees.** However, before the African tribes could fully absorb and assimilate this addition to their ethnic complex, the fugitives from the Assyrians must have begun to arrive in a steadily growing stream. Women and children were included among these refugees, and centers of Jewish culture must now have begun to grow up, and a white aristocracy no doubt commenced to establish itself and assert its superiority over the various tribes of Blacks along the upper reaches of the Nile.

Speaking of the period 342–339 B. C., Talbot says: "Many Egyptians migrated to the south and west when their country was

[32] Note:—Doctor Haddon writes: "The general impression that one gets is that Hamitic (or Ethiopian) peoples in Upper Paleolithic times began to spread westwards along the grasslands and open forest country right across Africa. The earliest of them doubtless mixed with Negroes of various sorts and produced ameliorated Negro strains. Movements of this kind probably took place repeatedly over a very long period of time."—*Races of Men and Their Distribution,* p. 50. And again: "Traditions point to successive waves of people advancing from North-east Africa to Angola by various routes."—l. c., p. 52.

attacked and conquered by the Persians under Ochus." [33] These may have joined the early Jewish emigrants, or what is more probable in view of the ancient enmity between Jew and Egyptian, have driven the partially Judaized tribes before them to the interior of Africa.

**Kokia.**

Some such state of affairs may well have started the evolution of the Songhois people, then dwelling at their first Kokia on the Nile, whence a Pharaoh had summoned the Magicians to contend with Moses. Their first two dynasties were clearly of a light complexion. And as the emigrants continued to arrive and accordingly increased the strength and power of the tribe, whatever its name at the time may have been, a process of absorption and conquest would naturally have started them on their long trek across the continent, even if no disorders from the North had brought any pressure upon them.

**Philae.**

Nor is this any mere vague conjecture. For it seems more than a coincidence that Felix Dubois, who apparently knows nothing of the Jewish colony at Elephantine, says: "The Songhois recall the Nubian rather than the West African negro, and I have studied both at leisure. Ethnography then, assists us in determining the point of departure of the emigration from the valley of the Nile. It is to the south of the island of Philae that we find a similar race, and there also has ancient Egypt left indelible traces. On the left bank of the river she has set up a magnificent series of her most characteristic monuments, and it is small wonder that its inhabitants should be so strongly inbued with them that they preserved the vision to the farthest point of their wanderings." [34] Now this Philae is situated at the First Cataract of the Nile close to the location of the Jewish Colony at Elephantine.[35]

**Commercial Enterprise.**

Their commercial spirit would further tend to carry the Jews, as individuals and in small groups, deeper and deeper into the interior until there must have been a chain of trading posts entirely across the con-

[33] Talbot, *Peoples of Southern Nigeria,* Vol. I, p. 26.
[34] Dubois, *Timbuctoo the Mysterious,* p. 97.
[35] Note:—Rene Francis writes: "Philae should be, strictly speaking, considered as the beginning of Nubia, of which the Cataract is really the borderline."—*Egyptian Aesthetics,* Chicago, 1912, p. 237. And again: "Nubia has perhaps more right to Philae than has Egypt."—l. c., p. 240.

tinent, which would explain the statuettes picked up among the Yoruba similar to those found in the foreign quarter of Memphis. And each center thus established, would only serve as an outpost and an easy means of advance, as their kinsmen among the Songhois aristocracy extended their sphere of influence and directed the western movement of the tribe.

**Songhois.** Thus we may visualize the evolution of the Songhois as a nation, that was in due time to become the dominant empire of Negro Land. Starting on their long trek to the West, perhaps shortly after the destruction of the Temple at Elephantine towards the close of the fifth century B. C., they doubtlessly would linger long around Darfur and later in the vicinity of Lake Chad, until their increasing numbers required broader fields and greater food supply, and so they would ultimately be drawn towards the great Niger bend, to found their latest Kokia about the year 300 A. D.

Later, as we know, the capital was changed to Gao which Lieutenant Hourst has described as "the most powerful city ever founded by negro civilization, the metropolis from which radiated the various routes bringing to the Niger the produce of the Tchad districts and of Egypt." [36] Of the Songhois themselves, referring to the third dynasty (1494–1591) the same author asserts: "The Askias had united under their banner all the African states from Lake Tchad to the Senegal, and from the desert to Say. The Songhay empire was then not only the most powerful in Africa, but of the whole contemporary world." [37] This praise seems fulsome, and the traveller has probably allowed his enthusiasm to lead him into gross exaggeration. The Songhois had certainly risen to great power and influence, and had made Timbuktu a remarkable seat of learning and a rendezvous of scholars.[38] But, while a contemporary declared, "It was a six-months journey to cross this formidable empire," [39] it would appear wanting in probability to

[36] Lieut. Hourst, *Personal Narrative of his Exploration of the Niger,* trans. Mrs. Arthur Bell, New York, 1899, p. 165.

[37] Idem, p. 165.

[38] Note:—After the destruction of the seat of learning at Timbuktu, in 1594, as we are told by General Barrows, the famous black Jurist and scholar Ahmed Baba, who had been carried off to Morocco by the invaders, "lamented not his captivity, but only the loss of his great library of sixteen hundred tomes, which his unfeeling and barbarous master destroyed."—Cfr. Barrows, *Berbers and Black,* p. 83.

[39] Dubois, *Timbuctoo the Mysterious,* p. 113.

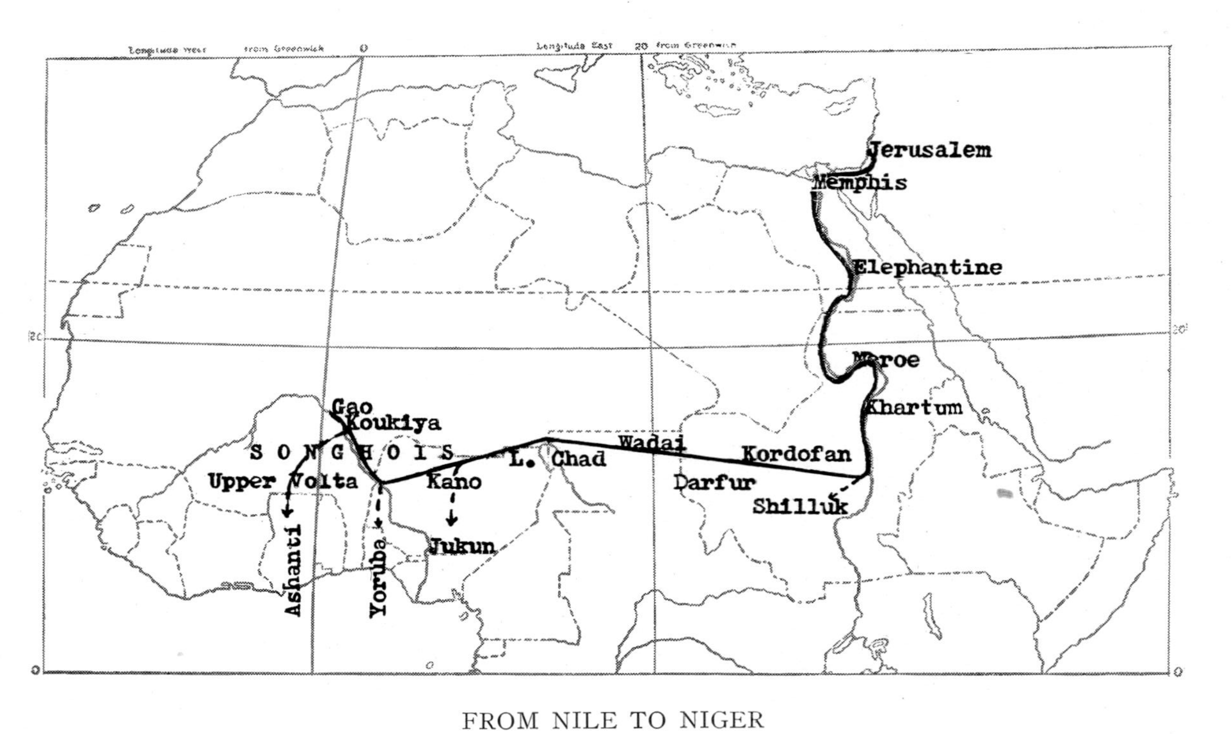


FROM NILE TO NIGER

*(Solid line marks the suggested course of migration. Broken lines indicate possible diversions with resultant tribes.)*

claim that any confederation of African tribes could surpass, for example, the Empire of Charles V, which reached its height at this period.

When Ibn Batoutah visited Gao, which he calls Caoucaou, in 1352, he speaks of the Chief of the Mosque of the Whites, implying that they were fairly numerous.[40] On the previous page he has described the city as "One of the most beautiful cities of the Negroes, one of the largest and most populous." [41]

**Kindred Peoples.** From time to time, there must have been a breaking-off of bands of varying strength, while the nation was in its formative state; perhaps of those who lingered behind at each new advance along the line of trek; perhaps of adventurers or malcontents, who in due course would develop into other tribes of similar culture and traditions. This would be especially the case, when the main body of the Songhois became converted to Islamism at the beginning of the eleventh century. In view of their antecedents, it would be only reasonable to expect that entire families or clans within the tribe must have clung to their old form of worship, and severed their connections with the parent-stock.[42]

[40] Ibn Batoutah, *Voyages,* Vol. IV, p. 436.

[41] Idem, Vol. IV, p. 435.

[42] Note:—In the heart of the Congo Basin, situated about S. 5°; E. 21°, and quite as remote from Egypt as are the Ashanti and the Songhois, we find the Bakuba. Internal evidence shows that this tribe must have ultimately come from the borders of Ethiopia. Conway T. Wharton says of them: "Is it too fantastic to suppose that the comparatively advanced civilization possessed by the Bakuba may be explained by being an indirect reflection of ancient Egypt? The beetle or scarab design so often seen in their carving, the carving itself in base relief, the distinctly Egyptian cast of countenance manifest in their wood sculpture, all lend credence to the supposition. Yet, again, there is the fascinating possibility at least, that the rude image of the Semitic religion, so remarkably preserved in the mythology of these people, is a corrupt infiltration of the religion of the Hebrews as it was in Egypt." And again: "Other of their legends, not heretofore cited, bear strong resemblance to certain incidents in scriptural history. For instance, this one: 'In the course of our wanderings we crossed a great water in a boat without oars, that was propelled by the hand of God 'Ncemi.' Is this too far a cry from the story of the ark? Then listen to this: One day in preparing materials for this book, I was sitting in a small thatch hut in Mushonge, listening to the old grey-haired 'Mbami Bushongo,' as he told me stories of his people. Suddenly, without prompting or leading question of any kind, he volunteered: 'We, too, once had white skins like yours; we are now black because of a curse put upon us by our forefather, Wota. He did it because one of the sons of Wota rolled up the door of his father's hut without ceremony and under circumstances that were improper. Wota put a curse upon him, and since then we have been black.' I checked this story over with another ancient chief, a son of a king, and while his account

**Jukun and Ashanti.**

In this way, perhaps, the Jukun, and many other tribes, such as the Yoruba, may well have derived their Hebrewisms, which to-day are seeking explanation. For, while the Songhois themselves would necessarily lose much of their Hebrew culture and tradition, first when they embraced Mohammedanism in 1009 A. D.[43] and possibly even more so, when the Negro Askias displaced the light-complexioned Sunni dynasty in 1494,[44] still many offshoots of the tribe, that clung tenaciously to their ancient faith and resisted Islamism to the present day, must have preserved these traces of their origin.

**Later Infiltrations.**

The Songhois then, present the most reasonable solution of the problem as to how the Hebraic influence found its way from the Nile to the Niger. Unquestionably, there must have been many other waves of influence of greater or less degree following along all the lines of commerce, and the steady infiltration has necessarily left its impress here and there despite the tendency of Mohammedanism to obliterate all preceding cultures wherever it gains the ascendancy.

With this constantly repeated surge of Hebraic culture from Upper Egypt, there may, without doubt, have been intermittently associated, especially in mediaeval times, a companion element that had its origin in Abyssinia among the parent-stock of the present day Falashas, and thus parallelisms to Abyssinian culture may have grown up intermingled with the Hebrewisms of West Africa, but we are inclined to think, that if such a contact ever was established, its effects must have been almost negligible.

**Ghana.**

From the Kingdom of Ghana, too, we admit, as well as from the later arrivals across the desert of Judeo-Berber tribes, many of the Hebrewisms of West Africa may be explained. But in the case of the Ashanti at least, we are convinced that their Hebraic influence was derived from the far East and that in all probability it is the Songhois people who con-

differed in some particulars, the conclusion drawn was the same, namely, that the Bakuba are now black because of the curse of their forefather. It caused an unforgettable sensation to hear the old Mbami gravely begin telling the following: 'Ncemi (God) is not one but three!; first there is Ncemi the Creator, next there is Kofangana, who acts as mediator between Ncemi and man, and last, there is Nyonyi Ngana, assistant of Kofangana, and acting for him when he is away. These three are all one in power and honour.' "—Wharton, *The Leopard Hunts Alone*, p. 79 ff.

[43] Meek, *Northern Tribes of Nigeria,* Vol. I, p. 67.

[44] Idem, Vol. I, p. 67.

stitute the living contact, and that we have here a truly remarkable instance of real cultural diffusion.

**Judaized Tribes.** The Judaizing of the Berber tribes in North Africa may well have had its counterpart in Upper Egypt where small groups of Jews may have won over entire tribes and after establishing themselves as a priestly aristocracy to govern them, have guided them to the interior of the continent where they might more freely carry on their religious practices free from persecution.

**Judeo-Negroes.** Some such tribe, the Songhois might conceivably have been in the days of its inception—a Judeo-Negro tribe with the real Jewish element, probably already mixed with an Egyptian or Nubian strain, constituting at the start, the white aristocracy; and adoption into the tribe being accomplished by proselyting. Its tribal unity would thus be established, not on ethnic but solely on religious lines.

**Final Conclusion.** In any case, it is the writer's personal conviction that, explain it as you will, a Jewish element is to be found in the parent-stock of the Ashanti, whether that parent-stock is to be associated with the Songhois or not. This element, too, has every indication of being lineally connected with the Hebrews of pre-Babylonian days, presumably through the refugees in Egypt. Yame the Supreme Being of the Ashanti is to all appearances none other than the Yahweh of pre-exilic times, and the ancient tribal religion has much in common with the divided worship of Yahweh in the reign of King Manasses as revived at Elephantine and then passed on, in course of time, by the Jewish influences which found their way across the continent.

**Nile to Niger.** We cannot postulate any degree of certitude for this theory. It must for the present remain a theory, and nothing more. Time, however, the writer believes, will strengthen its credibility, if it does not eventually establish it as a fact. This much, however, may be safely claimed as proven at the present writing: Hebrewisms, real or apparent, actually do exist among the Ashanti, and the most plausible explanation of them as a collective entity appears to be a diffusion of Hebraic culture that found its way, long centuries ago, from the Nile to the Niger.

## *Chapter XIII*

## CONFIRMATION OF THE THEORY

**Divine Name.** We have a truly remarkable confirmation of the plausibility of our theory in the various names for the Supreme Being to be found among the Pagan tribes of Africa.

**African Nomenclature.** Thus, the Reverend Sogismond W. Koelle, writing in 1853, published a comparative vocabulary of nearly three hundred words and phrases in more than one hundred distinct African languages. Since the data were gathered at Sierra Leone from natives of the various tribes, many of whom had left their original haunts at an early age, inaccuracies must be expected both as regards the location of tribes and word-equivalent, as well as in pronunciation. However, the general scope of the work throws much light on the subject now under consideration.

The name of the Supreme Being is given for an even two hundred tribes, although many are probably different dialects of the same language. As we would expect, among the Mohammedan tribes the word is commonly Allah, or a close derivative, such as Yala among the Jollops near Cape Verde. As regards the strictly Pagan tribes, however, there is a great variety of form. For frequently, instead of naming the Supreme Being directly, they refer to Him by one or other of His attributes, as, for example, the Creator. It is surprising then, to note the number of instances, over widely separated districts, where there exists an indication of a possible derivation from the Yahweh of the Hebrews, making due allowance for the consonants that are commonly interchangeable, such as M and W. Thus in the Cameroons we find Nzamba, Nzambe, Monyama, and Nyama. In French Equatorial Africa, Anyambe and Nyama. Further south in Belgian Congo, Nzambi, Ndzambi, Ndsambe, Ndsami, Ndzama and Ndsambi. While still further south in Angola, we find Nsambi, Ntsambi and Ndzambi. In other words, the more we withdraw from the Niger, the more remote the derivation appears. At Pika in North-East Nigeria, besides Alla, Yamba was also used; and at Timbuktu, Alla had not yet crushed out the predominant Yerkoi or Yarkui of the Songhois.[1] Caron spells the Songhois word Yerkoy, to be pronounced as French, (i. e. Yerkwa), and remarks that the language at Timbuktu is not as pure as at Gao.[2]

In other parts of Africa a like similarity is noted. Thus among the Barotse of Upper Zambesi, the word is Niambe,[3] and Nassau calls attention to the fact that "this name Niambe is almost exactly the same as Anyambe, in Benga, two thousand miles distant," [4] in Spanish Guinea, on the West Coast, just north of the Equator.

With the Fans of the Gabon forest, the Supreme Being is Nzame,[5] and in the Grebo country further to the north, He is known as Nyiswa.[6] Again in the vocabulary gathered by Captain Tuckey during his expedition to the Congo in 1816, the word for God is given as Zambe in Malemba, and Yambee in Embomma. The latter place is near the mouth of the Congo River.[7]

John Clark also furnishes us with several examples in his *Specimens of Dialects* published in 1848, wherein he states: "These specimens are the result of eighteen years' attention to this interesting subject in the West Indies, and in Africa." [8] Most of his information, however, is merely from hearsay, although he gives it the approval of his experience. Thus he records as the name of the Supreme Being in French Equatorial Africa, Anyambe, Anyambi and 'Nyambi. At the mouth of the Gaboon River, Anyambe; and on an island off the Gaboon coast, we find Anyambi. On the River Cameroon, about thirty miles from the sea, it is Niambi.

In speaking of the Supreme Being among the Northern Tribes of Nigeria, Meek observes: "Nyama is also among the Mumbake

[1] S. W. Koelle, *Polyglotta Africana,* London, 1854.
[2] E. Caron, *De Saint Louis au Port de Tombouktou,* Paris, 1891, p. 366.
[3] Lionel Declé, *Three Years in Savage Africa,* London, 1898, p. 74.
[4] Robert Hamill Nassau, *Fetichism in West Africa,* London, 1904, p. 34.
[5] Alexander Le Roy, *The Religion of the Primitives,* New York, 1922, p. 115.
[6] Wilson, *Western Africa,* p. 209 Note.
[7] J. K. Tuckey, *Narrative of an Expedition to Explore the River Zaire, usually called the Congo, in South Africa, in 1816,* London, 1818, p. 395.
[8] Clarke, *Specimens of Dialects,* p. 3.

identified with the Sun. Under the name of Nan, Nen, Nyan, he is the Supreme God of the Angas, Yergum, Pe, Montoil, Sura, and Mumbeke, and is also, I believe, as Yamba, recognized as the sky-dwelling God by the Kamu, Awok, Bolewa, Tangale, Waja, and by a great many non-Nigerian Bantoid tribes. Nyambe is, in fact, the high God of the Western Bantu. . . . That Nan is regarded as the Supreme Ruler of the world is shown by the willingness of the Angas to apply to him, and him only, the Muslim title of Allah." [9] Here we should notice that the Nyan of Northern Nigeria whence the Ashanti came, is identical with the compounding form of the Ashanti Nyame, as it appears, for example, in Nyankopon, Nyamekopon, Nyame alone great one.

A. W. Cardinall, treating of the Natives of the Northern Territories of the Gold Coast, speaks of a tribe called Kassena or Awuna, that is now almost extinct. It has many characteristics in common with the Ashanti. For example, "ye" or "yeh" is the verb "to be" in both; and in regards to both we find the same balance structure in their poetry that is also characteristic of the Hebrew.[10] With the Kassena, the name of the Supreme Being is We, which looks like what Cowley calls the earliest form from which Yahweh is derived, namely Yau [11] or else a corrupted form of YahWEH itself,[12] the verbal component "Yah" being dropped.

**Yahweh Derivatives.**

The Jewish Colony at Elephantine, as we have seen, used the form Ya'u for Yahweh,[13] and in places in North Africa, such as Carthage and Hadrumentum, many inscriptions have been found, where the God of the Hebrews is named Iao,[14] just as excavations at Samaria show the form Yo.[15] These are evidently survivals of old forms of the terragrammaton. For while Yah [16] occurs in poetry

[9] Meek, *Northern Tribes of Nigeria,* Vol. II, p. 30.

[10] Cardinall, *Natives of the Northern Territories,* p. 107, 156. Note:—"As a general rule, though not always, the Hebrew poet strives to establish, in his verse, a certain parallelism of ideas."—Charles Latourbeau, *L'Évolution Littéraire dans les Diverses Races Humaines,* Paris, 1894, p. 285

[11] Cowley, *Aramaic Papyri,* Introduction, p. xviii.

[12] Cardinall, l. c., p. 22.

[13] Cfr. page 272.

[14] Paul Monceaux, *Les Colonies Juives dans l'Afrique Romaine—Revue des Études Juives,* Tome XLIV (1902), p. 5 f.

[15] Cambridge *Ancient History,* Vol. III, p. 362.

[16] יָהּ

of the Old Testament,[17] in the composition of proper names Yeho [18] and Jo or Yo [19] are the usual forms. Thus we have it recorded in connection with the determination of the courses of the priests by lot [20] that the twenty-third fell to Delayahu,[21] "Yahu hath drawn," [22] and the twenty-fourth and last to Ma'azyahu,[23] "Consolation of Yahu." [24] So too, we have many compounds of Jo or Yo[25] such as Joab,[26] "Jo (or Yahweh) is father," [27] a family name after the Exile.[28] Now, no less an authority than Brown, Driver and Briggs' Lexicon takes care to note: "Bonk seems to show that as prefix in the composition of proper names, Yeho [29] is the oldest and the latest form, and that Yo [30] is intermediate, belonging to the earliest post-exilic period until the time of Christ; occasional copyists' mistakes being taken into account." [31] This might well indicate that just as Ya'u of the Elephantine Temple is connected with the pre-exilic Jews, so the Iao of North Africa, as we would expect, is derived from a later offshoot of migration subsequent to the return from Babylonia. Furthermore, Charles Bruston has shown that Greek inscriptions found at Carthage and its vicinity are really Hebrew words in Greek letters, and in these the form Iao occurs as well as other modifications of the Tetragrammaton.[32]

**Nyame.** With the Ashanti, as we have seen, the Supreme Being is Nyame. The Agni, supposedly of com-

[17] Brown, Driver and Briggs, *Hebrew and English Lexicon,* p. 219.
[18] יְהוֹ
[19] יוֹ
[20] I Paral. xxiv, 18.
[21] דְּלָיָהוּ
[22] Brown, Driver and Briggs, *Hebrew and English Lexicon,* p. 219.
[23] מַעַזְיָהוּ
[24] Gesenius, *Hebrew and Chaldee Lexicon,* trans. Tregelles, London, 1847, p. CCCCXCII.
[25] יוֹ
[26] יוֹאָב
[27] Brown, Driver and Briggs, l. c., p. 222.
[28] I Esdras ii, 6.
[29] יְהוֹ
[30] יוֹ
[31] Brown, Driver and Briggs, l. c., p. 219 Note.
[32] Cfr. *Revue Archéologique,* 5 Serie, Tome X (1919), p. 28 ff; Tome XII (1920), p. 47 ff; Tome XVI (1922), p. 77 ff; Tome XVIII (1923), p. 624.

mon origin with the Ashanti, call Him Niame,[33] and the Sanwi, also of the Ivory Coast, invoke Him as Niamene.[34] As Roger Villamur attributes many of the customs of both the Agni and the Sanwi to an impress of what he calls "Ashanti culture," this similarity in the names of the Supreme Being is easily explained.[35]

**Bantus.** Doctor Walter Addison Jayne, speaking of the local Egyptian deities, remarks: "The real names of the gods were known only to the priests, if at all; they were too sacred to be mentioned, whence the deities received substitute names, some being best known by their home seats, as 'he of Edfu' (Tbot) or 'she of Dendera' (Enet)." [36] A somewhat similar condition exists among many of the Bantu tribes, where the Supreme Being is indicated by an invariable radical signifying heaven,[37] or its equivalent meaning "on high" or "the firmament" or "the air," joined with a variable prefix that determines the precise meaning. Thus the Swahili, M-ungu, He of Heaven; the Pokomo, Mu-ungu, He from on high; the Tabwa, Mu-gulu, He of Heaven; the Herero, Mu-kuku, He of on high; etc.[38]

**Monotheists.** Monsignor Le Roy has well said: "It is beyond question or doubt that the Negrillos and the Bantus as well as all the Blacks of Africa acknowledge and proclaim the existence of a Being superior to all, to whom a special name is given, who is distinguished from other spirits, from the manes, shades, and elements, and whom we can identify only with God." [39]

[33] Louis Tauxier, *Le Noir de Boudoukou,* Paris, 1921, p. 624.

[34] Cl. Gaube, *Étude sur le Côte d'Ivoire,* Paris, 1901, p. 78. Note:—Tauxier gives as the Abron word for God Niangouboun.—Cfr. *Le Noir de Boudoukou,* p. 588. This is evidently the Nyankopon of the Ashanti with whom the Abron are racially connected.

[35] Roger Villamur, *Notre Colonie de la Côte d'Ivoire,* Paris, 1903, p. 170.

[36] Walter Addison Jayne, *The Healing Gods of Ancient Civilization,* New Haven, 1925, p. 8.

[37] Note:—Kortleitner remarks how Semites quite commonly use the words for God and Heaven indiscriminately, and adds: "Even among the Talmudists Heaven is frequently used for the name of God."—*De Polytheismo Universo,* p. 29.

[38] A. Le Roy, *La Religion des Primitifs,* Paris, 1911, p. 500 f. Note:—The same may be said of some of the distinctively Negro tribes of West Africa. Thus Samuel Crowther, a native missionary among the Yoruba, literally translates the word for God, Olorun, as "the owner of heaven," deriving the word from "lorun," "to have or possess heaven."—Cfr. *Grammar of the Yoruba Language,* p. 8.

[39] Le Roy, *Religion of the Primitives,* p. 120.

J. Leighton Wilson had already written in the middle of the past century, when treating of Northern Guinea, which he places along the West Coast of Africa between Cape Verde and the Cameroon Mountains: "The belief in one great Supreme Being, who made and upholds all things, is universal. Nor is this idea imperfectly or obscurely developed in their minds. The impression is so deeply engraved upon their moral and mental nature, that any system of atheism strikes them as too absurd and preposterous to require a denial." [40]

J. G. Christaller in his dictionary states: "The heathen negroes are, at least to a great extent, rather monotheistic, as they apply the term for God only to one supreme being." [41] And Mungo Park writing at the close of the eighteenth century is equally outspoken, when he says: "Some of the religious opinions of the Negroes, though blended with the weakest credulity and superstition, are not unworthy of attention. I have conversed with all ranks and conditions, upon the subject of their faith, and can pronounce, without the smallest shadow of doubt, that the belief of one God, and of a future state of reward and punishment, is entire and universal among them." [42]

Captain Rattray's testimony need not be repeated here, as it has been given in detail in the Chapter on the Supreme Being of the Ashanti. But quite recently another Ethnologist of standing has unequivocally aligned himself against the popular theory of

[40] Wilson, *Western Africa,* p. 209. Note:—This is precisely the point of view taken by David Livingston. Writing of Bechuanaland, he says: "There is no necessity for beginning to tell even the most degraded of these people of the existence of a God or of a future state, the facts being universally admitted. . . . On questioning intelligent men among the Bakwains (situated near the head-waters of the Limpopo River) as to their former knowledge of good and evil, of God and the future state, they have scouted the idea of any of them ever having been without a tolerably clear conception on all these subjects."—David Livingston, *Missionary Travels and Researches in South Africa,* New York, 1858, p. 176. And again: "But, though they all possess a distinct knowledge of a deity and of a future state, they show so little reverence, and feel so little connection with either, that it is not surprising that some have supposed them entirely ignorant on the subject."—l. c., p. 177. Finally, writing at Tete on the Zambesi River, Livingston later adds: "As Senhor Candido holds the office of judge in all disputes of the natives, and knows their language perfectly, his statement may be relied on that all the natives of this region have a clear idea of a Supreme Being, the maker and governor of all things. He is named 'Morimo,' 'Molungo,' 'Raza,' 'Mpambe,' in the different dialects spoken. The Barotse name him 'Nyampi,' and the Balonda 'Zambi.' All promptly acknowledge him as the ruler over all."—l. c., p. 686.

[41] Christaller, *Dictionary of Asante and Fante Language,* p. 342.

[42] Park, *Travels in the Interior of Africa,* p. 406.

Colonel Ellis. C. K. Meek writes: "All the tribes, however, devoted to naturism and fetishism, are sufficiently theistic to believe in the existence of a Supreme Ruler of the world." [43]

All this, of course, goes counter to the prevalent school of evolutionists who place unlimited confidence in the observations of Sir Alfred Burton Ellis. As an admirer of Herbert Spencer,[44] Ellis follows his guide in his evolution of religious belief among the West African tribes. And while his value as a witness in this particular matter has been thoroughly discredited,[45] yet he and his disciple Miss Mary Kingsley are the great authorities quoted by the modern school.

To meet, then, any criticism of our theory which may be brought to bear from that source, it may be well to go into the question here at some length.

Professor Mercer positively asserts: "The existence of a nation of atheists has never been demonstrated. The most primitive peoples, both historically and culturally, have been found to be theists (in the broad and non-technical sense of the term). The oldest human records we possess, as well as the oldest and most reliable traditions of the most ancient peoples, bear witness to the universality of theism in ancient times." [46]

[43] Meek, *Northern Tribes of Nigeria,* Vol. II, p. 29.

[44] Ellis, *Yorouba-Speaking Peoples,* p. 282.

[45] Cfr. page 69 ff.

[46] Samuel A. B. Mercer, *The Ethiopic Liturgy: Its Sources, Development, and Present Form,* Milwaukee, 1915, p. 15. Note:—Even Ellis is finally forced to admit that degenerate African worship, as shown for example in the veneration of the serpent, is not idolatry in the strict sense of the word. For speaking of the Ophiolatry of Dahomey, he writes: "The snake itself is not worshipped but rather the indwelling spirit; the outward form of the python being considered the manifestation of the God."—Cfr. *The Ewe-Speaking Peoples of the Slave Coast of West Africa,* p. 54. Then after explaining that its title Danh-gbi implies "life-giving snake," he continues: "Danh-gbi is the god of wisdom, and of earthly bliss. He is also the benefactor of mankind, for the first man and woman that came into the world were blind, and mankind would have been blind to this day had not Danh-gbi opened their eyes."—l. c., p. 56. Diederich Westerman in treating of "Conceptions of God found in West Africa," is even more specific. He says: "The God of Heaven is also connected with a natural body, namely the visible heaven. But this God holds a unique position, he is above everything and is everywhere. . . . Everything owes its existence to him. Local deities are his children, they derive their power from him. He is the creator, the guide and preserver of the world and all that is in the world. His characteristic qualities are power, justice and goodness, and they find expression in a number of 'praise names,' sayings and songs."—Cfr. *Gottesvorstellungen in Oberguinea—Journal of the International Institute of African Languages and Cultures,* Vol. I, (1928), p. 283.

**Rationalists' Error.** Professor Wallis discloses the fundamental error in the Rationalists' mode of procedure, when he writes: "Much attention has been paid to the false science of primitive man and the ethnologist has given little heed to the correct science. We are more prone to emphasize his superstitions than his knowledge, his errors of judgment than his correct inferences." [47]

**Radin's View.** This is also in keeping with what we are told by Doctor Paul Radin, late Professor of Anthropology at the University of California and sometime Fellow of Harvard and Columbia Universities. He says: "The problem, in short, that confronts us is not as has always been erroneously assumed, the origin of monotheism. That is one which I would say antedates Neanderthal man.[48] The historical problem connected with monotheism implicit and explicit, is, as I see it, not how monotheism arose but what made it the prevailing and exclusive official religion of a particular people." [49] And again: "Most of us have been brought up in the tenets of orthodox ethnology and this was largely an enthusiastic and quite uncritical attempt to apply the Darwinian theory of evolution to the facts of social experience. Many ethnologists, sociologists and psychologists still persist in this endeavour. No progress will ever be achieved, however, until scholars rid themselves, once and for all, of the curious notion that everything possesses an evolutionary history; until they realize that certain concepts are as ultimate for man as a

[47] Wallis, *An Introduction to Anthropology,* p. 482.

[48] Note:—We might here call attention to a remark of A. L. Kroeber: "It is conceivable that the people of the Upper Paleolithic spent at least as much time on ceremonial observances as in working flint. Analogy with modern uncivilized tribes would make us think that this is quite likely. But the stone tools have remained lying in the earth, while the religious customs went out of use thousands of years ago and the beliefs were forgotten. Yet this is known: as far back as the Mousterian, thirty thousand years ago, certain practices were being observed by the Neanderthal race of western Europe which modern savages observe in obedience to the dictates of religion. When these people of the Mousterian laid away their dead, they put some of their belongings with them. When existing nations do this, it is invariably in connection with a belief in the continued existence of the soul after death. We may reasonably conclude therefore that even in this long distant period human beings had arrived at a crude recognition of the difference between flesh and spirit; in short, religion had come into being."—Kroeber, *Anthropology,* p. 171. Why is it that Kroeber cannot go a step further and admit the existence of religion from the beginning of the human race?

[49] Paul Radin, *Monotheism among Primitive Peoples,* London, 1924, p. 65.

social being as specific physiological reactions are for him as a biologial entity." [50]

**Lang's Contention.**

While entirely disagreeing with some of his conclusions, Doctor Radin thus writes of Andrew Lang: "In 1898 he published *The Making of Religion,* in which he claimed that the evolutionary school in ethnology was hopelessly wrong in one of its fundamental assumptions, that namely a belief in a Supreme Deity did not now and never had existed among so-called primitive tribes. He contended that ethnologists, misled by certain preconceptions, had misinterpreted those indications pointing in such a direction, crediting to Christian influences those definite instances where the facts could not possibly be denied. But he went much further. He contended that the fairly elevated conception of a Supreme Deity found much among such simple tribes as the aborigines of Australia could only be understood by assuming that the traces of monotheism there encountered, represented a definite degeneration of an older and purer faith partially contaminated to-day by animistic beliefs. In other words, monotheism had preceded animism and a purer faith had secondarily been contaminated by the superstitious accretions of a later degenerate time." [51]

This last statement of Lang's, Doctor Radin positively rejects, and yet he admits: "Twenty-five years have elapsed since Lang wrote his book and his intuitive insight has been abundantly corroborated. The Ethnologists were quite wrong. Accurate data obtained by trained specialists have replaced his rather vague examples. That many primitive peoples have a belief in a Supreme Creator no one to-day seriously denies." [52]

[50] Idem, p. 66.

[51] Radin, *Monotheism among Primitive Peoples,* p. 19. Note:—Radin immediately adds: "As was the case in so many of Lang's theories or intuitions, if you wish, he was only partially right."—l. c. His own personal theory concerning "the existence among primitive people of monotheism," a theory with which, as is evident, we must disagree, is thus briefly summed up: "Such a belief, I cannot too often repeat, is dependent not upon the extent of knowledge nor upon the elaboration of a certain type of knowledge, but solely upon the existence of a special kind of temperament. When once this has been grasped, much of the amazement and incredulity one inevitably experiences at the clear-cut monotheism of so many primitive peoples will vanish and we shall recognize it for what it is—the purposive functioning of an inherent type of thought and emotion."—l. c., p. 67. While then, we disagree with Doctor Radin as to his own conclusions, his admissions, particularly of the "clear-cut monotheism of so many primitive peoples" is useful for our present purpose.

[52] Radin, l. c., p. 21. Note:—Friederich Hertz, too, pays tribute to Lang in

**Dawson's Testimony.** It is interesting, then, to find the Oxford Historian Christopher Dawson clearly stating: "Among the pastoral peoples all over the world, from Siberia to Africa, we find the Sky God as a vague and often impersonal power which is yet conceived as the creator and supreme ruler of the universe. It is characteristic alike of the ancient Aryans, the Turks, the Mongols, the Hamites, and many of the Negro peoples of Africa; and even among peoples of the higher culture such as the Sumerians and the Chinese it appears as one of the earliest elements in their religion, inherited perhaps from an older phase of barbarism. Even the lower peoples of the hunting culture are not entirely devoid of the conception, and it has a good claim to be considered the oldest and most universal religion of the world." [53]

**Retrogression.** R. E. Dennett, too, absolutely rejects the suggestion that the Negroes gradually evolved from a state of fetishism to whatever concept they have of God to-day. On the contrary, it is his firm opinion that "the people have well nigh lost the knowledge of God which once their forefathers possessed." And he adds: "I should infer from the long study of the people that I have made . . . that this superstition called fetishism is an overgrowth imposed upon the purer knowledge they once certainly possessed." [54]

the following words: "The religious notions of primitive peoples appear to us as full of inordinate imagination and gross superstitions. Yet recent research by A. Lang and others has made the surprising discovery that the notion of a supreme deity is also found in peoples at a very early stage of civilization, though this particular deity is mostly imagined as enthroned so high as not to take any care of the things of this earth and laying no claim to worship."—Hertz, *Race and Civilization,* p. 246. In the present volume we have seen that this last statement is not borne out by facts.

[53] Dawson, *The Age of the Gods,* p. 243. Note:—Kortleitner is very clear on this point. He maintains: "It is evident that even such races as later became pagans, at the beginning worshipped one God, and afterwards passed eventually to the worship of many gods. That the African Negroes once venerated one God, Creator of the world, they who best understand the affairs of these peoples, know both from the names by which the Divinity is designated among these savages and by other indications as well."—Kortleitner, *De Polytheismo Universo,* p. 32.

[54] R. E. Dennett, *At the Back of the Black Man's Mind,* London, 1906, p. 168. Note:—Professor Elliot Smith in his recent little volume on the origin of civilization admits: "The gigantic ruins found in Central America, Java, Cambodia, Rhodesia, and in many of the centers of still older cultures afford impressive testimony of the fact that civilization is apt to undergo a process of degradation, or even local destruction, more or less complete. The fact has often promoted the suggestion that the communities of so-called natural men

**African Judaism.** This last observation is well confirmed by the present condition of North African Judaism. In fact with all their fetishism, the tribal religions of the Ashanti and other Negro peoples are no more gross and independent of a Supreme Being, than the cult of avowed Jewish tribes and groups remote from Negro Land. The degradation to which the Mussulman domination has reduced the once prosperous Jewish tribes is well illustrated by Nahum Slouschz, who is certainly a sympathetic witness. Of certain Jews at Tafilelt he writes: "The mysticism of these people is extraordinary. Their jubilant antics with the Torah on the morning of Simhat Torah was a scene never to be forgotten. For them the Torah was no longer the mere symbol of a sacred thing—in their ecstasy it became a mystic fire—in itself an object of worship; it was the purest fetichism." [55] When treating of the manners and customs of the Tripolitan Jews, he records: "When a dead body makes a motion as if to rise, it is said to be moved by an evil spirit, and must be struck violently to prevent it from rising again. Under the head of a corpse a sackful of sand is placed. If the death took place on the Sabbath, a knife and a piece of bread are placed on the breast of the body. If the deceased leave no male issue, they make the cover of the coffin out of the top of his table. The hair-band is always buried with a dead woman. If two members of the same family die in one year, they release a cock in the field before the coffin to ward off a third calamity. (This is a variant of the Morocco custom mentioned before). On returning from the cemetery, they drive a nail into the door of the house. Indeed religion in Tripoli has a large admixture of superstition." [56] In the Atlas Mountains, Slouschz found "the cult of the dead plays an important part." [57] At one village the "Genius of the river," is worshipped.[58] Elsewhere "women made rendezvous with spirits and danced with them." [59] Moreover, "the Jews of the Sahara are exceedingly superstitious and believe in demons and in sor-

were not really primitive, but simply people who had lost the culture they formerly enjoyed." G. Elliot Smith, *In the Beginning,* New York, 1928, p. 24 f.

[55] Slouschz, *Travels in North Africa,* p. 349.

[56] Idem, p. 208.

[57] Idem, p. 469.

[58] Idem, p. 472.

[59] Idem, p. 284.

ceries of every kind."[60] And, "the Sachai is a sorcerer who comes originally from Morocco. By the use of kameot, conjuring books and talismans (talmes), he learns all secret things. He cures, curses, and uncovers springs and secret treasures."[61] And yet these degraded devotees of superstition and fetishism justly claim descent from the Chosen People who were expressly called to safeguard and perpetuate the service of Yahweh.

**Cultural Development.** The evolutionist, then, is in error when he takes it for granted that the low state of civilization to be found in out-of-the-way corners of the world must be a survival of the early conditions of the human race, and not a deterioration from early standards. Experience shows that a group does not always tend towards its betterment when left to itself, but on the contrary too frequently degenerates physically and intellectually, as well as spiritually.

Thus, for example, some twenty years ago a decidedly undesirable element flocked into the State of Maryland. They were presumably what is known as " White trash" from the West Virginia Mountains. They passed for such at any rate. A small colony, or perhaps a single family, would suddenly appear in a neighborhood and without leave or license take possession of a vacant house or even a hovel in the woods. Dirty, unkempt, their horror of water seemed only second to their aversion for work. Their propensity for begging earned for them the title of "Gim-mes" (Give me). Their open disregard for the ordinary standards of decency and the accepted norm of morality was notorious. Legal marriage in the strict sense of the word was unknown to them. A certain natural bond was sanctioned among them, but at night men, women, and children would sleep huddled together on the floor in a manner

[60] Idem, p. 357.

[61] Idem, p. 285. Note:—Slouschz states: "There are many kinds of kameot, talismans and amulets, which the Jewish child wears from the day of its birth. First comes the hand (or hand of Fatma) with five fingers, worked in metal with strange designs. This hand is found engraved in all the houses of the more backward Jews. It is worn as an amulet round the neck or on the heart. Children wear besides a horn of coral, a collar containing a small cypress to protect them from evil, a little bag of black cumin, incense, grains of carob, and silver plates with the words Shaddai, Siman Tob, etc."—*Travels in North Africa,* p. 282. Slouschz further reports that when Rabbi Isaac ben Shishet reached Algiers in 1391, "he began a campaign against the ignorance and superstitions of the native Jews. . . . Still all his efforts did not succeed in dispelling either the superstitions which are the peculiar possession of the natives, or their worship of the dead, the dominating African cult."—l. c., p. 320.

no whit more civilized than was customary in darkest Africa before the advent of what we flatter ourselves by calling modern civilization. And yet, this "White trash" from the West Virginia Mountains, if they did actually come from there, was descended from as good stock as ever settled in the United States. Isolation and hardships and no doubt local conditions that can only be surmised led to neglect of religious practices, God was forgotten in time, and His moral law disregarded, until there was evolved a type of degeneracy that is better left undescribed. Just how far physical and moral uncleanness had advanced the decay of civilization, it is hard to say. Without question the hook-worm had much to do with the bodily lassitude and spiritual decreptitude of the poor unfortunates. In any case, here at least, the tendency of the race was not to self-betterment but rather to decay.

**Civilization.** It is not surprising then, to find Christopher Dawson in his chapter on the Decline of Archaic Civilization, emphatic in his statement: "The Archaic Civilization, which has been described in the preceding chapters, reached its full development in the third millenium B. C. Thereafter the note of civilizations of the Near East was conservation rather than progress. In fact, in many respects the general level of material culture stood higher in that age than at any subsequent period. All the great achievements on which the life of civilization rests had been already reached, and there was no important addition to its material equipment until the rise of the great scientific and industrial movements in Western Europe in modern times. The most important inventions which characterise the higher culture, such as agriculture and the domestication of animals, the plough and the wheel vehicle, irrigation and the construction of canals, the working of metals and stone architecture, navigation and sailing ships, writing and the calendar, the city state and the institution of Kingship, had been already achieved by the fourth millenium, and by the third we find organised bureaucratic states, written codes of laws, a highly developed commerce and industry, and the beginnings of astronomy and mathematics." [62]

[62] Dawson, *The Age of the Gods,* p. 237. Note:—Doctor Frederick Tilney, Professor of Neurology at Columbia University, whose recent work, *The Brain from Ape to Man,* is professedly a defense of the evolutionary theory, is constrained to make certain admissions that are worth recording here. While

**Criteria.** Dawson had previously said: "Judged by purely physical standards, such as the size of their brain, fossil man of the later palaeolithic period was equal and sometimes even superior to the average modern man. The modern average of cranial capacity lies between 1400 and 1500 cubic centimeters, while that of the fossil man of Cromagnon has been estimated at 1650 cc., that of Chancelade at 1710 cc., and that of Barma Grande, near Mentone, higher still. This result is not flattering to our pride in the progress of modern man, but it is cu-

claiming for mankind in general a steady, if spasmodic, progress (Vol. II, p. 932), he contends, however, that this is accomplished only by a succession of races, each of which in turn is doomed to decay and extinction. Thus he states: "As in the first flush of any renaissance, so with the awakening of a new race, the initial period is usually the most fertile in productive ingenuity. . . . The same familiar cycle of juvenescence, maturity and decline which characterised the development of earlier races did not fail to apply its inevitable formula to the Cro-Magnon." (Vol. II, p. 761 f). He had already said: "The Cro-Magnon ranks high among the races of mankind in intellectual development and known capacities of production. He belongs to the species Homo Sapiens, the same species of man that has made modern history." (l. c., p. 759). And again: "The Cro-Magnon were a race which developed in Asia but seem to have had no connection of an ancestral kind with the Neanderthals. They possessed a brain capable of more complex ideas, greater comprehension, more reasoning powers, a wider, more facile imagination. Above all, they were endowed with a highly artistic sense which had not been present in any of the previous races of man. Indeed, they seem to have possessed a cerebral capacity which was nearly if not quite equal to that of modern man. They were capable of advance education and had strongly developed esthetic as well as religious feelings." (l. c., p. 760.) Later Doctor Tilney adds: "The treasures of their art galleries upon the walls of the ancient caves, their remarkable drawings, sculptures and paintings fully warrant the distinction which has been conferred upon them in the title of Paleolithic Greeks." (l. c., p. 763). Yet, speaking of Cro-Magnon Industry, he observes: "The Solutrean was the high noon of his cultural achievement just as the middle Mousterian was for the Neanderthal. In this era the flint industry attained its culminating stage but its flourishing activities soon began to wane. Through the Magdalenian all of the artistic and industrial development sank slowly toward the horizon of its disappearance. At length in the Azilian Period the last survivors of the greatest race in the Old Stone Age, senescent in their industries, decadent in their art, saw the setting of the Cro-Magnon sun and the passing of their kind into the darkness." (l. c., p. 762.) Once more he returns to the subject: "Cro-Magnon destiny was no exception to what had gone before and what would follow many times thereafter. It embraced the irresistible tendency towards racial decline with final extinction, and this was the fate which did at length befall Cro-Magnon man." (l. c., p. 766.) All this raises the question: Independent of experimental knowledge which necessarily is ever on the increase, just how far has man advanced intellectually, especially in the power of deduction, since Cro-Magnon times? The question is especially pertinent as regards the religious beliefs of so-called primitives. Moreover, if Doctor Tilney is consistent in his theory, he should admit that the present race of man has been recrudescing, and that primeval cultural conditions were of a higher order than those of the present day.

riously borne out by the recent discoveries of Fossil man outside Europe." [63]

**Cro-Magnon Man.**

Kroeber, too, adds his tribute of praise to the high standard of civilization to which the Cro-Magnon man attained. Thus he says: "The Cro-Magnon race of Aurignacian times, as represented by the finds at Cro-Magnon and Grimaldi, was excessively tall and large-brained, surpassing any living race of man in both respects." [64] And again: "This race was not only tall, but clean-limbed, lithe, and swift. Their brains were equally large. . . . If these individuals were not exceptional, the figures mean that the size and weight of the brain of the early Cro-Magnon people was some fifteen or twenty per cent greater than that of modern Europeans. . . . The Cro-Magnon peoples used skilfully made harpoons, originated a remarkable art, and in general attained a development of industries parallel to their high degree of bodily progress." [65] Certainly from a civilizational standpoint the comparison of Cro-Magnon man with our so-called primitive of to-day, does not lend support to the theory of the evolution and betterment of the human race.

**Primitive Man.**

The Reverend Philo L. Mills has said in his monumental work on Prehistoric Religion: "There are those who have dabbled with Tyler's Primitive Culture, with Frazer's pretentious work on Totemism and Exogamy, and who are firmly convinced that primitive man was either entirely

[63] Dawson, *The Age of the Gods,* p. 10. Note:—Naturally size of brain alone has been cast aside as an index of the scale of civilization, and other criteria, such as complexity of cerebral convolution, and the like, have been introduced in the scheme of evolution. Thus Professor Tilney first mentions: "Statistics indicate that the brain weight of distinguished and talented individual members of the race is somewhat in excess of the average adult brain. Thus in one hundred distinguished men, the average weight of the brain was 1469.65 gm., about 100 gms. above the average weight of European brains."—*The Brain from Ape to Man,*" Vol. II, p. 777. He then takes care to add, when he is distinguishing the brain of a man from that of an ape: "Two facts are impressive upon inspection of the cerebral hemisphere in man when compared with all the lower primates: first, the marked increase in size; second, the great complexity of convolutional richness and intricacy of fissural pattern."—l. c., p. 778. To which he adds later: "If a single statement might cover the characteristic features of the lateral aspect of the human hemisphere in contrast to all other primates, it is that the complexity of the convolutions and the tortuousness of the fissures render impossible a uniform description in man, while the relative simplicity of these features in all simian brains discloses the discrete territorial boundaries almost at first glance."—l. c., p. 789.

[64] Kroeber, *Anthropology,* p. 27.

[65] Idem, p. 28.

atheistic, or if in possession of any religion at all, that the idea of God was developed out of the ghost or the magical nature cult. To them we shall oppose an enormous array of religious facts which have only recently been unearthed but which in their united force point to conclusions of precisely the opposite character—it is the all-Father belief which precedes the totemic or animistic cult by indefinite ages. *Primitive man believed in God,* and only in later times was the belief corrupted." [66]

So, too, the Reverend Joseph Rickaby: "It is not unlikely that the savage state of what anthropologists and geologists know as 'primitive man' was part of the punishment of original sin." [67]

It is not surprising then, to find even so pronounced an advocate of the evolution of religious beliefs as Professor Lynn Thorndyke, actually forced to admit: "Instead of simply having failed to progress from a lower stage of civilization, savages may have retrogressed from a once higher state of culture. It is, therefore, none too certain that their customs and thought are those of primitive man." [68] And again: "The view that man once lived promiscuously in hordes and that the family developed only gradually, perhaps with settled life, has now been abandoned, and the family, usually monogamous, is recognized as the oldest human institution and 'omnipresent at every stage of culture.' " [69]

**Final Conclusion.**

Wherefore, we conclude, that, the Supreme Being not only of the Ashanti and allied tribes, but most probably of the whole of Negro Land as well, is not the God of the Christians which, at a comparatively recent date, was superimposed on the various tribal beliefs by ministers of the Gospel: but, the Yahweh of the Hebrews, and that too of the Hebrews of pre-exilic times, that either supplanted the previous concept of divinity in the African mind, or else clarified and defined the original monotheistic idea which may have lain dormant for many centuries, or even perhaps been buried for a time in an inexplicable confusion of polytheism and superstition. It was the tri-

[66] Philo L. Mills, *Prehistoric Man,* Washington, 1918, Proleg. p. 4.

[67] Joseph Rickaby, *Waters that Go Softly,* London, 1923, # 51.

[68] Lynn Thorndyke, *A Short History of Civilization,* New York, 1926, p. 23. Note:—Christopher Dawson positively asserts: "The passing of the glacial age seems to have been in many respects a time of retrogression and cultural decadence."—*The Age of the Gods,* p. 45.

[69] Thorndyke, l. c., p. 29.

umph over the darkness of error of the original monotheistic idea, that had existed previous to the lapse from grace of the parents of the Human Race, and the reawakening of this primitive concept was the fruit of the Diaspora of the Chosen People of God that was to pave the way for Christianity.[70]

[70] Cfr. Henry Martin Battenhouse, *The Bible Unlocked,* New York, 1928, p. 406: "The Jews of the Dispersion formed the bridge across which Christianity entered the Roman World."

# BIBLIOGRAPHY

Anything like a critical Bibliography would require a volume in itself. We must here be satisfied with merely listing such references as have been found useful in preparing the present work. With the exception of periodicals, these may be found for the most part in the Boston College Library, Newton, Mass.

## GENERAL BIBLIOGRAPHY


ABOUL FARADJ, GREGORY.
*Supplementum Historiae Dynastiarum,* trad. Edward Pocock, Oxford, 1663.

ABULFEDA, ISMAEL.
*Annales Muslamici,* ed. Jacobus Georgius Adler, Hafniae, 1789.
*Historia Anteislamica,* ed. Henricus Orthobius Fleischer, Lipsiae, 1831.
*Géographie, I Partie,* trad. Reinard, Paris, 1848.
" *II* " trad. Saint-Goyard, Paris, 1884.

ABUTIBUS, GEORGIUS ELMACENIUS.
*Historia Saracenica,* red. Thomas Erpenius, Amsterdam, 1625.

BARTH, HENRY.
*Travels and Discoveries in North and Central Africa,* New York, 1857.

BARTON, GEORGE A.
*Religions of the World,* Chicago, 1919.

BASSET, RENÉ.
*Études Nord-Africaines et Orientales,* Paris, 1923–1925.
*Mélanges Africains et Orientaux,* Paris, 1915.

BOAS, FRANZ.
*Anthropology and Modern Life,* New York, 1928.

BOEMUS, JOANNES.
*Mores, Leges et Ritus Omnium Gentium,* London, 1541.

BRAWLEY, B. G.
*Short History of the American Negro,* New York, 1913.
*Social History of the American Negro,* New York, 1921.

BREASTED, JAMES HENRY.
*Ancient Times,* Boston, 1916.
*Conquest of Civilization,* New York, 1926.

Burton, Richard F.
*Select Papers on Anthropology,* London, 1924.
Casserly, Gordon.
*Africa To-Day,* Newcastle-on-Tyne.
Charton, Edouard.
*Voyageurs Anciens et Modernes,* Paris, 1867.
Clay, Albert T.
*Empire of the Amorites,* New Haven, 1919.
*Origin of Biblical Tradition,* New Haven, 1923.
Cleland, Herdman Fitzgerald.
*Our Prehistoric Ancestors,* New York, 1928.
Crawford, O. G. S.
*Man and His Past,* Oxford, 1921.
Cust, Robert Needham,
*Modern Languages of Africa,* London, 1883.
Dale, A.
*Dissertationes de Origine et Progressu Idololatriae,* Amsterdam, 1693.
Dawson, Christopher.
*The Age of the Gods,* Boston, 1928.
Denham, Clapperton and Oudney.
*Discoveries in Africa,* London, 1826.
Deniker, J.
*Les Races et les Peuples de la Terre,* Paris, 1926.
Dennett, R. E.
*At the Back of the Black Man's Mind,* London, 1906.
Dio, Cassius Cocceianus.
*Roman History,* trans, E. Cay, London, 1914.
Dixon, Roland B.
*Racial History of Man,* New York, 1923.
*Building of Cultures,* New York, 1928.
Dowd, Jerome.
*The Negro Races,* New York, 1907.
Dubois-Fontanelle, J. G.
*Anecdotes Africaines,* Paris, 1775.
Dufourcq, Albert.
*Les Religions Païennes et le Religion Juive Conparées,* Paris, 1923.
Fillion, L. Cl.
*Histoire d'Israel Peuple de Dieu,* Paris, 1927–1928.
Fowler, Henry Thatcher.
*Great Leaders of Hebrew History,* New York, 1920.
Frazer, James George.
*Totemism and Exogamy,* London, 1910.
*The Golden Bough,* London, 1920.
Gaffarel, Paul.
*La Conqûete de l'Afrique,* Paris, 1892.

GARNIER, NOËL.
*L'Afrique: Anthropologie Géographique,* Paris, 1894.
GOLDENWEISER, ALEXANDER A.
*Early Civilization,* New York, 1926.
GRAY, GEORGE BUCHANAN.
*Studies in Hebrew Proper Names,* London, 1896.
*Sacrifice in the Old Testament,* Oxford, 1925.
HADDON, A. C.
*Races of Man and their Distribution,* New York, 1925.
HANKINS, FRANK H.
*Racial Basis of Civilization,* New York, 1926.
HARRIS, JOHN.
*Navigantium atque Itinerantium Bibliotheca,* London, 1764.
HARTMANN, JOANNES MELCHIOR.
*Edrisii Africa,* Göttingen, 1796.
HASTINGS, JAMES.
*Dictionary of the Bible,* (Edited), New York, 1924.
*Encyclopedia of Religion and Ethics,* (Edited), New York, 1913–1922.
HEEREN, A. H. L.
*African Nations,* Oxford, 1832.
*Historical Researches,* London, 1847.
HERODOTUS.
*Geography,* trans. A. D. Godley, London, 1921-1924.
HERTZ, FRIEDERICH.
*Race and Civilization,* London, 1928.
HOPKINS, E. WASHBURN.
*History of Religions,* New York, 1926.
IBN AT-TIQTAQA.
*Al Fakri,* trad. E. Amar, Paris, 1910.
IBN HAOUKAL, ABOU'L QASIM.
*Description de l'Afrique,* trad. Slane—*Journal Asiatique,* Paris, 1842.
JOHNSTON, HARRY H.
*History of the Colonization of Africa by Alien Races,* Cambridge, 1913.
JOSEPHUS, FLAVIUS.
*Antiquities of the Jews,* trans. William Whiston, New York.
*Against Apion,* trans. H. St. J. Thackery, London, 1926.
JUNKER, WILLIAM.
*Travels in Africa,* London, 1890.
JUSTEL, H.
*Recueil de Divers Voyages,* Paris, 1684.
KEANE, A. H.
*Africa,* London, 1895.
*Man, Past and Present,* Cambridge, 1920.

KOELLE, S. W.
*Polyglotta Africana,* London, 1854.
KÖHLER, KAUFMANN.
*Jewish Theology,* New York, 1928.
*Koran.*
Trans. J. M. Rodwell, London, 1871.
KORTLEITNER, FRANCIS X.
*De Polytheismo Universo et quibusdam ejus Formis apud Hebraeos Finitimasque Gentes Usitatis,* Innsbruck, 1908.
*Archaeologia Biblica,* Innsbruck, 1917.
KROEBER, A. L.
*Anthropology,* New York, 1923.
LAMMENS, HENRI.
*L'Islam: Croyances et Institutions,* Beyrouth, 1926.
LANG, ANDREW.
*Making of Religion,* New York, 1900.
*Magic and Religion,* London, 1901.
LE BLANC, VINCENT.
*The World Surveyed,* trans. F. B. Gent, London, 1660.
LEO AFRICANUS, JOANNES. (Hassan ibn Mohammed el-Ouzzan)
*Africae Descriptio,* Amsterdam, 1632.
LE ROY, ALEXANDER.
*La Religion des Primitifs, Paris,* 1911.
*Religion of the Primitives,* trans. Newton Thompson, New York. 1922.
LEROY, OLIVIER.
*La Raison Primitive,* Paris, 1927.
LETOURNEAU, CH.
*L'Évolution Littéraire dans les Diverses Races Humaines,* Paris, 1894.
LÉVY-BRUHL, LUCIEN.
*Les Fonctions Mentales dans les Sociétés Inférieures,* Paris, 1918.
*La Mentalité Primitive,* Paris, 1922.
*L'Ame Primitive,* Paris, 1927.
LOWIE, ROBERT H.
*Culture and Ethnology,* New York, 1916.
*Primitive Society,* New York, 1919.
*Primitive Religion,* New York, 1924.
LUCAS, CHARLES P.
*Partition and Colonization of Africa,* Oxford, 1922.
MACALASTER, R. A. S.
*Century of Excavation in Palestine,* London, 1926.
MAIMONIDES, MOSES.
*De Idololatria,* Amsterdam, 1675.
MARMOL, CARVAJAL.
*Description General de Africa,* Malaga, 1599.

*L'Afrique,* trad. D'Ablancourt, Paris, 1667.
MARTIN, BENJAMIN.
*System of Philology,* London, 1759.
MEILLET ET COHEN.
*Les Langues du Monde,* Paris, 1924.
MESNAGE, J.
*Le Christianisme en Afrique, Déclin et Extinction,* Paris, 1915.
MIGNE, J. P.
*Patrologiae Cursus Completus:—*
*Series Latina,* Paris, 1844–65.
*Series Graeca,* Paris, 1857–66.
MILLS, PHILO LAOS.
*Prehistoric Religion,* Washington, 1918.
MOORE, FRANCIS.
*Travels in Inland Parts of Africa.*
MOORE, GEORGE FOOT.
*History of Religions,* Edinburgh, 1914.
MORRISON, W. D.
*The Jews under Roman Rule,* London, 1890.
MÜLLER, W. MAX.
*Science of Languages,* London, 1861.
MUNTSCH, ALBERT.
*Evolution and Culture,* St. Louis, 1923.
MURET, M.
*Rites of Funeral, Ancient and Modern,* trans. Paul Lorrain, London, 1683.
MURRAY, HUGH.
*Discoveries and Travels in Africa,* Edinburgh, 1818.
NETTER, NATHAN.
*Israel et Son Talmud à Travers l'Histoire,* Paris, 1926.
OGILBY, JOHN.
*Africa,* London, 1679.
OUSELEY, WILLIAM.
*Oriental Geography of Ebn Haukal,* London, 1800.
PERRY, W. J.
*Children of the Sun,* London, 1927.
PHILO, JUDAEUS.
*Works,* trans, C. D. Young, London, 1890.
PLINY, THE ELDER.
*Natural History,* trans. Bostock and Riley, London, 1855.
POLYBIUS.
*Histories,* trans. W. B. Paton, London, 1922.
PORY, JOHN.
*Geographical Historie of Africa,* London, 1600.
PURCHAS, SAMUEL.
*His Pilgrimages,* London, 1614.

QUATREFAGES, A. DE.
*Human Species,* London, 1903.

RADIN, PAUL.
*Monotheism among Primitive Peoples,* London, 1924.

RASMUSSEN, JAMES LASSEN.
*Historia Praecipuorum Arabum Regnorum ante Islaismum,* Hanniae, 1817.
*Additamenta ad Historiam Arabum ante Islamismum, excepta ex Ibn Nabatah Nuveirio atque Ibn Koteibah,* Hanniae, 1821.

RAWLISON, GEORGE.
*Translation of Herodotus.*

RECLUS, ELISÉE.
*Africa and Its Inhabitants,* trans. A. H. Keane, London, 1878.

ROMMEL, CHRISTOPHER.
*Abulfedea Arabiae Descriptio Commentario Perpetua Illustrata,* Göttingen, 1802.

ROSS, ALEXANDER.
*Panseibia,* Little London, 1672.

ROSTOVTZEFF, M.
*History of the Ancient World,* trans. J. D. Duff, Oxford, 1926.

SAPIR, EDWARD.
*Language,* New York, 1921.

SAULCY, F. DE.
*Histoire de l'Art Judaïque,* Paris, 1858.

SCHMIDT, MAX.
*Primitive Races of Mankind,* London, 1926.

SCHMIDT, W.
"Origine de l'Idée de Dieu,"—*Anthropos,* Vienne, 1910.
"Les Religions de l'Afrique"—*Semaine d'Éthnologie Religieuse,* Paris, 1913.
*Die Sprachfamilien und Sprachenkreise der Erde,* Heidelberg, 1926.

SCHOLES, THEOPHILUS E. S.
*Glimpes of the Ages,* London, 1905.

SCHULTZ, ALFRED P.
*Race or Mongrel,* Boston, 1908.

SHAW, THOMAS.
*Travels and Observations,* Oxford, 1738.

SMITH, G. ELLIOT.
*In the Beginning,* New York, 1928.

SOUTTAR, ROBINSON.
*Short History of Ancient Peoples,* London, 1904

STRABO.
*Geography,* trans. Horace Leonard Jones, London, 1917.

SUMNER, WILLIAM GRAHAM.
*Folkways,* Boston, 1906.

SUMNER, KELLER and DAVIE.
*The Science of Society,* New Haven, 1927.
TALEB KAHN, MIRZA ABU.
*Travels,* trans. Charles Stewart, London, 1810.
TAYLOR, GRIFFITH.
*Environment and Race,* Oxford, 1927.
THORNDYKE, LYNN.
*Short History of Civilization,* New York, 1926.
TILNEY, FREDERICK.
*The Brain from Ape to Man,* New York, 1928.
TOUTAIN, J.
*Les Cultes Païens dans l'Empire Roman,* Paris, 1920.
TYLER, EDWARD B.
*Primitive Culture,* London, 1873.
*Anthropology,* New York, 1923.
UGOLINI, BL.
*Thesaurus Antiquitatum Sacrarum, Complectens Selectissima Clarissimorum Virorum Opuscula, in quibus Veterum Hebraeorum Mores, Leges, Instituta, Ritus Sacri et Civiles Illustrantur,* Venice, 1744–69.
VENDRYES, J.
*Languages,* London, 1925.
VIGOUROUX, F.
*La Bible et la Critique,* Paris, 1883.
*La Bible et les Découvertes Modernes,* Paris, 1884.
WALLIS, WILSON D.
*Messiahs: Christian and Pagan,* Boston, 1918.
*Introduction to Anthropology,* New York, 1926.
WEATHERFORD, W. D.
*The Negro from Africa to America,* New York, 1924.
WILLOUGHBY, W. C.
*Race Problems in New Africa,* Oxford, 1923.
*The Soul of the Bantu,* New York, 1928.
WISSLER, CLARK.
*Man and Culture,* New York, 1923.
WORK, MONROE N.
*Bibliography of the Negro in Africa and America,* New York, 1928.

## BIBLIOGRAPHY—FOR INTRODUCTION ON JAMAICA

*Abridgment of the Minutes of the Evidence taken before a Committee of the Whole House, to Whom It was Referred to Consider of the Slave-Trade,* London, 1789–1791.
BACON AND AARON.
*The New Jamaica,* Kingston, 1890.

BARCLAY, ALEXANDER.
*Practical View of Present State of Slavery in West Indies,* London, 1828.

BARKER AND SINCLAIR.
*West African Folk-Tales,* London, 1917.

BECKFORD, WILLIAM.
*Remarks upon the Situation of the Negroes in Jamaica, Impartially Made from a Local Experience of Nearly Thirteen Years in that Island,* London, 1788;
*Descriptive Account of the Island of Jamaica,* London, 1790.

BIGELOW, JOHN.
*Jamaica in 1850,* New York, 1851.

BLOME, RICHARD.
*Description of the Island of Jamaica from the Notes of Sir Thomas Linch, Knight, Governor of Jamaica,* London, 1672.

BRIDGES, GEOGRE WILSON.
*A Voice from Jamaica,* London, 1823;
*Annals of Jamaica,* London, 1828.

BROWNE, PATRICK.
*Civil and Natural History of Jamaica,* London, 1789.

BURDETT, WILLIAM.
*Life and Exploits of Mansong with a Particular Account of the Obi,* London, 1800.

BURGE, WILLIAM.
*Reply Relative to the Present State of Jamaica,* London, 1839.

CANA, FRANK R.
*Ashanti—Encyclopædia Brittanica,* 11th Edition, Vol. II, p. 725.

CLARK, A. H.
*Ingenious Method of Causing Death Employed by the Obeah Men of the West Indies—American Anthropologist,* Lancaster, Penn. Vol. XIV (1912).

COOK, E. M.
*Jamaica: The Lodestone of the Caribbean,* Bristol, 1924.

COOPER, THOMAS.
*Facts Illustrative of the Condition of the Negro Slaves in Jamaica,* London, 1824.
*Correspondence Relative to the Condition of the Negro Slaves in Jamaica,* London, 1824.

CRONISE AND WARD.
*Cunnie Rabbit, Mr. Spider and the Other Beef,* London, 1903.

CUNDALL, FRANK.
*Historic Jamaica,* London, 1915.
*Jamaica Under the Spaniards,* Kingston, 1919.
*Jamaica Handbook,* Kingston, 1924.

DALLAS, ROBERT CHARLES.
*History of the Maroons,* London, 1803.

DANA, M.
*Voodoo, Its Effects on the Negro Race—Metropolitan Magazine,* New York, Vol. XXVII (1908).
DAVIS, H. P.
*Black Democracy,* New York, 1928.
DE LISSER, H. G.
*In Jamaica and Cuba,* Kingston, 1910.
*20th Century Jamaica,* Kingston, 1913.
EDWARDS, BRYAN.
*Speech on the Slave Trade,* London, 1790.
*History Civil and Commercial of the British Colonies in the West Indies,* London, 1793.
*Proceedings of the Governor and Assemby of Jamaica in regard to the Maroon Negroes,* London, 1796.
FINLASON, W. F.
*History of the Jamaica Case,* London, 1869.
FRANCKLYN, G.
*Answer to the Rev. Mr. Clarkson's Essay on Slavery,* London, 1789.
FULLER, STEPHEN.
*Two Reports of the House of Assembly of Jamaica on the Subject of the Slave Trade,* London, 1789.
*New Act of Assembly of the Island of Jamaica; being the present Code Noir of that Island,* London, 1789.
*Proceedings of the Hon. House of Assembly of Jamaica, on the Sugar and Slave Trade,* London, 1793.
*Original Letter Books While Agent of Jamaica in England,* 1764–1795, MSS in Boston College Library, Newton, Mass.
GARDNER, WILLIAM JAMES.
*History of Jamaica,* London, 1909
GAUNT, MARY.
*Where the Twain Meet,* New York, 1922.
GLADSTONE, JOHN.
*Facts Relating to Slavery,* London, 1830.
HAKEWILL, JAMES.
*Picturesque Tour of the Island of Jamaica,* London, 1825.
HANSON, FRANCIS.
*Account of the Island of Jamaica—Prefixed to Laws of Jamaica,* London, 1683.
HARVEY AND BREWIN.
*Jamaica in 1866,* London, 1867.
HICKERINGILL, EDMUND.
*Jamaica Viewed,* London, 1661.
HILL, ROBERT T.
*Cuba and Porto Rico with the Other Islands of the West Indies,* New York, 1898.

JECKYLL, WALTER.
*Jamaican Song and Story,* London, 1907.
JOHNSTON, HARRY H.
*The Negro in the New World,* London, 1910.
JONES, JAMES.
*Acts of Assembly passed in the Island of Jamaica from 1770 to 1783,* Kingston, 1786.
KIDD, JOSEPH B.
*Illustrations of Jamaica,* London, 1840.
KNIBB, WILLIAM.
*Facts and Documents Connected with the Late Insurrection in Jamaica,* London, 1832.
LESLIE, JAMES.
*New History of Jamaica,* London, 1740.
LEWIS, MATTHEW GREGORY.
*Journal of a West Indian Planter,* London, 1834.
LIVINGSTON, WILLIAM P.
*Black Jamaica,* London, 1899.
LLOYD, WILLIAM.
*Letters from the West Indies,* London, 1837.
LONG, EDWARD.
*History of Jamaica,* London, 1774.
LOWE, JOSEPH.
*Inquiry into the State of the British West Indies,* London, 1807.
LUNAN, JOHN.
*Abstract of the Laws of Jamaica Relating to Slaves,* Saint Jago de la Vega, Jamaica, 1819.
LYNCH, MRS. HENRY.
*The Family Sepulchre,* London, 1848.
MADDEN, RICHARD. R.
*A Twelve-months Residence in the West Indies,* London, 1835.
MATSON, JAMES.
*Remarks on the Slave Trade and African Squadron,* London, 1848.
MCMAHON, BENJAMIN.
*Jamaica Plantership,* London, 1839.
MCNEILL, HECTOR.
*Observations on the Treatment of the Negroes in the Island of Jamaica,* London, 1788–1789.
MILNE-HOME, MARY PARMELA.
*Mamma's Black Nurse Stories,* Edinburgh, 1890.
MILNER, T. H.
*Present and Future State of Jamaica,* London, 1839.
MONTAGNAC, NOËL DE
*Negro Nobodies,* London, 1899.

MORETON, J. B.
*West India Customs and Manners,* London, 1793.
NELSON, WILLIAM S.
*La Race Noire dans la Démocratie Américane,* Paris, 1922.
NILES, BLAIR.
*Black Hayti,* New York, 1926.
NUGENT, MARIA.
*Journal of a Voyage to and Residence in the Island of Jamaica, 1801–1805,* London, 1839.
PHILLIPPO, JAMES M.
*Jamaica: Its Past and Present State,* London, 1843.
PIM, BEDFORD.
*The Negro and Jamaica,* London, 1866.
PITMAN, FRANK WESLEY.
*Development of the British West Indies, 1700–1763,* New Haven, 1917.
PRICE-MARS, DR.
*Le Sentiment et le Phénomène religieux chez les nègres de Saint-Domingue—Bulletin de la Société d'Histoire et de Géographie d'Hayti,* Port-au-Prince, Hayti, 1925.
*Ainsi Parla l'Oncle,* Compiègne, 1928.
PRINGLE, THOMAS.
*Suggestions Respecting the Apprenticeship of Negro Children,* London, 1833.
PULLEN-BURY, BESSIE.
*Jamaica as It Is in 1903,* London, 1903.
*Ethiopia in Exile,* London, 1905.
RADCLIFFE, JOHN.
*Lectures on Negro Proverbs with a Preliminary Paper on Negro Literature,* Kingston, 1869.
RAULIN, M.
*Histoire de la Jamaïque,* London, 1751.
RENNY, ROBERT.
*History of Jamaica,* London, 1807.
ROBY, JOHN.
*History of the Parish of St. James, Jamaica, to the Year 1740,* Kingston, 1849.
SCOTT, MICHAEL.
*Tom Cringle's Log,* Philadelphia, 1833.
*The Cruise of the Midge,* Edinburgh, 1834.
SCOTT, SIBBALD DAVID.
*To Jamaica and Back,* London, 1876.
SHERLOCK, P. M.
*Jamaica Superstitions—Empire Review,* 1924.
SHORE, JOSEPH.

*In Old St. James,* Kingston, 1911.
SLOANE, HANS.
*A Voyage to the Islands,* London, 1707.
*Natural History of Jamaica,* London, 1707.
STARK, JAMES H.
*Jamaica Guide,* Boston, 1898.
STERNE, HENRY.
*A Statement of Facts,* London, 1837.
STEWART, J.
*Past and Present State of the Island of Jamaica,* Edinburgh, 1823.
STUART, VILLIERS.
*Jamaica Revisited,* London, 1891.
STURGE AND HARVEY.
*The West Indies in 1837,* London, 1838.
TAYLOR, R.
*Negro Slavery Especially in Jamaica,* London, 1823.
THOMAS, HERBERT T.
*Untrodden Jamaica,* Kingston, 1890.
THOME AND KIMBALL.
*Emancipation in the West Indies,* New York, 1838.
TRAPHAM, THOMAS.
*Discourse of the State of Health in the Island of Jamaica,* London, 1679.
TURNBULL, DAVID.
*The Jamaica Movement,* London, 1850.
UNDERHILL, EDWARD BEAN.
*The Tragedy of Morant Bay,* London, 1865.
*A Letter on the Condition of Jamaica,* London, 1865.
WADDELL, HOPE MASTERSON.
*Twenty-nine Years in the West Indies and Central Africa,* London, 1863.
WHITEHEAD, HENRY S.
*Obi in the Caribbean—The Commonweal,* New York, June 1, 1927,
WHITELEY, HENRY.
*Three Months in Jamaica in 1832,* London, 1833.
WILCOX, ELLA WHEELER.
*Sailing Sunny Seas,* Chicago, 1909.
WILLIAMS, CYNRIC R.
*Tour Through the Island of Jamaica,* London, 1826.
WILLIAMS, JAMES.
*Narrative of Events,* London, 1837.
WILLIAMS, JOSEPH J.
*Whisperings of the Caribbean,* New York, 1925.
YOUNG, ROBERT.
*A View of Slavery,* London, 1825.

BIBLIOGRAPHY—FOR CHAPTERS I, II & III ON THE ASHANTI

ALLEN, MARCUS.
*The Gold Coast,* London, 1874.
ANCELLO, J.
*Les Explorations au Sénégal,* Paris, 1886.
ARCIN, ANDRÉ.
*La Guinée Française,* Paris, 1907.
AUDAIN, LÉON.
*Le Mal d'Haiti,* Port-au-Prince, Hayti, 1908.
BADEN-POWELL, R. S. S.
*Downfall of Prempeh,* Philadelphia, 1896.
BECKWITH, MARTHA WARREN.
*Jamaica Anansi Stories,* New York, 1924.
BEECHAM, JOHN.
*Ashantee and the Gold Coast,* London, 1841.
BELL, HESKETH J.
*Obeah Witchcraft in the West Indies,* London.
BISS, HAROLD C. J.
*Relief of Kumasi,* London, 1901.
BOWDITCH, T. EDWARD.
*Mission from Cape Town Castle to Ashantee,* London, 1819.
*Essay on the Superstitions, Customs and Acts, Common to the Ancient Egyptian, Abyssinians, and Ashantees,* Paris, 1821.
*Africa,* London, 1825.
BOWLER, LOUIS P.
*Gold Coast Palaver,* London, 1911.
BOYLE, FREDERICK.
*Through Fanteeland to Coomassie,* London, 1874.
BOYLE, VIRGINIA FRAZER.
*Devil Tales,* New York, 1900.
BRACKENBURY, H.
*Fanti and Ashanti,* Edinburgh, 1873.
BUDGE, E. A. WALLIS.
*The Divine Origin of the Craft of the Herbalist,* London, 1928.
BUXTORF, JOANNES.
*Synagoga Judaica,* Basel, 1641.
CAMPBELL-THOMPSON, R.
*Semitic Magic: Its Origins and Development,* London, 1908.
CARDINALL, A. W.
*Natives of the Northern Territories of the Gold Coast,* London, 1908.
*In Ashanti and Beyond,* Philadelphia, 1927.
CASTELLANFS, H. C.
*New Orleans as It was,* New Orleans, 1895.
CHANTRE, ERNEST.

*Contribution à l'étude des races humaines de la Guinée, Les Aschantis—Bulletin Société d' Anthropologie de Lyon,* 1919.

CHRISTALLER, J. G.

*Collection of Three Thousand and Six Hundred Tshi Proverbs,* Basel, 1879.

*Dictionary of the Asante and Fante Language,* Basel, 1881.

CLARIDGE, W. WALTON.

*History of the Gold Coast and Ashanti,* London, 1915.

CLIFFORD, LADY.

*Our Days on the Gold Coast,* London, 1919.

CONNOLLY, R. M.

*Social Life in Fanti-Land—Journal of the Royal Anthropological Institute of Great Britain and Ireland,* London, Vol. XXVI (1895).

CORY'S

*Ancient Fragments,* ed. E. Richmond Hodges, London, 1876.

CRUIKSHANK, BRODIE.

*Eighteen Years on the Gold Coast of Africa,* London, 1853.

DAVIES, T. WILTON.

*Magic, Divination and Demonology among the Hebrews and Their Neighbours,* London, 1898.

DEANE, JOHN BATHURST.

*Worship of the Serpent,* London, 1833.

DORSAINVILLE, J. C.

*Une Explication Philologique du Vaudou,* Port-au-Prince, Hayti, 1924.

DUPUIS, JOSEPH.

*Journal of a Residence in Ashantee,* London, 1824.

ELLIS, ALFRED BURTON.

*The Land of Fetish,* London, 1883.

*The Tshi-Speaking Peoples of the Gold Coast of West Africa,* London, 1887.

*The Ewe-Speaking Peoples,* London, 1890.

*History of the Gold Coast of West Africa,* London, 1893.

*The Yoruba-Speaking Peoples of the Slave Coast,* London, 1894.

*On Vodu-Worship—Popular Science Monthly,* New York, Vol. XXXVIII (1891).

*West African Folklore—Popular Science Monthly,* Vol. XLV (1894).

EMERICK, A. J.

*Obeah and Duppyism in Jamaica* (Printed Privately), Woodstock, 1915.

*Jamaica Mialism* (Printed Privately), Woodstock, 1916.

*Jamaica Duppies* (Printed Privately), Woodstock, 1916.

EPSTEIN, MOSHEH.

*Torah Verified in Science,* New York, 1928.

FARBRIDGE, MAURICE H.
*Studies in Biblical and Semitic Symbolism,* London, 1923.
FREEMAN, RICHARD AUSTIN.
*Travels and Life in Ashanti and Jaman,* Westminster, 1898.
FULLER, FRANCIS C.
*A Vanished Dynasty; Ashanti,* London, 1921.
GODWIN, THOMAS.
*Moses and Aaron, Civil and Ecclesiastical Rites used by the Ancient Jews,* London, 1678.
GRAVE, E. J.
*Fetishism in Congo Land—Century Magazine,* New York, Vol. XIX (1891).
GROS, JULES.
*Voyages, Aventures et Captivité de J. Bonat chez les Achantis,* Paris, 1884.
HADDON, ALFRED C.
*Magic and Fetishism,* London, 1906.
HAY, J. DALRYMPLE.
*Ashanti and the Gold Coast,* London, 1874.
HAYFORD, CASELY.
*Gold Coast Native Institutions,* London, 1903.
HOWEY, M. OLDFIELD.
*The Encircled Serpent,* Philadelphia, 1928.
HURWITZ, SOLOMON T. H.
*Root-Derivatives in Semitic Speech,* New York, 1913.
ILLUSTRATED LONDON NEWS.
*From Cape Coast to Coomassie,* London, 1874.
JOHNSTON, HARRY H.
*History and Description of the British Empire in Africa,* London, 1910.
KEMP, DENNIS.
*Nine Years at the Gold Coast,* London, 1898.
MACDONALD, GEORGE.
*The Gold Coast, Past and Present,* New York, 1898.
MARTIN, EVELINE C.
*British West Africa Settlements,* London, 1927.
MEREDITH, HENRY.
*Account of the Gold Coast of Africa,* London, 1812.
MORAND, PAUL.
*Magie Noire,* Paris, 1928.
MUSGRAVE, GEORGE C.
*To Kumassie with Scott,* London, 1896.
NASSAU, ROBERT HAMMILL.
*Fetishism in West Africa,* London, 1904.
*Where Animals Talk,* London, 1914.
NEWLAND, H. OSMAN.

*West Africa,* London, 1922.
OWEN, MARY A.
*Voodoo Tales,* New York, 1893.
PARK, R. E.
*Magic, Mentality and City Life—Publications American Sociological Society,* Vol. XVIII (1924).
PITTARD, EUGÈNE.
*Contribution à l'Étude Anthropologique des Achanti—L'Anthropologie,* Paris, Tome XXXV (1925).
PLAUCHUT, EDMOND.
*Les Anglais à la Côte d'Or,* Paris, 1875.
PRICE, HANNIBAL.
*Le Réhabilitation de la Race Noire,* Port-au-Prince, Hayti, 1900.
PUCKETT, NEWBELL NILES.
*Folk Beliefs of the Southern Negro,* London, 1926.
RAMSEYER AND KÜHNE.
*Four Years in Ashantee,* London, 1875.
RATTRAY, R. SUTHERLAND.
*Ashanti Proverbs,* Oxford, 1916.
*Ashanti,* Oxford, 1923.
*Religion and Art in Ashanti,* Oxford, 1927.
ROBERTS, H. H.
*Three Jamaica Folk Stories—Journal of American Folklore,* Vol. XXXV (1922).
*A Study of Folksong Variants based on Field Work in Jamaica—Journal of American Folklore,* Vol. XXXVIII (1925).
*Possible Survivals of African Folksongs in Jamaica—Musical Quarterly,* Vol. XII.
SAXON, LYLE.
*Fabulous New Orleans,* New York, 1928.
SCHAEFFER, HENRY.
*Hebrew Tribal Economy and the Jubilee,* Leipzig, 1922.
SCOTT, EDWARD.
*Dancing in all Ages,* London, 1899.
SHEPHEARD, H.
*Traditions of Eden,* London, 1871.
STANLEY, HENRY MORTON.
*Coomassie and Magdala,* New York, 1874.
*Autobiography,* ed. by his wife, Boston, 1909.
*Sub-Officers Guide of Jamaica.*
Publ. Harry McCrea, Kingston, 1908.
TROUILLOT, D.
*Esquisse Ethnographique de Vaudou,* Port-au-Prince, Hayti, 1885.
VAN HIEN, A.
*Totemism on the Gold Coast—Journal of the Royal Anthropo-*

*logical Institute of Great Britain and Ireland,* London, Vol. XXXVI (1905).
WERNER, A.
*Language-Families of Africa,* London, 1925.
ZELLER, RUDOLF.
*Die Goldgerwichte von Asante,* Leipzig, 1912.

BIBLIOGRAPHY—FOR CHAPTER IV ON WEST AND CENTRAL AFRICA

ABADIE, MAURICE.
*La Colonie du Niger,* Paris, 1927.
ADAMSON, M.
*Histoire Naturelle de Sénégal,* Paris, 1757.
AJISAFE, A. K.
*Law and Customs of the Yoruba People,* London, 1924.
ALEXANDER, HERBERT.
*Boyd Alexander's Last Journey,* London, 1912
ALEXANDER, JAMES EDWARD.
*Expedition of Discovery,* London, 1838.
ALLEN AND THOMPSON.
*Expedition to the River Niger,* London, 1848.
ALMADA, ALVAREZ D'.
*Traité Succinte sur les Rivières de Guinée et du Cap Vert* (1594), ed. Diego Köpke, Porto, 1841.
APPEL, JOSEPH H.
*Africa's White Magic,* New York, 1928.
AZURARA, GOMEZ EANNES DE.
*Chronicle of the Discovery and Conquest of Guinea,* trans. Beazley and Prestage, London, 1896–99.
BACKWELL, H. F.
*Occupation of Hausaland,* Lagos, 1927.
BAIKIE, WILLIAM BALFOUR.
*Exploring Voyage of the Rivers Kwora and Benue,* London, 1856.
BARATIER, GÉNÉRAL.
*Epopées Africaines,* Paris, 1918.
BARBOT, J.
*Histoire de la Guinée,* Paris, 1660.
BARNES, JAMES.
*Through Central Africa,* New York, 1915.
BARRET, PAUL.
*L'Afrique Occidentale,* Paris, 1888.
BASDEN, G. T.
*Among the Ibos of Nigeria,* Philadelphia, 1921.

BASSET, RENÉ.
*Essai sur l'Histoire et la Langue de Tombouctou et des Royaumes de Songhai et Melli,* Paris, 1889.

BASTIAN, A.
*Der Fetisch an der Küste Guineas,* Berlin, 1884.

BATEMAN, CHARLES SOMERVILLE LATROBE.
*The First Ascent of the Kasai,* London, 1889.

BATTY, R. B.
*Notes on the Yoruba Country—Journal of the Royal Anthropological Institute of Great Britain and Ireland,* London, Vol. XIX (1888).

BAUDIN, R. P.
*Fétichisme et Féticheurs,* Lyon, 1884.

BAUMANN, HERMANN.
*Division of Work according to Sex in African Hoe Culture—Journal of the International Institute of African Languages and Cultures,* London, Vol. I (1928).

BENEZET, ANTHONY.
*Some Historical Account of Guinea,* Philadelphia, 1771.

BENTLEY, W. HOLMAN.
*Pioneering in the Congo,* London, 1900.

BÉRENGER-FÉRAND, J. B.
*Les Peuplades de la Sénégambie,* Paris, 1879.

BERRY, ERICK.
*Black Folk Tales,* New York, 1928.

BINDLOSS, HAROLD.
*In the Niger Country,* Edinburgh, 1898.

BOSMAN, WILLIAM.
*Voyage de Guinée,* Utretcht, 1705;
*A New Accurate Description of the Coast of Guinea,* London, 1721.

BOUCHE, PIERRE.
*La Côte des Esclaves et le Dahomey,* Paris, 1885.

BOUET, F.
*Les Tomas,* Paris, 1912.

BOWDITCH, T. EDWARD.
*British and French Expedition to Teembo,* Paris, 1821;
*Essay on the Geography of North-Western Africa,* Paris, 1824.

BRUNACHE, P.
*Le Centre de l'Afrique,* Paris, 1894.

BRUNET ET GIETHLEN.
*Dahomey et Dépendances,* Paris, 1901.

BUELL, RAYMOND LESLIE.
*Native Problem in Africa,* New York, 1928.

BURDO, ADOLPHE.
*Niger et Bénué,* Paris, 1880.

BURROWS, G.
*The Land of Pigmies,* London, 1898.
BURTON, RICHARD F.
*Wanderings in West Africa,* London, 1863.
*Wit and Wisdom from West Africa,* London, 1865.
BUTT-THOMPSON, F. W.
*Sierra Leone in History and Tradition,* London, 1926.
CA DA MOSTO, ALUISE DE.
*Voyages à la Côte Occidentale d'Afrique (1455–1457),* Paris, 1895.
CAILLIÉ, RENÉ.
*Voyage à Tomboctou et Jenné,* Paris, 1830.
CALVERT, ALBERT FREDERICK.
*Togoland,* London, 1918.
CARBON, H.
*La Région de Tchad et du Ouadai,* Paris, 1912.
CARNEGIE, DAVID WYNFORD.
*Letters from Nigeria,* Brechin, 1902.
CARNES, J. A.
*Voyage from Boston to the West Coast of Africa,* Boston, 1852.
CARON, E.
*De Saint-Louis au Port de Tombouktou,* Paris, 1891.
CENDRARS, BLAISE.
*The African Saga,* New York, 1927.
CHATELAINE, HELI.
*Folk Tales of Angola,* Boston, 1894.
CHEVALIER, AUGUSTE.
*L'Afrique Centrale Française,* Paris, 190
CLARIDGE, C. CYRIL.
*Wild Bush Tribes of Tropical Africa,* London, 1922.
CLARKE, JOHN.
*Specimens of Dialects: Short Vocabularies of Languages and Notes of Countries and Customs in Africa,* Berwick-upon-Tweed, 1848.
CLOZEL, F. J.
*Dix Ans à la Côte d'Ivoire,* Paris, 1906.
CLOZEL ET VILLAMUR.
*Coutumes Indigènes de la Côte d'Ivoire,* Paris, 1902.
COLAS, A.
*Renseignements Géographiques sur l'Afrique Centrale et Occidentale,* Alger, 1880.
COLE, WILLIAM.
*Life on the Niger,* London, 1862.
COMMISSARIAT DE LA RÉPUBLIQUE FRANÇAISE AU CAMEROUN.
*Guide de la Colonisation au Cameroun,* Paris, 1923.
COMPIÈGNE, MARQUIS DE.

*L'Afrique Equatoriale,* Paris, 1875.
CORRY, JOSEPH.
*Windward Coast of Africa,* London, 1807.
CRAWFORD, D.
*Thinking Black,* London, 1912.
CROWTHER, SAMUEL.
*Grammar of the Yoruba Language,* London, 1852.
CULTRU, P.
*Premier Voyage de Sieur de la Courbe fait à la Coste d'Afrique en 1685,* Paris, 1913.
CUREAU, ADOLPH LOUIS.
*Savage Man in Central Africa,* trans. E. Andrews, London, 1915.
DALZEL, ARCHIBALD.
*History of Dahomey,* London, 1793.
DAYRELL, ELPHISTONE.
*Folk Stories from Southern Nigeria,* London, 1910.
DECLÉ, LIONEL.
*Three Years in Savage Africa,* London, 1898.
DELAFOSSE, MAURICE.
*Les Agni—L'Anthropologie,* Paris, Tome IV (1893).
*Sur les Traces probables de Civilisation Égyptienne et d'Homme de Race Blanche à la Côte d'Ivoire*—l.c., Tome XI (1900).
*Les Langues de l'Afrique*—l.c., Tome XXX (1920).
*Vocabulaires Comparatifs de plus de 60 Langues ou Dialectes Africaines parlés à la Côte d'Ivoire et dans les Régions Limitrophes,* Paris, 1904.
*Les Noirs de l'Afrique,* Paris, 1922;
*Les Frontières de la Côte d'Ivoire, de la Côte d'Or, et du Soudan,* Paris, 1908;
*L'Études des Langues Négro-Africaines de 1822–à 1922—Journal Asiatique,* Paris, 11e Serie, Tome XIX (1922).
DE LA SALLE, D'AUFREVILLE.
*Notre Vieux Sénégal,* Paris, 1909;
*Sur la Cotê d'Afrique,* Paris, 1912.
DEMANET, ABBÉ.
*Nouvelle Histoire de l'Afrique Française,* Paris, 1767.
DENNETT, R. E.
*Notes on the Folklore of the Fjort,* London, 1895;
*Nigerian Studies,* London, 1910;
*My Yoruba Alphabet,* London, 1916.
DOUVILLE, J. B.
*Voyage au Congo,* Paris, 1832.
DUBOIS, FELIX.
*Toumbouctou la Mysterieuse,* Paris, 1897;
*Timbuctoo the Mysterious,* trans. Diana White, London, 1897;
*Notre Beau Niger,* Paris, 1911.

Du Chaillu, Paul Belloni,
*Explorations and Adventures in Equatorial Africa,* London, 1861.
Duncan, John.
*Travels in Western Africa,* London, 1847.
Du Plessis, J.
*Thrice through the Dark Continent,* London, 1917.
Dupuis-Yakouba, A.
*Les Gow ou Chasseurs du Niger,* Paris, 1911.
Eddine, Nacer.
*Chroniques de la Mauritanie Sénégalaise,* Paris, 1911.
Elliot, G. F. S.
*Some Notes on Native West African Customs—Journal of the Royal Anthropological Institute of Great Britain and Ireland,* London, Vol. XXIII (1892).
Ellis, George W.
*Negro Culture in West Africa,* New York, 1914.
Emonts, John.
*Joys and Sorrows of the Pagan Children in the Land of Africa,* Sainte Marie (Illinois), 1927.
Equilbecq, F. V.
*Essai sur la Littérature Merveilleuse des Noirs, suivi de Contes Indigènes de l'Ouest-Africain Française,* Paris, 1915–16.
Es-Sadi, Abderraman ben Abdallah ben Iman ben Amir.
*Tarikh es-Soudan,* trad. O. Houdas, Paris, 1900.
Faidherbe, Louis L. C.
*Le Zenaga des Tribus Sénégalaises,* Paris, 1877;
*Langues Sénégalaises,* Paris, 1887.
Falconer, J. D.
*On Horseback through Nigeria,* London, 1911.
Falconer, Thomas.
*Voyage of Hanno translated and accompanied with the Greek Text,* London, 1797.
Forbes, F. A.
*Planting the Faith in Darkest Africa,* London, 1927.
Forbes, Frederick E.
*Dahomey,* London, 1851.
Foulkes, H. D.
*Angass Manual,* London, 1915.
Francois, G.
*Notre Colonie du Dahomey,* Paris, 1906.
Frazer, Douglas.
*Through the Congo Basin,* London, 1927.
Frobenius, Leo.
*The Voice of Africa,* London, 1913.
Froger, F.
*Étude sur la Langue des Mossi* (*Boucle du Niger*), Paris, 1910.

FULLERTON, W. T.
*The Christ of the Congo River,* London, 1928.
GATELET, LIEUT.
*Histoire de la Conquête du Soudan Français,* Paris, 1901.
GAUBE, Cl.
*Études sur la Côte d'Ivoire,* Paris, 1901.
GEARY, WILLIAM NEVILLE M.
*Nigeria under British Rule,* London, 1927.
GIDE, ANDRÉ.
*Voyage au Congo,* Paris, 1927.
*Le Retour du Tchad,* Paris, 1928.
GOLDBERRY, SILVESTER MEINRAD XAVIER.
*Fragmens du Voyage en Afrique,* Paris, 1802.
GOLLOCK, G. A.
*Lives of Eminent Africans,* London, 1928;
*Sons of Africa,* London, 1928.
GORJU, MGR.
*En Zigzags à travers l'Urundi,* Namur, 1926.
GRAY, FRANK.
*My Two African Journeys,* London, 1925.
GRIERSON, P. J. H.
*The Silent Trade,* Edinburgh, 1903.
GRIFFITH, T. R.
*On the Races Inhabiting Sierra Leone—Journal of the Royal Anthropological Institute of Great Britain and Ireland,* London, Vol. XVI (1885).
HAARDT and AUDOUIN-DUBREUIL.
*The Black Journey,* New York, 1927.
HACQUARD, AUGUSTIN.
*Monographie de Tombouctou,* Paris, 1900.
HALL, HERBERT C.
*Barrack and Bush in Northern Nigeria,* London, 1923.
HALL, LELAND.
*Timbuctoo,* New York, 1927.
HARDY, GEORGE.
*L'Art Nègre,* Paris, 1927.
HARRIS, JOHN H.
*Dawn in Darkest Africa,* London, 1914.
HAYWARD, A. H. W.
*Sport and Service in Africa,* London, 1926.
HAZZLEDINE, GEORGE DOUGLAS.
*The White Man in Nigeria,* London, 1904.
HELSER, ALBERT D.
*In Sunny Nigeria,* New York, 1926.
HILTON-SIMPSON, M. W.
*Land and Peoples of the Kasai,* London, 1911.

HINE, J. E.
*Days Gone By,* London, 1924.
HORN AND LEWIS.
*Trader Horn,* New York, 1927.
HOURST, LIEUT.
*Personal Narrative of the Exploration of the Niger,* trans, Mrs. Arthur Bell, New York, 1899.
HUTTON, WILLIAM.
*Voyage to Africa,* London, 1821.
IBN KHALDOUN, ABOU ZAKARYA YAHYA.
*Yaman: Abridged History of the Dynasties,* trans. Henry Cassels Kay, London, 1892.
ISERT, PAUL ERDMAN.
*Voyage en Guinée,* Paris, 1793.
JOBSON, RICHARD.
*The Golden Trade,* London, 1623.
JOHNSON, SAMUEL.
*History of the Yorubas,* London, 1921.
JOHNSTON, HARRY H.
*Pioneers in West Africa,* London, 1912.
JOSEPH, G.
*La Côte d'Ivoire,* Paris, 1917.
KEARTON AND BARNES.
*Through Central Africa,* London, 1915.
KINGSLEY, MARY H.
*Travels in West Africa,* London, 1897.
*West African Studies,* London, 1899.
KISCH, MARTIN SCHLESINGER.
*Letters and Sketches from Northern Nigeria,* London, 1910.
KLOSE, H.
*Togo,* Berlin, 1899.
LABAT, JEAN-BAPTISTE.
*Nouvelle Relation de l'Afrique Occidentale,* Paris, 1728.
LAING, ALEXANDER GORDON.
*Travels in Western Africa,* London, 1825.
LAIRD AND OLDFIELD.
*Expedition into the Interior of Africa by the River Niger,* London, 1837.
LANDER, RICHARD AND JOHN.
*Journal of an Expedition to Explore the Course and Termination of the Niger,* London, 1838.
LANGMORE, CONSTANCE.
*A Resident's Wife in Nigeria,* London, 1908.
LASNET, DR.
*Une Mission au Sénégal,* Paris, 1900.
LAVEILLE, E.

*L'Évangile au Centre de l'Afrique,* Louvain, 1926.
LE BARBIER, LOUIS.
*Dans la Haute-Guinée,* Paris, 1904.
LE HERISSÉ, A.
*L'Ancien Royaume de Dahomey,* Paris, 1911.
LEONARD, ARTHUR GLYN.
*The Lower Niger and the Tribes,* London, 1906.
LINSCHOTEN, J. H. VAN.
*Descriptio totius Guineae tractus, Congi, Angolae et Monomotapae,* Hagae Comites, 1599.
LLOYD, ALBERT B.
*In Dwarf Land and Cannibal Country,* London, 1907.
LUCAS, CHARLES P.
*Historical Geography of West Africa,* Oxford, 1913.
LUGARD, FREDERICK.
*Dual Mandate in Tropical Africa,* London, 1922.
LUGARD, LADY.
*Tropical Dependency,* London, 1905.
LUX, A. E.
*Von Loanda nach Kembundu,* Wien, 1880.
MACHAT, J.
*Les Rivières de Sud et le Fouta-Diallon,* Paris, 1906.
MACLEOD, OLIVE.
*Chiefs and Cities of Central Africa,* Edinburgh, 1912.
MADROLLE, CLAUDIUS.
*En Guinée,* Paris, 1895.
MALCOLM, L. W. G.
*Notes on Birth, Marriage, and Death Ceremonies of the Eyap Tribe, Central Cameroon—Journal of the Royal Anthropological Institute of Great Britain and Ireland,* London, Vol. LIII (1922).
MANGIN, EUGÈNE.
*Les Mossi,* Paris, 1921.
MARGOLIOUTH, MOSES.
*A Pilgrimage to the Land of My Fathers,* London, 1850.
MARGRY, PIERRE.
*Les Navigations Françaises,* Paris, 1867.
MARIN, EUGÈNE.
*Vie, Travaux, Voyages de Mgr. Hacquart,* Paris, 1905.
MARTONE, ED. DE.
*Atlas des Cartes Administratives et Ethnographiques des Colonies de l'Afrique Occidentale Française,* Paris, 1922.
MARTY, PAUL.
*L'Islam en Mauritanie et au Sénégal—Revue de Monde Musulman,* Paris, Tome XXXI (1915–16);
*Les Tribus de la Haute Mauritanie,* Paris, 1915;

*Étude sur l'Islam au Sénégal,* Paris, 1917;
*Études sur l'Islam et les Tribus du Soudan,* Paris, 1920.
*L'Islam en Guinée,* Paris, 1921;
*Études sur l'Islam en Côte d'Ivoire,* Paris, 1922;
*Études sur l'Islam au Dahomey,* Paris, 1926;
*Études Sénégalaises,* Paris, 1927.

MATTHEWS, JOHN.
*Voyage to the River Sierra Leone,* London, 1788.

McLEOD, JOHN.
*Voyage to Africa,* London, 1820.

MEEK, C. K.
*Northern Tribes of Nigeria,* Oxford, 1925.

MIGEOD, FREDERICK W. H.
*The Mende Language,* London, 1908;
*The Languages of West Africa,* London, 1911.

MILLIGAN, ROBERT H.
*The Fetish Folk of West Africa,* London, 1912.

MILLS, DOROTHY.
*Through Liberia,* New York, 1927.

MOCKLER-FERRYMAN, AUGUSTUS F.
*Up the Niger,* London, 1892;
*British Nigeria,* London, 1902.

MOLLIEN, G.
*Travels in the Interior of Africa to the Sources of the Senegal and Gambia,* London, 1820.

MONTEIL, CHARLES.
*Monographie de Djenné,* Tulle, 1903;
*Les Bambara du Segou et du Kaarata,* Paris, 1924.

MONTEIL, P. L.
*De Saint Louis à Tripoli par le Lac Tchad,* Paris, 1895.

MOREL, EDMUND D.
*Affairs of West Africa,* London, 1902;
*Nigeria: Its Peoples and its Problems,* London, 1911.

NORRIS, ROBERT.
*Mémoires du Regne de Bossa-Ahadée, Roi de Dahomé,* Paris, 1790.

NORTHCOTT, H. P.
*Northern Territories of the Gold Coast,* London, 1899.

OMBONI, TITO.
*Viaggi nell' Africa Occidentale,* Milan, 1845.

ORR, CHARLES WILLIAM JAMES.
*Making of Northern Nigeria,* London, 1911.

OSSENDOWSKI, FERDINAND.
*Slaves of the Sun,* New York, 1928.
*Cruel Gods Fill the African Olympus—New York Times Magazine,* May 13, 1928.

PARK, MUNGO.
*Travels in the Interior Districts of Africa,* London, 1810.

PARKINSON, J.
*Notes on the Asaba People of the Niger—Journal of the Royal Anthropological Institute of Great Britain and Ireland,* London, Vol. XXXVI (1905).

PAYEUR-DIDELOT.
*Trente Mois au Continent Mystérieux,* Paris, 1899.

PEYRISSAC, LÉON.
*Aux Ruines des Grandes Cités Soudanaises,* Paris, 1910.

PHILEBERT, CHARLES.
*La Conquête Pacifique de l'Intérieur Africain,* Paris, 1889.

PITT-RIVERS, GEN'L.
*Antique Work of Art from Benin,* London, 1900.

POOLE, THOMAS EYRE.
*Life, Scenery and Customs in Sierra Leone,* London, 1850.

POUTRAIN, DR.
*Contribution à l'Études des Négrilles, Type Brachycéphale—L'Anthropologie,* Paris, Tome XXI (1910);
*Les Négrilles du Centre Africain, Type Sousdolichocéphale—* l. c., Tomes XXII & XXIII (1911 & 1912).

POWELL, E. ALEXANDER.
*The Map that is Half Unrolled,* London, 1926.

RATTRAY, R. SUTHERLAND.
*Hausa Folk-Lore,* Oxford, 1913.

READE, WINWOOD.
*African Sketch Book,* London, 1873.

REEVE, HENRY FENWICK.
*The Gambia,* London, 1912.

REINDORF, CARL CHRISTIAN.
*History of the Gold Coast and Ashanti,* Basel, 1895.

ROBINSON, CHARLES HENRY.
*Specimens of Hausa Literature,* Cambridge, 1896;
*Hausaland,* London, 1900.

ROSCOE, JOHN.
*The Soul of Central Africa,* London, 1922.

ROSEROT, ALPHONSE.
*Dictionnaire Typographique du Départment de la Côte d'Or,* Paris, 1924.

ROUJET, FERNAND.
*La Guinée,* Corbeil, 1906.

SANDERVAL, OLIVIER DE
*De l'Atlantique au Niger par le Foutah-Djallon,* Paris, 1883;
*Les Rives du Koukouré de l'Atlantique au Foutah-Djallon,* Paris, 1900.

SAUGNIER, M.

*Voyages au Sénégal,* Paris, 1792.
SCHULTZE, A.
*The Sultanate of Bornu,* trans, P. A. Benton, London, 1913.
SCHULTZE, F.
*Der Fetischismus,* Leipzig, 1901–02.
SIBLEY-WESTERMANN.
*Liberia—Old and New,* New York, 1928.
SIMPSON, WILLIAM.
*Private Journal Kept during the Niger Expedition,* London, 1843.
SKERTCHLY, J. A.
*Dahomey as It Is,* London, 1874.
SMITH, J.
*Trade and Travel in the Gulph of Guinea,* London, 1851.
SMITH, WILLIAM.
*A New Voyage to Guinea,* London, 1745.
STANLEY, HENRY MORTON.
*The Congo,* New York, 1885.
SYDOW, ECKERT VON.
*African Sculpture—Journal of the International Institute of African Languages and Cultures,* London, Vol. I (1928).
TALBOT, D. AMAURY.
*Woman's Mysteries of a Primitive People,* London, 1915.
TALBOT, P. AMAURY.
*In the Shadow of the Bush,* London, 1912;
*The Peoples of Southern Nigeria,* Oxford, 1926;
*Some Nigerian Fertility Cults,* Oxford, 1927.
TANGYE, H. LINCOLN.
*In the Torrid Sudan,* Boston, 1910.
TARDIEU, A.
*Sénégambie et Guinée,* Paris, 1878.
TAUXIER, LOUIS.
*Le Noir du Soudan,* Paris, 1912;
*Le Noir du Yatenga,* Paris, 1917;
*Le Noir de Bandoukou,* Paris, 1921;
*Nègres Gouro et Gagou,* Paris, 1924.
THOMANN, GEORGES.
*Essai de Manuel de la Langue Néonolé Parlée dans la Partie Occidentale de la Côte d'Ivoire,* Paris, 1905.
THOMAS, CHARLES W.
*Adventures and Observations on the West Coast of Africa,* London, 1861.
THOMAS, NORTHCOTE W.
*Anthropological Report on the Edo-Epeaking Peoples of Nigeria,* London, 1910;
*Anthropological Report on the Ibo-Speaking Peoples of Nigeria.* London, 1913–14;

*Anthropological Report on Sierra Leone,* London, 1916.
TORDAY, E.
*On the Trail of the Bushongo,* Philadelphia, 1925.
TOUTÉ, GÉNÉRAL.
*Du Dahomé au Sahara,* Paris, 1914;
*Dahomé, Niger, Toureg,* Paris, 1917.
TRAUTMANN, RENÉ.
*La Littérature Populaire à la Côte des Esclaves,* Paris, 1927.
TREMEARNE, A. J. N.
*The Niger and the West Sudan,* London, 1900;
*Hausa Superstitions and Customs,* London, 1913;
*The Ban of the Bori,* London.
*Bori Beliefs and Ceremonies—Journal of the Anthropological Institute of Great Britain and Ireland,* London, Vol. XLV (1914).
TRILLES, H.
*Proverbes, Légendes et Contes Fang,* Neuchatel, 1905.
TUCKEY, J. K.
*Expedition to the River Zaire,* London, 1818.
VALDEZ, FRANCISCO TRAVASSOS.
*Six Years of a Traveller's Life in Western Africa,* London, 1861.
VERNEAU, R.
*Résultats Anthropologiques de la Mission de M. de Gironcourt en Afrique Occidentale—L'Anthropologie, Paris, Tome XXVII* (1916).
VILLAMUR, ROGER.
*Notre Colonie de la Côte d'Ivoire,* Paris, 1903.
WADSTROM, C. B.
*Précis sur l'Établissement des Colonies de Sierra Léone et de Boulama,* Paris, 1798.
WALLIS, C. BRAITHWAITE.
*Advance of Our West African Empire,* London, 1903.
WARD, HERBERT.
*Ethnographical Notes Relating to the Congo Tribes—Journal of the Royal Anthropological Institute of Great Britain and Ireland,* London, Vol. XXIV (1893).
*A Voice from the Congo,* London, 1910.
WEEKS, JOHN H.
*Anthropological Notes on the Bangala of the Upper Congo River —Journal of the Royal Anthropological Institute of Great Brittain and Ireland,* London, Vol. XXXIX & XL (1908 & 1909).
*Among Congo Cannibals,* London, 1913.
*Among the Primitive Bakongo,* Philadelphia, 1914.
WERNER, A.
*The Natives of British Central Africa,* London, 1906.
WESTERMAN, DIEDERICH.
*Gottesvorstellungen in Oberguinea—Journal of the International*

*Institute of African Languages and Cultures,* London, Vol. I (1928).
WHARTON, CONWAY TALIAFERRO.
*The Leopard Hunts Alone,* New York, 1927.
WHITFORD, JOHN.
*Trading Life in Western and Central* Africa, Liverpool, 1877.
WILSON, J. LEIGHTON.
*Western Africa: Its History, Condition and Prospects,* London, 1856.
WINTERBOTTAM, THOMAS MASTERSON.
*Account of the Native Africans in the Neighborhood of Sierra Leone,* London, 1803.
ZÖLLER, H.
*Forschungsreisen in der Deutschen Colonie Kamerun,* Berlin, 1885.
ZUCCHELLI, ANTONIO.
Missione di Congo, Venice, 1712.

## BIBLIOGRAPHY—FOR CHAPTERS V & VI ON THE DIASPORA OF THE JEWS

ABBOTT, G. F.
*Israel in Europe,* London, 1907.
ABRAHAMS, ISRAEL.
*Campaigns in Palestine from Alexander the Great,* London, 1927.
ABULFEDA, ISMAEL.
*Chorasmiae et Mawalnahrae hoc est Regionum extra fluvium Oxum Descriptio,* trad. Joannes Gravius, London, 1650.
ACOSTA, JOSÉ DE.
*Natural and Moral History of the Indies,* London, 1880.
ADDISON, LANCELOT.
*Present State of the Jews: More Particularly Relating to Those in Barbary,* London, 1675.
ARENDZEN, J. P.
*Men and Manners in the Days of Christ,* London, 1928.
ARIÉ, GABRIEL.
*Histoire Juive,* Paris, 1923.
ASKOWITH, DORA.
*Toleration of the Jews under Julius Cæsar and Augustus,* New York, 1915.
BANCROFT, HUBERT HOWE.
*Native Races of the Pacific States of North America,* New York, 1875.
BARROW, R. H.
*Slavery in the Roman Empire,* New York, 1928.

BARTON, GEORGE A.
*Sketch of Semitic Origins,* New York, 1902.
BASKERVILLE, BEATRICE C.
*The Polish Jew,* London, 1906.
BELL, H. IDRIS.
*Jews and Christians in Egypt,* London, 1924.
BELLOC, HILAIRE.
*The Jews,* Boston, 1922.
BEN GORION, JOSEPHUS.
*The Wonderful and Most Deplorable History of the Latter Times of the Jews,* London, 1662.
BENIAMINIS, D.
*Itinerarium,* ed. Constantini L'Empereur, Amsterdam, 1633.
BENTWICH, NORMAN.
*Philo-Judaeus of Alexandria,* Philadelphia, 1910.
*Hellenism,* Philadelphia, 1919.
BEVAN, ELWYN.
*Jerusalem under the High-Priests,* London, 1924.
BLUNT, A. W. F.
*Israel before Christ,* London, 1926.
*Israel in World History,* Oxford, 1927.
BOURBOURG, BRASSEUR DE
*Histoire des Nations Civilisées et de l'Amérique-Centrale durant les Siècles Antérieurs à Christophe Colomb,* Paris, 1857.
BREREWOOD, EDWARD.
*Languages and Religions through the Chief Parts of the World,* London, 1674.
BROWN, BRIAN.
*Wisdom of the Hebrews,* New York, 1925.
BROWNE, LEWIS.
*Stranger than Fiction,* New York, 1925.
*The Believing World,* New York, 1926.
BUDGE, E. A. WALLIS.
*Book of the Cave of Treasures,* London, 1927.
BURTON, RICHARD F.
*The Jew, the Gypsy and El Islam,* Chicago, 1898.
*Cambridge Ancient History,* New York, 1925, especially Vol. III.
CASANOWICZ, I. M.
*The Jews of Mzab—American Anthropologist,* Lancaster, Penn. Vol. VII (1905).
CAUSSE, A.
*Quelques Remarques sur les Origines de la Diaspora et son Rôle dans la Formation du Judaisme,* Paris, 1924.
COHON, SAMUEL S.
*B'nai B'rith Manual,* Cincinnati, 1926.
COOK, G. A.
*North Semitic Inscriptions,* Oxford, 1903.

COOK, STANLEY A.
*Israel and Totemism—Jewish Quarterly Review,* Philadelphia, Vol. XIV (1923).
CORDIER, HENRI.
*La Chine,* Paris, 1921.
*Les Juifs en Chine—L'Anthropologie,* Paris, Tome I (1890).
DANBY, H.
*The Jew and Christianity,* London, 1927.
DELITRA, C. E.
*Recherches sur les Vestiges d'un Culte des Morts chez les Anciens Hébreux,* Geneva, 1903.
DE ROO, P.
*History of America before Columbus,* Philadelphia, 1900.
DOS REMEDIOS, J. MENDES.
*Os Judeus em Portugal,* Coimbra, 1895.
DUBNOW, G. M.
*History of the Jews in Russia and Poland,* Philadelphia, 1916.
DUBNOW, SEMION MARKOVICH.
*History of the Jews,* Philadelphia, 1903.
DUSSAUD, RENÉ.
*Le Sacrifice en Israel et chez les Phéniciens,* Paris, 1914.
*Les Origines Canaanéenes du Sacrifice Israélite,* Paris, 1921.
EDREHI, M.
*An Historical Account of the Ten Tribes Settled beyond the River Sambatyon in the East,* London, 1836.
EINSTEIN, DAVID G.
*The Indestructible Faith,* New York, 1927.
ELBOGEN, ISMAR.
*History of the Jews after the Fall of the Jewish State,* Cincinnati, 1926.
EWALD, HEINRICH.
*History of the Jews,* London, 1878.
FINN, JAMES.
*The Jews in China,* London, 1843.
FLEURY, M.
*Les Mœurs des Israélites,* Liege, 1777.
FREDERIC, HAROLD.
*The New Exodus,* London, 1892.
GALE, THEOPHILUS.
*Court of the Gentiles,* London, 1669–82.
GASTER, MOSES.
*The Samaritans: Their History, Doctrines and Literature,* London, 1925.
GEIGER, ABRAHAM.
*Judaism and Its History,* New York, 1911.
GLOVER, F. R. A.

*England the Remnant of Judah,* London, 1861.
GOLDSTEIN, MOSES.
*Dietary Barbarisms,* Brooklyn, 1926.
GOLDZIHER, IGNAZ.
*Mythology among the Hebrews and Its Historical Development,* trans. Russell Martineau, London, 1877.
GRAETZ, H.
*History of the Jews,* Philadelphia, 1891.
GRANT, ASAHEL.
*The Nestorians; or the Lost Tribes,* London, 1841.
HA-COHEN, JOSEPH.
*La Vallée des Pleurs,* Avignon, 1881.
HALL AND COHON.
*Christianity and Judaism Compare Notes,* New York, 1927.
HEREDIA, ANGEL TINEO.
*Los Judios en España,* Madrid, 1881.
HINE, EDWARD.
*Oxford Wrong in Objection to the Anglo Saxons Being Identical with Israel,* New York, 1880.
HONOR, LEO L.
*Sennacherib's Invasion of Palestine,* New York, 1926.
HORN, GEORGE.
*De Originibus Americanis,* Hague Comites, 1652.
HOWLETT, THOMAS ROSLING.
*Anglo-Israel, The Jewish Problem and Supplement,* Philadelphia, 1894.
HUNTING, HAROLD B.
*Hebrew Life and Times,* New York, 1921.
HYAMSON, ALBERT M.
*History of the Jews in England,* London, 1907.
JASTROW, MORRIS.
*Hebrew and Babylonian Traditions,* New York, 1914.
KASTNER, ADOLPHE.
*Analyse de Traditions Religieuses des Peuples Indigènes de l'Amérique,* Louvain, 1845.
KAUTSKY, KARL.
*Foundations of Christianity,* New York, 1925.
*Are the Jews a Race?* New York, 1926.
KINGSBOROUGH, LORD.
*Mexican Antiquities,* London, 1829.
KITTLE, RUDOLPH.
*History of the Hebrews,* trans. John Taylor, London, 1895–96.
KUENEN, A.
*The Religion of Israel,* London, 1874.
LEITE, SOLIDONIO.
*Os Judeus no Brasil,* Rio de Janerio, 1923.

L'ESTRANGE, HAMON.
*Americans no Jewes,* London, 1652.
LEWISOHN, LUDWIG.
*Israel,* New York, 1925.
LIGHTLEY, J. W.
*Jewish Sects and Parties in the Time of Jesus,* London, 1925.
LINDO, E. H.
*History of the Jews of Spain and Portugal,* London, 1848.
LOFTHOUSE, W. F.
*Israel after the Exile,* Oxford, 1928.
LUMNIUS, JOAN FREDERICUS.
*De Extremo Dei Judicio et Indorum Vocatione,* Venice, 1569.
MAAS, ANTHONY J.
*A Day in the Temple,* St. Louis, 1892.
MANASSEH BEN ISRAEL.
*Thesouro dos Dinin,* Amsterdam, 1647.
*Esperança de Israel,* Amsterdam, 1649.
MANN, JACOB.
*The Jews in Egypt and Palestine Under the Fatamid Caliphs,* Oxford, 1920.
MARGOLIN, ARNOLD D.
*The Jews of Eastern Europe,* New York, 1926.
MARGOLIS AND MARX.
*History of the Jewish People,* Philadelphia, 1927.
MCCURDY, JAMES FREDERICK.
*History, Prophecy and Monuments,* New York, 1914.
MENDELSSOHN, SIDNEY.
*The Jews in Africa,* London, 1920.
*The Jews in Asia,* London, 1920.
MERCER, SAMUEL A. B.
*Extra-Biblical Sources for Hebrew and Jewish History,* New York, 1913.
MILMAN, HENRY HART.
*History of the Jews,* London, 1846.
MOORE, GEORGE.
*The Lost Tribes,* London, 1861.
MOORE, GEORGE FOOT.
*Judaism in the First Centuries of the Christian Era,* Cambridge, 1927.
MOSES, LEVI.
*Histoire de la Religion des Juifs, et de leur Etablissement en Espagne et autres parties de l'Europe, où ils se sont retirés après la destruction de Jerusalem,* Amsterdam, 1680.
MURR, C. G. VON
*Versuch einer Geschichte der Judan in China,* Halle, 1806.
NEWMAN, LOUIS ISRAEL.

*Jewish Influence in Christian Reform Movements,* New York, 1925.

OESTERLEY, W. O. E.

*The Wisdom of Egypt and the Old Testament,* London, 1927.

ORTEGA, MANUEL L.

*Los Hebreos en Marruecos,* Madrid, 1919.

OTTLEY, R. L.

*Short History of the Hebrews in the Roman Period,* New York, 1923.

PARAVEY, CHEVALIER DE

*Dissertation sur le Nom Antique et Hiéroglyphique de la Judée ou Traditions Conservées en Chine sur l'Ancient Pays de Tsin,* Paris, 1836.

PEAKE, ARTHUR S.

*The People and the Book,* Oxford, 1925.

PEDERSEN, JOHS.

*Israel: Its Life and Culture,* London, 1926.

PEET, T. ERIC.

*Egypt and the Old Testament,* Boston, 1923.

PHILO JUDAEUS.

*Libri Quatuor jam primum de Graeco in Latinum conversi: Ioanne Christophorsono Anglo, interprete,* Antwerp, 1553.

*Biblical Antiquities,* trans. M. R. James, London, 1917.

PICCIOTTO, JAMES.

*Sketches of Anglo-Jewish History,* London, 1875.

PITTARD, EUGENE.

*Race and History,* London, 1926.

POOLE, W. H.

*Anglo-Israel,* Toronto, 1882.

RADIN, MAX.

*The Jews amongst the Greeks and Romans,* Philadelphia, 1915.

RAISIN, MAX.

*History of the Jews in Modern Times,* New York, 1919.

*Recueil d'Observations Curieuses,* Paris, 1749.

REINACH, THEODORE.

*Jewish Coins,* London, 1903.

RENAN, ERNEST.

*History of the People of Israel,* London, 1888.

ROBINSON, A. K.

*Predestination as taught in the Bible and verified in History,* Leeds, 1895.

ROGERS, EGDAR.

*A Handy Guide to Jewish Coins,* London, 1914.

ROSENAU, WILLIAM.

*Jewish Ceremonial Institutions and Customs,* New York, 1925.

SAMUEL, JACOB.
*The Remnant Found,* London, 1841.
SAYCE, A. H.
*Early History of the Jews,* New York, 1897.
SCHWARZ, SAMUEL.
*Inscricoes Hebraicas em Portugal,* Lisbon, 1923.
SENIOR, H. W. J.
*The British Israelites,* London, 1885.
SHARP, JOHN T.
*North Americans of Antiquity,* New York, 1880.
SIMON, MRS.
*The Ten Tribes of Israel and Mexican Antiquities,* London, 1836.
SKINNER, JOHN.
*Prophecy and Religion,* Cambridge, 1922.
SMITH, HENRY P.
*Religion of Israel,* New York, 1914.
SMITH, J. M. POWIS.
*The Prophets and Their Times,* Chicago, 1925.
SMITH, W. ROBERTSON.
*Lectures on the Religion of the Semites,* London, 1923.
STANLEY, ARTHUR PENRHYN.
*Lectures on the Jewish Church,* London, 1863–76.
STERLING, ADA.
*The Jew and Civilization,* New York, 1924.
STEVENS, J. C.
*Genealogical Chart, Showing the Connection Between the House of David and the Royal Family of Brittain,* Liverpool, 1877.
STODDARD, LOTHROP.
*The Rising Tide of Color against White Supremacy,* Introduction by Madison Grant, New York, 1921.
TALMUD, BABYLONIAN.
Trans. Michael J. Podkinson, Boston, 1918.
TALMUD DE JERUSALEM.
Trad. Moïse Schwab, Paris, 1871–90.
THACKERY, H. ST. JOHN.
*The Septuagint and Jewish Worship,* London, 1921.
THOROWGOOD, THOMAS.
*Jewes in America,* London, 1648.
TOBAR, PÈRE.
*Inscriptions Juives de Kai-Fung-Fu,* Shanghai, 1900.
TRIGAULT, NICALAUS.
*De Christiana Expeditione apud Sinas suscepti ab Societate Jesu ex P. Matthaei Ricii ejusdem Societatis Commentariis,* Augsburg, 1615.
TURNER, SHARON.
*Sacred History of the World,* London, 1833.

WELLHAUSEN, JULIUS.
*History of Israel,* Edinburgh, 1885.
WILD, JOSEPH.
*The Lost Ten Tribes and 1882,* London (Ontario), 1879.
WILSON, JOHN.
*Our Israelitish Origin,* London, 1845.
WISE, ISAAC M.
*History of the Israelitish Nation,* Albany, 1854.
WORRELL, W. H.
*A Study of Races in the Near East,* New York, 1927.
WORSLEY, ISRAEL.
*A View of the American Indians Showing them to be the Descendants of the Ten Tribes of Israel,* London, 1828.
ZANGWILL, ISRAEL.
*Children of the Ghetto,* London, 1895.

## BIBLIOGRAPHY—FOR CHAPTER VII ON ABYSSINIA, EAST AND SOUTH AFRICA

ABU SALIH.
*The Churches and Monasteries of Egypt and Some Neighbouring Countries,* trans. B. T. A. Evetts, Oxford, 1895.
AL-HAKAMI, NAJM AD-DIN OMARAH.
*Yaman: Its Early Mediaeval History,* trans. Henry Cassels Kay, London, 1892.
AL-JANARDI, ABU ABD ALLAH BAHA AD-DIN.
*Account of the Karmathians of Yaman,* trans. Henry Cassels Kay, London, 1892.
ANSORGE, W. J.
*Under the African Sun,* London, 1899.
BAINES, THOMAS.
*Gold Regions of South Eastern Africa,* Cape Colony, 1877.
BAKER, SAMUEL WHITE.
*Albert N'Yanza, Great Basin of the Nile,* London, 1866.
*Nile Tributaries of Abyssinia,* London, 1867.
BASSET, RENÉ.
*Etudes sur l'Histoire d'Ethiopie,* Paris, 1882.
BEKE, CHARLES T.
*Abyssinia—Journal of the Royal Geographical Society,* London, 1884.
BENT, J. T.
*The Sacred City of the Ethiopians,* London, 1893.
BRADLEY, MARY HASTINGS.
*Caravans and Cannibals,* New York, 1926.
BRUCE, JAMES.
*Travels to Discover the Source of the Nile,* Edinburgh, 1804.

Also Third Edition, Edinburgh, 1813 (New Matter).
BRYCE, JAMES.
*Impressions of South Africa,* London, 1897.
BUDGE, E. A. WALLIS.
*The Queen of Sheba and her only Son Menyelek,* Liverpool, 1922.
BURKITT, M. C.
*South Africa's Past in Stone,* Cambridge, 1928.
BUXTON, M. ALINE.
*Kenya Days,* London, 1927.
CALLAWAY, HENRY.
*Unkulunkulu,* Natal, 1868.
DARLEY, HENRY.
*Slaves and Ivory,* London, 1926.
DONNITHORNE, FRED A.
*Wonderful Africa,* London, 1924.
DRAKE-BROCKMAN, RALPH E.
*British Somaliland,* London, 1912.
DU TOIT, S. J.
*Rhodesia Past and Present,* London, 1897.
EL-QADER, CHIHAD EDDIN AHMED BEN.
*Histoire de la Conqûete de l'Abyssinie,* trad. René Basset, Paris, 1909.
FREJUS, R.
*Relation of a Voyage made into Mauritania in Africa,* London, 1671.
GOGARTY, H. A.
*In the Land of the Kikuyus,* Dublin, 1920.
*Kilima-njaro: An East African Vicariate,* New York, 1927.
HALL, R. N.
*Great Zimbabwe,* London, 1905.
HARRIS, W. CORNWALLIS.
*The Highlands of Aethiopia,* London, 1844.
HODSON, ARTHUR WIENHOLT.
*Seven Years in Southern Abyssinia,* London, 1927.
HOLLIS, A. C.
*The Masai,* Oxford, 1905.
HONE, PERCY F.
*Southern Rhodesia,* London, 1909.
HOSKINS, G. A.
*Travels in Ethiopia,* London, 1833.
JOHNSON, T. BROADWOOD.
*Tramps round the Mountains of the Moon,* Boston, 1909.
JOHNSTON, HARRY HAMILTON.
*British Colonial Africa,* London, 1906.
KEANE, A. H.
*The Gold of Ophir.*

KRAPF, J. LEWIS.
*Travels, Researches and Missionary Labors during Eighteen Years Residence in Eastern Africa,* Boston, 1860.
LAGAE, C. R.
*Les Azande ou Niam-Niam,* Brussels, 1926
LAVINE, DAVID.
Introduction to *Buston Al-Ukal* by Nathanael ibn Al-Fayyumi, New York, 1908.
LEPSIUS, R.
*Briefe aus Aegypten, Aethiopien und der Halbinsel des Seriai,* Berlin, 1852.
LE ROUX, HUGUES.
*Chez la Reine de Saba,* Paris, 1914.
LEUTHOLF, JOB.
*Historia Aethiopica,* Frankfort, 1681.
MACCREAGH, GORDON.
*The Last of Free Africa,* New York, 1928.
MACDONALD, DUFF.
*Africana,* London, 1882.
MACRIZI.
*Historia Regum Islamiticorum in Abyssinia,* ed. Frederick Theodore Resick, Amsterdam, 1790.
MAUGHAM, REGINALD CHARLES FULKE.
*Portuguese East Africa,* London, 1906.
MERCER, SAMUEL A. B.
*Ethiopic Liturgy: Its Sources, Development and Present Form,* Milwaukee, 1915.
MORIÉ, LOUIS J.
*Histoire de l'Ethiopie,* Paris, 1904.
PARKYNS, MANSFIELD.
*Life in Abyssinia,* London, 1853.
PERRUCHON, JULES D.
*Les Chroniques de Zar'a Ya Eqob et de Ba'eda Maryam, Rois d'Ethiopie, de 1434 à 1478,* Paris, 1893.
PETERS, CARL.
*The Eldorado of the Ancients,* New York, 1902.
PLOWDEN, WALTER CHICELE.
*Travels in Abyssinia and the Gala Country,* London, 1868.
POWELL, E. ALEXANDER.
*Beyond the Utmost Purple Rim,* London, 1925.
RANDALL-MACIVER, DAVID.
*Mediaeval Rhodesia,* London, 1906.
RANKIN, DANIEL J.
*Zambesi Basin and Nyassaland,* Edinburgh, 1893
REY, C. F.
*In the Country of the Blue Nile,* London, 1927.

Rossini, C. Conti.
*Notice sur les Manuscrits Ethiopiens de la Collection d'Abbadie,* Paris, 1914.
Russell, Michael.
*Nubia and Abyssinia,* New York, 1833.
Salt, Henry.
*Voyage to Abyssinia,* London, 1814.
Santos, Ioas dos
*Ethiopia Oriental,* Evora, 1609.
Sayce, A. H.
*Ancient Empires of the East,* London, 1884.
Schofield, J. F.
*Zimbabwe: A Critical Examination of the Building Methods Employed—South African Journal of Science,* Vol. XXIII (1926).
Skinner, Robert P.
*Abyssinia of To-day,* New York, 1906.
Smith, F. Harrison.
*Through Abyssinia,* London, 1890.
Stanley, Henry Morton.
*My Dark Companions and Their Strange Stories,* London, 1893.
Stern, Henry A.
*Wanderings among the Falashas in Abyssinia,* London, 1862.
Symons, R.
*What Christianity has Done for Abyssinia,* London, 1928.
Tellez, F. Balthazar.
*Travels of the Jesuits in Ethiopia,* London, 1710.
Walker, Eric A.
*History of South Africa,* London, 1928.
Wilson and Felkin.
*Uganda and the Egyptian Soudan,* London, 1882.

## BIBLIOGRAPHY—FOR CHAPTERS VIII & IX ON NORTH AFRICA THE FRENCH SUDAN

Abu Sereur, Mordecai.
*Les Daggatouns, Tribu d'Origine Juive demeurant dans le Désert de Sahara,* trad. Loeb, Paris, 1881.
Abu Zakariah.
*Chronique,* trad. Emile Masqueray, Alger, 1878.
Adams, Robert.
*Narrative,* Boston, 1817.
Al Farghani, Ahmed ibn Mohammed ibn Kathir.
*Brevis ac Perutilis Compilatio Alfargani,* Ferrara, 1493.
Al Garnati, Abu Hamid al Andalusi.
*Roudh el Qarthas,* trad. Beaumier, Paris, 1860.

*Le Tuhfat al-Albab,* trad. Gabriel Ferrand—*Journal Asiatique,* Paris, Tome CCVII (1925).

Amicis, Edmondo de
*Morocco,* trans. C. Rollin-Tilton, London, 1879

Anderson, Isabel.
*From Corsair to Riffian,* Boston, 1927.

Antar, Michael.
*En Smaala,* Paris, 1897.

Ashmead-Bartlett, E.
*The Passing of the Skereefian Empire,* New York, 1910.

Autran, C.
*Phéniciens, Essai de Contribution à l'Histoire Antique de la Méditerranée,* Cairo, 1920.

Barclay, Edgar.
*Mountain Life in Algeria,* London, 1882.

Barrows, David Prescott.
*Berbers and Blacks,* New York, 1927.

Basset, Henri.
*Essai sur la Littérature des Berbères,* Alger, 1920.
*Le Culte des Grottes au Maroc,* Alger, 1920.

Basset, René.
*Nédromal et les Traras,* Paris, 1901.

Bazin, René.
*Charles de Foucauld Hermit and Explorer,* London, 1923.

Beane, J. G.
*Cardinal Lavigerie,* Baltimore, 1898.

Beechey, F. W.
*Northern Coast of Africa,* London, 1828.

Bel, Alfred.
*Coup d'Œil sur l'Islam en Berbérie,* Paris, 1917.

Belgrave, C. Dalrymple.
*Siwa; The Oasis of Jupiter Amon,* London, 1923.

Ben Cheneb, Mohammed.
*Classes des Savants de l'Ifriqiya, par Abu l'Arab Mohammed ben Ahmed ben Tamim et Mohammed ben Al-Harit ben Asad Al Hosani,* Alger, 1920.

Benjer, G.
*Esclaves, Islamisme et Christianisme,* Paris, 1891.

Bensusan, S. L.
*Morocco,* London, 1904.

Bertholon, L.
*Étude Comparée sur des Crânes de Carthaginois d'il y a 2400 Ans et Tunisois Contemporains,* Tunis, 1911.

Bertholon et Chantre.
*Recherches Anthropologiques dans la Berbérie Orientale, Tripolitaine, Tunisie, Algérie,* Paris, 1912–13.

Besnier, M.
*Carthage Punique,* Caen, 1901.
Biarney, S.
*Etudes sur les Dialectes Berbères du Rif,* Paris, 1917.
*Notes d'Ethnographie et de Linguistique Nord-Africaines,* Paris, 1924.
Bloch, Isaac.
*Inscriptions Tumulaires des Anciens Cimetières Israélites d'Alger,* Paris, 1888.
Bodley, R. V. C.
*Algeria from Within,* Indianapolis, 1927.
Bonnel de Mézières, M. A.
*Recherche de l'Emplacement de Ghana—Mémoires présentés par Divers Savants à l'Academie des Inscriptions et Belles-Lettres, de l'Institut de France,* Paris, Tome XIII (1923).
Bovet, Marie Ann de
*L'Algérie,* Paris, 1898–99.
Broadley, A. M.
*Tunis, Past and Present,* Edinburgh, 1882.
Bruston, Charles.
*Une Tablette Magique expliquée par l'Hébreu—Revue Archéologique, 5 Serie,* Paris, Tome X (1919).
*Un Pierre Talismanique expliquée par l'Hébreu*—l. c., XII (1920).
*Essai d'Explication d'une Entaille gnostique*—l. c., XVI (1922).
*Encore une Amulette expliquée par l'Hébreu*—l. c., XVII (1923).
Buchanan, Angus.
*Exploration of Aïr Out of the World North of Nigeria,* London, 1921.
Calassanti-Motylinski, A de.
*Le Djebel Nefousa,* Paris, 1898–99.
Campbell, Dugald.
*On the Trail of the Veiled Tuareg,* Philadelphia, 1928.
Carette, E.
*Recherches sur l'Origine et les Migrations des Principales Tribus de l'Afrique Septentrionale,* Paris, 1853.
Carmoly, E.
*Relation d'Eldad le Danite,* trad. en Française, Paris, 1838.
Champion, Pierre.
*Le Maroc et ses Villes d'Art,* Paris, 1927.
Charvériat, François.
*Travers la Kabylie et les Questions Kabyles,* Paris, 1889.
Chudeau, R.
*Sahara Soudanais,* Paris, 1909.
Cochelet, Charles.
*Shipwreck of the Sophia,* London, 1822.

COHN, HERMANN.
*Mœurs des Juifs et des Arabes de Tétuan (Maroc)*, Paris, 1927.
CONTENAU, G.
*La Civilisation Phénicienne*, Paris, 1926.
COOK, GEORGE WINGROVE.
*Conquest and Colonization in North Africa*, Edinburgh, 1860.
DAMBERGER, CHRISTIAN FREDERICK.
*Travels through the Interior of Africa*, London, 1801.
DAPPER, O.
*Description de l'Afrique*, Amsterdam, 1686.
DAUMAS, MELCHIOR JOSEPH EUGÈNE.
*Le Sahara Algérien*, Paris, 1845.
*Le Grand Désert*, Paris, 1848.
D'AVEZAC, AUGUSTE.
*Etudes de Géographie Arabique sur une Partie de l'Afrique Septentrionale*, Paris, 1836.
DAVIDSON, JOHN.
*Notes taken during Travels in Africa*, London, 1839.
DAVIS, N.
*Carthage and Her Remains*, London, 1912.
DELAFOSSE, MAURICE.
*Haut-Sénégal-Niger*, Paris, 1912.
*Traditions Historiques et Légendaires du Soudan Occidental*, trad. d'un Manuscrit Arabe Inédit, Paris, 1913.
*Le Gana et le Mali, et l'Emplacement de leurs Capitales—Bulletin du Comité d'Études Historiques et Scientifiques de l'Afrique Occidentale Française*, Paris, Tome IX (1924). No. 3.
DELATTRE, PÈRE.
*Gamart ou la Nécropole Juive de Carthage*, Lyon, 1895.
DENNY, HAROLD M.
*Visiting Sahara's Lonely White Race—New York Times Magazine*, New York, Jan. 10, 1926.
DESFONTAINES, LOUICHE RENÉ.
*Fragment d'un Voyage dans les Régence de Tunis et d'Alger*, Paris, 1838.
DESPLAGNES, LOUIS.
*La Plateau Central Nigérien*, Paris, 1907.
DEVEREUX, ROY.
*Aspects of Algeria*, London, 1912.
DOUIS, CAMILLE.
*Voyage dans la Sahara Occidental*, Rouen, 1888.
DOUTTÉ, EDMOND.
*Magie et Religion dans l'Afrique du Nord*, Alger, 1909.
DUVEYRIER, HENRI.
*Les Toureg du Nord*, Paris, 1864.
*Journal de Route*, Paris, 1905.

Edrisi, Abou Abdallah Mohammed ibn Mohammed ibn Abdallah.
*Description de l'Afrique et de l'Espagne,* trad. R. Dozy et de Goege, Leyden, 1866.
El-Abbassi, D'Ali Bey.
*Voyage,* Paris, 1814.
El-Bekri, Abdallah ibn Obeid ibn Abd el Aziz.
*Description de l'Afrique Septentrionale,* trad. MacGuckin de Slane, Alger, 1913.
El-Djaznai, Abou Hasan Ali.
*Zahrat el-As,* trad. Alfred Bel, Algiers, 1923.
El-Eghwaati, Hadji Ebn-ed-din.
*Notes on a Journey into the Interior of Northern Africa,* trans. W. B. Hodgson, London, 1831.
El-Hachaichi, Mohammed ben Otsmane.
*Voyage au Pays des Senoussia,* trad. Sarras et Lesram, Paris, 1912.
Epstein, Abraham.
*Eldad ben Mahli ha-Dani,* Presburg, 1891.
Erskine and Fletcher.
*Vanished Cities of Northern Africa,* Boston, 1927.
Estry, Stephen d'
*Histoire d'Alger,* Tours, 1845.
Ezziani, Aboulquasem ben Ahmed.
*Le Maroc, de 1631 à 1812,* trad. O. Houdas, Paris.
Faidherbe, Louis L. C.
*Notice sur la Colonie du Sénégal,* Paris, 1859.
Fallot, Ernest.
*Par Dela la Méditerranée,* Paris, 1887.
Flamand, G. B. M.
*La Position Géographique d'In-Salah,* Paris, 1913.
Foucauld, Charles de
*Reconnaissance au Maroc,* Paris, 1888.
Foureau, Fernand.
*Une Mission au Tademayt,* Paris, 1890.
*Ma Mission de 1893–1894 chez les Toureg Azdjer,* Paris, 1894; *Rapport sur Ma Mission au Sahara et chez les Toureg Azdjer,* Paris, 1894.
*Documents Scientifiques de la Mission Saharienne. D'Alger au Congo par le Chad,* Paris, 1903–05.
Fromantin, Eugène.
*Une Année dans le Sahel,* Paris, 1925.
Gaden, Henri.
*Note sur le Dialecte Foul parlé par les Foulbé de Bagnirmi—Journal Asiatique,* Paris, 10e Serie, Tome XI (1908);
*Le Poular. Dialecte Peul du Sénégal,* Paris, 1913–14.

GASTINEL, G.
*Carthage et l'Enéide,* Paris, 1926.
GAUTIER, ÉMILE F.
*Sahara Algérien,* Paris, 1908.
*L'Algérie et la Métropole,* Paris, 1920.
*Le Sahara,* Paris, 1923.
*La Conqûete du Sahara,* Paris, 1925.
*L'Islamisation de l'Afrique du Nord,* Paris, 1927.
GAUTIER ET LASSERRE.
*Les Territoires du Sud de l'Algérie,* Alger, 1922.
GRAMMONT, H. D. DE
*Histoire d'Alger sous la Domination Turque* (*1515–1830*), Paris, 1887.
*Correspondence des Consuls d'Alger* (*1690–1742*), Alger, 1890.
GRANT, CYRIL FLETCHER.
*Studies in North Africa,* New York, 1923.
GRUVEL ET CHUDEAU.
*A Travers la Mauritanie Occidentale,* Paris, 1909.
GSELL, STEPHEN.
*Histoire Ancienne de l'Afrique du Nord,* Paris, 1921–
GSELL, MARÇAIS ET YVER.
*Histoire d'Algérie,* Paris, 1927.
HAMAKER, H. A.
*Miscellanea Phoenicia, Leyden,* 1828.
HAMET, ISMAEL.
*Les Musulmans Français du Nord de l'Afrique,* Paris, 1906.
*Histoire du Magreb,* Paris, 1923.
HAMILTON, JAMES.
*Wanderings in North Africa,* London, 1856.
HANOTEAU, A.
*Essai de Grammaire de la Langue Tamachek,* Paris, 1860.
HANOTEAU ET LETEURNEUX.
*Le Kabylien,* Paris, 1893.
HARDY, GEORGES.
*Géographie de la France Extérieure,* Paris, 1928.
*Histoire de la Colonisation Française,* Paris, 1928.
HARRIS, LAWRENCE.
*With Mulai Hafid at Fez,* London, 1909.
HARRIS, M. W.
*Le Tafilelt,* Maroc, 1909.
HARRIS, W. B.
*The Berbers of Morocco—Journal of the Royal Anthropological Institute of Great Britain and Ireland,* London, Vol. XXVII (1896).
HILTON-SIMPSON, M. W.
*Among the Hill-Folk of Algeria,* New York, 1921.

HORNE, JOHN.
*Many Days in Morocco,* New York, 1927.
IBN ADARI AL MARRAKOCHI.
*Histoire de l'Afrique et de l'Espagne,* trad. E. Fagnan, Alger, 1901.
IBN BATOUTAH, ABOU ABD ALLAH IBN MOHAMMED AL LAWATI.
*Voyages,* trad. Defrémery et Sanguinetti, Paris, 1922.
IBN KHALDOUN, ABOU ZEKARYA YAHYA.
*Histoires des Berbères et des Dynasties Musulmanes de l'Afrique Septentrionale,* trad. De Slane, Alger, 1852–56.
*Prolégomènes Historiques,* trad. De Slane, Paris, 1868.
IBN KHORDADBEH, ABOUL KASIM OBAIDALLAH IBN ABDALLAH.
*Kittab el Masalek wa't,* ed. De Goege.
*Le Livre des Routes et des Provinces par C. Barbier de Meynard—Journal Asiatique,* Paris, 1865.
IBN SA'ID, ABOUL HASAN ALI IBN MOUSA.
*Kitab al-Mugrib fi Hula al-Magrib, von Dr. Knut L. Tallquist,* Leyden, 1899.
JACKSON, G. A.
*Algiers,* London, 1817.
JAUBERT, AMÉDÉE.
*Relation de Ghanat et des Coutumes de ses Habitants,* Paris, 1825.
JEAN, C.
*Les Toureg du Sud-Est, L'Aïr,* Paris, 1909.
KATI MAHMOUD (BEN EL-HADJ EL MOLAOUAKKIL KATI).
*Tedzkiret en Nisean,* trad. O Houdas, Paris, 1900.
*Tarikh el-Fettach,* trad. Houdas et Delafosse, Paris, 1913.
KEARTON, CHERRY.
*The Shifting Sands of Algeria,* London, 1924.
KERR, ROBERT.
*Morocco after Twenty-five Years,* London, 1912.
LANDER, RICHARD.
*Records of Captain Clapperton's Last Expedition to Africa,* London, 1830.
LEARED, ARTHUR.
*Morocco and the Moors,* London, 1891.
LEMPRIÈRE, WILLIAM.
*Tour from Gibralter to Tangier,* London, 1791.
*Tour through Morocco,* Newport, 1813.
LENZ, OSKAR.
*Timbuktu, Reise durch Marokko, die Sahara und den Sudan,* Leipzig, 1884.
LEYNADIER ET CLAUZEL.
*Histoire de l'Algérie Française,* Paris, 1856.
MACMICHAEL, H. A.
*History of the Arabs in the Sudan,* Cambridge, 1922.

MARTY, PAUL.
*L'Emirat des Trarzas,* Paris, 1919.
MASQUERAY, EMILE.
*Note concernant les Aoulad-Daoud du Mont Aures (Aouras),* Alger, 1879.
*Formation des Cités chez les Populations Sédentaires d'Algérie,* Paris, 1886.
MEAKIN, BUDGETT.
*The Moorish Empire,* London, 1899.
MEAKIN, J. E. B.
*The Morocco Berbers—Journal of the Royal Anthropological Institute of Great Britain and Ireland,* London, Vol. XXIV (1893).
MÉLIA, JEAN.
*La France et l'Algérie,* Paris, 1919.
*La Ville Blanche Alger,* Paris, 1921.
MENDOZA DA FRANCA, JORGE DE.
*Al Eccelentissimo Señor el Marques de Velada,* Madrid, 1648.
MERCIER, ERNEST.
*Histoire de l'Afrique Septentrionale (Berbérie),* Paris, 1888–91.
MONCEAUX, PAUL.
*Histoire Littéraire de l'Afrique Chrétienne depuis les Origines jusqu'à l'Envasion Arabe,* Paris, 1901.
*Païens Judaisants,* Paris, 1902.
*Les Colonies Juives dans l'Afrique Romaine—Revue des Études Juives,* Paris, Tome XLIV (1902).
MONNIER, MARCEL.
*France Noire,* Paris, 1894.
MONTBARD, G.
*Among the Moors,* New York, 1894.
MOORE, M.
*Carthage of the Phoenicians in the light of Modern Excavations,* London, 1905.
MORGAN, J.
*History of Algiers,* London, 1731.
MUIR, WILLIAM.
*The Caliphate: Its Rise, Decline and Fall,* Edinburgh, 1924.
NACHTIGAL, G.
*Sahara and Sudan,* Berlin, 1879–81.
O'CONNOR, V. C. SCOTT.
*A Vision of Morocco,* New York, 1924.
ODINOT, PAUL.
*Les Berbères—La Géographie,* Paris, Tome XLI (1924).
OLON, PEDIN DE S.
*Estat Present de l'Empire de Maroc,* Paris, 1694.
OSSENDOWSKI, FERDINAND.

*Oasis and Simoon,* New York, 1927.
PANANTI, SIGNOR.
*Narrative of a Residence in Algiers,* London, 1818.
PEYSSONNEL, JEAN ANDRÉ.
*Relative d'un Voyage sur les Côtes de Barbarie en 1724 et 1725,* Paris, 1838.
PIQUET, VICTOR.
*Les Civilisations de l'Afrique du Nord,* Paris, 1921.
PLAYFAIR, ROBERT LAMBERT.
*Travels in the Footsteps of Bruce in Algeria, and Tunis,* London, 1877.
POULET, GEORGES.
*Les Maures de l'Afrique Occidentale Française,* Paris, 1904.
POWELL, E. ALEXANDER.
*In Barbary, Tunisia, Algeria, Morocco and the Sahara,* London, 1927.
PROCOPIUS,
*English Translation* by H. B. Dewing, London, 1916.
PROROK, BYRON KUHN DE.
*Digging for Lost African Gods,* New York, 1926.
PULSKY, FRANCIS.
*The Tricolor on the Atlas,* London, 1854.
RAWLINSON, GEORGE.
*History of Phoenicia,* London, 1889.
*Ancient History from the Earliest Times to the Fall of the Western Empire,* New York, 1899.
RECLUS, ELISÉE.
*La Phénice et les Phéniciens,* Neuchâtel, 1900.
RECLUS, ONÉSIME.
*L'Atlantide,* Paris, 1918.
REICHERT,
*Monumenta Ordinis Fratrum Praedicatorum Historia,* Louvain, 1896.
RENÉ, LE MORE.
*D'Alger à Tombouctou,* Paris, 1913.
RICHET, ETIENNE.
*La Mauritanie,* Paris, 1920.
RILEY, JAMES.
*Authentic Narrative,* Hartford, 1817.
RIVIÈRE, JOSEPH.
*Recueil de Contes Populaires de la Kabylie du Djurdjura,* Paris, 1882.
RIVOYRE, DENIS DE
*Aux Pays du Soudan,* Paris, 1885.
ROCHEFORT, JEANNEQUIN DE
*Voyage de Lybie au Royaume de Sénéga,* Paris, 1643.

RODD, FRANCIS RENNELL.
*People of the Veil,* London, 1926.
ROHLFS, G.
*Reise durch Nord-Afrika von Tripoli nach Kuka,* Gotha, 1868.
*Reise von Tripolis nach der Oase Kufra,* Leipzig, 1881.
RONCIÈRE, CHARLES DE LA
*La Découverte de l'Afrique au Moyen Age,* Cairo, 1925–27.
RONDET-SAINT, MAURICE.
*En France Africaine,* Paris, 1914.
ROUTH, E. M. G.
*Tangier,* London, 1912
ROY, RENÉ.
*Au Pays des Mirages,* Paris, 1911.
ROZET, M.
*Voyage dans la Régence d'Alger,* Paris, 1833.
RUNNER, JEAN.
*Les Droits Politiques des Indigènes des Colonies,* Paris, 1927.
SAINT-MARTIN, VIVIEN DE
*La Nord de l'Afrique dans l'Antiquité Grecque et Romaine,* Paris, 1873.
*Histoire de la Géographie,* Paris, 1873.
SALA, GEORGE AUGUSTUS HENRY.
*Trip to Barbary,* London, 1866.
SALLUST, CRISPUS.
*Jugurthan War,* trans. J. C. Rolfe, London, 1921.
SAN JUAN, FRANCISCO DE
*Mission Historical de Marruecos,* Seville, 1708.
SARRAZIN, H.
*Races Humaines du Sudan Français,* Chambéry, 1902.
SCHIRMER, G.
*Le Sahara,* Paris, 1893.
SCHWAB, MOISE.
*Phéniciens, Judéo-Hellenes, Berbères, dans le Bassin de la Méditerranée, Journal Asiatique,* Paris, 10e Serie, Tome XIII (1909).
SCOTT, A. MACALLUM.
*Barbary the Romance of the Nearest East,* New York, 1921.
SCOTT, COL.
*The Esmailia of Abd-el-Kadir,* London, 1842.
SCOTT, M. D.
*The Real Algeria,* London, 1914.
SÉDILLOT, L. A.
*Histoire des Arabes,* Paris, 1854.
SHALER, WILLIAM.
*Sketches of Algiers,* Boston, 1826.
SLOUSCHZ, NAHUM.

*Étude sur l'Histoir des Juifs au Maroc,* Paris, 1905.
*Hébraeo-Phéniciens et Judéo-Berbères,* Paris, 1908.
*La Civilisation Hébraïque et Phénicienne à Carthage,* Tunis, 1911.
*Travels in North Africa,* Philadelphia, 1927.
*Un Voyage d'Études Juives en Afrique-Mémoires présentés par divers savants à l'Académie des Inscriptions et Belles-Lettres de l'Institut de France,* Paris, 1913.
*Étude sur l'Histoire des Juifs au Maroc—Archives Marocaines,* Paris, Tome IV & VI (1906–08).

TILHO, COL.
*Documents Scientifiques de la Mission Tilho,* Paris, 1906–09.

TRISTRAM, HENRY BAKER.
*The Great Sahara,* London, 1860.

TULLY, RICHARD.
*Ten Years Residence at Tripoli,* London, 1817.

VAN NOSTRAND, JOHN JAMES.
*The Imperial Domains of Africa Proconsularis,* Berkeley (California) 1925.

VERNON, PAUL E.
*Morocco from a Motor,* London, 1927.

VILLOT, E.
*Mœurs, Coutumes et Institutions des Indigénes de l'Algérie,* Alger, 1898.

VUILLOT, P.
*L'Exploration du Sahara,* Paris, 1895.

WALCKENAER, C. A.
*Recherches Géographiques sur l'Intérieure de l'Afrique Septentrionale,* Paris, 1821.

WALMSLEY, HUGH MULLENEUX.
*Sketches of Algeria, during the Kabyle War,* London, 1858.

WILKIN, ANTHONY.
*Among the Berbers of Algeria,* London, 1900.

WILSON, ALBERT.
*Rambles in North Africa,* Boston, 1926.

WINDUS, JOHN.
*Journey to Mequinez,* London, 1725.

WINGFIELD, LEWIS.
*Under the Palms in Algeria and Tunis,* London, 1868.

YPRIATE, CHARLES.
*Souvenir du Maroc,* Paris, 1863.

ZELTNER, F. DE
*Les Toureg du Sud—Journal of the Royal Anthropological Institute of Great Britain and Ireland,* London, Vol. XLIV (1913).

ZWEMER, SAMUEL M.
*The Moslem World,* Philadelphia, 1908.

BIBLIOGRAPHY—FOR CHAPTERS X & XI ON EGYPT AND THE ENGLISH SUDAN

AL-HAKAM, IBN ABD.
*Futuh Misr,* ed. Charles C. Torrey, New Haven, 1922.
ANNELER, H.
*Zur Geschichte der Juden von Elephantine,* Bern, 1912.
ARTIN, YACOUB PASHA.
*England in the Sudan,* trans. George Robb, London, 1911.
BAKER, SAMUEL WHITE.
*Ismailia,* London, 1874.
BARTON, GEORGE A.
*Religion of Israel,* New York, 1918.
*Archæology and the Bible,* Philadelphia, 1925.
BATE, H. N.
*The Sybilline Oracles,* London, 1918.
BONNEL DE MÉZIÈRES, M. A.
*Rapport de M. Bonnel de Mézières chargé de Mission sur le Haut-Oubangui, le M'Bomon et Bahr-el-Ghazel,* Paris, 1901.
BREASTED, JAMES HENRY.
*History of Egypt,* New York, 1905.
*Development of Religion and Thought in Ancient Egypt,* New York, 1905.
*Ancient Records of Egypt,* London, 1907.
*History of the Ancient Egyptians,* London, 1908.
BROSSES, CHARLES DE
*Du Culte des Dieux Fétiches ou Parallèle de l'Ancienne Religion de l'Égypte avec la Religion Actuelle de la Négritie,* Paris, 1760.
BROWNE, W. G.
*Travels in Africa, Egypt and Syria, from the Year 1792 to 1798,* London, 1806.
BRUGSCH, HENRI.
*History of Egypt under the Pharaohs,* trans. Henry Danby Seymour, London, 1879.
*Dictionnaire Géographique de l'Ancienne Égypte,* Leipzig, 1879.
BUDGE, E. A. WALLIS.
*The Egyptian Sudan,* London, 1907.
*Egyptian Magic,* London, 1908.
*Egyptian Ideas of the Future Life,* London, 1908.
*The Book of Opening the Mouth,* London, 1909.
*Legends of the Gods,* London, 1912.
*Annals of Nubian Kings,* London, 1912.
*The Book of the Dead,* London, 1923.
*Short History of the Egyptian People,* London, 1923.
*Dwellers on the Nile,* London, 1926.

BURCKHARDT, JOHN LEWIS.
*Travels in Nubia,* London, 1819.
CAILLAUD, FRÉDÉRIC.
*Voyage à Méroe, au Fleuve Blanc,* Paris, 1826.
CAPART, JEAN.
*Lectures on Egyptian Art,* Chapel Hill (N. Carolina), 1928.
CHAMPOLLION, J. F.
*Système Hiéroglyphique des Anciens Egyptiens,* Paris, 1827–28.
*Grammaire Egyptienne,* Paris, 1836–41.
CHAMPOLLION LE JEUNE.
*L'Égypt sous les Pharaons,* Paris, 1814.
COWLEY, A.
*Aramaic Papyri of the Fifth Century B.C.,* Oxford, 1923.
DOMVILLE-FIFE, C. W.
*Savage Life in the Black Sudan,* Philadelphia, 1927.
DUGMORE, A. RADCLYFFE.
*The Vast Sudan,* Bristol, 1924.
EBERS, GEORG.
*Egypt,* trans. Clara Bell, London, 1878.
EDWARDS, AMELIA B.
*A Thousand Miles up the Nile,* London, 1891.
EL-TOUNSY, MOHAMMED IBN OMAR.
*Voyage au Darfour,* trad. Perron, Paris, 1845.
*Voyage au Ouaday,* trad. Perron, et Jamard, Paris, 1851.
FALLS, J. C. EWALD.
*Three Years in the Libyan Desert,* St. Louis.
FRANCIS, RENE.
*Egyptian Aesthetics,* Chicago, 1912.
GAYET, ALBERT.
*Coins d'Egypte Ignorés,* Paris, 1905.
HASSANEIN, BEY, A. M.
*The Lost Oases,* New York, 1925.
HINDE, SIDNEY LANGFORD.
*The Last of the Massi,* London, 1901.
JAYNE, WALTER ADDISON.
*Healing Gods of Ancient Civilization,* New Haven, 1925.
JEQUIER, GUSTAVE.
*Histoire de la Civilisation Egyptienne,* Paris, 1925.
JOHNSTON, HARRY H.
*The Nile Quest,* New York, 1903.
LEEDER, S. H.
*The Desert Gateway,* London, 1910.
*Veiled Mysteries of Egypt,* New York, 1913.
*Modern Sons of the Pharaohs,* London, 1918.
MACKENZIE, DONALD A.
*Ancient Civilizations,* London, 1927.

MAGE, M. E.
*Voyage dans le Soudan Occidental,* Paris, 1868.
MAHAFFY, J. P.
*History of Egypt under the Ptolemaic Dynasty,* London, 1899.
MARESTAING, PIERRE.
*Les Écritures Égyptiennes et l'Antiquité Classique,* Paris, 1913.
MASPERO, GASTON.
*Passing of the Empires,* London, 1900.
*History of Egypt,* trans. M. L. McClure, London, 1906.
*Egypt: Ancient Sites and Modern Scenes,* trans. Elizabeth Lee, New York, 1911.
*Popular Stories of Ancient Egypt,* London, 1915.
*Etudes de Mythologie et d'Archéologie Egyptiennes,* Paris, 1916.
MEYER, E.
*Geschichte des Alten Aegyptens,* Berlin, 1887.
MORET, ALEXANDER.
*In the Times of the Pharaohs,* New York, 1911.
*Kings and Gods of Egypt,* New York, 1912.
*The Nile and Egyptian Civilization,* London, 1927.
MYER, ISAAC.
*Oldest Books in the World,* New York, 1900.
NEWBOLD, D.
*Rock-pictures and Archæology in the Libyan Desert—Antiquity,* Gloucester, Vol. II (1928).
NORDEN, FREDERICK LEWIS.
*Travels in Egypt and Nubia,* London, 1757.
NORDEN, HERMANN.
*White and Black in East Africa,* Boston, 1924.
PALLME, IGNATIUS.
*Travels in Kordofan,* London, 1844.
PETHERICK, MR. AND MRS.
*Travels in Central Africa,* London, 1869.
PETRIE, W. M. FLINDERS.
*History of Egypt,* New York, 1896.
*Religion and Conscience in Ancient Egypt,* New York, 1898.
*Syria and Egypt,* London, 1898.
*Hyksen and Israelite Cities,* London, 1906.
*Memphis,* London, 1909.
*Personal Religion in Egypt before Christianity,* London, 1909.
*Egypt and Israel,* London, 1911;
*Status of the Jews in Egypt,* London, 1911.
*History of Egypt from the Earliest Kings to the XVIth Dynasty,* New York, 1924.
POLLARD, JOSEPH.
*The Land of the Monuments,* London, 1898.
ROSELLINI, J.

*I Monumenti dell' Egitto e della Nubia,* Pisa, 1832–44.
SAYCE, A. H.
*Egypt of the Hebrews and Herodotus,* London, 1896.
SCHURÉ, EDOUARD.
*Sanctuaires d'Orient,* Paris, 1926.
SCUTELLIUS, NICALAUS.
*Iamblicus de Mysteriis Aegyptiorum,* Rome, 1556.
SELIGMAN, C. G.
*Cult of Nyakang and the Divine Kings of the Shilluk,* Khartoum, 1911.
SLADEN, DOUGLAS.
*Queer Things about Egypt,* Philadelphia, 1911.
SLATIN PASHA, RUDOLF C.
*Fire and Sword in the Sudan,* trans. F. B. Wingate, London, 1896.
SONNINI, C. S.
*Travels in Upper and Lower Egypt,* London, 1799.
SWANN, ALFRED J.
*Fighting the Slave-Hunters in Central Africa,* London, 1910.
THOMSON, J.
*Through Massi Land,* Boston, 1885.
THOMSON AND RANDALL-MACIVER.
*Ancient Races of the Thebaid,* Oxford, 1905.
TREATT, STELLA COURT.
*Cape to Cairo,* Boston, 1927.
VAUPANY, H. DE.
*Alexandrie et la Basse-Egypte,* Paris, 1885.
WEIGALL, ARTHUR.
*Life and Times of Akhnaton,* London, 1922.
*Glory of the Pharaohs,* London, 1923.
*History of the Pharaohs,* London, 1925–27
WESTERMANN, DIEDRICH.
*The Shilluk People: Their Language and Folklore,* Philadelphia, 1912.
WILKINSON, F. M.
*Manners and Customs of the Ancient Egyptians,* London, 1847.
WRIGHT, CHARLES H. H.
*Light from Egyptian Papyri on Jewish History before Christ,* London, 1908.

# *Index A—Individuals.*

# *Index B—Places, Peoples, etc.*

*(To indicate on the maps the localities mentioned in the text would make them unreadable. It was deemed preferable to use the latest maps with little detail and to give latitudes and longitudes in this Index.)*

# *Index C—Topics.*

# Index D—References.

MISSION LIBRARY S.V.D.